Sales Management

The Complete Marketeer's Guide

By The Same Author

PRACTICAL EXPORT MANAGEMENT
Developing International Business

Sales Management

The Complete Marketeer's Guide

Chris J Noonan

London
GEORGE ALLEN & UNWIN
Boston   Sydney   Wellington

© Chris J Noonan 1986
This book is copyright under the Berne Convention. No reproduction without
permission. All rights reserved.

George Allen & Unwin (Publishers) Ltd
40 Museum Street, London WC1A 1LU, UK

George Allen & Unwin (Publishers) Ltd
Park Lane, Hemel Hempstead, Herts HP2 4TE, UK

Allen & Unwin Inc
8 Winchester Place, Winchester, Mass 01890, USA

George Allen & Unwin Australia Pty Ltd
8 Napier Street, North Sydney, NSW 2060, Australia

George Allen & Unwin with the
Port Nicholson Press
PO Box 11-838 Wellington, New Zealand

First published by George Allen & Unwin 1986

British Library Cataloguing in Publication Data

Noonan, Chris J.
    Sales management: a complete marketeer's guide.
    1. Sales management
    I. Title
    658.8'1   HF5438.4
    ISBN 0-04-658254-1

Library of Congress Cataloging-in-Publication Data

Noonan, Chris J.
    Sales management.
    1. Sales management.   I. Title.
    HF5438.4.N66   1986   658.8'1   85-28590
    ISBN 0-04-658254-1

Set in 12 point Baskerville by Fotographics (Bedford) Ltd
and printed in Great Britain by Hazell Watson and Viney Ltd,
Member of the BPCC Group, Aylesbury, Bucks

Contents

Contents

List of Examples

Introduction

How often do we hear the phrase 'He's a born salesman', usually with the implication that the person referred to is able to converse freely and with confidence? Although that may be an admirable quality, it is far from the salesperson's main role, which is to influence customers and contacts to buy, stock, display and promote the products offered by his company. I take the position that a salesperson is not born, but made, through effective training to harness and develop the natural qualities and attributes that may be a necessary part of the ideal salesperson's personality profile. The sales manager therefore needs all the skills and qualities of the salesperson and more besides in order to get things done by effective management of an often quite diverse team of people. The emphasis in his role is on planning, controlling, monitoring, managing and motivating subordinates.

Many people enter a sales career by default, in that they are unable to decide on an alternative career or are unwilling to undertake the necessary training for the alternatives that are available to them. To such people selling perhaps has the image of a soft option, with little control, much independence, and good rewards. Nowadays, that approach will rarely lead a person into a major company, where great attention is paid to the careful selection and training of salespersons. Companies are often under pressure to achieve adequate volume to keep plants utilised to a capacity that will generate profits, and the sales team are at the sharp end in having to accept responsibility for achieving the necessary sales targets for existing and new products.

Selling has long since lost the image of being an 'easy number'. Hours are frequently long, pressures great, disruption of domestic plans all too common (although rewards both in monetary terms and in the sense of achievement can be greater than in many other careers). The salesperson is only as good as his next order, not his last. The sales manager is in turn only as good as his success in constantly motivating his subordinates to higher standards of professionalism and achievement.

Many large companies are very sophisticated in their sales management and sales training structures and programmes. But equally there are many smaller companies that are not in the position to have a well-developed and trained sales organisation. In such companies the sales manager may double in another function, possibly including general management and marketing.

This book is intended to serve as a practical guide to the principles of sales management – whatever the sales manager's personal background, experience, industry, product group or company size – in order to help the sales manager build a stronger sales team through the late 1980s and on into the 1990s, by developing his own organisation's role and structure to meet the changing market conditions and buyer needs as buying control becomes more centralised and sophisticated.

This text may be of interest to:

- sales and marketing directors and senior sales managers, who may like to use it as a one-volume reference work and summary of the many facets of sales management for which they have responsibility. Whilst its content might perhaps not be particularly new to such experienced managers, it might nevertheless serve to consolidate knowledge and experience and to enable them to 'see the wood from the trees';
- field sales managers, in particular, whether having titles such as District, Regional or Area Manager, or other such designation, who may find the text has practical applications by adapting the principles to their own particular environment. Some aspects of their job functions may be covered in this text to an extent not found in many sales management courses;
- salespersons and students of sales and marketing, who will find that the text provides a comprehensive coverage of sales management principles that will provide a firmer base for their entry into sales line management.

How to use the book

This text combines breadth and depth of coverage in one readable volume. The reader may like to adopt the following system of reading, depending on his own particular needs and reading objectives:

- Read the book quickly from cover to cover, particularly noting chapter summaries and checklists, to get a broad understanding of the subject matter and scope of the text. This may well be all that is needed by the most experienced manager seeking just to consolidate his knowledge and experience.
- Those with particular learning or training needs may then benefit by selective in-depth reading and study of chapters of special interest. I would advise the reader carefully to relate the principles and practices covered to his own products, company and markets and to develop a personalised case study approach to problems within his own experience.
- Where examples, illustrations and checklists appear, the practising sales manager and salesperson or student not so familiar with such systems may benefit by creating his own examples.

- It might also be useful to produce your own summaries and check-lists relating specifically to your own environment and needs, or simply to make margin notes on points of interest or of practical application in your own organisation.
- The book may also serve as an occasional reference point when you experience problems in areas covered by the text.

Sales management is a profession, and one to which many of us are very committed. I trust that this text will contribute to the profession and serve as an aid to those who wish to develop professional sales management skills further.

Part I

Organising and Managing for Results

---

1 Functions and Organisation of the Sales Force

In this first chapter of the text I shall consider the functions of the sales force and the factors that impact on how it might be structured and organised. Whilst there may not be a definitive way to organise a sales force, its functions will tend to be similar between companies and industries, and the discussions and guidelines presented in the text will generally have relevance and applicability in most organisations, big and small, and most industries, whether fast moving consumer goods (f.m.c.g.), industrial or service oriented.

SALES FORCE FUNCTIONS

I would first like to illustrate a typical corporate organisation (Example 1.1), in which each functional director has a specialist organisation reporting to him. Although I show each division separately, some might be merged (for example, production and engineering), with one senior manager or director responsible for the combined functions, while in some smaller organisations or those where development was not a priority (such as retail operations or certain service industries) there might be no research and development division at all.

Example 1.1 A typical corporate organisation

It is customary in the larger fast moving consumer goods companies for the sales and marketing functions to be separated, each with greater specialisation and more narrowly defined responsibilities. In many smaller companies, and often in industrial or service product environments, the two functions may be combined,

Example 1.2 Major organisational functions

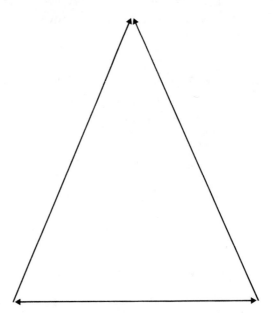

Board
- sets corporate objectives and
  develops policies

- prepares annual and longer-term
  plans and related budgets and profit
  performance targets

- develops corporate strategies

- measures performance against plans
  and develops corrective action
  programmes to counter deviations

Sales division
- forecasts potential sales volumes
  and prices incorporating marketing
  and promotional activity for existing
  and new products

- develops strategies to achieve sales
  forecasts

- develops a sales force organisation
  and structure to achieve the planned
  forecasts and implement the strategies

- converts division plans and forecasts
  into specific sales targets, programmes
  and tactics for subordinate personnel

Marketing division
- analyses user/consumer needs in relation
  to market opportunities for new and
  existing products and their attributes
  and benefits

- develops marketing strategies and
  programmes, including advertising and
  promotional activity

- conducts or commissions market
  research into aspects of existing and new
  products, including test marketing

- provides marketing support to assist
  the sales division achieve sales volume
  and profit forecasts

4

either because budgetary limitations do not permit expansion of personnel resources and separation of functions, or because the nature of the products, industries or markets favours a combined sales and marketing function and effort. Where the functions are separated, both might be represented by a director on the main board or by equally senior managers on other internal policy-making committees. Whilst in the following I shall tend to treat the sales and marketing functions as if they were separate departments, the reader who operates in an environment where they are combined within the sales organisation should easily relate to the discussion.

Whatever the structure and organisation you have experience of, the main functional responsibilities of the board of directors and the separate or combined sales and marketing divisions are likely to be as illustrated in Example 1.2. In essence, the sales division is ultimately responsible for achieving the sales volumes prescribed in company plans at prices yielding acceptable gross profit contributions.

Example 1.3 Principal sales and marketing functional responsibilities

Sales	Marketing
MANAGEMENT	
Sales volume	Current brand management (including profitability)
Distribution	Market research and analysis
Product display/merchandising	Public relations
Call/account coverage	Advertising and promotion
Sales force recruitment	
Sales force training	
Provision of feedback	
• bulletins	
• conferences	
• personal contact	
Trade terms	
Performance measurement	
ADMINISTRATION	
Credit control	Product performance & market share analysis
Collection of payments	Packaging supplies
Customer service	Product & packaging compliance with existing legislation
Order processing	
PLANNING	
Sales forecasting	Sales & marketing forecasts
Pricing policies & profit planning	Pricing policies & profit planning
Sales promotions & competitions	New product development
Sales force rewards & incentives	New product test marketing
Management training	Product design (physical attributes, including packaging, size and shape, etc.)

5

Within either the separate or combined sales and marketing divisions are a range of specific tasks that generally fall into one of three broad functional categories:

MANAGEMENT
ADMINISTRATION
PLANNING

Example 1.3 illustrates which of the broad categories might apply to the various sales and marketing functional responsibilities, but clearly there is some flexibility. On the whole I prefer to consider functions more concerned with the present as **management** and those more concerned with the future as **planning**.

A brief comment on each of these functions is warranted at this point, although additional detailed subject coverage will be given to a number of them at appropriate stages of the text.

Sales volume
Once a target or forecast is set or agreed under the broad planning function, the sales manager is responsible for its achievement. Generally a multitude of other interrelated company plans and programmes are dependent on achievement of plan volumes and prices.

Distribution
A distribution target by product may be set independently of volume targets, but achievement of any distribution target is more usually related to volume targets; i.e. higher sales volume is a function of increased distribution as well as a function of increased levels of offtake in existing outlets.

Volume and distribution are both variable factors in the marketing and sales programme that impact on the total marketing mix, including pricing policies, advertising and promotional activity, product design, and other consumer awareness and acceptance boosting programmes, all of which are amongst the more traditional marketing department responsibilities. Given any particular product marketing mix and programme, the sales manager must aim at achieving the requisite levels of volume and distribution.

Product display and merchandising
These are both traditional sales force functions and responsibilities. While the marketing department may design display aids and promotions aimed at improving display at the sales points, the sales-person responsible for contact with the retail outlet, wholesaler, cash and carry warehouse, or other forms of account must achieve the **display objectives**, since offtake and volume levels are a function of

effective display. Product display may be in two main forms: regular shelf space and display; and promotional or feature displays. The activity of maintaining or creating these displays at the store level of contact is most commonly referred to as **merchandising**. The merchandising function may be performed by the appropriate sales-person covering the territory, or by a separate individual or team specially charged with display and merchandising activity. Many companies now prefer to use agencies that specialise in providing in-store merchandising support to the regular sales team, or recruit and train their own team of part-time merchandisers (frequently a good source of such labour is the abundant talent of housewives who have no family commitment during certain hours of the day). Such an approach to obtaining and maintaining display is often more cost-effective than using the scarcer and more costly resource of highly trained salespersons.

Call coverage

The physical act of calling on retailers or other types or levels of customers is referred to as covering the customer base or achieving **call coverage**. Many sales departments now supplement the physical calls of the salespersons with a system of telephone selling from a specially trained team of telephone salespersons whose main task is to generate repeat orders from regular customers who can operate an effective system of stock control; however, they may also have a supplementary task of making initial calls to potential customers on whom a salesperson or manager could make a subsequent personal selling call. For the purposes of discussion here I shall consider only actual physical calls to customers as part of the planned coverage programme.

Coverage means more than just making calls at random or even calling on every customer at the same frequency. It should be a carefully planned activity that relates the frequency of call on any one customer to the potential level of sales through that customer (or his current actual sales), the amount of stock the customer can or will hold at any one time, frequency of required delivery, factors such as shelf life of a product, customer creditworthiness, limitations on storage space, and so on. High-volume supermarkets or department stores may require more frequent calls than a wholesaler, not because they are selling more product but more because they operate restrictive policies of carrying minimum back-up stock.

Sales recruitment and training

The identification and subsequent training of a company's sales force must be the responsibility of the sales management. They must prepare job specifications and job holder profiles, probably with the aid of a personnel manager, who may also assist with other aspects of recruitment such as advertising, interviewing, candidate correspon-

7

dence, terms and conditions of appointment, etc. Sales training is likely to take two main forms in larger companies: initial theoretical sales training, including company and product knowledge at the head office or central training school; and practical field training under the supervision of the recruit's new line manager. Supplementary training will generally take place at sales meetings and conferences. Smaller companies may have to rely solely upon recruiting persons who have already been trained in other companies.

Provision of feedback

This function is essential to communicate achievements and objectives, and to provide support and motivation. It usually takes the form of regular bulletins from head office or field management, and occasional area sales meetings or more comprehensive national sales conferences, which can provide a broader forum for feedback, training, communication of plans and programmes, motivation and a general opportunity for colleagues to interrelate. New product launches are usually communicated at major sales conferences because that provides an excellent programme theme.

Trade terms

The sales managers will liaise with the marketing and financial departments in assessing what terms of trade can and will be offered to satisfy normal trade practices and customer expectations. Generally there are well-established industry norms that impose some limitations on any one manufacturer who might try to reduce margins. Careful reviews of competitive pricing, trade terms and promotional offers need to be regularly undertaken with attention to:

- quantity discounts and allowances
- special promotional activities
- payment periods
- early or prompt payment discounts
- wholesaler/distributor discounts or rebates
- key account performance-related discounts or rebates
- conditions of sale and warranties
- size and frequency of deliveries.

Performance measurement

The sales management team must develop statistical measures of performance to relate achievements to targets, budgets and plans, and as part of the programme to provide feedback. Such measurements are often developed in conjunction with the marketing and marketing research departments, and statistics produced will be broken down to give meaningful information to each management tier in the sales organisation (e.g. national, regional, area, territory statistics), and with a separate measurement for each key account function or manager.

Comparative figures for performance against plans may cover:

- **sales volumes** by product and by customer
- **sales values** by product and by customer
- **call coverage** achieved against scheduled call coverage
- **distribution** achieved by product, territory, etc.
- **display achievements** by product, territory, etc.

Any other relevant comparisons for particular industries, products or promotional activities can also be monitored and produced.

Credit control

This functional responsibility is usually either shared with or controlled by the finance division. In the final analysis, however, the sales force must be held accountable and advise on the suitability of customers for credit and set credit limits and any other restrictions or variations from the standard trading terms. Contact may frequently be made with other suppliers and creditors as part of the credit checking process. Many food and consumer goods producers have learned to be cautious in extending credit as the rise and boom of cash and carry operations in the late 1960s and 1970s produced its share of bad debts. A company may decide on a policy to limit the outstanding credit permitted a new customer for, say, the first year of trading. This does impose severe restrictions on a genuinely successful new trader, with the result that a sales force has to provide more frequent call coverage to maintain in-stock positions. Field managers tend to take a close interest in all such new accounts to reduce the risk of over-extending credit and incurring bad debts.

Collection of payments

The normal practice in companies is for payment for goods despatched to be remitted directly by mail or other direct transfer mode to the customer service or credit control department. However, the sales force may rightly be involved in chasing payments where a customer fails to remit payment by the due date, because a visit from the sales person or field manager may be less likely to produce ill-will at this stage than a terse reminder letter. Many companies adopt the practice of sending a polite reminder where a payment is not received on time, with a copy to the appropriate field manager for his personal follow-up with the customer or salesperson. Where payment is not forthcoming, the sales manager will again be involved in decisions whether or not to terminate supplies and proceed with other legal action or debt collection methods.

Customer service

This function may encompass such duties as credit checking and control and the collection of payments. Additionally the customer service department is likely to be delegated the responsibility of handling customer enquiries, complaints, requests for spare parts and service information, as well as order processing duties.

Order processing

In some companies this function is separate from the customer service department or function, and will involve all the stages of processing the order from the receipt of the salesperson's written order (or customer's telephone order) through the preparation, packing, despatch and invoicing stages.

In a small company all the support functions may be the responsibility of very few persons, whereas a large company may have the resources and need for a number of support staff or departments.

Sales forecasting

The sales management have a major contribution to make to the process of forecasting sales volumes and related budgets, as they manage the achievement of related distribution and display objectives. This function involves careful study of the past performance history and prediction of the effects of marketing programmes, seasonal trends and external factors such as competitive activity or changing tastes or economic trends.

Pricing policies

The marketing and sales departments will both be closely involved in developing and implementing market price policies and strategies that achieve the dual objectives of satisfying profit objectives whilst being competitive.

Sales promotions and competitions

Although the development and planning of sales promotions aimed at increasing demand for a product, display and/or distribution may be a joint sales and marketing team effort, the design and control of sales force incentives and competitions will largely be an exclusive sales management function. Such programmes can generally be closely directed to the achievement of specific short- and longer-term strategic objectives.

Sales force rewards and incentives

The sales manager is responsible, in conjunction with personnel colleagues, for ensuring that the rewards and incentives of his subordinates maintain high levels of morale, motivate his staff to high levels of performance and achievement, encourage excellence, and ensure that the good performers desire to remain in the company's employ. Although this may be considered as either a management or a planning function, I prefer to insert it under the heading of planning because of my belief that correct programmes within this function probably have great bearing on the future success of the sales team.

Management training

Many sales managers give attention to the training of the territory salespersons but neglect management training. Management training to meet the future needs of the business and demands of the job is a key function, and a well-trained team of sales managers will contribute greatly to their own development, to company performance and to the morale and training of their sales teams.

Marketing
functions

As this work is not intended to be a specialist marketing text I shall touch only briefly on the main marketing functions listed in Example 1.3 in order that the reader develops an understanding of the inter-relationships between sales and marketing functions.

Brand management

Broadly this will include the regular preparation and analysis of marketing and market research data and statistics relating to the performance of each product, including distribution and offtake analysis, consumer product and advertising awareness, consumption patterns and preferences, purchasing frequencies, taste preferences and trends. Marketing analysis is particularly concerned with identifying and quantifying trends that impact on sales volumes, distribution, usage, offtake, and profitability. The profitability of each product in relation to assets employed in its production (plant and equipment, financial, and human) and market prices is of particular concern to product brand managers fulfilling their catch-all functional role of brand management.

Whilst a fast moving consumer goods company might have all the sophistication to undertake comprehensive brand management along the lines outlined above, many industrial or service companies have neither the personnel resources, expertise nor access to sophisticated market data.

Market research

This will normally be designed and implemented under the control of the marketing department to monitor performance, tastes, trends, and awareness in relation to existing products, and to assess market acceptance and sales potential of new products or processes. The actual market research programme will often be contracted out to specialist market research agencies.

Again, in many non-fast moving consumer goods sales organisa-tions and markets, market research plays a lesser role and any market

11

research that is conducted might be geared simply to generating information upon which marketing programmes can be based.

Public relations
This marketing function has grown rapidly over the last decade and is complementary to the advertising and promotion functions. Suppliers of goods and services frequently now find that a positive public relations programme can be more cost-effective than advertising to certain target groups. They thus seek favourable editorial comment on their company and products, and offer sponsorship or endorsements to events and programmes likely to attract publicity. Specialist public relations companies can generally develop a tailor-made programme within budgetary limits.

Advertising and promotions
These are traditional responsibilities of the marketing department in fast moving consumer goods companies, but might be a sales responsibility in industrial or service company environments. Advertising is designed to create user or customer awareness and trial, repeat usage habits, and favourable company and product images to the target market. Media used may be any or all of radio, television, cinema, press, other publications or specialist journals, posters, etc. (the choice depending on the nature of the products and markets). Obviously media that can provide visual as well as aural impact will be likely to generate increased awareness or recall at any particular level of advertising frequency. Radio advertising is less costly than television, and if there is a broad variety of stations accepting advertising it may be possible to target a market sector selectively.

Promotional activity is generally in the form of consumer or trade promotions, competitions, redemption or self-liquidating pro- grammes (where possibly labels are redeemed with some cash for special offer products not directly related to the promoted product), and sponsorships (e.g. where a manufacturer offers to contribute money to a charity for each label returned to a stated address). Promotions also have the objective of increasing display, distribution and trial. Advertising additionally can inform the target market on aspects of product use, design, benefits and attributes.

The written media may be more cost-effective in targeting certain specialist products to specialist markets – e.g. advertising a new anti- biotic to the medical profession through medical journals, or promoting industrial products through trade or professional journals.

Product performance, market share and position analysis
Much of the marketing department's time is allocated to obtaining and interpreting data that can be used to monitor performance of

previous or current marketing programmes or in the design and implementation of future programmes.

Packaging supplies

The control over the design and supply of packaging material is a normal marketing function (although actual orders may be placed by a purchasing department) because the marketing team are generally charged with ensuring that all packaging material is functional, is appealing, and complies with all relevant legislation and trade practices.

Legislative compliance

Governments, local authorities and self-regulatory trade associations increasingly take an interest in aspects of product design, use, and safety, and impose a multitude of regulations on the marketing of products. As mentioned above, the marketing department need to keep abreast of all requirements and ensure compliance.

Sales and marketing forecasting

The forecasting of sales potential and the setting of targets will normally be a shared function with the sales manager.

Pricing policies

The marketing department, who are primarily concerned with strategic aspects of the sales and marketing programme, are likely to have more input to product pricing considerations as pricing is a critical factor in product positioning against competitors.

New product development

Although many novel product ideas may be generated from within a research and development department, the responsibility for identifying market gaps and new product launch opportunities will normally rest with the marketing team. They will be charged with relating the product of research to the needs of the market.

New product test marketing

The launch of a new product into a market requires extensive product and market research followed by a sufficient period of test marketing to establish the viability of the concept, product acceptance, and sales potential. The test marketing period enables any teething problems to be identified and resolved. The greater the investment required to develop a product and the necessary production facilities, the more intensive is likely to be the test marketing and related market research.

Product design

Engineers and scientists may develop the mechanics or concept of a

13

product and its functional characteristics, but it will generally be the responsibility of the marketing team to design the product presentation, as market acceptance and sales potential may depend heavily on aesthetic presentation. Design will need to take account of the environment of usage, the functions to be performed, size and shape limitations, handling and storage factors, safety, regulatory considerations and servicing requirements.

THE SALES MANAGER

The discussion of the functions of the sales division or department within the company organisation leads into a more detailed review of the sales manager's role, functions and personal qualities.

The sales manager's role

Management has often been described in general terms as MAKING THINGS HAPPEN and GETTING THINGS DONE THROUGH OTHER PEOPLE. The sales manager is no different from any other company executive in that he works both with and through others to promote activity, change and decision taking that lead towards the achievement of objectives and plans. Indeed, the sales manager is perhaps the key operational manager in a corporate organisation. He may not have control over the level or amounts of investment in assets employed in the business in total, but he *is* responsible for managing the resources directly under his control (which include finance, personnel, sales force equipment, product, possibly distribution equipment and facilities, and marketing programmes) and for improving the return both on those resources and on total company assets. Moreover the sales manager and his team provide the interface between the retailer and/or other customers, direct purchasing end users and trade contacts and the other parts of the management team involved in the marketing, production, research and designing of both existing and new products. They can provide feedback on all relevant aspects of products and market conditions to interested departments. They are also in the best position to obtain and provide market intelligence on all aspects of competitors' products, prices and policies as well as on trade acceptance of the company's own activities and programmes.

As the **leader of a team** with varying levels of skills, experience, functional responsibilities and seniority, the sales manager's primary responsibility is for the **management, motivation** and **morale** of his subordinate staff. This role will include:

- accepting responsibility for achieving objectives both with and through his team
- maximising the effective sales effort of his team by providing **training, counselling** and **feedback**

14

- exercising control and maintaining discipline within his team
- interpreting and filtering company policies, which are normally set by a main board or top management team and might be communicated downwards only on a 'need to know' basis
- communicating effectively with subordinate managers through regular sales management meetings and briefings (including bulletins)
- ensuring that each subordinate is provided with a high level of **job satisfaction** in terms of:

  - job content
  - team spirit and membership
  - management
  - pecuniary and non-pecuniary rewards
  - recognition of achievements
  - quality of products sold
  - the company as a good employer.

In order to be effective in his role the sales manager should:

- ensure he is well briefed in, and has a comprehensive understanding of, company policies and objectives in order to be in a position correctly to evaluate alternative action courses and initiate corrective action when necessary
- put his subordinates first in his priorities in order to maximise the effective effort of his team.

Most of the resources controlled by the sales manager are tangible and replaceable. Only the less tangible resource of **time** is irreplaceable, and that is the key resource the effective sales manager must optimally manage and control to improve returns on the assets employed in the business. For the sales manager that critical but limited resource is often most effectively used in making contact with persons and organisations outside the company head office rather than within the company office environment. Time spent on internal committees and organisational matters is time lost in the selling and motivational functions of the sales manager. Only the sales manager and his team have the function and ability to generate the orders that produce the income that ensures the company operates as a viable production unit. Any time spent in non-selling or non-trade contact activities must constantly be questioned at and by each level within the sales management structure.

Sales functions   Earlier in this opening chapter I reviewed the principal functional responsibilities of a sales division and a marketing division, whilst recognising that these might be combined. At this point I would like, at the risk of a little repetition, to summarise the main functions of particular sales positions found in a typical sales force. Whilst the particular job titles might be more common to a fast moving consumer goods company, the reader will understand that the actual job functions will generally be performed in any sales organisation, including suppliers of both industrial and service products.

Sales manager/director

This would be the person at the head of the sales organisation, either on the main company board or with access to it through reporting in to a main board director. The main functions of this position would include:

- forecasting potential sales volumes and prices
- identifying, setting and achieving sales objectives, targets, budgets and profit plans
- assigning sales force priorities in line with objectives and plans
- developing programmes for field implementation of the company's marketing, promotional and advertising plans for existing and new products, including developing sales promotions within budgetary limits
- developing a sales force organisation and structure to achieve company plans and objectives and suited to the company, industry and markets (which might include the selection and training of agents or distributors)
- converting overall plans and objectives into specific standards of performance, sales targets and programmes for subordinate functions and managers, including regional/area managers and key account executives (and possibly agents and distributors if part of the system), ensuring each is allocated his fair share in relation to historical performance or potential
- developing a head office sales support organisation, which may include:

  - operational planning and forecasting
  - sales recruitment and sales training
  - sales force rewards and incentive programmes
  - sales performance monitoring and feedback reporting
  - customer service departments
  - order processing departments
  - product distribution (if under sales force control)
  - sales promotional department (planning promotions and providing all sales aids including product literature, display aids, product merchandising aids and equipment)

- selection and training of all subordinate managers
- liaison with departments concerned with forecasting, product marketing, product development, budgeting, production

16

planning and scheduling, distribution, and possibly those
concerned with input supplies

- setting the terms of trade, including basic prices, scale discounts
  and allowances, promotional allowances, etc.
- communicating with both the sales force and customers
  (including agents and distributors if appropriate) as necessary on
  matters concerned with plans, programmes, policies, products
  and performance
- assisting in the development and test marketing of new products.

Field sales managers

Reporting in an appropriate hierarchical fashion to the sales
manager/director would normally be one or more levels of field
sales managers (who might be termed regional or area managers if
organised geographically, or other suitable titles relating to specific
areas of responsibility if organised functionally, e.g. grocery trade
manager; industrial sales manager; public sector sales manager).
These management levels would normally provide the link between
the top (head office based) sales management and the salespersons
actually calling on accounts and customers, and functions would
include:

- liaising with superior managers and subordinate salespersons in
  setting sales performance standards and targets in terms of
  volume by product and by customer within his geographical or
  functional sphere of responsibility, and building these into
  territory, area or functional plans and targets
- responsibility for achieving assigned objectives, targets, forecasts,
  budgets, etc.
- responsibility for planning and monitoring the call coverage of all
  outlets or accounts under his sphere of control to optimise the
  effective frequency of coverage in relation to sales potential
- field implementation of the company's marketing and
  promotional programmes and activities
- selecting, training, managing, motivating and controlling
  subordinate managers and field salespersons under his line
  authority (or, possibly, agents or distributors if used)
- advising superiors on competitive activity, products, promotions
  and terms of trade
- liaising between and communicating with head office departments, functions and personnel and field salespersons and
  customers (or agents and distributors) as appropriate and
  necessary.

Key account managers

This function, if appropriate to the organisation, industry and
markets, is likely to be a management position, responsible for

17

dealing with major accounts or trade sectors of the particular markets (whether fast moving consumer goods, industrial or service oriented), and concerned more with negotiation and planning than with man-management. The job holders might have geographical responsibility for major accounts, or cover a trade sector spanning the nation. Whether the particular job title is simply key accounts manager or related to specific functional responsibility, such as industrial sales manager, functions will generally include:

- liaising with the sales manager/director, sales planning and marketing departments in setting forecasts/targets for all major/key accounts (often termed 'national accounts') under his control by product
- liaising with buyers to agree annual sales volume forecasts consistent with company forecasts/targets
- advising on or setting terms of trade for each account or trade sector, including pricing levels, discounts and allowances (possibly related to performance against agreed standards and targets)
- conducting negotiations on prices and quantities for standard products, special products, special offers, private label products and in-store promotional activity where appropriate
- implementing at the account level the company's general marketing and promotional programmes
- negotiating any special distribution requirements
- achieving satisfactory profit contributions from accounts
- advising senior management on, and implementing at the account level, any special promotional activity
- ensuring that agreed programmes, prices and policies are implemented at the level of individual branches or stores by liaison within his own supporting sales organisation, and with appropriate key account personnel including branch or store managers
- developing relationships and liaising with the key account's own buyers and other managers involved in the testing or use of products (if an industrial or service product), or with the account's store management structure if the product is for resale through wholesale or retail outlets
- liaising internally with other field and head office personnel to ensure that the field sales force provide supporting coverage at the individual branch or store level (if that is appropriate for the nature of the products), including the merchandising of products or booking store-level orders for direct delivery or supply from the customer's central warehouse or distribution centre, and that head office departments correctly produce, pack, deliver and price products and supply any requisite promotional materials, etc.
- monitoring the performance of the key account and each branch,

store or subsidiary within the key account organisation to identify
deviations from forecasts and plans and following up to ascertain
causes of performance variations, and communicating results and
findings back to buyers.

Territory salesperson

At the bottom of the sales force pyramid is the person who makes the
calls on each individual account or customer and presents the
company's products and programmes. His functions are likely to
include:

- converting the company's sales and marketing programmes to
  specific and relevant objectives at the level of each individual
  account or customer
- agreeing with superior sales managers the individual customer
  and territory objectives, targets and programmes on a product-by-
  product basis
- maintaining planned call coverage
- maintaining full and accurate customer account data (including
  stock and sales history, calls made, orders received, products
  presented and listed, etc.)
- avoiding out-of-stock situations at all accounts or customers within
  his sphere of responsibility
- developing professional customer relations with all buyers and
  other personnel within customer or account organisations who
  can influence the purchase and/or use of the company's products
- identifying potential outlets for existing and new products
- achieving maximum levels of distribution (or use) in current and
  potential worthwhile outlets
- achieving optimum levels of product display at key sites in wholesale trade or retail stockists
- providing feedback on competitive activity, promotions, prices
  and products.

**Sales
management
qualities**

Chapter 6 deals at length with the qualities to look for in considering
sales force selection, but at this early stage of the text it would seem
appropriate to summarise some key personal qualities, such as:

- being a good **organiser** and **administrator** in order to ensure
  that plans and programmes are developed, implemented and
  monitored
- being a good **communicator** with colleagues, subordinates,
  customers and trade contacts at all levels
- being demonstrably **decisive**, thereby inspiring colleagues and
  subordinates with a sense of leadership, direction and confidence
- being **fair, objective** and **impartial** in allocating objectives and

targets, handling issues and disputes, and dealing with colleagues, subordinates and trade contacts

- having a high level of **initiative** to identify and take advantage of opportunities, and develop corrective action programmes when performance deviates from plans
- providing **leadership**, an often intangible quality that inspires others to follow or take instruction.

STRUCTURES AND ORGANISATION

The foregoing summary of the major sales and marketing functions should help in creating an awareness of the need to develop a sales structure and organisation to encompass these particular functions and any others that may be particular to an individual company, industry or management style.

This section will consider several alternative organisational structures, with the aid of pictorial organisation charts. The presentation of an organisation in chart format serves several functions:

- it shows how tasks or function are grouped
- job holders can identify reporting relationships and sources of instructions and communications
- it helps create a team environment under a common name, such as 'sales division', and identifies each role in the team such that each job holder can relate his role to the total team structure function and objectives.

In presenting an organisation chart it is common to depict specialisation by function horizontally across the chart, and to use vertical levels of management and non-management positions to add capacity within the span of effective control of each tier of functional management. I shall initially develop the more traditional hierarchical pyramid reporting structures and then consider variations that take more account of different market environments.

**Analysis of
activity needs**

When designing an organisational structure, activities that are all working towards a common objective are usually grouped together. In this approach there may be a series of sub-organisations where lower tiers of objectives are sub-grouped together. For example, the sales organisation is a sub-group of the company organisation; and the national accounts function may be a sub-group of the sales organisation. The objectives accepted by a group will be a determining factor in setting the strategies to achieve these objectives. Once the strategies are agreed they become a major factor influencing the development of specific functional activities.

20

However, the design of a sales organisation does not just centre on the internal functional needs of the company relating to the sale (and perhaps marketing) and distribution of the products (some of which were listed in Example 1.3). Perhaps of greater importance are the types of sales-related service the purchasers of the products might require, and the tasks the sales organisation must perform to sell, distribute and display product effectively. Sales force activities to be considered in organisational design might be developed from an analysis of special needs in these three categories, as in Example 1.4. In this example I have not listed under company needs the functions included in Example 1.3, preferring to concentrate on factors affecting field sales force rather than head office organisation. But the reader can expand the list or develop his own to suit his own company, industry and market needs.

Example 1.4 Analysis of company, customer, and product sales activity needs

Company	**Customer**	**Product**
• soliciting orders	• product presentations	• sampling
• outlet coverage	• surveys of needs	• demonstrations
• product distribution	• product modifications	• point of sale merchandising
• product display	• special packaging (incl. private label)	• after-sales service
• profit	• special unit/pack sizes	• advertising/ promotional support
• credit control	• promotional support	• special handling/ storage (protective packaging, refrigerated storage, etc.)
	• special price negotiations	
	• central warehouse delivery	
	• delivery to branches/ subsidiaries	
	• (long-term) supply contracts	
	• technical support relating to usage/functionality/ maintenance	
	• guaranteed supply continuity	
	• extended credit	

The needs analysis may not be the same for each customer type or trade sector, and the resultant sales organisation might become complex, as demonstrated in some of the examples developed below. But the analysis stage can be followed by assigning responsibility for satisfying a need or performance of a task to certain specific job functions. Generally the more concentrated the buying at fewer buying points (i.e. major accounts) the more senior the level of sales manager required to perform the actual selling and customer liaison tasks, possibly supported by other members of the sales team performing support tasks (such as merchandising) not directly related to product presentation and order negotiation or supply terms. In

21

some industries contract negotiation is a protracted process, as in heavy engineering, and sales teams may have to be formed to handle all stages of needs analysis, product presentations and/or modification and negotiation, and the team might include a mixture of skilled individuals from selling, technical and possibly financial backgrounds.

**Developing
a structure**

In a small company the management structure will necessarily be limited possibly to a sales manager, one or two other office-based managers, a secretary or clerical assistant, and a small field sales force. This team may have to embrace all of the functions previously outlined to whatever greater or lesser degrees are practical until growth in sales volume and profits justifies an increase in manpower and management.

A basic traditional organisational structure may resemble Example 1.5. Such a limited organisation may be suitable where there is a limited product range, few customers for the products (such as with industrial products or products marketed through a network of appointed agents or distributors), or in a wholesaling organisation where most of the sales and marketing functions are performed by the manufacturer.

Example 1.5   A basic organisation structure

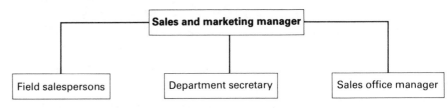

As sales volume increases, or the product range or complexity expands, a larger and more sophisticated organisation may be required to handle workloads or provide additional support functions (see Example 1.6). A number of staff roles, such as **sales training**, that do not have line management authority but that relieve line or field managers of some functions, enabling them to increase their span of control over subordinates, can be developed and separated. Functions such as control over sales force vehicles, equipment and stationery may well fall into a clerical job category within the sales planning manager's department, perhaps reporting to the display and promotions manager.

It is important to mention at this point that management titles are of little practical importance. They are largely designed to indicate a person's functional responsibilities within an organisation; they do not necessarily denote rank or seniority. It may fairly be assumed that the person holding the title *sales director* or *vice-president, sales* is at the

Example 1.6 A developing organisation structure

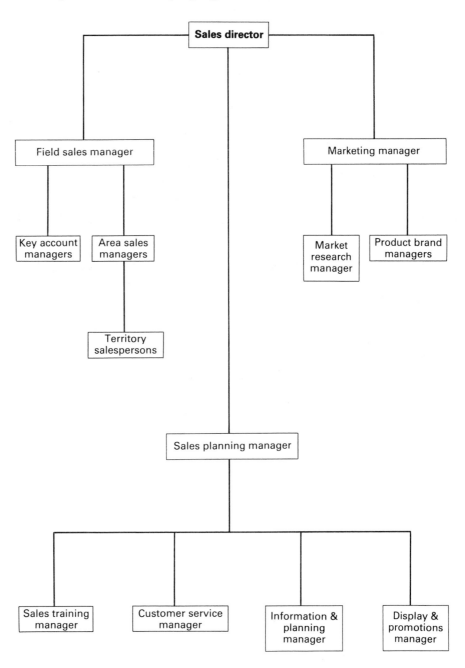

head of the selling organisation, but other titles such as *area* or *regional* sales manager will not obviously reflect the seniority order. A formal job evaluation process, normally conducted with the help of a personnel department, will aid in establishing the seniority of jobs based upon measurable criteria in terms of skills, responsibilities, accountabilities, subordinate functions controlled, and a variety of

23

other objective factors. Smaller companies will necessarily arbitrarily assess levels of seniority according to the sales manager's judgement of each subordinate's responsibilities and contribution to the overall achievement of objectives, and rewards will be allocated accordingly.

A further stage in organisational development may occur as sales volumes grow further, workloads increase, product ranges expand, product complexity increases, market structure and segmentation changes or becomes more defined, product servicing support needs develop. Any or all of these developments could result in changes in an organisational structure or increases in its size with greater emphasis on functional specialisation to ensure accomplishment of the necessary activities that will aid in pursuing strategies and achieving goals and objectives.

The organisational structure will also vary according to the market and distribution structure and service needs of an industry. For example, the organisation required to mass-market fast moving consumer goods (f.m.c.g.) may be very different from that required to market a non-perishable product, an industrial product, or a service to consumers or industry. The skills and qualifications of job holders will vary according to the nature of the products and markets. For example, in an organisation marketing sophisticated engineering products it is highly likely that even within the sales organisation many or most job holders will need a minimum engineering qualification. Chapter 6, on the selection process, will deal at more length with job holder skills, but at the stage of considering an organisational structure and its functions thought needs to be given to whether persons either can be found with the relevant skills or could acquire them through training.

In Example 1.7, I am now assuming that the marketing function is performed by a separate marketing division under the control of a marketing director, as is often the case in f.m.c.g. companies. I have not attempted to put the number of persons at any particular job level or function. That is determined by workloads and management span of control at each level. The example illustrates how some of the job functions previously discussed can be allocated to individual managers with a limited range of specific responsibilities, either as part of their personal workload or as the workload of subordinate managers or clerical support staff.

Any particular organisational structure should have scope for **flexibility** to take account of and develop with the environmental changes. For example, the buying needs and practices of retailers and/or wholesalers or other users of the products or services may change; product distribution patterns may significantly change if a new tier or type of distribution outlet develops – such as cash and carry outlets, voluntary buying groups, speciality shops, etc. Similarly, the final organisational structure should reflect the skills of individuals and the particular accountabilities of managers. For

24

Example 1.7 Separate sales and marketing organisations

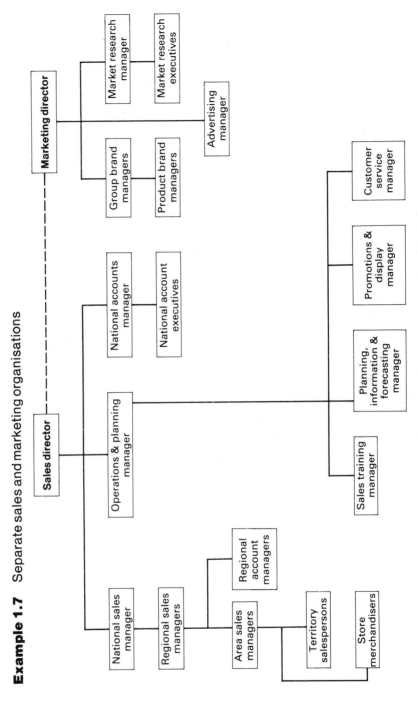

Marketing director

- Market research manager
  - Market research executives
- Group brand managers
  - Product brand managers
- Advertising manager

Sales director

Operations & planning manager

- National accounts manager
  - National account executives

- Sales training manager
- Planning, information & forecasting manager
- Promotions & display manager
- Customer service manager

National sales manager

- Regional sales managers
  - Regional account managers
  - Area sales managers
    - Territory salespersons
    - Store merchandisers

Note: it is assumed that, within each function, the necessary lower management and clerical support will be assigned and developed according to workloads.

example, in Example 1.7 it could well be argued that the sales training manager should actually report in to the national sales manager as he is the user and beneficiary of the services. That is a perfectly valid approach and a final decision will rest with the sales director. If the sales director actually has a specific national sales manager, he may be happy for the training function to report in to the senior field sales manager; if, on the other hand, he has only a subordinate network of regional sales managers, he may well wish not to delegate the overall company sales training function to any single regional sales manager, but to retain it as a central staff role.

The marketing department is likely to be very much smaller than a sales department. In Example 1.7 it has been assumed that each product manager would have overall responsibility for all aspects of the marketing mix for products under his control, possibly with a central advertising function to ensure optimum buying of time and space.

In looking at Example 1.7 it is apparent that three factors dominate or determine the final structure. These are: horizontal, vertical and geographical specialisation.

Horizontal specialisation
This is where functions that can be separated or considered mutually exclusive, yet relevant and important to the achievement of objectives, are identified as a sub-division of an organisation (e.g. sales training, customer service, forecasting, etc.). This functional separation is independent of geographical considerations or the vertical levels of management required to fulfil satisfactorily the responsibilities of a functional department.

Vertical specialisation
As the workload of any department or individual grows beyond the available capacity, then decisions must be taken to relinquish functional responsibilities to a new specialised section, or to add tiers of management or support staff so that authority for some aspects of activities can be delegated down the chain of command. Each level in the chain must have clearly defined objectives and performance standards to ensure that the delegated functions are being satis-factorily performed. Final accountability for performance will always rest with the delegator or department head.

Geographical specialisation
In the sales division this could be as simple as dividing the country up into similar-sized regions, areas and territories, in terms either of population, land area, number of outlets for the products, or of some more sophisticated workload analysis, such as measuring the time required by call to achieve optimum sales. (This will be discussed in

26

Chapter 9.) In a large organisation, certain staff or other non-line management roles may also need to be expanded with specific geographical emphasis (e.g. regional sales trainers); depending on the nature of the function, it may either report in to field line management or remain an offshoot of the appropriate head office function. Typically, in the distribution division or function, a network of depots or regional warehouses may be necessary to fulfil order and delivery requirements. These depots may come under the line responsibilities of the head of the distribution function yet have very close liaison and cross-functional relations with the local field sales management. For example, customer orders may be sent by the salespersons to the local depot for handling and despatch, with copies only to head office for control purposes.

Management span of control

No one manager can effectively manage, train, motivate and control an infinite number of subordinates. The **span of control** is dependent on:

- the nature of work being performed (skilled versus unskilled)
- the knowledge and experience of the persons involved in managing or being managed
- the physical proximity of the jobs
- the similarity of content of the jobs being managed
- the time available and required for training, planning, communicating and supervising.

The traditional view of sales management is that a single manager can effectively manage and control only a small number of separate and mutually exclusive functions, perhaps as few as four–six functions, or a small team of subordinate field operatives. Limitations are encountered within the factors listed above.

In Example 1.7, the sales operations manager has four distinct subordinate functional departments, but all in the close geographical proximity of the head office environment. The national sales manager has two functions – the field sales force and regional accounts – but these are spread over a vast geographical area, which imposes different pressures and limitations on the supporting management structure. The national sales manager can probably effectively manage up to about eight regional sales managers, each of whom in turn can probably effectively control around six subordinate managers (the number of subordinates being assumed to be less because of additional training and supervisory needs over a wide geographical area). Each area manager may be responsible for a team of six–eight territory salespersons depending on the limits of his span of control, which are identified with consideration to the limiting factors listed previously.

Example 1.8 illustrates how the size of a field sales force may vary with the number of management tiers and the effective span of control at each level. It is assumed that there is one national sales manager, who starts with a network of area sales managers, and gradually adds tiers of regional and then divisional sales managers to the organisation. The figures in each column show, for each span of control limitation, the size of the sales force below the national sales manager.

Example 1.8 Relationship between sales force size and span of control

Span of control	Area manager	Area manager and regional manager	Area manager, regional manager and divisional manager
4	20	84	340
5	30	155	780
6	42	258	1554
7	56	399	2800
8	72	584	4680

In practice, as mentioned previously, an organisation would not develop so simply as to have the same effective span of control at each management level. For example, there might eventually be a structural need for four divisional sales managers, each with five subordinate regional sales managers, each of whom has one regional account executive and five area managers reporting to him. If each area sales manager has a span of control of eight territory representatives, then the overall sales force reporting to the sales director is 944 persons – large by any standards. The sales organisation developed in this discussion might look like Example 1.9. Terms such as divisional, regional or area manager are used only to denote greater geographical spans of responsibility; frequently it might be appropriate to add a more definitive notation, such as 'Northern' divisional sales manager or 'London' regional sales manager.

The actual number of territories and territory salespersons required to provide requisite levels of coverage will be established only after careful workload analysis (this will be reviewed in Chapter 9). In fact, in designing the organisation it is common first to establish the number of territories, and then to add tiers of management subject to span of control limitations.

Product specialisation

I have so far concentrated on a company with a single sales organisation. Even in the fast moving consumer goods industry sectors, however, changing markets and distribution patterns have resulted in companies adopting sales force formats that recognise the different structures needed to develop product sales potential effectively.

Example 1.9   Development of a geographical organisation

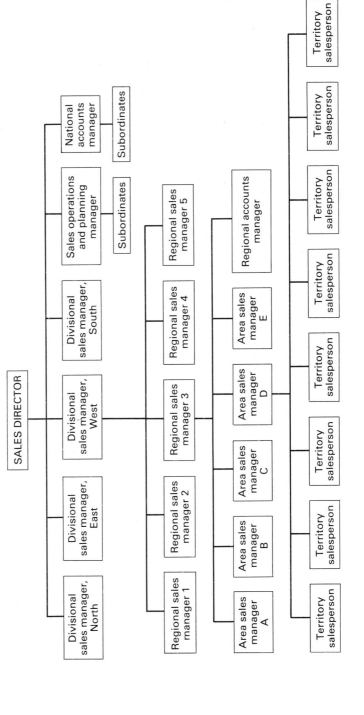

For example, in the food and pharmaceutical industries, products may be sold through more than one type of retail outlet, each having different sales service needs. A confectionery product may reach its major markets both through the traditional smaller confectionery/ tobacconist/newsagent (CTN) outlets and also through multiple supermarket groups. Selling through the CTNs is likely to require significant attention to the wholesale trade, which redistributes to the smaller retail outlets, and limited retail display activity at the level of those outlets justifying a direct call. Supermarkets move high volumes but tend to hold little off-shelf stock, and thus require significant levels of merchandising support to generate display and motivate ordering. Much attention needs to be paid to promotional activity, which is normally organised by the key account sales managers through head offices of the multiple retailers.

A manufacturer of a non-prescription medicine will also find he has both potential sales through the traditional pharmaceutical outlets, many of which are still independently owned, and mass merchandising opportunities through the growing network of drug stores, in addition to sales through the supermarket household medicines and patent cures sections.

There may be a common product marketing and promotion programme in the above examples, but the servicing needs of the different outlet types may be different, and each outlet type will require different amounts of time and labour to achieve sales potential. The management of key accounts in each sector may also be quite different, and involve greater specialisation than is possible in an organisation with a single sales force format. Example 1.10 reflects an organisation developed to service the same products through different retail channels of distribution.

National account management

Several of the examples illustrated show a separate **national accounts** management function within the sales organisation that is charged with the responsibility to develop sales through major retail groups or large industrial product users. Some key accounts may be only regional in coverage, and have a direct impact on the sales volume only over a limited geographical area covered by the manufacturer's sales organisation. In such cases a specialist position of *regional accounts manager*, reporting to an appropriate level of field sales manager, might effectively service the account.

Over recent decades, however, there has been a trend towards more concentration of retailing in most industry sectors, including food, pharmaceuticals and associated products, furniture supplies, clothing, electrical goods, stationery supplies, travel services, household goods and do-it-yourself materials. This growth may result from mergers of existing but smaller retail groups seeking economies of scale and greater profit potential by rationalisation. Additionally

30

Example 1.10 Organisation developed to serve different market sectors

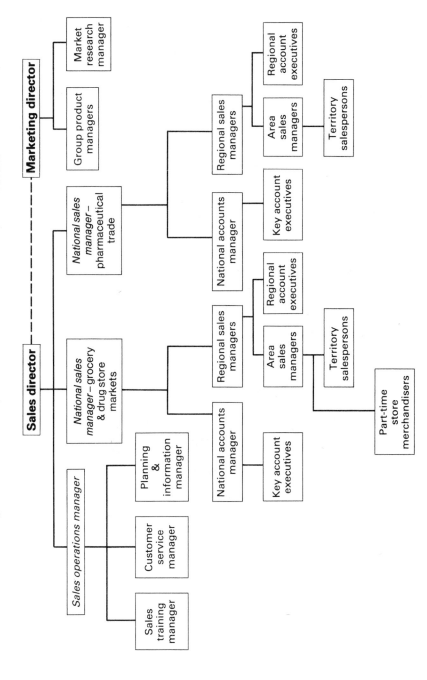

many of the giant retail groups are recent ventures formed by
entrepreneurs who have seen opportunities to discount prices, offer
wider product ranges, and improve the sales facilities and environment by locating at convenient suburban sites in competition with
the traditional smaller high street retailers. It is for the consumer to
judge whether the standard of service offered is better, but the
consumers clearly are heavily motivated to purchase from these
newer outlets. Smaller independent retailers have, in some
industries, responded by joining voluntary buying groups, which are
able to centralise buying and warehousing, obtain more favourable
prices from manufacturers, and pass on lower prices and more
promotional activities to members of the buying group.

Mergers of industrial companies to form larger groups benefiting
from synergy of operations and markets have also resulted in more
concentration of buying in a number of cases as a central buying unit
seeks to manage the purchase of supplies for all subsidiaries or, if not
actually to place the physical orders for the subsidiaries, at least to
negotiate the terms and conditions under which suppliers of inputs
will provide goods and services.

Obviously the concentration of buying is seen as advantageous by
the major industrial and multiple retail groups. Many manufacturers
initially responded with a degree of despair, fearing their margins
would be eroded and terms dictated to them to the point where they
were effectively working for the buyers. There is no doubt that a
manufacturer should have concern that one or few buyers dominate
his sales programme; the major retail buyers will surely expect and
demand that a large part of savings be passed on to them in the form
of lower prices, discounts, rebates or other supporting promotional
activity in order that they, in turn, can remain more competitive and
attractive to the buying public. In general, however, experience
would seem to show that the major buying groups have no interest in
dictating terms that would force suppliers out of production.
Concentration may actually have provided a stimulus, with direct and
indirect benefits to suppliers, such as:

- an improved ability to forecast sales
- better production planning and plant utilisation
- improved control over supplies of inputs and inventories
- lower physical distribution costs to fewer delivery points
- more flexibility and control in developing specific sales
  promotions to support ongoing marketing programmes
- new opportunities to supplement production of branded goods
  with private label production runs utilising spare production
  capacity (I do not propose in this text to debate the marketing
  merits of branded versus private label merchandise)
- concentration of the key selling function to few individuals at few
  locations, with greater professionalism from buyers

32

- the concentration of the sales function may result in the need for smaller field sales forces, with cost savings, or (in the case of f.m.c.g. products) a changed structure to provide more merchandising services at the store level rather than normal selling activities.

The result has often been the recognition of the need for a specialist **national accounts** function within the sales organisation to centralise and concentrate the effort directed towards major industrial groups and multiple retailers operating across a wide geographical area.

Within a national accounts department it would be normal to make one **accounts manager** totally responsible for all aspects of business development through particular key accounts. The job of the account manager does not finish when he agrees a programme with a buyer. In fact, most of his time is spent following up to ensure that programmes are implemented according to plans, and monitoring results to provide feedback to buyers and within his own organisation. Moreover, prior to any meeting with a buyer there is usually a considerable period spent planning the call, since a call without a specific objective is counterproductive.

The key account function thrives and develops on mutual respect, professionalism in all aspects of conducting sales negotiations, and close mutual liaison between buyers and sellers. Neither party benefits by ignoring apparent or potential problems, and both have a strong interest in the satisfactory resolution of matters standing in the way of profitable business development. The account manager must above all be an efficient and effective communicator, and able to motivate and influence persons not under his direct line management authority.

Example 1.11 A national account sales structure

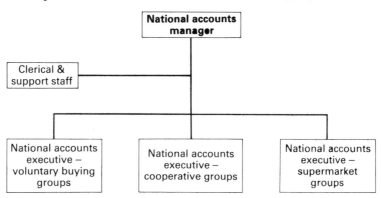

The size of a national accounts function will depend on the number of key multiple retail accounts or industrial buying groups that represent potential markets and the supporting workload to service those accounts effectively as sales develop. A smaller company with few actual or potential outlets may need only one key account manager; a larger mass market product manufacturer may need a hierarchical organisation (Example 1.11), where each market sector is covered by a different account manager.

An industrial sales organisation is likely to be much less complex, although the limitations related to the span of control of individual managers will still apply. I shall give an example of a sales organisation for an electrical components manufacturer (see Example 1.12). It is assumed that the organisation must be developed to manage the sales of electrical switches of various types to the different end-use markets, which might encompass a range of switches suitable for sale through retailers and wholesale distributors for home light fittings, and a different range of switches that would find use only as components in other electrical manufactured products. The nature of the products might require coverage of public sector departments concerned with approvals and specifications (including safety aspects and products approved for use in public sector buildings), architects who might specify or recommend products, builders or construction companies who might actually incorporate products in development programmes, and electrical goods manufacturers.

Example 1.12 Sales organisation for an electrical switch manufacturer

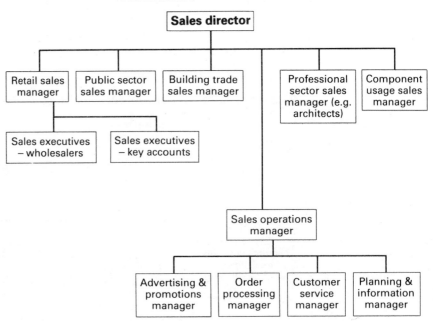

In the example, the company has chosen to organise by market sector, so that each key sales executive is specialised in a particular

34

market sector and is not limited by geographical boundaries. This form of organisation may be advisable if the skills and qualifications for any particular market sector are different from those for another market sector. For example, the sales executive calling on architects may benefit from or need an architectural training in order to relate to clients; the executive covering electrical goods manufacturers may need to be a qualified electrical engineer; the sales executive dealing with the public sector may need to have worked within that sector to know the approval processes and contacts. The retail sales manager may have a more conventional subordinate sales structure to provide coverage of key retail and wholesale accounts. I have not included a sales force for coverage of independent retailers on the assumption that the company has determined that this would not be cost-effective and has decided to concentrate efforts on widening distribution by providing significant support to the wholesale trade. The sales operation manager also has a fairly conventional range of subordinate responsibilities, but with an additional responsibility for advertising and promotion, on the assumption that the product is commodity- rather than brand-oriented, and does not yet warrant a significant and separate marketing function. Such products are mainly promoted through trade literature and advertising in specialist trade journals, and through presentation at trade exhibitions. In such a limited sales organisation, sales training may not warrant a full-time functional specialisation, but might be the responsibility of one of the operational managers. In this example I have deliberately chosen to use the term 'sales operations manager' and not 'sales office manager', since the latter might suggest largely clerical subordinate functions, whereas the key person in line control of head office support functions should have significant control of and input into a number of important operational areas including planning, policies, strategies and forecasting, in addition to the operational functions. Perhaps a broader term could be 'operations and planning manager'.

Specialised designs

The basic principles involved in developing an organisation can be applied to a number of specialist products. Some products may not need regular coverage cycles, for example if there is normally a once-only sale such as may be the case in selling certain financial and related services. Such organisations may not benefit from geographical territory limitations, particularly where sales achievements relate closely to the salesperson's range of contacts and connections. An insurance company specialising in normal household insurance may find that a geographically structured organisation gives it the required control over representatives, who each have a fixed-boundary territory to cover. Another insurance company selling pension schemes may prefer to organise in a manner that identifies and provides coverage to separate market

35

sectors, where individual salespersons would benefit by specialist knowledge or skills. Example 1.13 illustrates an insurance company providing a range of services.

Example 1.13   Basic sales organisation of an insurance company

In this example, the household insurance cover department would be organised on traditional geographical lines with the number of managers related to the number of separate territories and effective span of control at each management level. The life assurance and pension plan departments may require very different approaches. Even though the market coverage overlaps, it may be decided that the very different specialist insurance knowledge is such that the two departmental functions could not effectively be merged. Both departments may identify two target market sectors: private clients, often identified through contacts of the sales executives who are free to operate over a wide geographical area without defined boundaries; and professional advisers to individuals, such as lawyers, bankers and accountants, who can recommend programmes and influence clients. At first glance it may appear that there is little, if any, difference between the two market sectors. However, the sales executives calling on professional advisers may need a far greater knowledge of complex subjects such as tax regulations. They may also be more effective if they do not use 'pressure' sales techniques.

Indeed, professional advisers may be more influenced by sales executives who hold a professional qualification. The private client market, on the other hand, may respond better to the more traditional sales approach of creating attention, interest, desire and action, as the client is the decision maker.

Retail sales structures

In discussing sales organisations and structures, it is too easy to forget that the major sales area in industry is at the retail level. Each store exists only to sell to shoppers. Selling at the store level may be **active** – where sales assistants offer advice and seek to identify a customer's needs and preferences, relating these to goods available – or **passive** – where a range of goods is mass-merchandised in display racks and the customer is left to choose, and the first contact with staff is normally at a check-out point.

Example 1.14   Basic organisation of a retail department store

A typical department store organisation will relate to the types of goods sold, with each department having a manager and subordinate sales staff. In Example 1.14 the electrical goods section of the store organisation is sub-divided into four departments each with a manager responsible for all aspects of product merchandising and sales effort and performance. The floor sales staff are at the front end of contact with the consumers and need specialist sales training (just as much as any manufacturer's representatives) in aspects of company policy, product knowledge, effective selling, handling objections, customer relations, and so on. The department managers will have a range of other functional responsibilities including ordering, display, personnel matters, department profit performance, training and customer contact. They may have some flexibility in pricing, but this is likely to be a head office function. The store management are thus fundamentally responsible for achievement of sales volume targets at agreed prices. Although the organisation at store level may be very basic, there is likely to be a whole range of support services at a head office, mainly related to buying and merchandising.

This book is mainly aimed at those managing sales operations for manufacturers, but much of the content could have relevance for the retail trade, particularly aspects of recruitment, training and motivation. A recognition by any retail organisation of the significance of selling and the benefits of effective sales training within their organisation would perhaps create a new emphasis on staff training.

Matrix organisations

Many companies have found that the traditional pyramidical organisational hierarchy is not effective or easy to manage as the company grows in size, diversity, product ranges and market sectors served. Products are often becoming more complex to design and use, and therefore also to sell and market, with much more liaison and inter-departmental teamwork within both selling and buying organisations at all stages of the planning, decision-taking, controlling and monitoring processes. Sales and marketing managers may find they cannot manage their departments and functions in isolation from other specialist functions.

The result has been the development in some organisations of a form of **matrix** management, where planning, controlling, decision taking, evaluation, resource allocation, etc., are delegated downwards to the management levels where specialist functional inputs are available. A team may be formed for each market sector or product group, possibly led by a sales or marketing manager of suitable experience and seniority, and the team would report in to the sales and marketing division department heads and divisional directors who might make up the sales and marketing policy committee. Example 1.15 shows an example of a matrix format.

However, as those readers who have experience of it may already know, and those who choose to develop such an organisational format may discover, it often takes some years for a matrix organisation to develop and function effectively because of the traditional interpersonal and interdepartmental differences and conflicts, and there is often benefit in stability of membership on any committee grouping.

Example 1.15 Matrix management

	SALES DIRECTOR			MARKETING DIRECTOR			
POLICY COMMITTEE	National sales manager	Operations & planning manager	National accounts manager	Market research manager	Marketing manager		
PRODUCT GROUP A	Regional manager 1	Customer service manager	Accounts manager 1	Market research analyst 1	Product manager 1 (Team leader)	Financial analyst 1	Production manager 1	Advertising agency account exec 1
PRODUCT GROUP B	Regional manager 2 (Team leader)	Sales training manager	Accounts manager 2	Market research analyst 2	Product manager 2	Financial analyst 2	Production manager 2	Advertising agency account exec 2

Notes: Within each department and division there will be a hierarchical management pyramid, although membership of any particular matrix group need not depend on seniority but upon the person's functional contribution to that group. If, for example, it is felt that particular functions need to be represented on several matrix groups, then one functional representative might sit on all groups, or subordinates (e.g. assistant to the customer service manager) might attend the group.

Each matrix group would have a team leader, probably from either sales or marketing departments or divisions.

ORGANISATIONAL CONSIDERATIONS

A variety of possible organisational structures have been considered and reviewed in this chapter. It is worth attempting to establish some guidelines to consider in developing an effective sales organisation.

Span of control
A key factor determining the number of managers a sales organisation needs is the limit on the effective span of control of each manager over functions, skills, job content, job proximity and utilisation of time.

Workloads
The number of positions within any sales force will also be a function of workload capacity within each particular functional activity identified. As the workload of a functional activity increases, that function may require to be separated as a sub-department or delegated to a specific new subordinate position.

Functional activities
Identification of those specialist functional activities requiring separate management input, control and development will increase the quantity and quality of output from the organisation.

Communications
Effective and efficient communications systems between the functional activities and management levels are a prerequisite to a good organisation structure to ensure coordination of separate and related activities, provision of feedback, effective planning, and the recognition and achievement of common objectives through coordinated strategies.

Flexibility
Any organisation is basically intended to make people more productive and to improve group and individual performance. Although the organisation provides continuity by recognising and emphasising functional activities, which are supported by a vertical management and non-management structure, there is an essential need to maintain flexibility to adapt to changes in the environment and marketplace. Senior managers should constantly be aware of barriers to flexibility and resistance to change within their subordinate organisation and seek to counter this, possibly by encouraging the decentralisation of decision making where this is practical and prudent.

Role clarification
An organisation will only operate effectively where there is an

absence of internal conflict. This is a rather difficult, if not impossible, ideal to achieve, but conflict can be reduced by avoiding duplication or overlapping of line or functional responsibilities. The preparation of formal job specifications aids in identifying potential areas of conflict or role misperception.

In a field sales organisation, management control and motivation are more likely to be effective in an environment of 'one man, one boss'. One salesperson is generally responsible for the sales through each particular account, and needs to know to whom and for what he is responsible. Various forms of functional or matrix management structures that may be effective within a head office environment need very careful evaluation in terms of control, accountability and motivation if applied to a field sales environment. Any factor that could inject confusion into the field management equation may adversely affect performance. For example, where a specific position as a field sales trainer has been introduced, those field sales trainers rapidly become aware of the need not to usurp the authority of line managers and be seen as an 'alternative manager'.

Organisational format

The actual organisation of a sales force may generally take one of three formats:

- **geographical**, where each manager and salesperson is respon-sible for sales activity and outlet coverage in a clearly defined geographical area;
- **market sector**, where the markets for the product are in more than one market sector (e.g. grocery and pharmaceutical outlets for a typical drug store type of item) and where a different sales force is developed to cover each market sector with greater specialisation and effectiveness;
- **end-use**, where a product has sales potential in more than one industry or market sector, and where effective penetration into each target market or industry would require significantly different skills or qualifications or organisational structures.

SUMMARY

- The sales team are responsible for achieving the sales volumes prescribed in company plans at prices yielding acceptable profit contributions.
- Sales management functions can usually be broadly categorised into areas of **management, administration** and **planning**.
- Field organisations should reflect the needs of the product and the customers in respect of:

  - ability to provide adequate outlet coverage
  - solicitation of orders and efficient order processing
  - provision of sufficient product knowledge and information
  - provision of customer-level promotional support
  - understanding the business and trading environment of the customers
  - provision of any necessary product merchandising support
  - after-sales service where necessary.

- The sales manager is primarily responsible for the **management, motivation** and **morale** of his subordinate team.
- He identifies and sets goals and objectives in conjunction with the marketing function aimed at achieving targets and forecasts, and structures a sales force organisation that can implement sales and marketing programmes, provide training, feedback and all other necessary support services required to aid field sales force achievement of its goals and objectives.
- He must also ensure that the subordinate positions in the sales organisation provide high levels of **job satisfaction** in terms of job content, team spirit and membership, management, training, rewards and incentives, recognition, quality products, and a positive company image.
- The key irreplaceable resource the sales manager must most effectively manage is **time**.
- He needs to be seen to be decisive, fair and impartial, demonstrate initiative, provide leadership, be a good communicator, organiser and planner.
- The organisation of the sales force must reflect the functional requirements of the company, the service requirements of the customers, and particular activity needs of the products, and the sales manager can usefully prepare an analysis which will help in evaluating if his organisation provides satisfaction of needs in all three categories.
- The organisation must also reflect the functions that are the responsibility of the sales director and his subordinate managers, which relate to the overall achievement of company and sales force objectives.

- The size of any sales organisation will be a function of actual or potential sales volumes, the coverage of customers needed to generate those volume profitably, and the workloads within each tier of functional or line responsibility.
- The number of field sales management positions is particularly governed by the effective span of control of each tier of management required. By working backwards from an assessment of the territory workloads it becomes possible to identify the numerical requirements for primary, secondary and tertiary line managers, taking account of factors limiting the span of control.
- Organisations are generally designed to provide management and outlet coverage on the basis of:

  - geography
  - market sector
  - end-use.

- Traditionally the pyramidical 'one man, one boss' field sales organisation is preferred for effective management, motivation, communication and control.
- An organisation structure is primarily concerned with arranging and correlating tasks in such a fashion that the assignment of individuals to those tasks will result in effective and efficient team work towards common objectives, each team member/job holder having his own subordinate and specific objectives as part of the group objective.
- To be effective the organisation should be flexible, assign clear roles to job holders to avoid the risk of conflict, and have clearly defined reporting relationships as well as an absence of barriers to communications within the organisation.

CHECKLIST   A SALES MANAGER'S PERSONAL AUDIT

1   Either on your own or preferably with the help of colleagues or superiors assign points to each of the listed management factors such that the total of all points equals only 100. This is effectively giving an estimate of the relative import- ance or weighting of each factor in the sales management process and function.

2   Next, rate yourself, or preferably ask colleagues to rate you, on the scale 1 to 6 for each of the listed factors, multiply the rating figure by the points weighting, and enter the total in the last column.

3   Add your last column figures to give a total at the bottom. You can compare your total score with an average of 350, and see if you are scoring above or below average.

This exercise has limited application, but may help you to identify or recognise training needs. It can have more serious application where a number of persons (say all the area sales managers) have attached weightings to these or another internally prepared list of key sales management factors, and average weightings are entered on a separate audit sheet for each participant who then is rated on each factor.

	Weightings	Score						Weighting × score
		1	2	3	4	5	6	
DO YOU...								
• provide leadership?								
• motivate the team?								
• set goals and objectives?								
• develop strategies and tactics?								
• prepare forecasts, plans, or set targets?								
• develop promotional programmes?								
• recruit the right people?								
• provide training to meet all needs?								
• communicate effectively?								
• measure performance?								
• provide feedback?								
• exercise control and discipline?								
• recognise or anticipate problems?								
• exercise initiative?								
• take decisions promptly?								
• develop corrective action programmes?								
• manage resources cost effectively?								
• delegate effectively?								
• develop organisational structures to suit the business and environment?								
• develop support functions?								
• develop systems and procedures?								
• have all the necessary skills for the job?								
• design motivating reward and incentive schemes?								
TOTALS	100							

44

CHECKLIST EFFECTIVE ORGANISATIONAL STRUCTURE

Is your organisation designed to:

- prepare sales forecasts, plans, budgets, and sales programmes?
- increase and/or maximise distribution?
- merchandise and display product optimally?
- provide 100% scheduled call coverage?
- identify and develop new customers?
- recruit the most suitable sales personnel?
- provide comprehensive sales and management training?
- measure performance?
- provide feedback and effective communications?
- control customer credit and collect late payments?
- provide support services to the sales force?
- provide customer service support?
- process orders promptly and efficiently?
- effectively distribute product to all customers?
- provide the necessary support and service to key accounts?
- provide customer after-sales service?
- reflect customer needs in terms of distribution, buying practices and trade terms?
- have in-built flexibility to meet changing markets and environments?

Are the following effective and realistic for all sales force operatives?

- reporting relationships?
- spans of control?
- workloads?
- number/mix/range of functional activities?
- internal and external communications?
- organisational format?
- reporting procedures, administrative systems, and controls?

If the answer to any of these questions is 'no', or a qualified 'yes', then there may be scope for organisational modifications or improvements that might increase the productivity and effectiveness of the sales organisation.

45

2 Motivational Management in the Sales Force

WHAT IS MOTIVATION?

Motivation is generally seen as the process of getting people to work towards the achievement of an objective. Management may often take a rather limited or perhaps selfish approach to motivation, seeing it only as getting subordinate employees to work towards the achievement of a company objective through the achievement of targets, plans, or forecasts. However, traditional motivational theory (Maslow, *Motivation and Personality*, New York, Harper & Row, 1954) postulates that individuals are motivated only when they see an opportunity to fulfil some personal need, which may be either positively satisfied in that something is added (such as a new or bigger automobile), or negatively satisfied in that a source of dissatisfaction is reduced or removed (such as the achievement of an objective that stops the pressures from the manager and gives the achiever a quieter life for a while).

We should thus consider motivation as the process of getting people to act willingly towards the achievement of greater satisfaction of personal needs through the achievement of company goals and objectives.

MOTIVATIONAL FACTORS

Broadly speaking, motivational theory has recognised two main types of need: (i) primary or physiological needs; (ii) secondary or social needs.

The lower-level primary or **physiological** needs include:

- the satisfaction of basic survival requirements, including nourishment, shelter, clothing and, nowadays, the basic material comforts of life;
- physical and emotional security.

Companies attempt to satisfy basic needs by providing continuous employment, which enables the individual to earn an income that fulfils basic comfort and survival needs to acceptable social standards. The company frequently extends its satisfaction of basic needs by acting as a security blanket for the individual employee and his family, giving security of employment and earnings, protection of earnings during periods of sickness, the provision of health and life

46

assurance, pensions, and safe working environments. In less developed economic environments, as found in some third world nations, the individual may never progress beyond the level of satisfying the most basic survival needs of food, shelter and clothing on a day-to-day basis.

Once there is a basic satisfaction of primary needs, the individual may start to consider what else he looks for and values in life, and develop or recognise a range of secondary needs. These secondary needs may initially be mainly **socially** orientated and then graduate on a scale towards **self-esteem**. They include the needs for:

- **recognition** as an individual and for personal achievements
- **acceptance** within the social and group environment
- **independence** of thought and action
- **achievement** of something he sees as worthwhile
- **status** in society and the work environment
- **power** through position and responsibility
- **economic strength**, which might manifest as greed or a drive for acquisition of material things.

PRACTICAL MOTIVATION

As the emphasis of the text is on the practical rather than the theoretical approach to sales management and motivation, this discussion of needs or drives should be related to the sales environment; comments are as relevant to the motivation of managers as to that of territory salespersons.

Establish
goals and
objectives

Before anyone can be motivated to produce or achieve anything he must know exactly what he is expected to produce or achieve. That means the manager must set clear and definitive goals and objectives, communicate these to the people expected to contribute to their achievement and, where necessary, break down the overall goals and objectives into lower stages or levels of objectives.

Within each individual job function **standards of performance** should be set and communicated in writing and accepted by each job holder as his personal standards to aim for and measure performance and achievement against. The more clearly each job holder understands the relationship between his own job performance and the company goals and objectives, the easier it will be for the manager to develop individual effort into team commitment. The individual also needs to understand how achievement of company goals and objectives will actually benefit him by increasing his satisfaction of needs. This will encourage self-motivation and self-development.

47

Although everyone has needs, the manager must recognise and accept that each of his subordinate team members is an individual, with a personal blend of needs and drives, strengths and weaknesses. The manager's task is to form objective judgements on the magnitude, priorities, interrelationships, and balance between the individual personal needs of each of his subordinates; and then to increase productivity and performance by offering means by which the individual can increase his satisfaction of an individual need or greater satisfaction of a range of needs. The manager may do this in isolation on the basis of his experience and observation, or he might attempt to form a motivational needs analysis (illustrated later in this section) by discussion over a period of time with an individual. Clearly many people do not recognise or acknowledge their own motivations and needs hierarchy, and the following discussion of needs may assist managers in the analysis process.

Survival
The basic survival of the individual and his dependants necessitates the individual earning a wage to meet his minimum requirements. However, what is minimum for one person may be insufficient for another. In selecting salespersons, account should be taken of the current living standards of each candidate, and a manager should assess if the position will yield an income level high enough to meet those standards; if this is not possible then it is likely the person will not stay long in the position, but will use it as a stepping stone to other employment.

The individual who wants to provide more than minimal living standards for his family can be motivated by opportunities for him to increase earnings. An individual who has little interest in material comforts is unlikely to be motivated to increase productivity and performance through financial and other material rewards, so that if such motivators are in common use in the sales force it is essential that managers ensure that the acquisition drive and related drives are strong in job candidates.

Health
This is closely linked with survival as a physiological drive, and one we tend to take for granted. By health I mean the general physical and mental well-being of the employee and his family, including the illness preventative measures of good nutrition and physical activity, no excesses of stressful pressures, access to treatment when sickness does occur, and income continuity during sickness. An individual who finds his health suffering because of job content or work-related pressure may present a long-term problem unless the manager can remove the causes of the health problems, for example through training that increases skills to the point where the individual no longer feels the job to be a source of pressure. In some instances,

48

continuing ill-health in the family might serve as a motivator or demotivator. If it affects the salesperson's productivity or performance, perhaps because he feels obligated to rush home early at the end of the day, then it will be a demotivating influence. It might prove a motivator if the salesperson prefers to work even harder either to earn more to meet the extra costs of an unwell family member, or to avoid going home to face the problematic home environment.

Security

Most people have some degree of security drive – for income and job security, or for a stable home environment. An established position, along with the income and fringe benefits that brings (such as sickness cover, life assurance, holidays, pensions, etc.), helps satisfy certain security needs. Some sales managers may question whether a highly security-driven person is right for a sales environment where security is related to an ongoing ability to achieve measurable results. On the other hand, a person driven by certain security needs may be motivated to improve performance by fear of loss of tenure of his position (but constant motivation using the threat of job loss is ineffective as the demotivational effects will generally come to override the motivational effects).

Acceptance

This drive might encompass acceptance by family, friends, peer groups, colleagues and supervisors. Some people are strongly driven by a need to belong to a group, and will work hard to do what is necessary to achieve acceptance, including responding to training and counselling that will raise their own standards to levels acceptable to the group. At the other end of the spectrum is the person who refuses to cooperate in a group environment and thrives on being seen as a maverick, possibly also projecting the image that he is superior to other group members. The manager who encounters such a subordinate will have to evaluate if that is the real person – in which case he is probably motivated to retain his independence and self-image of superiority through results achieved – or if the individual is scorning group membership and acceptance because he actually fears that he might not be successful if he attempted to gain acceptance.

Affection

The need to give or receive affection is another drive that can impinge on the work situation. Many people perhaps satisfy their strongest affection needs within the family, but a person having the strong need to be liked can be motivated in the work situation by an awareness of what he can do that will increase his popularity within the work group. This may be particularly relevant where sales effort depends on team activity.

49

Respect

Again, this drive factor has degrees and counter-drives or needs. One person may be strongly driven to receive respect from colleagues, friends, family and so on. Another may be driven by a need to show respect for authority and those who represent it. Others disdain showing respect for authority or those who represent it, and might even cynically boast that 'it takes a good man to earn my respect'. A man might feel that he deserves respect because of his present position; or that he would receive more respect if he had a better position or different job title. He might increase job productivity and performance in order to increase the level of respect he will be shown by colleagues. The cynic might well become respect-motivated if he actually finds there is something his manager can do better, after he has previously experienced failure in his attempts to achieve the objective.

Harmony

The need for order is strong within some people. Such a person may be motivated to do whatever is necessary to avoid disharmony in the environment. At the opposite end of this need spectrum are those who thrive on disharmony in any form. Occasionally there will be a team member who appears to thrive on bringing disharmony into a harmonious team environment. Such a person may respond to counselling, or may have other needs that can be played on to bring his behaviour into line with the group needs (such as a need for respect, or acceptance, or responsibility).

Dependence

Individuals may be highly dependent and need much support from the manager or, at the other extreme, may be very independent and able to operate with minimum supervision and attention whilst demonstrating decisiveness and initiative.

Consolidation

At some point, some people become satisfied with their present role and status in life and want to consolidate that position rather than chase higher goals or levels of achievement. Such a person might prove rather resistant to change unless that change helps his own need for consolidation. A consolidator might be satisfied to be seen as an elder statesman of the sales force and might actually be motivated by being drawn into roles that use his experience in training younger people; in such a training role the elder statesman/consolidator may even agree to learn new skills or techniques.

Change

The opposite of the consolidator is the person who constantly seeks change and challenge, seeking to diversify his skills, interests,

50

experiences, environment, and so on. If such a salesperson responds to change in a highly results-oriented fashion, he may be ideal to handle special assignments and sales research projects, or fulfil other one-off roles to supplement his routine (such as organising conferences and meetings or training meetings for wholesalers).

Activity
Some people must be always 'on the go', unable to sit down and relax for long. Such a salesperson may well thrive on extra-curricula activities such as running evening training sessions for distributors' salesmen. Other people might simply be concerned with getting through the tasks of the day as quickly as possible in order to rest and relax. In addition, whereas one person might have activity drives in a physical sense, another may be driven towards intellectual activity.

Knowledge
The drive for knowledge also varies greatly between persons. One person may accept the minimum level of product and company knowledge to perform his job functions satisfactorily; another may be driven to read advanced sales and marketing texts in the quest for knowledge and excellence.

Achievement
The need to achieve something lasting is a major drive in many persons. The need might be satisfied by achieving tangible perform- ance results, material benefit, increased status or recognition, a contribution to knowledge or history. Within the sales environment the need to achieve must be matched with other qualities, qualifications and drives that will actually lead to positive achieve- ment, otherwise the achievement-driven salesperson will become frustrated at not making progress.

Recognition
The drive or need for recognition also varies between persons. One may be happy with an obscure role; another needs to be in the forefront, recognised by associates and peers for personal qualities, achievements or skills. There are many avenues open to the sales manager who has recognition-motivated subordinates, including mentions at meetings and in bulletins, or the assignment of special projects and promotion. The recognition-motivated salesperson may well satisfy his need by achieving results that will ensure that he is recognised.

Responsibility
Some people have a strong need to have and accept responsibility; others seek to avoid it. Responsibility has many dimensions. The person who seeks responsibility may have the attributes and

51

characteristics for a man-management role in the organisation;
alternatively he may be high in technical and sales skills, and perhaps
satisfy his needs through project work or key account management
or other changes in functional activities.

Status

The salesperson's needs in terms of status interrelate closely with a
number of the other drives, including recognition, achievement and
responsibility. Higher status needs might be easily satisfied by
changing a job title from, say, 'territory salesperson' to 'installation
consultant'. However, changing a title is often only a cosmetic
exercise that produces other internal problems. The need for more
status may relate to a person's feelings of low self-worth in his present
role. A recognition by customers and colleagues in other departments that the sales function is an essential and highly valued role in
the organisation, and one that greatly contributes to communications, distribution and the achievement of goals and objectives, might
lessen any self-worth doubts.

Some people may satisfy their status needs through the normal
career progression channels within the organisation if they possess
the necessary characteristics and skills. Otherwise, alternative
approaches to conferring status need to be examined.

Power

For some people the drive for power grows as other needs are
satisfied. This is more than just a desire for responsibility. It is a need
to be at or close to the apex of a hierarchical pyramid. This drive may
be sublimated to other needs that are more readily satiable, such as
recognition, responsibility, activity, or knowledge. Indeed, to some
people knowledge is power.

Acquisition

The physiological drives for survival extend at a more advanced need
stage to a desire for acquisition just for its own sake. This need often
covers collectibles of little functional use. Increasing material rewards
through incentive schemes may offer a means to satisfy acquisition
needs.

A chart of some basic motivational needs can be drawn up as in
Example 2.1. The line manager might attempt a rating on the scale to
identify the stronger needs within each individual in the team.

A manager might develop this chart by adding his own observed
motivations for each team member. A study of what a person does in
his spare time often gives a good lead to less obvious drives and
motivations, because if basic needs are not being satisfied in the work
environment many persons will seek to satisfy those needs

Example 2.1 Motivational needs audit

	Rating								Notes
	1	2	3	4	5	6	7	8	

Survival
Need for income to meet more than
minimum requirements

Health
Physical and mental well-being of
self and family

Security
Need for stability of income,
employment, homelife and
environment

Acceptance
Need for acceptance by family, friends,
peer groups, colleagues, supervisors

Affection
Need for close relationships within
home, social and work environments

Respect
Need to receive or show respect in
home, social or work environment

Harmony
Preference for order/harmony rather
than disharmony/conflict

Dependence
Need for support and supervision

Consolidation
Satisfaction with present role/status

Change
Need to diversify skills and interests
and find new challenges

Activity
Need for physical and/or intellectual
activity beyond minimum job inputs

Knowledge
Desire to pursue new knowledge and
excellence

Achievement
Need for tangible achievements in
terms of results, status, benefits,
recognition, knowledge, etc.

Recognition
Preference for public recognition
rather than obscurity

Responsibility
Need to have and seek responsibility
rather than avoid it

Status
Need for a feeling of self-worth or
recognition of status

Power
Need for power through position or
knowledge

Acquisition
Need for additional material things
beyond survival needs, and these
need not be functional

in extra-curricula activities. For example, an active man in a sedentary job might pursue aggressive sporting hobbies in his spare time; an adventurous person with lower physical security needs might seek his outlet through participation in armed forces reserve units at weekends; the person whose status or authority needs are not satisfied at work might be very active on various committees or hold responsible positions in social groups outside of work.

A person who has no unsatisfied needs will prove near impossible to motivate, but rather than the sales manager saying 'that man cannot be motivated' he should be asking 'what unsatisfied need has he got that I have so far failed to recognise?' All too often, less experienced managers look for or only recognise in others the drives and motivations they believe they recognise in themselves (the 'halo' effect), which are probably more highly oriented towards responsibility, status, achievement, improved materials benefits, and so on. They may find it hard to accept the more passive drives such as consolidation, harmony and security.

Articles on motivation and motivational factors tend to develop certain common theories on the basic needs and hierarchy of needs, and seek to isolate individual drives or needs. But the individual is a complex blend of many needs, with the balance constantly changing as certain satisfactions are achieved or the person's circumstances or environment change. The sales manager who seeks to understand the motivational needs of each of his sales team will quickly learn that he must develop a flexible approach to increasing the needs satisfaction of each team member.

JOB SATISFACTION

Every job is made up of a number of interesting (motivating) and uninteresting (demotivating) factors; each individual may have differing views as to which factors he places in these broad categories. To get the greatest productivity and performance out of each individual, managers have to provide a job and a working environment seen by each person as motivating and providing the satisfaction of his personal drives and needs. The work and theories of Frederick Herzberg published in the 1950s provide a useful basis for considering satisfying and unsatisfying aspects of jobs in the sales environment.

Demotivators Before motivation can commence it is necessary to identify and eliminate or neutralise demotivating factors. General demotivators can be categorised under the headings of:

- job uncertainties
- job imbalances
- inadequate management
- inadequate working environment
- poor compensation
- poor prospects

Job uncertainties

Insecurity of tenure   A salesperson who feels his job may not last long – either because it is seasonal or contractual in nature, or because the company may cease operations, or there is a threat of redundancy for any reason, or the job holder is under a disciplinary warning – may not feel motivated to give of his best. The sales manager must work to minimise or remove the feelings of insecurity and the causes.

Ill-defined roles and responsibilities   If a job description either does not exist or inadequately defines the role, relationships, duties, responsibilities and limits of authority of the job holder, then he is likely to be demotivated by the lack of clarity. The sales manager must also be realistic and reasonable in his expectations or demands. A person who sees an objective as quite unachievable will frequently make only a token effort.

Poor training   It is not sufficient just to recruit a person to a position and present him with a job description. Inadequate orientation and training in the functions of the job may act as a demotivator.

Absence of performance standards   The job holder wants to know what is expected of him and what standards of performance are considered as satisfactory so that he can measure himself against those standards, and to experience consistency in demands by members of management. If standards of performance do not exist, or measurements are not provided enabling him to compare his performance against standards, then it may be demotivating. A thorough feedback of data to support comparisons with standards of performance is essential.

Job imbalances

Qualifications   If the job holder is over-qualified for a position and feels he is working below his level of experience and expertise he may feel demotivated (he might have taken the job knowing it was below his level yet needing current employment). Occasionally an under-qualified person may be put into a job for which he is inadequately trained or experienced, and will be demotivated by the constant problem faced in striving to perform satisfactorily. It is important to match the job holder to the job holder profile (as reviewed in Chapter 6).

Incorrect assignment By placing a person in a job for which he is unsuited, in terms of either experience, qualifications or interest, there is a danger of demotivation as the person struggles to perform satisfactorily in an unwelcome or unsatisfactory environment. The managers responsible for selection must evaluate carefully the characteristics, skills and experience needed in a position and fill positions only with matched persons.

Limited self-development Demotivation may result if the job holder feels that the position offers little or no scope for expansion of experience and skills and growth in stature and maturity for other more senior positions.

Job-content variety Wherever possible, jobs should be designed and structured to give variety of content and activity to reduce demotivation through boredom. Clearly each individual's threshold at which boredom might set in or demotivation occur will vary according to the person's skills, experience, intelligence, potential, ambition, and so on. The line manager will need to be sensitive of this in planning to stretch each person in a job through training and the addition of extra functions or responsibilities to eliminate or delay demotivation.

Inadequate management

Poor skill credibility If the manager is not seen as having the necessary skills and experience to perform the functions of his subordinates then his lack of credibility may become a demotivator. Salespersons traditionally like to know that their line manager can sell.

Poor control A salesperson expects to be controlled, and will lose respect for a manager who does not implement or exercise controls, or controls inefficiently, or is not seen to be 'on top of his job'. On the other hand, a manager should beware of stifling initiative and effort through over-control (discussed at more length in Chapter 11).

Prejudices A manager who is seen to act in any way that throws doubt on his neutrality in dealing with a subordinate may face a demotivating reaction from team members, who need to know their manager will always be objective and impartial.

Lack of recognition The manager who fails to recognise the efforts and achievements of any of his team members in a manner that satisfies that person's need for recognition may demotivate the individual. Acts of recognition need to match the requirement for recognition. Some salespersons may be happy with a quiet 'well done, John, on selling in that feature display'; others will need more visible

56

recognition in bulletins or at sales meetings to satisfy their needs and ego.

Inadequate communications The manager who fails to keep in constant touch with each of his subordinates – in person, by telephone, or through meetings or bulletins – and to provide informed communication and feedback of company progress, policies and programmes, as well as feedback on the individual's results and achievements, may find some salespersons demotivated. Each individual has different needs for involvement and communication, and the sales manager must identify and recognise the level of contact and communication needed for each team member.

The sales manager should also be scrupulously consistent in the content of his communications to individuals, because the team members will talk with each other regularly. If a manager has been untruthful, manipulative or deceptive in his dealing with team members this will become apparent to his subordinates before too long and weaken his credibility and leadership. Promises should never be made that cannot or will not be fulfilled. Whenever a genuine mistake occurs then the manager should not seek to transfer the blame for the mistake but should accept his own involvement or responsibility.

Inadequate development programmes A manager who fails to train and develop each salesperson to the extent of their potential and ability to accept and absorb training is not doing them justice, and could expect a demotivated reaction from those who feel not enough is being done to promote their development. This becomes a serious problem when, in addition to not providing development training (as a supplement to current job skill training), the sales manager also fails to nominate candidates from amongst his team for consideration for more senior positions. Many personnel officers and senior sales managers have experienced feedback from salespersons leaving the company that certain area managers are not considered within their team to be developing or progressing individuals with potential. Such a problem needs to be countered with training and counselling of the managers involved.

Inadequate working environment
This is a very broad subject that covers many of the factors that do not fit specifically into other categories.

Work equipment Every person likes to have the right quantity and quality of equipment satisfactorily and comfortably to perform his job functions. In the case of a sales force this will include good-quality

57

(and in adequate quantity) sales and promotional aids, probably a nice briefcase, and a good standard of car comparable to those supplied by competitors to their salespersons and that gives that status and recognition the salesperson needs. Whenever possible or practical it can often be motivating to offer a limited choice of company vehicles suited to the requirements of the job (such as a choice between saloon or estate versions). Attention should also be given to any work-related aspects of safety in considering equipment.

Work location   An office-based person will probably be concerned that he has an adequate-sized work area that enables him to work comfortably and gives recognition to his status and seniority in the organisation. Office-based staff may show great interest in such facilities as staff canteens, rest areas, sports or social facilities, and the overall standards of decoration and company equipment. Everyone likes to work for a concern that looks as if it is successful and run in an organised fashion.

A field operative may well be more concerned with the company vehicle, as just mentioned, and with the type of outlet he has to visit. If all the territory outlets are small, dingy, backstreet shops this may be demotivating. Calls on big, modern, industrial or multiple retail outlets add to interest and motivation.

Distractions that draw a person's attention away from work can be demotivating and reduce productivity and performance. This happens when a salesperson is asked to leave what he sees as his job and do something that to him seems quite unrelated, unimportant, or simply not his function (and possibly reducing his commission-earning potential). Other demotivating distractions might be more physical or environmental in nature, such as a noisy office or a desk located alongside what is effectively an office thoroughfare. Distractions in the field sales environment should be avoided as they are normally particularly time-consuming and of limited productive benefit.

Work relations   It is important for each person to work with a group of people he likes and respects. This is perhaps much more critical for office-based persons who are in constant close contact with many colleagues. The sales force personnel operate in a lonelier environment as far as contact with colleagues goes, but should be able to look forward to harmonious contact with colleagues. The salesperson has a mixture of relationships to build and cope with: the person-to-person relations with colleagues and customers; the salesperson-to-company relationship on which depend loyalty and ongoing satisfaction with the employer; and his relationship with society and the outside environment.

58

Poor compensation

The compensation package offered to each person will be demotivating if:

- it offers a lower regular income from salary and incentives than the individual values himself at
- it is less than comparable companies offer for similar positions, job functions and responsibilities
- the fringe benefits normally associated with employment – such as pensions, holiday time and pay, sickness cover, long-term disability incomes, medical insurance schemes, lunch allowances, subsidised canteens, etc. – are not competitive and comparable with those normally offered in the industry or general job market-place
- the incentive and bonus schemes are considered inadequate, unfair or unachievable
- improved results and performance through increased skills, productivity or other effort are not recognised through some form of merit income increase or other bonus. Compensation increments are one common way of demonstrating recognition for above-average achievement.

This subject is so critical in the sales environment that it will be dealt with in much more detail later in this chapter.

Poor prospects

If the prospective opportunities for advancement in a position or company do not match the ambitions of the job holder, then he may well become demotivated over time as the realisation sets in that high performance and effort do not increase his satisfaction of status and ambition or power needs. A converse situation is where the job and company do offer significant development and promotion prospects, but the job holder, while performing very satisfactorily in his present position, is not seen as having the qualities, skills or other characteristics considered necessary for higher positions. The sales manager faces alternatives of counselling the individual towards realism, with possible demotivating effects, providing corrective and development training (if that will reduce the imbalance between expectations and potential), and finding other avenues to use the skills and characteristics that the person exhibits and that might offer scope for development if correctly channelled (possibly in another job environment). A company needs to have a career development programme that ensures the satisfaction of competent and ambitious younger managers if such talent is not to be lost to the company. Some companies recognise the needs to tap and develop internal resources, and institute early retirement programmes to create opportunities.

59

These demotivating factors are not mutually exclusive. They are intricately interrelated and a balance must be achieved between them. It is possible to go to extremes with no incremental benefit. An office can be changed from an efficient working environment to such levels of luxury and comfort that the sense of work pace, urgency and need to produce is actually reduced.

The field sales manager should constantly be aware of any signs that there are problems in the motivational aspects of his sales team. Frequent symptoms may include:

- increased absence
- higher claimed sickness incidence
- complaints about demotivating factors
- deteriorating performance
- requests for transfer
- active hunting for alternative jobs by members of the team
- increased staff turnover
- less compliance with administrative systems and procedures
- increased cynicism (perhaps more apparent at meetings)

and a host of attitudinal indications through changed or modified behaviour.

It is always a useful management control to plot factors that can be objectively measured (such as absence, sickness, staff turnover) on charts or graphs that highlight variances from levels considered normal.

Motivators The guidelines for creating a good environment in which motivation can develop effectively can be summarised from the foregoing analysis of demotivators as:

- clarify the job
- set standards of performance
- recruit only qualified people
- train thoroughly
- compensate fairly
- manage efficiently and effectively
- communicate information
- provide feedback and formal appraisal
- promote staff development
- use advanced technology, systems and procedures.

Job description
Prepare a thorough, detailed and definitive job description covering the main duties, functions and responsibilities, including limits of authority and key result areas. Remove any ambiguity about the sales-

60

person's role and any potential source of conflict between two or more persons over who should be doing what or who is senior to whom.

Standards of performance

Clearly identify key result areas from the job description and set objective, achievable and measurable standards of performance against which the job holder can personally measure his performance.

Recruitment

Do not compromise at the selection stage. Recruit only people who match the characteristics, skills and experience detailed in a job holder profile.

Training

Avoid frustration, failure or demotivation through inadequate skills or poor company loyalty by providing thorough orientation to the company and training in all aspects of the job functions. Personal analysis of skills and needs, strengths and weaknesses, and the preparation of personal objectives and self-development programmes will raise confidence and increase the satisfaction of each individual's needs.

Compensation

Direct and indirect compensation (wages, salaries, bonuses, fringe benefits) should equitably represent reward for the responsibilities, duties and functions compared with competitive companies. Participation in formal and informal salary surveys with competitors is extremely beneficial to provide a source of confidential comparative data.

Management and control

Recruit and train managers who have the qualifications, skills and experience to provide leadership, training and motivation whilst gaining the respect of the team members through effective control, objectivity, impartiality, and empathy with subordinates. To ensure that each person is working towards the goals and objectives that have been set, managers need to exercise control both through the various continuous controls that can readily be operated in the sales organisation, and through the warning controls that alert management to deviations from the plotted course towards objective achievement (see Chapter 11).

Communication

Whilst there may sometimes be a limit to what information can be communicated to subordinates, generally the more a salesperson

61

knows and understands about his company, its goals, objectives, policies and programmes, and his role in ensuring the achievement of each of these, the greater his involvement and commitment.

Feedback

This should be provided through training, audits of skills and training needs, counselling, and measuring performance against standards and objectives.

Formal appraisal

This is the most effective form of feedback if properly conducted in that it tells a person at prescribed intervals exactly how he has performed on the tasks and duties assigned to him over the period since the last appraisal. It enables him to establish to what degree his superiors are satisfied with his work performance and obtain feedback on strengths, weaknesses, skills and potential. The factors communicated in a formal appraisal should never be a surprise to the appraisee if effective and frank communications exist between the manager and the managed.

Staff development

Recognise the needs of all levels of employees to grow with the job and into other and bigger jobs, and prepare continuing training and development programmes to advance existing skills and add new skills and experiences that stretch managers and salespersons alike. The cliché 'there will be plenty of opportunities with us in the future' must be seen by all to be a reality. Internal promotion can be a major motivator, just as external recruitment to internal positions, while being necessary in some circumstances, is a frequent demotivator.

Advanced technology, systems and procedures

Everyone takes pride in working for an organisation that is seen in the marketplace as modern, progressive, innovative, and so on. A new product, new advertising, new systems (which offer tangible benefits to all those involved) and the company's reputation as a market leader can all be major motivators. If the sales manager knows his organisation is seen as conservative by the trade and competitors, he can be sure his sales team are very aware of and sensitive to their own image in relation to the company's image.

MANAGEMENT'S MOTIVATIONAL ROLE

The manager clearly is the key to the motivational process. He identifies the motivational drives of his subordinates and offers the opportunity and means to increase certain satisfactions. In addition to the motivators already listed, the manager can also make use of:

- counselling
- recognition
- praise
- involvement/participation
- delegation
- promotion.

Counselling

Ongoing review discussions and counselling of each team member provide an opportunity to increase or direct motivation towards key result areas and the counsellee's personal increase of satisfactions. Frank, honest communication in the counselling process will build trust and a relationship of respect between the sales manager and his salespersons.

Recognition

The field sales manager is the key to providing a forum for recognition of the specific efforts and results of each of his team members. Recognition may help the satisfaction of other drives, such as status, achievement, acceptance.

Praise

Praise (which should be specific and not general as that may seem insincere) is a form of personal recognition and can help to increase the satisfaction of drives such as: security, harmony, recognition, affection, acceptance.

Involvement/participation

The manager can involve his team members in a variety of tasks and activities beyond day-to-day functions. Some people may initially avoid any extra involvements, perhaps out of lack of confidence (possibly, in turn, resulting from the person's concern that he lacks the necessary skills) or because of a reluctance to disturb the present balance of need satisfactions. The more each person is involved in a wider range of functions, particularly those that hold an interest, the greater the commitment to achievement of goals and objectives. Area meetings give an excellent forum for participation, possibly with each salesperson having a particular role or project under his control to review at such meetings.

Delegation

Delegation of the authority to take decisions and act positively may serve with many people to increase their commitment and motivation, especially those who have strong needs for responsibility, power, achievement, and so on.

63

Promotion

The line manager is the key to the salesperson's satisfaction of needs for increased status, material rewards, recognition, power, etc., through promotion. It is essential that members of a sales team see that their manager both trains and develops people for positions of greater responsibility and puts forward candidates for more senior positions as vacancies occur.

The good manager sees, knows and notes everything going on within his organisational environment; he controls much of the activities through his formal system of continuous and warning controls; he overlooks a lot of non-critical happenings; and he corrects, through counselling and training, a few points that particularly impact on key result areas.

MANAGEMENT'S LEADERSHIP ROLE

The manager's role is to lead. The authority that accompanies leadership may derive from any of several sources:

- **election** by peers to hold a position of authority or power over peers
- **appointment** by higher-placed persons who believe they are in a position to exercise judgement and appoint a person to provide a leadership role to persons at a lower level in the hierarchy
- **knowledge**, where an individual has a degree of specialist knowledge on a subject that causes peers to listen, seek, and accept guidance
- **structure**, where an organisation is structured such that it is clear which jobs are more senior to others, and which subordinate positions report to each higher management tier
- **personal authority**, where the individual has particular characteristics and attributes that command attention and cause people to want to listen to his guidance, such as unusual levels of energy, drive, enthusiasm, integrity, intelligence, loyalty, commitment, determination, communications skill, and factors relating to bearing and appearance.

Any manager's claim to leadership will normally be based on a mixture of these factors. However, whatever the source of his authority, a manager's recognition as leader comes, not when he claims authority by virtue of the position or title given to him, but when his subordinates realise that through him they can each increase the satisfaction of personal needs; only then will they accept his guidance, direction and leadership.

The manager must:

64

- achieve fulfilment of the group's functional tasks, goals and objectives
- maintain a team committed and motivated to achieving the group objectives
- satisfy the personal needs of individual team members through fulfilment of the group objective
- lead in a fashion that motivates subordinates through their personal commitment
- be seen by subordinates as decisive, rational and consistent
- be objective and impartial
- accept full responsibility for the actions, activities and performance results of team members
- lead by example and exhibit the highest standards in personal characteristics such as integrity, reliability, dependability, loyalty, etc.
- be seen to be a constant source of motivation and stimulation while exhibiting high levels of personal energy, enthusiasm, commitment and work effort.

MANAGEMENT STYLES

How a person uses his authority in a leadership role to motivate others to accept direction and guidance towards the achievement of common objectives is of concern here. The manager may follow or prefer any single or mixed style of:

- **autocracy**, where the manager takes his decisions alone and without consultation with subordinates and expects their total commitment in implementing decisions – practitioners of this style of management tend to prefer to communicate on a 'need to know' basis,
- **democracy**, where managers permit the team to decide its own course, perhaps by seeking a vote on each significant issue or set of alternatives,
- **consensus**, where the manager will communicate and discuss the merits of options or alternative courses of action, without taking a formal vote, and act as a chairman in recognising the consensus of views and opinions or support for any course of action.

Within each of these broad categories is a range of points, such as from total authoritarian dictatorship to paternalistic dictatorship. It is important that a manager understands his own style and balance of his sources of authority in his efforts to motivate subordinates, and is also sensitive to his impact upon both them and other colleagues. For example, the manager may be more or less people-oriented, or more or less results-oriented, or at any point of a matrix of these two

65

factors. (Whatever the management style, in the case of most managers the goals and objectives are set at higher organisational levels, and lower levels of management are generally more concerned with strategies and tactics to achieve them.)

What is the right style? There may not be a simple answer to this question. Broad motivational guidelines would suggest that:

- a person who works from a sense of threat or fear will seek to produce a satisfactory result, but will not be motivated to outstanding performance because threats provide a major distraction of attention and effort;
- participation and involvement at each stage of the evaluatory and decision-making process increase understanding and commitment of individuals in a team to the achievement of satisfactory results;
- fuller communications and feedback on objectives, plans, policies, programmes and results increase team involvement and commitment to the group goals and objectives.

The manager's style will also be influenced by his own views on the ability of his team members to understand issues and make constructive comment: some managers always believe that they alone are the best judges of action, and that their subordinates do not wish to be involved in the planning or decision-making processes. Such viewpoints tend to the cynical and are unlikely to be very motivational. In addition, the style may vary according to the situation. In deciding whom to involve in the management decision-making process, the manager should ask himself a series of questions:

- Whose problem is it?
- Have I the authority to decide and act?
- Is there time to consult and communicate?
- Are there alternative courses of action?
- Who else has information, knowledge or experience that can contribute to an evaluation of alternatives?
- Who else is being committed to involvement, participation, action or decisions?
- Who might benefit from or suffer from any course of action?
- Who might benefit from the experience of involvement in management decision-making processes (as a training exercise)?

This self-questioning process might help a manager move away from a highly autocratic management style and increase team commitment to action and results.

The word **MICRO** might sum up the manager's task:

66

Motivation to provide a source of satisfaction of personal needs;

Involvement of each team member in activities and decisions leading towards achievement of common goals and objectives;

Commitment of each team member to the common goals and objectives;

Recognition of the needs of the individuals and of their individual contributions to the achievement of group goals and objectives;

Orientation of each team member so that he knows and understands his role, job, duties, responsibilities and relationships.

REWARDS AND INCENTIVES

Much has been written on the role of rewards and incentives in motivating a sales force. It is a critical subject that warrants special attention in this chapter, but at the outset I do feel it is important to make two points:

(i) financial rewards and incentives satisfy only some of the many personal needs for survival and security or the more advanced economic/acquisition needs;

(ii) any effort after a certain point to increase productivity and performance through increased rewards and incentives is likely to cost more in real terms than using alternative motivational means to satisfy the other needs and drives to produce a similar increase in productivity and effort.

These points made, the position has already been taken in this chapter that poor or inadequate levels of financial reward will serve as a major demotivator. The compensation programme must provide a degree of security, offer flexibility to motivate persons through merit and incentive schemes, and respond to changes in the job and product marketplace.

Gross income and benefits might include some or all of the following:

- a fixed wage or salary
- commission on sales
- bonuses or other performance-related incentives
- other incentives, such as competitions or award schemes
- life assurance
- medical insurance
- pension schemes
- disability insurance and other short- and long-term income protection during sickness
- paid vacations
- expense allowances and subsidised meals, sports or social facilities
- company vehicles.

67

The system of rewards will vary according to local practice and culture. In some communities people who enter the sales profession expect little security of earnings and work largely or entirely for commission. If this is the only source of income or reward then the salespersons are effectively freelance sales agents, in that there is little or nothing to hold them to an employer if adequate earnings do not materialise.

In most western countries, salespersons expect at least a basic salary to meet certain accepted or expected living costs and standards, and this is usually in the range of two-thirds to three-quarters of total income. Together with benefits such as the normal fringe benefits of sickness cover, life assurance, medical insurance, pension schemes, vacations, company cars, etc., the basic salary tends to act more as a **maintenance** than as a **motivational** factor, satisfying the security and survival needs of the individual and his dependants.

The compensation programme must meet not only the needs and expectations of the individual employees, but also the needs and means of the company. The company's needs are to employ suitably qualified, skilled and experienced salespersons to fulfil the sales functions and to retain those employees who continually perform satisfactorily.

The basic salary

In summary, the basic salary should:
- be competitive with that for similar positions in similar-sized companies (there is merit in participating in inter-company salary surveys and watching job advertisements)
- fit in with a company job-grading scheme that reflects the differing duties and levels of responsibility of positions within the company
- be related to the skills, experience and responsibilities required of the position.

The position of an individual within the job-graded salary scale will depend on the level of skills, experience, and other attributes the job holder brings to the position, and the merit awards given to the job holder as a result of performance-based appraisals and performance against accepted and measurable standards.

If a chartered accountant is recruited to sell insurance and pension programmes he will expect to be rewarded not solely by a salary competitive with those of normal door-to-door household insurance salespersons, but on a scale that reflects his forgone earnings in his area of expertise, i.e. the accountancy profession. If, for particular reasons, it is considered necessary to recruit the Rolls Royce equivalent person to do a job that might be performed (maybe not as well) by a Mini, then you accept the running costs and maintenance expenses of the Rolls Royce.

Many companies still keep salary structures a secret. In that case, there is a danger of distraction as individuals worry about whether a colleague is on a different reward scale and package from themselves for basically similar work. A structured and published salary scale, whereby the individual sees the bottom and top of the range and any fixed incremental points and also the salary range for at least one more senior level, can both serve as a motivator to show how performance and promotion can increase the material needs satisfaction, and clarify concerns about colleagues' earning ranges. Of course, published data would not show the actual position of any person within a job income range. There is no reason why the top of one salary grade might not overlap the bottom of the next higher grade, although some companies do have a policy that a manager should always earn more than his highest-paid subordinate, since he does have the overall responsibility and accountability for results: and that is a positively motivating reward policy.

Incentives Not every sales job is suitable for additional incentives. It might be felt that only those persons actually negotiating direct orders can be rewarded on a results-oriented basis. In that case part-time store merchandisers in the manufacturer's employ might be paid purely a fixed hourly rate (although they could be rewarded partly by a fixed hourly rate of pay plus a bonus relating to the number of cases actually merchandised). Similarly, the jobs of salespersons involved in arranging transfer orders for branch delivery systems or supply through other distributors might not lend themselves so readily to incentive or performance-based rewards as it is difficult to measure actual results. Straight salary is a more normally accepted reward system where selling is a group effort, orders take a long time to materialise, or individual performance-related results are very hard to separate and measure.

The general principles and guidelines sales managers should consider in designing incentive schemes are:

- the scheme should be relevant to and compatible with established goals and objectives
- the rewards should be based on criteria that are subject to specific quantifiable measurement
- the basis of awards, i.e. the achievements required, should be realistic and achievable
- the incentive awards should be based on effort and performance from activities that are specifically controlled or influenced by the individual salesperson or manager
- the scheme should be fair and equitable to all team members, and offer benefit and rewards to all team members related to individual productivity and performance

- the scheme should not penalise participants (or if it penalises one it should penalise all equally) if factors outside their control disrupt the achievements or environment (such as strikes, other disruptions or production problems)

- the scale and level of rewards should relate to the specific potential of the territory or job function (industrial sales or key accounts) under the salesperson's direct control (i.e. it will not be motivational to set the terms of achievement in standard absolute values or volumes of product for all territories if it is historically demonstrated that some territories produce more sales or have more potential than others – it might be fairer to have a scheme based on percentage improvement from a base period

- the earnings of incentives for salespersons doing a regular job should be evenly spread over a longer term, rather than all or nothing on one or a few orders, or highly cyclical in producing incentive earnings (as might be the case with seasonal items), so that recipients of incentive-based earnings can budget earnings and expenditure

- the critical measurement date to assess earnings and pay incentives should be at regular intervals (weekly or monthly) to facilitate individual planning and budgeting, and therefore the basis of measurement of incentive schemes needs to be on activities and results that occur at reasonably frequent intervals

- Reward, like punishment or correction, should quickly follow the activity to which it relates; frequent smaller bonuses are more likely to be motivational than, say, year-end bonuses at the lower levels in the sales organisation (and possibly also at higher levels!)

- the ongoing reward scheme should not be an 'all or nothing' reward system, where unless a target or goal is met in full there is no bonus earned, or where only one or few persons might qualify for the bonus or incentive. Restrictive programmes serve as demotivators to those who realise a short way through the incentive period that they are low in the performance league tables and simply stop competing. Constant motivation of all participants is only maintained where everyone has a real chance to earn an incentive award

- the incentive scheme should:

  - be simple in structure
  - easy to administer
  - require minimum management control time
  - require minimum special training
  - dovetail with existing systems, procedures and practices within the sales force.

The most usual types of incentive schemes are:

70

- commission on sales
- bonuses
- contests.

Commission on sales

A common scheme of incentive reward is simply to pay a straight commission on the value of all sales achieved. This might be at a standard percentage, say 1 per cent, or might be graduated, say 1 per cent up to a certain sales level and 2 per cent thereafter. The commission scheme and potential must ensure that each salesperson can and does at least earn at a level to give a reasonable standard of living. The company has the advantage that payments relate directly to sales volumes, but the disadvantage in a multi-product company that rarely will each product have a similar gross margin (except perhaps in the wholesale trade if the wholesalers work on a fixed percentage margin). If the high-volume sellers pushed by the salespersons to boost commission earnings have lower gross margins, the company will face an overall margin erosion. This can be countered by varying the commission levels according to the profitability of the product (which is particularly important if the salesperson has authority to vary prices) or setting minimum sales levels by product before commission becomes due and payable. Commission schemes also tend to encourage salespersons to concentrate on established repeat business from existing outlets rather than pioneer calling, unless there is a special bonus or incentive for each new pioneer outlet that places an initial order.

Commission-only reward schemes, while not offering security, are often simpler for a company starting with new products or in new markets as the company has lower fixed costs, and costs per currency unit sold are predictable.

Commission schemes are very difficult to structure and manage where product sales are cyclical or where an individual is only one of a number of persons involved in generating business, i.e. a key account executive. Attention also has to be given to such factors as returns or allowances for credit. To reduce the risk of overselling (particularly of perishable goods), returns and allowances should be deducted from gross sales before the commission is calculated.

Bonuses

Traditionally bonuses are awarded as a lump sum for the specific achievement of an objective, such as a sales or profit target or return on capital employed in the business, usually within an agreed time frame. Bonuses might be instead of or in addition to other commissions or incentives, and they can readily be geared to team efforts, i.e. each person in the team gets a bonus if the team achieves its goals or objectives. Whereas commission on sales is ongoing, paid regularly with salary, bonuses are usually awarded less frequently, such as quarterly or annually, or on an *ad hoc* basis when there is a particular activity or result that warrants bonus incentives.

If bonuses are intended to reflect or reward team effort, then a **bonus pool** can be established. Awards from this pool should reflect the contribution or seniority of each person who contributed to a particular achievement. It might be considered inappropriate that each person receive the same absolute bonus, and that it should rather be awarded as a percentage of base income.

Bonuses, like commissions, should relate to a result area where individual effort can impact on the outcome, if not control it. For example, every person's productivity and cost-saving efforts can impact on the return on capital employed and company profitability. I often feel there is a lot more scope in the sales environment for bonus schemes to relate to the profitability of individual territories and higher-tier profitability in the organisation.

Unfortunately, when it comes to deciding bonus levels, all too frequently managers have to take subjective decisions because some external factors outside the control of participants impacted on results (usually negatively). My own personal view is that external environmental and economic factors are as likely to benefit as detract from bonus earnings opportunities, and that bonuses should not be subject to subjective discussions such as 'well, he would have got the bonus except for . . .'.

Contests

Many companies favour the use of competitions and contests as a means of rewarding salespersons for effort and results against short-term priorities and objectives. This is an effective way of drawing attention to certain aspects of performance, but has the negative effect that few or perhaps only one person can win, and other participants frequently reduce effort once they see or feel they cannot catch a colleague who appears to have established a clear lead. It is absolutely essential that the structuring of each contest or competition gives each participant a fair and equal chance of winning (which would be unlikely, as mentioned previously, if each territory had to obtain the same absolute levels of achievement) to ensure that all eligible participants do put in extra effort. Also, the structuring of the competition should consider whether for any reason one territory might be expected to have favourable factors that would let it take too large a lead too early, and demotivate other participants (such as multiple account buying offices).

There are several useful points to note in structuring competitions:

- Many companies find that prizes of goods rather than cash can be more motivating in the short term, and give a more lasting memento of success (e.g. a new video recorder or a holiday for the family).

- There should be a range of prizes so that all eligible participants feel motivated to strive for necessary performance results until the last moment.
- Prizes of family interest often prove particularly attractive and motivating.
- An ongoing award programme, possibly where points are accumulated by all participants that can lead to the acquisition of a range of prizes or merchandise when redeemed, can be a major motivator. Such schemes can be organised in conjunction with outside specialist promotion agencies.
- Contests should not be geared always to the same goals and objectives, but varied frequently (possibly monthly) to avoid stale-ness or the feeling that the points gained (or prizes collected) are just a salary supplement. And contests should be designed to home in on particular functional activities or achievement areas that do impact in the short term on key result areas.
- It is essential that any contest be structured in a fashion that minimises abuse. Contests are subject to abuse if only because some of the objectives are often less concrete or measurable (e.g. related to product display or distribution). If it is related to new distribution of a product, should the base be a customer who was out of stock on the salesperson's arrival at the store, or one who never previously stocked and sold the product? Or should the base be taken as the recorded distribution on entry or exit as recorded on the daily activity reports for the most recently completed journey cycle? A penalty for detected abuse should be sufficiently large as to discourage it.
- A danger in a competition geared to one objective is that it invariably distracts from other goals and objectives and activities. The structuring of a contest may need to consider penalties for under-performing against criteria other than those being promoted in the contest or, possibly, participation in a contest may depend upon certain minimum achievements of a range of key result areas.

Other incentives

Apart from the foregoing, there are many other motivational rewards with varying weaknesses or merits. It is common in some industries (such as insurance) to have exclusive '**clubs**' (such as a 'President's Club') for high achievers. Entry into the club is certainly a status motivator, and other ongoing benefits might accrue. However, the problem is what to do with people who do not continue to perform adequately to maintain club membership, or had an abnormal year's sales performance for whatever reasons and cannot sustain that performance. To use such schemes as continuing motivators, management must be prepared to remove benefits conferred: whilst entry to the 'club' might require a million dollars of sales in one year, continued membership might set annual ongoing sales at no less than three-quarters of a million dollars in any succeeding year, and failure to achieve at that minimum level would result in the loss of any benefits.

The use of larger vehicles or an extra week's holiday as a reward incentive is only useful if management can and do remove the benefit on subsequent failure to maintain performance. I personally do not favour giving additional status trappings, such as bigger cars, that can be difficult to remove (because of public loss of status, demotivating effects on the beneficiary of the 'perk', or legal or union problems that might result). Generally rewards and incentives should be such that once given they are kept.

The structuring of a motivating reward system might use any or all of the foregoing systems (a summary checklist is given at the end of this chapter). However, if too much incentive activity is going on at any one time, the benefit of any scheme is reduced and there will be conflict between short- and long-term goals and incentive programmes. Therefore, where more than one incentive reward programme operates it should be planned that each separate objective is compatible with all others. For example, a commission scheme that gives varying ongoing commission relative to the profitability of different products and subject to a minimum level of profit per account would conflict with a bonus or contest linked to opening pioneer accounts, because salespersons would be reluctant to withdraw attention from existing accounts which they have to strive to keep at a minimum profit level to be eligible for commission. However, if the sales force received a commission on all sales to new pioneer accounts, and not just above a minimum profitability level, for at least the first year, this might offset any lost commission from established accounts and provide the motivation to seek new accounts with development potential. Clearly, the balance is very complex when rewards and incentives are used to avoid or minimise conflict between objectives and priorities, and also to avoid introducing an element of demotivation.

In addition, management must be clear that the introduction and use of incentive reward schemes is no substitute for personnel training and development, and should not impose an extra control burden on management.

APPRAISALS

The role
and purpose
of appraisals

I prefer to deal with the very important subject of appraisals within this chapter rather than the subsequent chapters on management control (Chapter 11) or communication (Chapter 3), because a well-

74

structured and effectively used appraisal system is a source of motivation.

The role and process of appraisal is the comparison of individual performance against agreed standards and objectives. Where performance is not at least at acceptable levels or standards, corrective action may generally be triggered, including counselling to identify problems and development needs and programmes and training. Where performance exceeds standards, then reward in the form of merit pay increases, promotion, or more advanced training and development might be appropriate.

Certain principles should be applied to any good appraisal system:

- the appraisor (line manager) should communicate very clearly (in writing) to an appraisee (salesperson) at the beginning of each appraisal period his specific objectives and performance standards for the current appraisal period
- objective measurements should be provided on a regular basis to enable the appraisor and appraisee constantly to review performance and to implement corrective action as appropriate
- the appraisor should review performance not in isolation but in cooperation and conjunction with another involved person (normally the second or next level of line manager) at the end of the appraisal period, and agree the appraisal objectively on measurable criteria and subjectively on any factors that do not lend themselves to objective measurement
- where an appraisal involves both objective and subjective factors, then a weighting system needs to be developed to give greatest weight to the objective performance standards and achievements
- the appraisee should be involved in his own appraisal and invited to submit, prior to the evaluatory meeting between first and second line managers, his own comments on achievement against standards and objectives, and on strengths, weaknesses and development needs and on any external factors that have impacted on his performance including obstacles and problems encountered and relationships.

Appraisal is not a once- or twice-yearly activity: like effective training, it is a continuing exercise. The communications and evaluations of an appraisal should never come as a surprise to the appraisee (particularly if the field sales manager is constantly counselling and training salespersons). Some companies prefer to separate the timing of formal appraisals from the implementation of merit increases.

The appraisal system formalises the need for the appraisor and appraisee to identify and recognise the needs of the appraisee (for promotion, status, recognition, material rewards, job satisfaction and enrichment, feedback, security, and so on) and his ability to satisfy those needs by achieving and exceeding performance standards and through the establishment of personal and company development programmes. Formal appraisal should therefore act as a summary of performance and development feedback communicated over the appraisal period.

The performance environment

If a formal appraisal is conducted every six months, as would be the practice in many companies, then without doubt there will be a number of changes in circumstances and the environment during the appraisal period. Changes may occur in the competitive market place; in the work environment; in company policies, strategies or organisation; in sales territory workloads or boundaries; and as a result of legislation and regulatory control. Most, if not all, changes might be outside the control of the individual salesperson or appraisee, but impact on his performance or ability to perform; the appraisors must make objective judgements taking account of changes. The basis of an appraisal may therefore need review and discussion between appraisor and appraisee before it is formalised so that both parties understand the account taken of any known environmental changes. The final appraisal should be based on those aspects of performance that were within the control of the appraisee for the duration of the appraisal period, and on agreed and accepted standards of performance.

What to measure and appraise

In preparing for an appraisal each appraisor should review documents, data or other available information that might contribute to assessment under the various appraisal form headings developed. Such data sources include:

- previous appraisal forms
- training assessments and reports and records of training given
- field check reports relevant to the territory
- agreed objectives and standards of performance
- company published statistics or measurements kept personally by the line manager for all his subordinates
- particularly important correspondence (or bulletins referring to the appraisee's performance)
- notes on any special activities or contributions, e.g. organising a wholesaler training meeting
- notes on any critical events or occurrences (good or bad).

Appraisal ratings can be given in each of the areas listed below.

Standards of performance
Objective measurements can be made on any job factor for which there is an agreed standard of performance, such as:

76

- call rate
- call coverage
- pioneer calling
- conversion ratio of calls to orders
- distribution
- display
- market share
- territory/area profitability
- sales value/volume targets or forecasts
- complaints.

Skills

The appraisor can review the appraisee's particular skills and rate his standards in this respect. Essential and optional skills need particularly to be recognised and some form of objective standards set. In the sales environment skills might include:

- selling
- administrative
- organisational
- communications
- planning
- decision making
- motivational.

The appraisal should not normally be concerned with too much detail, but the appraisor should always have specific examples to bring forward in an appraisal meeting or subsequent counselling meeting with an appraisee.

Subjective factors

Although the emphasis in an appraisal is upon the objective, it may also fairly take account of subjective factors such as the **characteristics**, **attributes** and **attitudes** of the appraisee as they relate to his job performance in the present position, and his **potential** to take on increased responsibility.

Personal characteristics The strengths and weaknesses in individual characteristics and behavioural factors can be commented on by reference to characteristics identified in a job holder profile, particularly drawing attention to how they impact on actual performance or development potential. For example, if the salesperson is abrasive or insensitive then that should be communicated, and counselling given on how to minimise the impact on his performance or future potential.

Development needs   The appraisal should identify the development needs of the individual in respect of both current job skills and his development for future (more senior) positions in the organisation. The appraisee should also be encouraged to assess and comment on his own development needs and training requirements. The appraisor and appraisee should then specifically identify priority development needs and prepare a programme for the next appraisal period consisting of both self-development and company development elements.

If the company part of the development programme is not implemented, it is not only most frustrating for an appraisee (and reduces his faith and credibility in management) but also serves to demotivate the appraisee from pursuing the self-development aspects of the programme. If it is agreed at an appraisal that specialist training is needed (say on an accounting course for non-financial managers) then the appraisor (line manager) should ensure that the appraisee is put forward for such a course, even if a suitable course is not immediately available. A common problem is that managers, having identified training and development needs, either postpone action or take no action, with the standard excuse that 'we cannot afford to let you go just now'. That shows insincerity and lack of commitment to the appraisee's development.

Promotability   The appraisal should clearly identify the appraisee's strengths and weaknesses in relation to other jobs that he might do in the organisation, and his suitability and eligibility for promotion. Such assessments and counselling should be realistic and honest. A salesperson who has no further potential within the organisation should not be misled with false promises that he is 'next in line' for consideration. Frank but sensitive communication lets a person come to terms with his situation, re-assess his drives in relation to opportunities, and take conscious decisions that reduce the risk of demotivation in the longer term (e.g. to seek other employment opportunities or to remain in the present role and become an 'elder statesman' of the sales force, giving priority to satisfying other drives and needs).

Developing an appraisal form   Many companies already have an established, effective and credible appraisal system. The forms used may be suitable for sales positions at either the territory salesperson level or sales management level. If forms do not exist or require some modification, then some guidelines are as follows:

- the form should be simple in structure and format and clear in the instructions for completion
- the form should identify key aspects of performance, personality and potential

- criteria listed should be relevant to the particular job being appraised and be capable of objective measurement
- the design should encourage consistency in rating between different raters who are familiar with the job and appraisee
- the form should encourage consistency in rating between subsequent appraisals.

Appraisal forms generally use rating scales against key criteria; these might be either **numerical** (i.e. 1 to 6) or **verbal** (i.e. poor, unsatisfactory, satisfactory, good, very good, outstanding). It is essential that each appraisor in the system operates to the same standards in assigning ratings; that requires training, counselling and control of appraisors, perhaps by a neutral personnel officer.

Because an appraisal is mainly concerned with actual performance against standards and objectives, there is a danger, in any counselling, that both parties get too involved in a discussion and debate on the more subjective areas, such as promotability considerations, which is why it is essential that clear weighting must go to performance. Some companies take the position that actual on-the-job performance as measured by performance statistics, etc., should carry at least 70 per cent weight in the overall rating and 100 per cent weighting in consideration for merit pay increases. (See Example 2.2 for a sample form.)

Counselling The most difficult part of an appraisal is not the assessments and preparation/review discussions between first and second line managers, but communicating the contents of the appraisal to an appraisee in a counselling meeting. The intention of a counselling meeting is to improve or modify performance and behaviour, so it should:

- let the appraisee see, understand and agree his actual performance in relation to agreed standards
- ensure that the appraisee learns his manager's views of his role and performance
- advise the appraisee what prospects he might have and how to realise those prospects through further development
- confirm and consolidate with the appraisee the ongoing mini-appraisals communicated at counselling and training sessions
- increase the personal motivation of the appraisee to improve his productivity and performance through agreed objectives and development programmes.

The appraisee should be notified well in advance of the time and place of the counselling meeting, and counselling should:

79

Example 2.2 Example of a basic sales force appraisal form

Name of appraisee:		Date of appraisal:		
JOB PERFORMANCE **Key result area**	**Standard of performance**	**Actual achievement**	**Rating**	**Comment**
Call rate Call coverage Conversion ratio Pioneer calling Distribution Display Sales targets Market share Territory profitability Complaints				
Overall rating	1 2 3 4 5 6 7 8 9	**Comment**		

Technical skills	**Rating**	**Comment**
Selling skills . . . . Administration Organisation Communications Planning Decision making Time management		
Overall rating	1 2 3 4 5 6 7 8 9	**Comment**

Job performance summary

Overall rating	1 2 3 4 5 6 7 8 9

Example of a basic sales force appraisal form (contd.)

SUBJECTIVE FACTORS	
Strengths	**Development areas**

Personal characteristics and attitudes	Rating	Comment
Initiative Integrity Decisiveness Adaptability Flexibility Judgement Tenacity Enthusiasm Reliability Energy Motivation Right mental attitude		

Overall rating on subjective factors

1 2 3 4 5 6 7 8 9

Potential

Training and development

OVERALL APPRAISAL RATING

1 2 3 4 5 6 7 8 9

OVERALL APPRAISAL COMMENT

Signed: 1st line manager   Appraisee
        2nd line manager   Date

Notes to appraisors: Ratings should be given on the 1 to 9 scale (1 being least satisfactory, 9 most satisfactory).
Job performance should carry 70% weighting in overall appraisal rating.

- be conducted in a relaxed informal manner, away from the normal work environment (not in the salesperson's car)
- be unbroken by interruptions and distractions
- have plenty of time specifically allocated to the appraisal so that the counselling and discussions are not rushed. It may be wise to allow at least two hours per appraisal
- be a two-way exchange of views, comment and opinions.

It is frequently a good opening to lead in to the general appraisal counselling with a question that instantly involves the appraisee in the self-assessment process, such as 'Tell me, John, what do you think have been your main achievements over the last six months?' As the review discussion proceeds, it is most useful to compare the appraisee's self-evaluations of performance, potential, motivations, etc., with your own evaluations, getting understanding and agreement where there are differences.

When the appraisal counselling is complete, appraisor and appraisee should write up their summary notes, and each should sign a copy of the appraisal form as acknowledgement that the appraisal has taken place, the contents communicated and accepted, and the objectives, standards of performance and development plans for the next period set.

SUMMARY

- Motivation in a business environment can be considered as the process of getting people to act willingly towards the achievement of greater satisfaction of personal needs through the achievement of company goals and objectives.
- Needs may be categorised into **physiological** and **social** needs. Physiological needs are those primarily concerned with economic and physical survival and security; social needs include recognition, status, acceptance, respect, harmony, consolidation, change, knowledge, responsibility, achievement and power.
- The manager must identify and recognise the balance of needs and drives in each of his subordinates and their respective priorities in seeking further satisfaction of needs.
- Before motivational efforts can be effective, it is necessary to remove or neutralise any demotivators, such as those resulting from job uncertainties, job imbalances, inadequate management, the working environment, poor compensation and poor prospects.
- Managers should ensure that the environment is conducive to effective motivational practices by: setting clear goals and objectives and standards of performance for each person; recruiting only suitably qualified persons to positions; thorough training; fair compensation; efficient and effective management and control; and providing feedback and staff development programmes.
- Managers can also motivate through: counselling, recognition, praise, involvement and participation, delegation, and career progression.
- Managers may derive their authority from any of several sources, including: election, appointment, knowledge, organisational structure, or personal characteristics of authority; and might practise management styles that are predominantly autocratic-, democratic- or consensus-oriented.
- Whatever the source of authority, managers will not be effective leaders unless they win the confidence of subordinates that, through their leadership, guidance and direction, each subordinate can increase the satisfaction of needs.
- In developing reward and incentive programmes the level of total rewards for any particular position needs both to be competitive in relation to the reward programmes offered by other comparable companies and industries, and meet the needs and expectations of persons recruited to positions. Income generally consists of some or all of: fixed salaries, commissions on sales, bonuses and other performance-related incentives. In addition, fringe benefits may include: life assurance, medical insurance, pension schemes, long-term disability and sickness income protection, vacations, company vehicles, etc.

83

- Incentive schemes should: base reward on effort and measurable performance; include only measurable performance criteria whose achievement is within the control of the participants in the scheme; be equitable to all participants with each having a fair and equal chance of winning or earning; provide regular feedback on progress and reward regularly.
- Appraisal is the process of comparing individual performance against agreed standards and objectives and should be ongoing. The appraisee needs to be clear what those standards and objectives are at the beginning of each appraisal period. The greater weight in an appraisal assessment should be given to objective measurements rather than to subjective factors, and account needs to be taken of changes in the environment that are outside the control of the appraisee.
- Frank, honest, appraisal counselling should be conducted in a relaxed, less formal atmosphere, unbroken by interruptions, and with plenty of time allocated to the two-way communication process.

CHECKLIST   PRACTICAL MOTIVATION

	Notes	Action

Have **goals and objectives** been established?

Have **standards of performance** been set and agreed?

Have **job descriptions** clearly identified the job functions, duties, responsibilities, and relationships?

Has a **needs audit analysis** been prepared for each team member?

Is the manager's **motivational environment** right in respect of:

o correct selection of suitable job holders?
o training programmes
  – self-development?
  – company development?
o fair reward and incentive programmes?
o control systems and procedures?
o formal appraisal systems?
o communication and feedback systems?
o career development?

In addition to the foregoing, does the manager make use of opportunities for:

o counselling?
o expressing recognition?
o giving praise?
o involvement/participation in planning and decision processes?
o delegation?
o promotion?

CHECKLIST   DEMOTIVATORS

	Notes	Action

Check if potential or actual DEMOTIVATORS have been identified and removed or neutralised, including:

Job uncertainties:
o insecurity of tenure
o ill-defined roles and responsibilities
o poor training
o absence of performance standards

Job imbalances:
o personal qualifications
o incorrect job assignment
o limited self-development opportunities
o poor job-content variety

Inadequate management:
o limited management skills and experience
o poor management control
o manager's prejudices
o lack of recognition or appraisal systems
o inadequate communications
o inadequate company personnel development programmes

Inadequate working environment:
o poor equipment
o poor location
o poor relations

Poor compensation:
o uncompetitive income and incentive rewards
o inequitable incentive programmes
o absence of merit reward recognition
o uncompetitive fringe benefits

Poor prospects:
o limited internal promotion opportunities
o limited opportunities to increase knowledge or skills or experience

CHECKLIST   REWARD SYSTEMS

What	When	Advantages	Disadvantages
Salary only	• sales projects take a long time to produce orders • it is not practical to identify the real contribution of any one person, and sales activity and results are a team effort • sales force tasks and objectives are not related to direct product sales, e.g. merchandising or technical product briefings • individual salesperson's activity has little direct impact on sales levels, e.g. very established repeat purchase products	• administratively simple • equitable rewards system • promotes and satisfies security-driven motivations • predictable incomes and sales force budgets • rewards can be linked to longer-term objectives • rewards reflect longer-term merit and loyalty	• does not relate territory sales costs to sales volumes • favours security-motivated rather than achievement-motivated salespersons • no flexibility to direct longer- or shorter-term effort to objectives through the use of incentives • the sales force costs are relatively fixed whereas performance may exceed or fall short of targets set when budgets are prepared
Commission only	• products are not cyclical in sales pattern • for newer products or companies with limited resources • pre-trained experienced salespersons are recruited • attention is to be devoted only to new or repeat sales orders and not to non-selling related activities	• directly links sales costs to sales values or profitability, as a percentage figure • differential commission levels can direct effort to certain products or markets • motivates materially orientated sales-persons	• limits recruitment largely to salespersons not strongly security-motivated • higher sales force turn-over of less productive staff, possibly with higher ongoing training costs • insecurity of individual earnings • unsuitable where it is not feasible specifically to identify the individual sales contribution of each salesperson • requires adjustment for product returns and other credit allowances
Bonuses	• it is difficult to separate each individual's contribution to an objective or result but where an incentive is considered an essential motivator • for achievement of longer-term objectives • results depend on the effort of a team of salespersons	• good motivator to longer-term goals and objectives • useful team incentive programme • encourages the development of a system to recognise individual contributions to team efforts to achieve objectives and results (e.g. sales and profits)	• not ideal for short-term objectives or corrective action • less easy to budget the costs of an incentive programme • more complex administratively to measure and control in relation to performance and results • subjectivity may enter the final evaluation process of allocating bonuses as

Reward systems (contd.)

What	When	Advantages	Disadvantages
		• useful as a reward for territory or area profit performance	consideration is given to external disruptive factors that impacted on performance
Contests	• to direct attention to short-term objectives or limited goals, or to motivate activity and attention towards corrective action	• a good short-term motivator to limited goals and objectives • frequently more motivationally beneficial where goods rather than cash form the reward • acts as an ongoing motivator where a points or other ongoing accrual system for recognising effort and achievement is developed so that all participants receive benefit	• may distract from longer-term objectives and activity • if there is one or few winners this acts as a demotivator to all other participants • generally very complex to structure and administer a fair and equitable contest system • often more open to abuse than other incentive programmes • can distract management control time and effort unless it can be centrally controlled or managed by external specialists

3 Developing Sales Force Communications

Any member of a sales force spends much of his time communicating with others, both internally and externally. Effective management, control, measurement and motivation are dependent on efficient and effective communications. In this chapter I propose to consider the broad communication process and link this with the main internal sales management methods of communicating through memoranda, bulletins, meetings and conferences so that an efficient and practical communications system can develop.

THE ROLE AND PROCESS OF COMMUNICATION

The process of communication is fundamentally the sending and receiving of signals. In the sales environment the signals are normally transmitted:

- **verbally**, in the form of telephone conversations or face-to-face discussions, presentations and meetings,
- in **writing**, as in letters, memoranda and such aids as product literature,
- **pictorially**, as in advertisements, product brochures, charts and graphs and other illustrative communications,
- **numerically**, as in the issue of sales forecasts, targets, and performance data, often now through computer printouts where the information systems are computerised,
- **demonstrably**, by showing how to perform a task or use a product,
- **physically**, through body language (posture and gesture) and facial expressions,
- **attitudinally**, through the attitudes demonstrated or expressed by any of the foregoing means.

It is generally useful or necessary to use a combination of these means of communication to ensure that the meaning and purpose of a communication is received and to maximise the likelihood that the appropriate action and results materialise.

In the sales environment probably around three-quarters of a first line manager's communications are on a one-to-one basis with subordinate salespersons, colleagues or customers, but the percentage of one-to-one contacts would be expected to decline further up the management hierarchy. Both the salesperson and the sales manager should beware of the unintended effects of **involuntary** communications that they can or might transmit by body language and facial expressions.

The first stage of the communication process is for the communicator (the initiator of a communication) to clarify in his own mind the purpose of the communication he is about to issue or transmit. He should ask himself what he seeks to accomplish, and give careful consideration to the media to be used in the communication.

Communications in the sales and management environment frequently relate to:

- the established or newly adopted **policies** of the company that provide a source of guidance to employees and that might govern actions at all levels within the organisation
- the range of **programmes**, plans, strategies and tactics developed within the organisation that comply with the broad policies and that contribute to the achievement of company goals and objectives
- the operational **procedures** and practices that enable programmes to be effectively implemented
- the **preceding** actions, policies and programmes and their outcomes or impact on the company or its environment, and their relationship to current policies, programmes and procedures.

The means of communication chosen will depend on such factors as:

- the amount of time available to the communicator to achieve his purpose and the degree of urgency in the need to communicate
- the range of media that are available to both the communicator and the recipient of the communication – do both parties have access to a telephone or postal services, or can they practically arrange a personal meeting within the time constraints imposed on the communication?
- the complexity of the subject matter of the communication. The more complex is the subject matter, the more necessary it becomes that the communication medium can transmit complex data accurately.

The more common communication media used in business today include:

- face-to-face meetings
- written and illustrative communications (letters, memoranda, reports)

- computers (direct computer-to-computer links, desk-top visual display units linked to central computers, computer data input terminals, etc.) that receive or transmit or produce numerical and statistical data, reports or analyses
- telephone, telex, or telegraphic services
- telephonic document and data transmission services.

The future will see growth in television/video conference linking systems enabling geographically separated parties to see each other while conducting discussions or negotiations. For the purpose of this text we are concerned with sales management communications through **memoranda, bulletins, meetings** and **conferences**.

What to communicate

Managers clearly have much discretion in deciding what to communicate and to whom, but some guidelines can be summarised as follows.

Essential information
A person needs to receive communications on everything that concerns the performance of their specific job functions; that impacts on their ability to comply with procedures and practices and fulfil their functional activities, responsibilities and duties; and that provides feedback and measurement against standards of performance, forecasts or targets, and other goals or objectives.

Optional information
Information could be communicated that adds to each employee's understanding of the company and its operations, or of its results and achievements; or improves the employee's understanding of the working environment or the marketplace. For example, it might be appropriate to let some or all employees have access to company financial data of various types or performance data (product costing data, management accounts, financial accounts, market share information, etc.). If the company is a public company, employees may well have free access to published information. It is then often beneficial to present the market and financial performance data separately to employees in a readily comprehensible fashion to facilitate understanding of such factors as the sources and uses of funds and the broad cost and value added parameters.

Information that might be of benefit or interest, or a source of training or development of employees, but that is not directly relevant to current job functions and job performance (such as new product and technology information) could also be communicated. Some companies pay employee contributions to a range of trade or professional journals or institutions to encourage broader interest, involvement and self-development through exposure to information and knowledge sources from outside the immediate work environment.

90

A manager who believes in communicating only on a 'need to know' basis would be losing much of the opportunity to motivate through communications. The sales manager should never forget that in his environment **communication is a major source of motivation**.

It is always a problem to know or decide what should *not* be communicated because there will always be matters or information that cannot or should not be communicated to either salespersons or field sales managers.

Information should generally not be communicated if the disclosure of that information could in any way be harmful to the company or its employees. The harm might come from the effect of the disclosure of information on employees' attitudes, activities, morale or productivity. For example, would some employees react in a negative or disruptive fashion if they were aware that goods were being produced for certain foreign markets that pursued policies those employees did not approve of, whilst the managers knew the particular order was essential to keep the overall operation running. In addition, certain information (e.g. certain market research data, or forward marketing plans and programmes, including advertising and promotional plans or new product launches), if obtained by competitors either through employees or other sources, could be used by competitors to develop programmes designed to counter the company's market activities.

Information should not be disclosed to employees, except on a 'need to know' basis, where it is covered by any non-disclosure or secrecy agreement with third parties, as might be the case if a product is being manufactured under licence from another party that has imposed conditions that the fewest company employees possible have access to plans, specifications, procedures, processes, formulas, etc.

Any information covered by any other security restriction imposed by other parties for whom the company is working on work being done for them (such as government agencies concerned over defence-related work, or other companies that sub-contract work that relates to projects they consider confidential) should not be communicated. There could, in some cases, be very severe restrictions on who can have access to information on a project, each individual perhaps needing a security clearance. Private contractors who sub-contract part of a project may seek similar assurances, with contractual penalty clauses for breach of confidentiality.

Communications should be restricted or otherwise limited where premature communication could be disruptive or lead to activity that might impact negatively on the outcome of the subject of the communication (as might happen in the case of acquisitions, mergers or divestment of assets). In general terms this could extend to limited communication (on a 'need to know' basis) of many plans and programmes when they are still in the formative stages or incomplete or not yet ready for implementation.

91

Communications should go to:

- everyone who has an established 'need to know' the content of a communication in order to perform their own sales organisation job functions effectively and efficiently – for example, the territory salesperson has a definite 'need to know' all the procedural practices and systems required of them, and to be updated every month on any procedural changes; and also needs to know the sales promotional objectives and plans, and sales forecasts and targets as they relate to the territory
- people who are required by the communication either to take personal action or to direct others to take action – for example, a bulletin to salespersons requiring them to make certain recordings or notations on daily activity reports must also be copied to the persons or departments required to make any analysis or prepare any feedback information (and those parties should have been involved in and agreed with proposals for any field recording procedure)
- people who may need to see a communication and its contents for information purposes – for example, a copy of a disciplinary note might go to a personnel officer, and a copy of a note of praise might go to a senior sales manager or even a personnel officer concerned with staff development.

Communications generally should not be sent to people who do not need to know the content, or act on it, or store it for information purposes. Such unnecessary communications are likely to serve as a source of distraction for the recipient.

Where there is an established and effective system of communications, such as through the hierarchical management structure, then communications should be routed through the correct channels (i.e. a research scientist should not be gossiping over a beer to a salesperson about next year's new product launches if the field sales manager himself is unaware of future plans and activities, as that can reduce management credibility).

Within the sales force environment, **formal communications** are generally between:

- managers and subordinate salespersons
- salespersons and customers
- customers and head office customer service functions
- head office management functions and field managers.

Additionally, of course, there is usually significant **informal communication** between colleagues at similar levels or in similar functions, such as salespersons exchanging contacts and field sales managers exchanging copies of bulletins and ideas or reviewing field management problems. These informal communications can be motivational if they are more positive than negative in nature and purpose.

Everybody has personalised aspects in their style of communications. Some people dislike writing letters or memoranda, feeling written communications are too impersonal, and prefer to use the telephone instead. Others prefer to put everything in writing, perhaps commenting that it helps them collect their thoughts. A communicator should be very sensitive to the purpose of the communication or the impact of the content of a communication upon the recipient, and I would offer some broad comments and guidelines as follows.

Where the subject of the communication is not good news (such as a failure to succeed in a promotion candidacy), the first communication is often better by face-to-face contact or, if that is impractical, at least by telephone. Then the communicator (perhaps an area manager) can judge his timing and delivery and impact of the news and also provide feedback, counselling or motivational support. In matters of appraisal or discipline, then initial contact and discussions should always be through personal meetings, with appropriate written communications to follow (such as an appraisal form or warning letter).

Where a communication sets out policies, procedures and practices, or relates to plans, forecasts, targets, performance feedback or measurements, standards of performance, product information, prices, or is in any way factual and possibly needed for reference, then it should be in writing (even if the contents have already been discussed or communicated over the telephone or at a meeting).

If the purpose of a communication is to give recognition for achievement, whilst personal praise might be beneficial and effectively transmitted by a private verbal communication, recognition within a peer group will be more effective and lasting either by inclusion of a comment in a bulletin and/or by public comment at a sales meeting or conference.

Although there is a broad spectrum of styles in written or verbal communications on the formal/informal scale, managers need to develop a style that is effective in promoting action or providing a source of motivation, yet reflects sensitivity.

Arbitrary issuing of orders without explanation, information or involvement of those supposed to carry out the instructions should be avoided. Most employees and subordinates in any work environment, not just sales, want to do a good job and receive recognition for it, and therefore expect to receive fair and reasonable instructions. In particular, they need to understand the objective of the instruction and the benefit (including personal benefit in terms of needs satisfaction) to be expected by following instructions. In general, communications by whatever means need to be:

- **empathetic**, i.e. demonstrate an understanding of the environment within which the salesperson operates,
- **sincere** in content and expression,
- **informative**, i.e. provide all the information the salesperson needs to fulfil all his duties and functions effectively,
- **clear** in content, structure and format to aid understanding and implementation,
- **concise**, i.e. home in on the key issues,
- **meaningful**, in that the content must relate to the recipient's skills, experience, environment or activities,
- **simple** in structure and format so that even complex data and information can be grasped.

Whenever anything beyond a basic person-to-person letter is prepared, it is always useful to seek comment on the draft communication from other persons who might have valid comments to make, who are also familiar with the recipients, or who might help judge it against the above criteria. A poorly prepared or structured communication can do more harm that good if recipients waste time and attention complaining about the incomprehensibility, the irrelevance to the job in hand, the nuances, grammar or whatever other factors serve to distract them.

Communication breakdowns

As practising managers, we often hear comments to the effect that there was 'a breakdown of communications'. Why do communications break down? Basically they break down either because people communicate inadequately or inefficiently, or because people who could and should communicate fail to realise or accept the need to communicate. If communication breakdowns appear to be the result of deliberate action or non-cooperation, managers can only effectively stop that by identifying the underlying causes and then removing or neutralising them. It is vital to do this, because problems in communicating cause the performance of both the company and its employees to suffer.

Some causes of communication breakdowns and blockages are:

- Internal rivalries or jealousies between persons and departments. Perhaps one manager was jealous of another's success, status, role or achievements. Such problems seem quite common in many medium–larger organisations, possibly because of the failure of senior management to recognise and satisfy the needs and drives of all the individuals involved or to reconcile imbalances between needs and the realities of performance and potential.

94

- Failure to understand the need to communicate in the first place, as might happen with a specialist (perhaps a researcher) who tends to operate rather in a vacuum or isolation, or with a salesperson who does not understand the impact of his actions upon others, and who does not tell his manager when the branch manager of a multiple account throws him out of a store (with the key account executive first hearing of it from the account's store controller).
- Simple oversight, as when a key account executive forgets to tell the territory salespersons of activity he is arranging in the stores on which they make the field calls.

Good communications are essential to good management, especially within a sales force, because sales managers and salespersons operate mainly away from a head office environment and will often be unaware of what they have missed in the way of communications because they are not party to the interpersonal or interdepartmental gossip and cross-flow of contact and information exchanges. The sales manager needs to prepare a briefing folder to cover all general matters of relevance or interest and that have not yet been the subject of specific communications so that he can communicate these matters to his subordinate managers at the regular sales management meetings (a field manager might act similarly in respect of his salespersons).

In addition, managers responsible for monitoring the activities and actions of their subordinates should insist that they make a clear note on all written communications of whom it was addressed to and who received copies; they might also check that all who should have received a copy did actually do so (not just relying on a secretary's judgement). Some managers like to make master lists (either for their own use or for their secretary's reference purposes) of who should receive copies of each type of correspondence or communication prepared and issued by that manager. If, for example, only one copy of a communication is sent to a department then perhaps it should either be addressed to the department head with a note to circulate it as appropriate, or be marked with a circulation list of those who should see it within that department (it is often wasteful to send a separate copy to all readers if some only need to read for background information).

It is therefore useful for all sales managers to be trained in communication skills, both written and verbal, by attending either outside courses or internal courses prepared and run by company specialists, or by having external consultants develop tailor-made training programmes to improve skills and increase sensitivity to the whole communication process.

SALES BULLETINS AND MEMORANDA

Much of the preceding general discussion on communications applies particularly to written communications, so I do not propose to repeat it in this section but to summarise:

- the role and purpose of bulletins and memoranda
- their content and structure.

The role and purpose of bulletins and memoranda

The main uses of these communications are to:

- **issue instructions** or guidelines for action, procedures, or operating methods and systems
- **inform** recipients of events, developments, plans, policies, programmes, targets, forecasts, etc.
- **provide feedback** on results and achievements against objectives, forecasts, targets, or standards of performance
- **motivate** recipients to improved productivity and performance
- **confirm** discussions or agreements on programmes, courses of action and projects
- **give recognition** to people who have achieved noteworthy results.

Letters or memoranda will, most often, be directed to one person and deal with one topic or set of related subjects (but could, of course, be directed as an open letter to several members of a sales team).

Sales bulletins are a very useful means of communicating matters of general interest, and might cover just one topic or several topics within the content matter. The purpose of sales bulletins is usually to provide a lift in morale and motivation. It should therefore generally be **positive** rather than negative (negative or critical bulletins tend to serve as demotivators). Bulletins more usually are issued to all the members of a sales team or perhaps to the entire sales organisation. For example, a bulletin from an area sales manager would typically be sent to each member of the area sales team, possibly with copies for information purposes to other area sales managers or certain interested head office support management; a bulletin from the national sales manager might be sent to every member of the sales force at all levels of seniority, or just to subordinate sales managers – the approach would depend on purpose and content.

Content and structure

The length, content and structure of a memorandum or bulletin will depend on such factors as:

- its purpose (as identified in the last section)
- the complexity of the subject matter

96

- the experience and abilities of the recipients to assimilate, comprehend, interpret, analyse or act on the content matter
- the impact its receipt is intended to or might have upon the recipients and the environment in which it will be received.

In general, the more complex the subject matter of a communication, the more likely that it should be the subject of a separate memorandum rather than included in a regular area or national sales bulletin.

The more private or personal the subject matter, such as criticism of certain activities or inactivities or results, the more it lends itself to communication through a private letter or memorandum with fewer, if any, copies to other persons or departments. I have never favoured putting routine critical comments to a salesperson in writing, preferring to discuss them in face-to-face counselling situations where corrective action can be considered, agreed, and implemented. I prefer to reserve the written critical communication for such rare occasions as the issue of a formal warning or where breaches of procedures or discipline are serious and recurrent.

Although recognition and praise can be expressed in a personal memorandum, probably with copies to more senior line management, a mention in an area or national sales bulletin will be more effective in motivating the individual and stimulating his colleagues to greater competitive effort.

Sales bulletins will usually be used to communicate:

- current advertising programmes and promotional plans
- key account summary activity
- competitive activity and general market information
- summary company performance data (in particular noteworthy national, area or individual achievements)
- the introduction of new recording systems or procedures
- new product or market developments
- changes in product formulas, recipes or specifications, or price changes (which might be occurring between the issue times for new product data or price list sheets).

It is difficult to give clear guidelines on the frequency of issue of memoranda or bulletins, as the needs of each organisation will differ. But in principle the volume of communications issued to a sales force should be kept to a minimum while meeting the purposes and needs noted in the previous section. The sales force has a primary function of generating new and repeat business; the time given to active selling must be maximised and that to administrative functions minimised as far as efficiency will permit. I would strongly recommend that any general sales force bulletin from the head office go out only under the signature of the national sales manager, and

97

after he has checked and approved the contents. Field and national sales managers may find it useful to send out a monthly general bulletin to the sales force under their control (but only if there is something useful or necessary to say!) and specific memoranda as necessary. The sales manager could beneficially precede the issue of any memoranda or bulletin with the self-questioning process:

- Is the content interesting, and to whom?
- What purpose does it serve to communicate it?
- Is it essential that I communicate it, or just optional?
- How urgent is the need to communicate?

The answers to these questions will give an indication of the best means, style, format and timing of the communication.

At this point in the text I do not propose to consider other written communication used by the sales force. I shall give a brief review of sales promotional literature in Chapter 5.

AUDIO AND VISUAL COMMUNICATIONS

While written communications to the sales force are the most cost-effective method of communicating, especially where much numerical or instructional data must be transmitted and assimilated, managers should be sensitive to the considerable extra impact and motivational benefit that may at times be achieved through the use of audio or visual aids. Some companies with specialist products or services have developed sophisticated audio and visual communications particularly for standardising presentations to clients and ensuring that a good corporate image and standard of professionalism are communicated.

Both head office and field-based sales managers may find occasions where the use of audio cassette tapes gives variety in communications where there is no need for much data to be included in the communication (or where that might be transmitted through an accompanying instructional bulletin). They can supplement telephone contacts and be most useful where the level of direct field contact is low for any reason (including contact with foreign representatives). They are particularly useful for motivational contacts containing broad activity guidelines and special results, and where the recipients might be able to listen to the tapes whilst driving in the normal course of business.

Video cassettes are substantially more expensive to produce, and require a more professional standard of production and presentation. However, larger corporations may find occasional benefit in producing a 'mini conference' kit which could be viewed at home or at area or other local meetings when information needs to be communicated on a national level between national sales conferences. Clearly to be effective in the home environment it must be assumed each recipient has access to a home video system. Video cassettes are exceptionally useful at the time of new product launches, or where the motivational benefits are high and more complex data need to be illustrated on charts or graphs, and all can be accompanied by supporting worksheets incorporating the script.

SALES MEETINGS AND CONFERENCES

The main difference between a sales meeting and a conference might generally be considered the scale of the project. Sales meetings are usually conducted at the area or regional level as a regular means of communication between team members and the line managers. Sales conferences, generally on a national scale, are normally organised less frequently and planned to coincide with a more momentous event such as a new product launch or annual incentive awards, or to review the annual results and give a theme to the new sales year.

The purpose
of meetings
and conferences

There are a number of reasons for organising meetings within a sales organisation. Each purpose could be the single justification for a meeting, or a meeting or conference might cover a number of these objectives.

Motivation
A meeting might be designed to provide performance feedback and encouragement, to give ideas on means of improving productivity and performance, and to provide a conducive forum for sales colleagues to meet and exchange views and experiences.

Instruction
The main objective might be to impart new information, data, selling and marketing techniques, administrative systems and procedures relating to the company, its products or markets, policies and programmes.

Exploration
The purpose might be to elicit ideas (perhaps using brainstorming techniques, covered later in this chapter), suggestions, recommendations, etc., that could improve productivity and performance and further promote the achievement of goals and objectives through specific action courses, tactics and strategies. Such meetings might be intended to throw up a multitude of alternative points for consideration, and then reduce them through analytical or evaluatory

99

processes that identify and give appropriate weight to suitability, complexity, consequences, advantages and disadvantages.

Resolution

Such a meeting might be designed to identify and evaluate alternative courses of action to overcome or correct general problems, or problems specific to individuals, where other group members may have advice or experiences to draw upon to make meaningful contributions. The group might use the decision-making and evaluatory process and techniques reviewed in Chapter 9 to arrive at conclusions on specific courses of action.

In problem-solving meetings, just as in any form of contributory meeting, the attendees all need to:

- have experience relevant to the subject to draw on
- be interested in the subject matter of the meeting
- have the time and effort to devote to the meeting (not just attend for a short while, perhaps make a comment or two, and then leave)
- be in a position to take decisions or have the delegated authority either to make a recommendation that will be acted on or actually to implement group decisions and monitor the outcome.

Participation

Whilst a meeting for any of the above purposes may to a greater or lesser degree use individual and group participation to fulfil its role and achieve objectives, a meeting might have the particular function of team building through participation processes and techniques such as brainstorming sessions, team projects and group discussions. Or the participation might be aimed at increasing skills and experience through case study and role playing techniques. Such participatory meetings can usefully contribute to improved communication skills, sensitivity analysis (creating an awareness within the individual of his impact on and sensitivity to other persons – particularly fellow team members) in addition to improved sales and marketing skills. Some companies use team-building pro-grammes under modified structures and with such names as 'assess-ment centres'.

The meeting or conference controller or organiser (generally the senior sales manager attending) should clearly identify the purpose and objectives of the meeting or conference well in advance, and ensure that its design, structure and organisation are such as to achieve its objectives.

Organisation of
the meeting

In discussing matters such as the organisation of a meeting there is always the possibility that some readers may pass over the subject, considering that they are very familiar with it from practical experience, since even the most junior sales manager soon gets involved in running meetings. I hope readers of this text will at least review this section to consolidate their experience and knowledge, or use it to check if there are any points they could incorporate in their own meeting planning to provide a varied stimulus to team members.

Objectives

Decide upon and set meeting objectives as early as possible rather than just calling a meeting and then subsequently thinking what to cover in it. The content should be built around the objectives.

Theme

If there is to be a theme to the conference, choose that early and ensure that all speakers and those involved in planning the meeting are aware of the theme and relate to it in their presentations or room design and layout, etc.

Responsibility

Ensure that one person is immediately given the responsibility for all matters to do with the planning, organisation and administration of the meeting or conference (that person might well be yourself).

Venue

Identify and reserve a suitable venue, which might be simply a meeting room at the office or sales training school for a head office based sales managers' meeting, or a major resort hotel for a national sales conference. Conference facilities often need to be reserved one to two years in advance, and even small local meetings may still require the reservation of facilities a few months ahead of the date. The venue should be chosen only after a study visit of its facilities and services to ensure that these will enable you to accomplish the meeting objectives in a suitable environment. All requirements of the hotel and its staff should be listed, clarified and confirmed by an exchange of letters, including comments on room layout, seating, coffee and meal breaks, overnight accommodation where this is needed for any attendees, requisite car parking, and sundry equipment (such as overhead projectors, slide projectors, black-boards, lecterns and any other communication aids the hotel might be required to provide). Ideally a venue should be easy to reach by appropriate transport, relaxing and interesting in itself, and with a minimum of unwelcome distractions within sight or sound of meeting or conference room facilities. It should be sufficiently large to accommodate all attendees who need to stay overnight, and have suitable public or private (if that is what you require) dining facilities to accommodate all the attendees at the agreed meal break times.

Length

Decide how long the meeting should run for: frequently half a day or a full day will be needed to cover a typical sales force meeting agenda. A meeting should be no longer than is necessary to accomplish its stated objectives, should start promptly at the scheduled time and finish when it is supposed to. A sales manager who cannot start his meeting on time will have a problem persuading his salespersons to be at their first call on time.

Agenda

Prepare an agenda around the objectives and theme. The agenda should ensure that interest and attention are retained and controlled through the structure and variety of content and speakers.

Attendees

Decide who should attend the meeting or conference and ensure that they are available, notified of the date and venue, and given any other relevant instructions (such as a map showing how to get there, or suggested plane/train times). The attendees may include not just the appropriate salespersons and managers, but guest speakers, colleagues from other departments who might either benefit by the exposure to the sales force or contribute to the meeting or through future improved inter-department relationships, clerical and other non-managerial office staff who work with or for the sales division, and possibly even the spouses of the attendees if it is a reward-oriented occasion at a nice resort.

Layout

Consider the most suitable room layout to match the objectives. Seating might be theatre style in rows or behind tables (and the tables might be so placed that they can readily be moved or chairs turned round so that they can be used for other group activities such as discussions or assignments to be introduced as part of the programme). Whatever the arrangement it is essential that:

- all attendees can clearly see and hear each speaker and see all communication aids without physical contortions or discomfort
- the focal point (or points, if presentations are to be made from several locations in the room) is not near or in line with any source of distraction that could interrupt the attendees' attention (i.e. there are no doors or passageways or scenic view windows behind the speakers or in the line of sight of the audience) – frequently the speakers must be prepared to face the potential sources of distraction themselves
- heating and ventilation are set to ensure comfort but not to produce audience drowsiness (especially after lunch) or chilling – if ventilation is a problem (e.g. it is necessary to keep windows

closed because of outside noise), then other arrangements must be made to cope with smokers in the audience

- water or other beverages are available within reach of the speakers
- natural and artificial lighting are adequate and preferably variable, to ensure that the speaker and all his communications aids can be clearly seen and read, and that the audience can see to take any necessary notes
- the seating is such as to avoid creating a 'them and us' atmosphere (so the bosses should not all be lined up behind a head table) if team building is an objective, which it generally is at any meeting.

Example 3.1 illustrates several typical room layouts.

Example 3.1 Conference and meeting room layouts

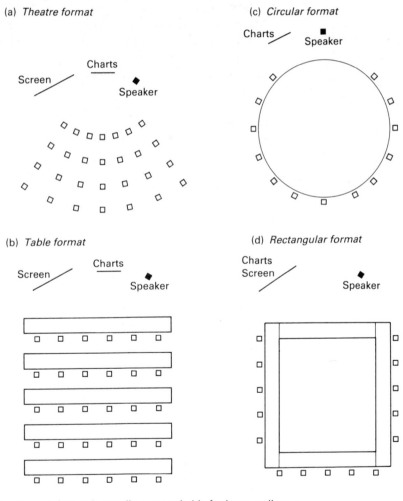

(a) *Theatre format*

Screen / Charts — ◆ Speaker

(c) *Circular format*

Charts / ■ Speaker

(b) *Table format*

Screen / Charts — ◆ Speaker

(d) *Rectangular format*

Charts Screen / ◆ Speaker

Note: Theatre format is usually more suitable for large audiences.
Circular and rectangular table formats are usually useful
for smaller groups, such as area meetings, of 6–20 people.

103

Communication aids

Plan which communication aids to use in the presentation (such as films, slides, photographs, video facilities, flip charts, magnetic boards, blackboards, charts with overlays, handouts, etc. – see separate section below) and ensure that these are both prepared well in advance and available at the meeting place. Ensure that the print is the right size to be read from the back of the room and in a legible colour. Speakers should rehearse talks, practising with the appropriate aids to ensure relevance and continuity. The meeting organiser should advise the speakers which aids are available for use, encourage use of a variety of aids in different presentations to give variety and retain interest, and ensure that speakers do prepare aids well in advance.

Review presentations

The conference organiser should review all planned presentations with the speakers in advance to ensure that the content is relevant, appropriate, gives continuity to the theme and promotes the achievement of the conference objectives.

Handouts

Wherever appropriate, handouts should be prepared and distributed summarising the content of talks and reproducing key charts or tables. At a major conference it will be useful to give each attendee a conference file or folder on arrival, which might include the agenda, writing paper and any other necessary materials. The attendee can then use the folder to collate and store all handouts and literature distributed during the conference and as a subsequent reference source. Because the overall purpose of most meetings is a mixture of instructional and motivational, at a minimum, with a view to modifying behaviour and improving productivity and performance, all handouts must be carefully prepared with those aims in mind, and conference manuals might include sections for personal goals and objectives and subsequent monitoring of personal performance.

Conduct of meetings A sales meeting should be treated by the organising sales manager in the fashion of a sales presentation, with the objectives of:

- gaining and retaining attention
- creating interest in the subject matter
- generating desire in the attendees to implement the content of the meeting in their everyday work practices because of the extra benefit through increased satisfactions of needs and drives
- provoking appropriate action from the attendees.

104

Meeting formats

The meeting might make use of a number of formats, depending on its purpose and objectives.

Presentations   Presentations and lectures can be given on specific subjects of interest to the whole group, with appropriate communication aids and handouts.

Group discussion   Projects related to the objectives, theme or content of the meeting can be discussed by groups, possibly geared to group resolution, recommendations or action plans relating to problematic aspects of the business environment covered in the meeting.

Planning sessions   Once the meeting organisers have communicated overall master plans or forecasts, the attendees can break up into groups or work as individuals under the guidance of their respective sales managers and develop their specific territory plans and programmes. Doing this at the conference or area meeting serves to maintain the momentum and attendees can leave the meeting with a ready-made set of objectives and action plans for each account rather than having to do the work at home or in the car later, when it will be done less thoroughly. For example, if the purpose of the meeting was to introduce new area and territory forecasts (or a new product), each attending salesperson ideally should have broken down his allocation on an account-by-account basis prior to leaving the meeting, taking account of any relevant factors and account knowledge. If the purpose of the meeting was to reorganise territory boundaries or reassign accounts, then each salesperson should have been instructed to bring all account files or folders; the salespersons can then exchange account folders, and all new journey schedule planning can be prepared that day.

Role playing   Where a meeting objective is to impart new management techniques or selling skills, then the normal training principles of explanation, demonstration, practice and consolidation should be followed. Role playing exercises should be conducted as part of the meeting training session, with appropriate props and other aids available to provide a suitable environment and motivation (i.e. product displays, display materials, sales literature). The role playing might extend beyond sales techniques to include training of managers in communications, counselling or recruitment interviewing. For example, if the purpose of the meeting is to brief managers on a forthcoming appraisal programme, it might be appropriate first to review the mechanism of the appraisal and the completion of the forms, and discuss the common measurement standards to be used, and then to have managers role playing counselling situations. If a lecture was given on public speaking

105

techniques, attendees should logically each be invited to prepare and present a short speech incorporating the principles given in the lecture. A session on effective interviewing techniques and procedures might suitably be followed by dummy interviews, with the attending managers in role playing situations, using as a script some prepared job application forms.

Case studies   The use of case studies is an excellent training and development technique. Case studies do not need to be limited to marketing and sales situations but can also cover general or specific management situations, including those concerned with aspects of motivation, counselling, discipline, and communications. They serve to sharpen analytical and problem-solving skills amongst both managers and salespersons.

Presentations by meeting attendees   Whether the meeting is an area meeting of territory salespersons or a regular sales management meeting, there is considerable benefit in attendees being invited (with advance warning generally) to make presentations or reports on subjects in which they have a particular interest, skill or experience (possibly projects or assignments for which they have overall responsibility). This serves to give recognition, increase knowledge and expertise, raise productivity and performance, and promote personal development.

Chairing the meeting

Generally a sales meeting or conference should have a master of ceremonies, main announcer or chairperson who controls and provides continuity, and who remains neutral and impartial in all discussions. At national conferences this is likely to be a senior sales manager, but at local meetings, while it might generally be an area sales manager, it might be beneficial occasionally to experiment by rotating the chair around team members. Since initially it is unlikely that any of the sales team would feel comfortable in the chairperson role, the sales manager can lead towards this objective by stages – for example, by having each salesperson responsible for a section or subject covered at the meeting with the salesperson leading the review and discussions of that section or subject.

Great care must be exercised by a sales manager to ensure that no attendee at a meeting is made to feel uncomfortable, foolish, incompetent, or otherwise a subject of derision or ridicule, otherwise such persons might suffer such a blow to their self-confidence and self-esteem as to obtain no benefit from the meeting and with a frequent subsequent loss of motivation and performance.

The meeting chairperson needs to retain effective control of the group and the direction and content of the meeting throughout the

106

proceedings. The actual opening of a meeting does more than anything to set the tone, and at the outset the chairperson should:

- introduce the topic clearly and definitively
- define the purpose and objectives of the meeting (in order that he may subsequently refer to these and use them to control the relevance of content and direction)
- limit the scope of the meeting or conference to matters that can be covered within the meeting time frame
- set the guidelines on rules and procedures to be followed in the course of the meeting and any resultant discussions (e.g. whether questions and comments are to be addressed through the chair)
- work to develop positive and receptive attitudes in the attending audience.

He must be particularly sensitive to the time parameters, holding the discussions or presentations to allocated time limits, and generally ensuring that there is always some time left at the end of each session for relevant questions. It is useful to give ongoing summaries as the meeting progresses so that all attendees see how the content and structure of the presentations flow in the direction of overall conclusions, programmes and points for action.

In a participatory meeting, the chairperson has the aims of:

- obtaining views and opinions
- gathering information on the nature and strength of individual or group feelings
- getting a reaction to the subject matter, discussion points and proposals
- developing the discussion so that it leads to the desired conclusions, action or acceptance of ideas or proposals
- producing the intended modification of attitudes, opinions, behaviour, activities, action or techniques.

Wherever possible, the meeting chairperson should get attendee involvement and participation to retain attention and interest. The chairperson needs to draw into the discussions people who might have a contribution to make or simply appear to be letting it all pass over their heads. This can often be accomplished by using questioning techniques, or by raising the ego, status or interest of particular persons by comments that publicly recognise their achievements or presence, or possibly their contributions to organising the meeting.

The frequent use of questions of a panel or audience will greatly help a chairperson to open discussions on relevant aspects of topics. The wording of questions should be sufficiently neutral so as not to appear to be a statement of the chairperson's own views or opinions, as that might stifle audience comment. Apart from retaining interest and involvement, suitable questions may also serve to elicit relevant factual information or other inputs that relate to the causes or consequences concerning the meeting subject matter. However, once a meeting is opened to public questions, the chairperson risks control problems, and must be firm in ensuring that comments and contributions are relevant, meaningful, well-presented and listened to (he may need to re-phrase or re-present worthwhile comments that might not have been well made by the commenting party). Generally a chairperson needs to avoid and control situations where a member of the audience actually seeks to make a speech under the guise of asking a question.

If questions are the order of the day to generate involvement, then it is better to use **open questions** and avoid those that require only a simple yes or no response. Any question that could cause particular embarrassment to any attendee should be avoided, as should questions that provoke confrontation or antagonistic reactions between the audience and the chairperson or other members of the audience. It is essential to avoid factions developing in an audience if a meeting is to achieve its objectives. Participants should not be 'put on the spot' with the 'what would *you* do?' type of questions (especially if the chairperson is aware that the participant's attention had drifted away – in which case he should be brought back to the meeting just by a casual comment that mentions his name, e.g. 'Tony made a useful comment to me last week about how he overcame the objection that our product had a longer delivery time than competitors'). More open questions, such as 'Do you have any ideas on ways we could look at or tackle this problem?', are more useful.

The chairperson at any meeting can, of course, expect to receive questions directed to himself. The sales manager chairing a meeting can generally expect more questions from his audience the more participatory is the style and format of the meeting. Questions may be relevant or irrelevant; if they are not relevant, it is better to explain that the question is outside the scope and purpose of the meeting (possibly offer to answer it privately subsequently), and bring the meeting back to relevant issues. Relevant questions may be intended to:

- give clarification to comments the speaker or chairperson has made in the course of presentations or discussions
- elicit more information on a subject of particular interest to the questioner
- seek a re-statement or re-phrasing of a question that the speaker or chairperson has put to the audience in general or to a particular person who has not grasped the sense or purpose of the original question

108

- seek the opinion, views or feelings of the speaker on a subject under discussion (or maybe even a subject quite unrelated to the discussion) – chairpersons and sales managers must be careful about expressing views or opinions that might negate their image of neutrality and impartiality
- put the chairperson or sales manager 'on the spot' or embarrass him, possibly where the questioner has more knowledge of a subject than the manager and asks a detailed or technical question – perhaps the manager's best defence is to field the question back to the questioner, and invite him to answer his own question.

In a participatory conference or meeting the chairperson must frequently compromise in order to gain acceptance. Attendees may have strong preconceived views, opinions and attitudes, and if the chairperson is also seen to be inflexible he may not retain the attention and interest of the audience or gain their involvement and so progress towards the objectives of the meeting. The chairperson must nevertheless retain control throughout the meeting, guide its direction and content, and organise the structure and format if it is to lead towards a meaningful and successful conclusion.

COMMUNICATION AIDS

The general aids to communications in meetings and conferences have been listed previously, and include:

- sound broadcasting facilities
- films
- video facilities
- slide presentations
- overhead projection facilities
- flip charts
- photographs
- models (material models not fashion models!) or samples
- overlay charts
- magnetic boards
- other charts and graphs
- blackboards.

The communication aids are generally used to:

- direct and retain attention and interest
- present often complex information in a meaningful and comprehensible fashion
- record audience inputs and comments
- involve the audience in participatory meetings

109

- increase assimilation and retention of information
- summarise main points of presentations
- provide a focal point as the meeting develops into a practical planning and implementation session.

When used effectively for presentation, control and planning purposes, they often save considerable time in meetings.

The aids used in a meeting will depend on the budget available to the sales manager, the size and nature of the audience, the venue facilities and the content and purpose of the meeting. Films and video facilities are very useful in training and role playing situations. Overlay charts and slides are often effective for presenting graphical or numerical data where there is a gradual build-up of information or data being presented, and each overlay adds to the previous discussion points. Overhead projectors offer the greatest flexibility at most meetings, and small portable units are a useful piece of equipment in any sales manager's armoury. Both overhead projectors and flip charts offer the advantage to sales managers of being relatively inexpensive, very portable, and flexible in use. They can be used for prepared presentations, with presentation data neatly incorporated on charts in advance; or flexibly during a meeting to give emphasis to points, get audience involvement, record and collate inputs, and clarify subject matter. They can be used to present original information, give comparisons, list advantages and disadvantages, gain consensus, and to summarise inputs, results, proceedings, objectives and action plans. They are the most useful aid to planning at sales meetings.

Whenever possible the presenter should generate more variety, attention and interest by using contrasting colours, although also ensuring that the notations are both clear and legible to all the audience.

The preparer of any aid to a presentation and communication (and the presenter himself, if they are not the same person) should ensure that he has all his aids in correct sequence and that they are suitable to the presentation environment (it would be useless to arrive at a meeting with the intention of showing slides only to find the meeting room could not be blacked out effectively). Maximum impact will normally be achieved by consideration of such design factors as:

- size
- legibility
- originality
- simplicity
- clarity
- colour
- realism
- relevance to the meeting content and the audience.

110

The information presented should be accurate (check for any errors in numerical charts), meaningful, and current.

MAKING A PRESENTATION

Many good courses and texts exist to give comprehensive training in the skills of making speeches and presentations. Salespersons and sales managers perhaps have an advantage over people in many other occupations as their daily existence revolves around inter-personal communications intended to exert influence on others. In this section, therefore, I propose to give only some summary guidelines that might help a sales manager in making an effective presentation of his subject matter and material.

Subject matter
The first task is to decide on the subject matter (or this may have been decided for you).

Group ideas
Jot down all your initial ideas on a sheet of paper, look for points that stand out as useful **key points** to build the speech around, and group related points together to aid the flow and continuity.

Information sources
Identify the sources of relevant information that you can tap while researching the subject matter of the presentation. These sources may include your own experience, the experience of associates, relevant literature, research reports, etc.

Audience
Consider who will form the audience. The content, structure and format of a presentation must take account of their present level of knowledge and experience, their likely levels of interest in the subject matter, their attitudes (will they be receptive, cynical, friendly, antagonistic, interested or uninterested?), their ability to assimilate the content and their rate of assimilation. The presenter must walk the line of neither 'talking down' to the audience nor aiming a talk over their heads.

Purpose
Before and during the preparation of the presentation consider what is the purpose of the talk. If it is just to give an overview of events or programmes, then less detail might be appropriate and the subject matter might be covered at a faster pace. If the intention is to impart a degree of expertise and new knowledge then more detail and supporting communication aids and handouts will probably be

necessary, and the talk may need to progress at a slower pace, with more time for questions and sufficient repetition to improve retention. If the purpose is to be instructional and impart new skills, then the talk probably needs to be broken down into stages that allow for audience participation and practice.

Perhaps the purpose is to put a new point of view or new course of action to overcome particular problems. Then the presentation may need to use some or all of the audience participation techniques previously discussed in this chapter to gradually influence the audience towards the new approach. An arbitrary decision that 'this is our new viewpoint' or 'this will be how we tackle the age old problem of . . . from tomorrow' will probably fall on deaf ears or fail because of lack of credibility, acceptance and commitment within the audience.

Presentation
The actual presentation needs a clear subject matter and theme to give continuity. A brief introduction will generally serve to gain attention and arouse interest so that everyone wants to hear what is to follow. The introduction should aim to show the audience what they might individually hope to get out of the talk.

The body of the talk should then develop the main theme, with each sequential step clearly explained in a meaningful and relevant fashion. It is always useful to relate talks to the experience of the audience, using examples and situations they might regularly encounter. Good use of communication aids will help assimilation and retention of the content, and retain general attention and interest.

The presentation should conclude with an effective and memorable summary, which might repeat key points, draw conclusions, or develop an action plan.

Script
Speakers normally find it useful to develop and write a complete presentation script from their initial notes, revise this and rehearse from it, possibly finally summarising the presentation onto pocket-sized prompt or cue cards.

Venue
Arrive at the venue early in order to familiarise yourself with the environment and facilities, and possibly also the audience. You need to ensure that the communication aids work, that sources of potential distraction are neutralised, that the audience will be comfortable during your talk (i.e. good ventilation, suitable room temperature, positioning so that no one will get a strained neck watching or listening), and that there is liquid refreshment beside you to lubricate your throat as necessary.

Impact

The first impression created by the speaker is critical to his impact on the audience and their subsequent attitude towards him. Avoid unnecessary flamboyance or distracting mannerisms or clothes, as any of these might divert attention away from the subject matter.

Positioning

Position yourself where the entire audience can see you without shifting their seats or twisting round, and within close proximity to your similarly visible communications aids. Avoid moving round unnecessarily as it detracts more from the talk than it contributes. Direct all speech clearly towards the audience (don't talk to the flip chart or notes). Be natural, enthusiastic and knowledgeable (well-rehearsed).

Timing

Control the timing to the allotted amount (otherwise a meeting chairperson may have to interrupt you) and limit the amount of information or knowledge being imparted to a level that can be assimilated and also effectively presented. Don't try to cover too much in a short time as nothing will then be retained by the audience. Frequent use of brief pauses may help slower members of the audience to catch up. At the end of each section or topic give a brief summary.

Questions

Always leave some time at the end for questions if these are not being taken during the course of the presentation. Questions relating to clarification of the presentation may sometimes best be taken during the presentation; questions on matters you know will be subsequently covered should not be taken at the time (as it will disrupt your flow), but the questioner should be told that you will shortly cover the point of his question, and that if it is not clear then can he raise the matter again.

Handouts

Where appropriate, prepare a handout covering the content and subject matter of the talk and any graphic illustrations or charts and tables used. Handouts can be particularly useful to highlight points that require action and to make practical suggestions for implementing proposals developed in a talk. If time has forced you to gloss over certain aspects in the talk, then the handout can serve to provide a little extra coverage.

To summarise this section: the key to effective presentation is thorough preparation; be clear on the purpose of your presentation

113

and its subject matter, and design the presentation to meet the needs, experience, knowledge and abilities of the audience.

BRAINSTORMING SESSIONS

I have chosen to separate this topic from the main body of the chapter and treat it in a little more depth because of my belief that it is a technique not sufficiently used or developed in many sales force environments. It can contribute much to team building, individual commitment and participation, and group and individual involvement in the direction and fortunes of the company. It also serves as a technique of improving individual analytical and evaluatory skills.

The purpose of brainstorming sessions is normally to elicit as much information as possible on a subject or as many alternative ways as can be found to tackle a situation or problem by drawing on the knowledge or experience of a group of people. The participants do not need to be from the same work environment. The emphasis in brainstorming sessions is not on analytical thought processes initially, but on creative thinking and exposition of ideas and alternatives.

Many persons or groups fail to produce creative ideas not because they lack creativity, but purely because they are inhibited by the norms, systems, values and so on in the environment. They are reluctant to be seen not to be conforming to peer group norms; afraid of being considered to be wrong or ridiculed by associates for expressing unconventional views or unproven theories; too ready to accept traditional systems and methods; unwilling to devote time and effort to seeking and evaluating alternatives; or simply jump to conclusions too rapidly without a real search for alternatives.

So in a brainstorming session the chairperson needs to encourage the participation of everyone and overcome these barriers to creative thinking by initially seeking only to elicit a multitude of ideas and comments, and not showing any personal reaction, attitude or other form of judgement himself. Nor should he permit any critical or evaluatory comment or judgement from the group at this stage. The most essential communication aid in a brainstorming session is a flip chart, and it would be quite normal, as ideas proliferate, to find the walls papered with sheets from the flip chart each listing comments and ideas.

As the flow of ideas lessens, usually after around 15–20 minutes, the time comes to start grouping ideas according to whatever common factors have been exhibited, and to remove any apparent duplication. Generally the brainstorming team would by now be quite relaxed and enjoying the fun spirit of the task, and showing little inhibition at the next stages of evaluation and criticism.

Once the ideas are suitably collated or grouped as seems most appropriate, they can then be discussed according to such parameters

114

as might be relevant to their suitability, operation or effectiveness. In a sales force environment, the parameters might be:

- cost
- ease of control
- ease of implementation
- lead times to implement
- acceptability to customers
- training required
- relevance to the products, markets, or competition
- ability to measure and monitor performance.

If a larger group, say of 12–20 people, was involved in the initial brainstorming session this could now be divided into smaller groups of 4–6 to develop and evaluate ideas within the broad categories identified. Alternatively, when the whole group has refined the ideas to a small number of concepts for further testing or evaluation, working parties can be formed to continue the programme and report back.

A sales manager might react initially by saying that brainstorming is not relevant to his environment or markets (he might even feel his team are called on not to be creative but just to follow established systems and procedures). That in itself represents an uncreative approach to an opportunity to build a team through brainstorming. The sales force is at the sharp end of the business environment, and there is always room for creative thinking in an effort to find new approaches to old problems. Often the very effort put behind a new approach may serve to improve performance as the old inhibitions are temporarily shelved.

A sales manager might start by trying a mini-brainstorming session around topics familiar to all the team, designed perhaps to identify interesting approaches to expanding distribution and trial, such as:

- Who uses or might use our products?
- Why do or might they use them?
- Where would they be likely to look to buy them?
- How would they actually use the products?
- How can we identify specific potential users?
- How can we reach potential users to introduce the products?
- What are the noteworthy features and benefits of our products?
- How can we promote our products to increase trial?
- How can we increase the space allocated to product displays?

Several questions relating to one topic or opportunity might be considered at one brainstorming session, and the session might form part of a larger-scale meeting such as a conference or area meeting. The sales manager should particularly encourage participatory

115

meetings and sessions where team involvement may either help find solutions to problems or increase commitment to proposals, projects or programmes.

SUMMARY

- The process of communication is the transmission and receipt of signals through such means as: demonstration and/or verbal, written, pictorial, numerical, physical and attitudinal communications. Involuntary communications occur through facial expressions and body language (posture and gestures), and in the sales environment the salesperson should be in control of both his voluntary and involuntary communications.

- Communications in the sales force generally centre round: policies, procedures, programmes and precedents.

- The means of communication will depend on the urgency of the subject matter, the communication media available to both the sender and the recipient, and the complexity of the content.

- Communications can cover **essential** communications on matters that relate to the specific performance of job functions, and **optional** communications that increase a salesperson's understanding of the company and its operations and environment, and of product or market developments. Managers who communicate only on a '**need to know**' basis are losing a major opportunity to use communications for motivational and personnel development purposes.

- Communications should be sent to those with a 'need to know' to perform job functions, those required to take supporting action, and those who benefit by seeing the communication for information and reference purposes.

- To be effective, communications should be empathetic, sincere, informative, clear, concise, meaningful and simple in format and structure.

- Communication breakdowns often result from internal rivalries or jealousies, failure to understand the need to communicate, or simple oversight. Because of their impact on morale, motivation and performance, sources and causes of communication breakdowns need to be identified and neutralised, using such means as corrective communication training and counselling.

- Bulletins and memoranda in the sales force environment are generally used to issue instructions, inform of events and programmes, provide feedback, motivate, confirm discussions and agreements, and give recognition for achievements.

- Meetings and conferences are generally designed in structure and content to fulfil such purposes as: providing a source of motivation, giving instruction and information, exploring new ideas and concepts, resolving current problems and implementing corrective action programmes, and promoting participation and team building.

- In organising meetings the senior sales manager should: define objectives, decide on a main theme, allocate overall organisational responsibility to one person, select a suitable venue, decide on the length of the meeting, prepare an agenda, notify all speakers and attendees of arrangements, plan a suitable room layout, select the communication aids to be used, review individual presentations with speakers, and prepare any necessary handouts and conference manuals.

- Meeting formats might include: lectures and presentations by sales managers and guest speakers, group discussions, planning sessions, role playing exercises, case studies, and other team involvement exercises such as presentations or assignments and projects conducted by individual attendees or smaller groups.

- The chairperson needs to remain neutral and impartial in all discussions and exercise firm control of time, the speakers and the audience while encouraging involvement and participation, including the use of questions and regular summaries as the meeting progresses. In a participation meeting he should seek to obtain the views and opinions of attendees, gather information and reactions, develop discussions on the subject matter, encourage participation by re-phrasing or re-presenting worth-while comments from individuals who might not have made a suitable impact with a comment, and lead towards conclusions or modifications of attitudes or behaviour that will promote higher productivity and performance.

- In preparing a talk, the presenter should: define his subject matter and objectives; group ideas into general sections or topics; identify key points and build a script around them with the objective of gaining attention, creating interest and retaining audience involvement throughout. The nature and experience of the audience must be taken into account in structuring a talk. Use of relevant communication aids (including handouts) promotes interest and attention, and aids retention. The speaker should address himself directly to the audience and not the charts, communication aids or personal notes (which might be summarised on to prompt cards), and refrain from distracting mannerisms, movement or flamboyance.

- Brainstorming sessions in the sales force aid the development of creative thinking skills and team building, and can usefully contribute new insights once barriers and inhibitions to such lateral thinking are broken down.

	Notes	Action

Set **objectives**

Decide main **theme**

Allocate organisational **responsibility**

Select a **venue**, considering:

- geographical location
- accessibility
- accommodation/parking
- leisure facilities
- meal facilities
- available communications aids
- billing arrangements
- communications/message facilities
- meeting room facilities, e.g.
  - size
  - location
  - ventilation
  - lighting
  - audio facilities
  - rest rooms
  - shape/layout

Confirm venue booking by letter

Prepare an **agenda** and circulate to all speakers

Invite guest speakers (confirm theme and subject of presentations)

Invite audience and advise of travel and accommodation arrangements

Plan **room layout**:

- theatre/table or other format
- water/beverages
- ash trays/waste bins
- lighting/audio
- communication aids
- theme displays

Review all speakers' presentation scripts

Prepare all **communications aids** and handouts for presentations

Prepare conference folders or manuals for audience (including writing materials, name tags, agendas, pre-conference reading, etc.)

Plan **reception** of all attendees:

- accommodation check-in
- welcoming committee
- book meals and beverages at break intervals

Rehearse all presentations, including the use and operation of communication aids

4 Sales Planning and Forecasting

Planning and forecasting are complex and broad subjects covered at length and in depth by many specialist texts, and this text will not attempt to go beyond summary coverage of practical aspects of sales planning and forecasting. It is particularly aimed at sales managers in smaller and medium-sized companies which may not have the sophisticated planning resources of larger corporations.

PLANNING

Why plan? I have often heard comments inside companies that the sales managers are the most reluctant to prepare plans and forecasts beyond the very short term, possibly claiming that they need to remain very flexible to take advantage of changing market conditions. Whilst I accept the need for flexibility in the sales environment, planning is an essential early stage in the management process. Planning gives a sense of purpose and direction to subsequent activities, by setting objectives, identifying priorities and key result areas, developing strategies and tactics, and monitoring results.

Stages in the planning process One approach to planning is that it occurs once a year (perhaps after much harassment from the finance division), consists of a collection of facts and figures presented to top management in a nicely bound 'annual plan' book and often then neatly filed in the bottom drawer. The first management realisation must be that planning is just as much 'ongoing' as any other management function. A well-prepared sales planning document should be a working guide, referred to at very frequent intervals, used to control actual performance against plans and to update forecasts as conditions change. It should be flexible to react to changing circumstances both internal and external to the company.

The full planning process encompasses the stages of:

- setting objectives;
- making specific programmes to achieve the objectives, including developing forecasts and/or targets, and initiating and refining tactics and strategies, including marketing and sales promotional activities geared to the achievement of objectives within the allocated time spans;
- developing controls that monitor results and ensure that strategies and tactics are implemented and produce results in line with the plans, or produce warnings at shortfalls or variances from plans;

120

● taking corrective action to return deviant results back towards the planned course.

This and the next chapter are concerned with the first two of these stages. Controls will be considered in detail in Chapter 11.

Example 4.1 The planning process

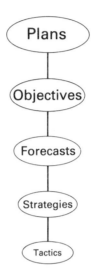

It is perhaps worth mentioning at this point of the text that effective sales planning and forecasting is not a one man task for the national sales manager, especially in larger companies. Many other managers and specialists can make a significant contribution in terms of:

● **market knowledge**
   – environment external to the company
   – economic environment (prices, interest rates, incomes, employment, production, distribution, demographic factors, etc.)
   – legislative and regulatory environment
   – competition (both domestic and foreign)
   – political considerations
   – distribution channel factors
   – trends and product preference patterns and changes
   – user attitudes, perceptions and expectations

● **company resources**
   – plant production capacity
   – raw material supplies and availability

– research developments (including new technology and
innovations, in-house company research and development
programmes, potential and 'ready made' new products)
– personnel resourcing and training
– financial resources and controls.

Therefore in medium to larger companies there may be considerable
scope for and merit in developing a small core '**strategy committee**'
that meets from time to time to monitor all of the above and any
other factors specific to the company, and to consider how developments in any or all of them might impact on company strategies and
objectives. The membership of such a committee is likely to include
(in addition to the key sales management functions of key accounts
and field sales management) representatives of marketing, market
research, corporate planning, production, finance and product
research departments, perhaps with a personnel representative
giving an input when matters of personnel resourcing are involved.
Obviously the objective would be to make advantageous use of
internal and external environmental factors whenever possible (e.g.
filling market gaps when a competitor experiences strikes or
production problems, including when importers face short-term
supply limitations).

Objectives **General sales objectives**
The first stage of planning is to set the **key objectives** for the
company. These might be set in terms of several criteria, including
turnover levels, profit contributions, returns on investment (capital
employed or shareholders equity), growth in investors' capital, unit
volumes of sales, market shares, and so on. Each company division
will, in turn, convert the company objectives into its own **subsidiary
operational objectives**. By working from the top down, a hierarchy
of objectives will be constructed. Each company division will interrelate its subsidiary operational objectives and plans to construct the
master company plan.

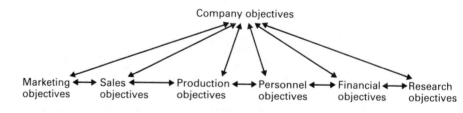

The plans of each division must relate to the overall company key
objectives. For example, various subsidiary operational objectives
can be set for field sales managers, salespersons and key account
executives that impact on the overall objectives:

122

Area	Subsidiary objective	Overall objective
Call coverage	• finding new productive productive outlets	• sales volume, profit growth
	• improve journey planning	• reduced costs, improved productivity
	• reduce call frequencies without volume loss	• improved productivity
	• increase coverage of worthwhile outlets	• higher volumes and profits through reduced out-of-stock positions
Distribution	• reduce out of stocks	• sales volume and profits
	• additional product listings in existing outlets	• sales volume and profits
	• new worthwhile accounts	• sales volume and profits
	• new products sold into existing or new accounts	• sales volume and profits
	• drop direct coverage of non-worthwhile accounts	• reduced costs
Display	• improve key site display positioning	• sales volumes
	• more display facings per product	• sales volumes
	• shift display emphasis from lower margin to higher margin products	• profits
	• greater use of point of sales display material	• sales volumes
	• feature promotional displays	• customer trial and sales volumes
Personnel/ training	• reduce staff turnover	• reduced recruitment costs
	• improve sales presentation skills	• higher productivity
Budgets/ equipment	• control over sales aids, materials usage and wastage	• cost savings
	• improve expense controls	• cost savings
	• reduce staffing levels	• cost savings
	• account/territory profit targets	• improved profitability

As can be seen from this table, most sales management and sales force objectives clearly relate to:

• higher sales volumes;
• improved profitability from sales activity; or
• cost control and reduction.

123

As a specific example, if the company has an objective of, say, increasing gross profit by 20 per cent pre-tax then the sales force has several alternative ways of achieving this:

- increasing prices of existing products
- increasing sales volumes of higher-margin products
- adding new products that will give a net increase in sales volume and gross profits (by more than costs increase and sales on other lines decline)
- increasing sales volumes at existing prices (through new or existing outlets)
- increasing sales volumes by selective price reductions (where additional gross profit contributions are more than the lost unit margin)
- reducing sales force costs.

The final plan might, and probably would, include a combination of these. In reality, it would be expected that some products would not support price increases without loss in sales volume partly or totally offsetting the increased contribution per unit. Other product lines, with correct market positioning, might be less price elastic, and capable of more exploitation. If new products are being added, then consideration must be given to whether they have high or low sales and profit potential and whether they will require more support services, including increases in sales or office staff.

The objectives within each of the above broad categories might be passed down the line to the individual territory level as:

- increase call rate by an average of one call per day
- reduce direct call coverage frequency on certain calls (booking increased orders per visit made or substituting telephone sales calls – see Chapter 12)
- identify 20 new worthwhile direct outlets and include them in the scheduled journey cycle, utilising capacity released as above
- increase sales to call ratios from a territory average of 60 per cent to 65 per cent
- increase distribution by 5 per cent for product 'Z'
- concentrate display and promotional activity on the higher-margin products 'X' and 'Y', and arrange at least three in-store feature promotions per month on each of these products.

In an industrial product environment, call rate may be a minor factor, particularly where many contracts take months of negotiating to produce the order. But an individual account manager might still be assigned quantifiable objectives of:

- increasing usage per customer by x per cent over a given period

(where the company is not already the sole supplier to a customer and there is still an opportunity to 'steal' some sales volume from competitors)
- finding new accounts/product users for a specified product (e.g. specifying y new users over the time period)
- increasing average prices achieved from sales by £z per unit volume or quantity.

To have credibility with those charged with achieving them, objectives must be **realistic, achievable** within the allocated time span, **measurable**, and with outcomes within the control of the person who set the objectives. The person responsible for the achievement of the objectives must accept them as his own objectives within his job functions and responsibilities, and should be involved in discussing the objectives with his line manager and agree that they comply with the foregoing criteria. It is only through the sales team that the company objectives will be achieved. The field sales manager's objectives should therefore include a strong emphasis on personnel training and development.

Key account objectives

In most companies a few customers dominate sales, and those few customers may have the greatest impact on both sales volume and profitability. If the benefits from supplying goods or services to major accounts directly relate to cost savings then it might be reasonable to pass on some or all of these savings.

Cost savings might relate to such factors as:

- lower physical distribution costs (fewer delivery points)
- larger average order sizes
- reduced order processing and administrative costs (larger average order value)
- lower credit control costs
- lower packaging costs (if bulk goods are supplied)
- lower sales force costs (through reduced coverage for any level of sales)
- lower management/sales force staffing requirements

However, key accounts also have their additional servicing costs because of the demands they make upon manufacturers, including:

- higher promotional expenditure and activity level for any level of sales volume
- discounts and rebates that are in excess of measurable cost savings
- a frequently higher incidence of claims in connection with product returns

125

- high individual store servicing costs to support product listings with in-store promotional activity and product merchandising
- increased costs of administration if the account requires special data or analyses of information particular to their business
- the frequency with which large accounts take advantage of their size in arbitrarily extending payment times
- higher sundry expense costs for sales management, including customer entertainment.

Many companies face a constant balancing act between the benefits and costs of operating distribution through key accounts, but it is a reality of any industry or market sector that any supplier of goods or services will find that a small proportion of regular customers are the source of most of the demand for a product. On the basis that this situation must be accepted, there are three main considerations to take into account when setting objectives in respect of key accounts:

- limit the percentage of output to be sold to or through any one customer
- limit the total share of production output to be offered for sale to the major accounts (say the top 20 customers)
- set profit performance related objectives as a priority for each key account rather than just volume related objectives.

The first two of these points are concerned with limiting the exposure of the company to risks. If the fortunes of a manufacturer depend totally on one or very few customers then there may be a question about how long the supplier can remain independent (or if there is any benefit in trying to remain independent rather than seeking a merger). The benefits of measuring account profitability will be touched on again later in the text to reinforce the point that field sales managers need to be very sensitive to matters of profitability that depend on factors within their control, such as price levels, sales product mix, key account terms, promotional expenditures, sales volumes and sales force costs.

SALES FORECASTING

Once general or specific objectives have been set, the next stage is to develop forecasts and strategies to achieve those objectives within an allocated time span. It might seem that strategies and forecasts and targets are interrelated in the proverbial chicken and egg, 'which came first' fashion. Some sales managers feel they need to decide on the strategies for the market place before they can prepare a forecast;

others prefer to develop forecasts or targets and then consider the means to achieve them. I believe there is benefit in working from both ends.

In this text I take the view that there is an essential difference between forecasts and targets:

- **forecasts** are projections of expected sales over a particular future time span based upon known parameters such as historical sales achievement data in a base period, and adjusted for any known or predicted environmental changes or factors that might impact on future performance, both internal and external to the company.
- **targets** are fundamentally a statement of what the sales force want to achieve and may be based (as in the case of a new company without a sales history to use as a basis for more sound forecasting) mainly upon data external to the company. Achieve-ment of targets is heavily dependent upon the development and implementation of suitable strategies and tactics in the form of sales activity and promotional programmes. As with any other objective, targets need to be seen by the sales force responsible for their achievement as **realistic** and **achievable** within the allocated time span.

I do not favour the targeting games played in some companies where targets are set at levels for each separate territory that are higher than is necessary to total the overall company targets or forecasts. If that were to result in shortages against orders for any reason, or cancellation of orders because production could not match sales, then the credibility of the salespersons with customers could be seriously harmed with a major demotivating effect on salespersons.

Sales forecasts generally aim at various time spans from the base point:

- **short-term forecasts** usually cover one year to eighteen months ahead
- **medium-term forecasts** usually attempt to project sales trends and forecasts between one and three years forward (and with a lower expectation of accuracy than would normally be sought in a short-term forecast)
- **long-term forecasts** normally attempt to forecast forward for around five years (with obviously rather limited accuracy, as environmental factors, both internal and external to the company, are likely to impact on the company and product markets the further into the future forecasts and projections are made).

Forecasting takes account of the **past, present**, and the **future**. To

127

consider the historical performance in relation to the future it is essential that accurate and comprehensive sales performance records and statistics are kept by volume and value, by geographical markets, by market segment or sector, and by customers for each separate product and variety. Notes should be available on promotional and marketing activity timing and results (where any quantifiable measurement was attempted), and on relevant **external** data, including competitive activity and performance, total market data and published economic data.

What to
forecast

The first task is to assess the current size of the potential market for any product or product category, and then to attempt to relate the company's potential **sales volumes** and **values** to this estimate. The task becomes more complex and less quantitatively accurate as attempts are made to forecast both the future market sales potential and trends and the company's future market share. There are limits to the size of every market: the potential demand for any product has a finite limit, and forecasters are often very concerned with the total market size and growth potential once their company's market share becomes significant. At that point many companies develop positive diversification strategies as the main route to growth. A small company may be less concerned by the market size limits, as in its initial stages much growth comes from steal from competitors through the marketing means at its disposal, including price competitiveness, quality factors, design, delivery, service, etc.

The volume and value forecasts should take account of the factors listed in the later section of this chapter, 'developing sales strategies'. Where exports occur or are planned to commence, company sales forecasts should incorporate a section on **export sales forecasts**. Company plans also need to take account of the impact of **imports** of competitive goods and services upon domestic sales, whether those imports come from new or existing sources.

These forecasts can then be interpreted in terms of the resources/ costs needed to achieve them:

- **sales force operating costs and expenses**, including:
  departmental costs for:
  - sales training
  - recruitment
  - customer service
  - order processing
  - sales planning
  - export department (where applicable)

  operating costs for:
  - promotional and display materials
  - sales force vehicles

128

  – sales force expenses
  – wages and wage increases
  – sales promotional activities

- **staffing levels**, taking account of
  – natural wastage
  – retirement
  – sickness
  – holidays
  – changes in qualifications, experience or skills needed for the job

- **profits**, by:
  – product
  – customer
  – territory
  – market sector

- **pricing levels and movements**:
  – nationally
  – regionally
  – internationally.

Forecasts of cost factors need to take account of inflation and other cost increases (or decreases) if the sales forecast is taking account of expected future product price movements rather than being in constant price terms. The company's accountants will advise the sales manager how they wish to treat future price and cost movements. An industry selling on a 'cost plus' pricing basis will have different budgetary considerations from one facing prices dictated by market conditions. It is just as necessary for companies, such as agents and distributors, that receive their income as a commission on sales to prepare forecasts and budgets to ensure that the level of income due to be generated more than covers the costs of operating the business, or that adjustments in the level of resources are made in response to changes in market conditions or sales expectations.

Sales forecasts also need to give consideration to:

- seasonal trends
- cyclical trends
- random fluctuations
- product life cycles.

Seasonal trends

Many industries face seasonal sales trends, such as the holiday and leisure industries or those with strongly seasonally related goods. In some instances it may be practical to gear staffing to the peak sales periods where special training and experience is less critical than in a more complex product industry. Toy and cosmetic companies

129

relying heavily on in-store promotional activity around the Christmas season may be able to use temporary workers to act as in-store product advisors and demonstrators. Seasonality of sales frequently has a major bearing on the structuring and operations of sales forces and the supporting distribution operations. The frequency of call coverage on some or all customers is likely to have to increase in the peak sales season, and this may put considerable pressure on the sales personnel resources at all levels. If there is purely a market shift in sales activity, say from an inland market area to coastal regions, then possibly the call frequency on inland outlets can be reduced and sales-persons temporarily transferred to the coastal regions to boost coverage operations there.

Cyclical trends

Such trends are well known in the building and construction markets, and in industries that rely heavily on agricultural inputs that are subject to varying annual output levels. It is difficult to rely heavily on commission incentive schemes for sales rewards where there is a strong cyclical or seasonal trend to sales. A company also faces the problem of erratic sales volume and profit earnings in a cyclical product market. The problems are perhaps accentuated where the cycles are not of predictable length or frequency. Usually market or company performance data must exist for a considerable historical time span if they are to be of any use in studying cycles and attempting predictions.

Not all markets will be subject to the same trends, movements or cyclical patterns: a supplier of a product, service, or ingredient that is used in many industries may experience less fluctuation in overall levels of product demand, whilst still being subject to fluctuations in sales to any one end use market.

Random fluctuations

These might occur for a number of reasons, such as the **positive** variations arising from additional sales promotions, short-term advertising campaigns, intermittent sales force incentive pro-grammes, export 'booms' (perhaps when the domestic currency weakens in relation to major international currencies), and unusual but beneficial weather conditions or fluctuations (very relevant for some seasonal types of products, such as umbrellas perhaps!). **Negative** variations might result from competitive short-term promotional activities, sales force personnel shortages (vacant territories), scheduled coverage lost for any unforeseen reason (including sickness), industrial disputes, adverse unpredicted weather conditions, raw material or input shortages, supply problems with imported inputs, export shortfalls against forecasts (perhaps resulting from unexpected currency fluctuations, or the imposition of foreign market import quotas or export licencing restrictions). In principle,

no allowance should be made for unpredictable random fluctuations
in preparing sales forecasts and budgets, since a forecast is based
upon known factors and conditions and on judgements on other
likely environmental changes. However, many companies do find it
beneficial to calculate the effects that a 5–10 per cent over- or under-
achievement against forecasts would have on profitability.

Product life cycles

Attempts should be made in longer-term forecasts to consider the life
cycle of a product. Most products have a limited life cycle before
market conditions dictate that change is necessary. Consumer tastes
and preferences change. Product developments and innovations, or
new technology or systems, all date established products. The
marketing team are likely to be concerned over modifications to
existing products (including packaging) that will extend the product's
life or give a new impetus to sales. The sales division needs to liaise
closely with the marketing team to recognise life cycle trends and
limits for longer-term forecasting purposes, although in the short
term the effect may be less obvious.

A typical product life cycle pattern

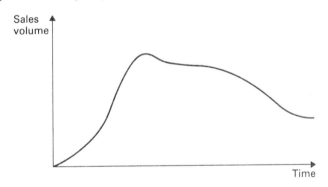

Forecasting
methods

Basically there are two ways of approaching the forecasting task –
looking down from the **macro** level of overall company performance
in relation to the environment, or building up from the **micro** level
of the recent historical performance of each account.

Macro forecasts

The macro forecast will look at figures such as historical overall
company achievements in relation to such environmental factors as
are demonstrably connected with company or market performance
and demand for the type of goods produced by the company and its
competitors. Demand for the industry and company products might
relate to overall national levels of production, prices, employment,
disposable income, the money supply, interest rates, imports and
distribution. Demographic factors (such as the size or growth rate of

131

the population, age and sex ratios, geographic population movements) might also have a bearing on sales potential and forecasting.

Forecasters concerned with preparing such forecasts will probably
refer to such officially published data as are available nationally or
regionally to cover the above factors and any others believed to affect
performance. Environmental factors that are not statistically
measurable – such as changes in regulations and legislation that
affect the industry (possibly concerned with health and safety,
advertising, labelling, ingredients, product structure, and so on) –
may also need to be taken into account.

Where a company is large and sophisticated then **macro** level
forecasting will frequently be a function of a separate corporate
planning department. This chapter is concerned with helping those
managers who do not have access to a corporate planning department but must still attempt to develop a company sales forecast.

Micro forecasts

In this system the individual salesperson or account executive would
be asked to study the performance of each of his customers over the
recent past (say, two–three years) on a product-by-product basis, and
prepare forward sales estimates for the next forecast period. Salespersons could try to produce such forecasts either by relying upon
their own judgement and sales records, or as a result of discussions
with each of their own customers on the customer's expectations and
plans for the forecast time period. The forecasts prepared for each
customer provide a basis for discussion and planning with the field
sales managers. Salespersons will tend to be more optimistic in
building up forecasts than the head office forecasters. However, such
forecasts are particularly good over the short term when most
external environmental factors are having less impact.

Consideration of the alternative starting points used to prepare
forecasts and the resulting levels of forecasts should give managers a
base for discussion and consensus of the final forecasts to accept and
work to in developing strategies and tactics.

In his attempts to develop acceptable and realistic assessments of the
future sales and potential, the sales manager might supplement his
judgement with statistical techniques such as **time series** or **causal**
studies.

Judgement

This will come into play in respect of historical performance factors
and market knowledge. Expert opinion may be available to comment
on the outside environment including economic, political, legislative
and technological factors that might impact on the broad markets for
the company's products or services. The internal sales management

team can exercise judgement in respect of the immediate trading environment, drawing on a wealth of knowledge derived from customer contact. Market research studies or 'user reports' might be available to indicate user attitudes, preferences, expectations and intentions under certain conditions.

Time series

These studies include the statistical techniques of:

- **trend fitting** – projecting forward from historical data
- **moving average** performance projections from the historical moving average data base
- **exponential smoothing**, where extra weighting is given to more recent data.

Causal studies

Such studies include such techniques as:

- **regression analysis**, where equations are developed that relate the volume of sales to a number of independent variables known to impact on sales performance (such as: advertising, call frequency, promotional expenditure, display activity),
- **econometric models**, which look at the interdependent relationships of a number of factors that affect sales and profits,
- **input/output models**, which might be very useful for ingredient or component forecasting where projections will encompass the demand for inputs in relation to outputs in user industries. In this case some knowledge is needed of the expected levels of user output.

The general sales manager may not have the facilities or the sophistication of data needed to develop comprehensive macro level forecasts, so in the subsequent discussions I shall mainly be concerned with data likely to be available to provide a basis for forward projections, such as moving average and moving annual total sales figures.

Whether forecasts are commenced and developed at the macro or micro level the end result will be that they must be definitive and broken down to the level of each separate account and geographical or organisational sales force tier in order that each member of the sales force has specific forecasts or targets to meet. Forecasts, therefore, will need to be prepared in respect of each:

- account or customer
- territory
- geographical area or region
- sales function, e.g. key accounts executive.

133

In addition, the forecasts need to be developed on a:

- product-by-product
- month-by-month
- volume and value

basis, taking account of changes in the product range or mix, advertising and promotional activity which might take place continuously or occasionally, and price changes projected.

Developing
a practical
forecast

Most recorded historical sales performance data can provide a base both for measurement against plans and for preparing forecasts of likely future performance or trends, in addition to serving to alert management of unwelcome variances that might need to be the subject of corrective action. Trend lines can be statistically fitted to historical data, and used as a guide in forecasting overall likely performance, although a straightforward projection made in this fashion does not make any allowance for any future environmental changes internal or external to the company (see Example 4.2). In Example 4.2 approximate trend lines have been fitted by inspection, because the statistical fitting of trend lines is beyond the scope of this text.

Wherever possible, it is worth trying to identify what data are available on the total market for the product category, and then plotting a graph including these data on one axis against time on the other (see Example 4.2 (c)). If data are not available on a sales units or volume basis (perhaps because suppliers all offer different sizes of product or packs), information on a value basis will still be valuable to identify trends or patterns. Information may sometimes be available through government agencies or trade associations concerned with recording production statistics or, if imports represent a large share of the market, it will be worth obtaining the historical product import data for quantity and landed value and analysing that for any apparent trends. Again, whilst approximate trend lines may be apparent to the eye, statistical techniques might be used to fit trend lines and project these forward.

There are, of course, practical problems and complications for a multi-product or multi-market segment supplier of goods or services. Such a company will need to forecast for each product into each separate market segment.

Assuming that historical sales information is available for each customer account on a product-by-product and month-by-month basis, as a starting point, an elementary planning sheet could be drawn up (as in Example 4.3) for each separate account, and the actual sales data inserted for the last two years along with the month-by-month forecasts for the next year. This example assumes the product line is for certain electrical household items. The source of

134

historical sales performance data for the territory salespersons might
be recordings on the customer call card or a centrally prepared and
issued computer printout.

Example 4.2   Fitting trend lines to historical data to aid forecasting

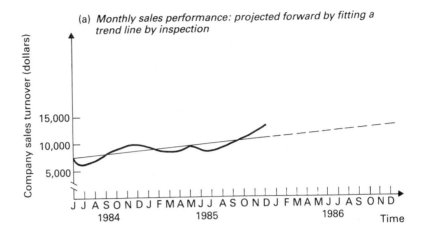

(a) *Monthly sales performance: projected forward by fitting a
trend line by inspection*

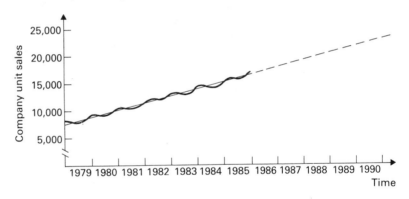

(b) *Moving annual total: trend line fitted by inspection*

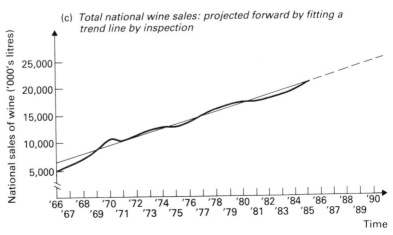

(c) *Total national wine sales: projected forward by fitting a
trend line by inspection*

135

Example 4.3   Customer sales forecast (all figures in units of product)

Customer	Territory:								
	Electric razors			Toasters			Percolators		
Month	'84 Act.	'85 Act.	'86 For.	'84 Act.	'85 Act.	'86 For.	'84 Act.	'85 Act.	'86 For.
January	40	45	50						
February	45	45	50						
March	50	60	60						
April	50	60	60						
May	75	70	70						
June	60	65	70						
July	60	70	75						
August	60	70	75						
September	75	75	80						
October	80	90	90						
November	100	105	110						
December	120	125	130						
Year total	795	880	920						

Act. = actual performance
For. = forecast

The next logical stage is to summarise all the individual customer forecasts on a simple tabulation sheet for each product, as in Example 4.4. This form of summary could either be produced manually by each territory salesperson, or be centrally prepared from the inputs supplied on each customer using the company's computer facilities, and then returned to the appropriate territory salesperson for review.

The data now available on a month-by-month basis by product and by customer for each territory can then be summarised on an annual forecast summary for each territory and customer, as in Example 4.5.

It is then purely a mechanical task to prepare the overall summary forecast sheets for each sales area, region, or nationally, noting both the sales volume and value forecasts.

At the level of **key account sales operations** and, if at all possible, at the level of each territory, a profit contribution forecast may be possible once the sales volume and value forecasts are made. Consideration needs to be given to directly attributable measurable costs, such as:

- discounts and allowances (including performance rebates)
- distribution costs
- direct selling operational costs and expenses
- product returns and other such allowances
- direct and specific promotional costs (i.e. excluding national advertising and promotion campaigns)
- manufactured costs of finished product shipped to a customer

Example 4.4 Territory sales forecast product summary sheet

Customer	Jan.	Feb.	Mar.	Apr.	May	Jun.	Jul.	Aug.	Sep.	Oct.	Nov.	Dec.	Totals
Territory: North Midlands 12							**Salesperson:** A. Jones		**Product:** Electric razors			**Year:** 1986
Lucas Dept Store, Newtown	15	15	20	20	25	30	40	30	30	35	50	70	380
Wilson's Dept Store, Hightown	20	20	25	40	30	35	40	40	50	55	70	100	525
Star Discount, Freetown	40	40	50	50	60	60	60	40	60	70	100	150	780
TOTALS	600	600	650	700	750	750	800	600	800	900	1,400	3,000	11,550

- attributable overheads (for either sales and marketing only, or an overall company overhead allocation)
- interest on average outstanding debts.

It may not be practical to allocate figures separately for a number of these factors at the level of each customer, or too cumbersome and costly to prepare such a detailed analysis. In this case a simple measure of gross contribution might suffice (i.e. the difference between the manufactured cost and the sales revenue). Whatever analysis is possible within the limits of a company's resources it is a useful management exercise to recognise the profitability or otherwise of servicing each account to ensure that the most cost-effective channel of distribution is used.

Example 4.5 Territory sales forecast volume/value summary sheet

Territory: **Salesperson:**   **Year:**

Customer	Electric razors Vol.	Val.	Toasters Vol.	Val.	Percolators Vol.	Val.	Totals Vol.	Val.
Lucas Dept Store	380	3,800	400	4,400	350	5,250	1,130	13,450
Wilson's Dept Store	525	5,250	600	6,600	550	8,250	1,675	20,100
Star Discount	780	7,800	500	5,500	500	7,500	1,780	20,800
TOTAL	11,500	115,000	9,500	104,500	9,900	148,500	30,900	368,000

139

Manufacturers of goods sold into several market sectors may particularly wish to see performance history and forecast sales by market sector, especially if cyclical fluctuations affect any one or all of these sectors. Analyses might be prepared on a month-by-month basis, and summary data tabulated as in Example 4.6, where the market sectors an electrical component company might sell into are identified for analysis. The manufacturer might have two fundamental markets — for replacement purposes (possibly in the local authority and retail/wholesale trade) and for new construction projects (the latter probably being very cyclical in nature).

Example 4.6 Sales analysis and forecast by market sector

Units	Light fittings	Wall switches	Wall sockets
Local authorities:			
Actual 1984	10,000		
Actual 1985	11,000		
Forecast 1986	12,000		
Construction industry:			
Actual 1984	25,000		
Actual 1985	20,000		
Forecast 1986	21,000		
Retail/wholesale trade:			
Actual 1984	15,000		
Actual 1985	15,500		
Forecast 1986	16,000		
Export:			
Actual 1984	10,000		
Actual 1985	15,000		
Forecast 1986	16,000		
Totals:			
Actual 1984	60,000		
Actual 1985	61,500		
Forecast 1986	65,000		

This example for light fittings indicates an export boom started in 1985, which might be a function of a weakening domestic currency, quite apart from a more aggressive export marketing programme.

Each territory, region or special function, such as key accounts, should have its forecast provided in a comprehensive but comprehensible format so that it may form the basis for setting objectives and measuring performance, and so that appropriate sales promotion planning may be instigated at the local level to ensure that forecasts are achieved within time spans and budgets. Salespersons who are involved in the preparation of the forecasts and planning processes will have a greater commitment to the achievement of those forecasts, since each of them will have already accepted that the forecasts are both realistic and achievable.

Developing sales strategies

Whatever the level a forecast or target is set at, there must be a strategic plan to ensure success. There are always limits in the short term on flexibility, because some strategies have much longer lead times than others (such as the development and launch of a new or modified product). Hence short-term limiting factors must be taken into account in preparing strategies.

Example 4.7 illustrates the key considerations the sales manager must take account of in developing his sales strategies.

Example 4.7 Considerations in developing strategies

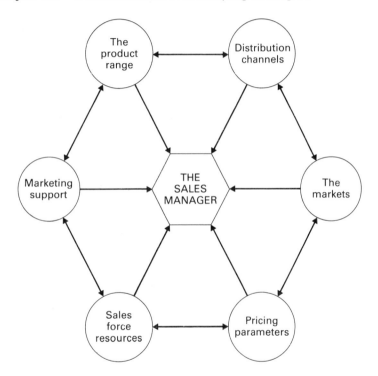

The product range

The marketing department, where a company is large enough to support a separate department, will have a major say in the range of products produced and offered for sale. In smaller companies the sales and marketing functions may well be combined, with the senior manager having overall control over both sales and marketing activities and decisions. Decisions have to be taken on:

- what market segments to target products at, or whether to try and cover all segments of any market (e.g. high, low and middle prices or qualities)

141

- whether to develop branded product images or to act as a private label supplier
- what range of products to offer any market segments.

Consideration of such matters depends on whether the products are intended for direct consumption by the public or are an industrial input as part of the processing of goods or services.

Distribution channels

Whatever the decisions taken concerning the product range, the sales manager will be responsible for arranging distribution channels to reach the target market, and structuring a sales force to supply and service those distribution channels. Goods may be sold and delivered direct to end users or retail establishments, or through a network of distributors, wholesalers, or service centres. Further consideration is given to these aspects in Chapter 12.

The markets

Once the markets are identified, the sales manager is responsible for identifying the persons or companies operating in that market. These will range greatly in size or potential product requirements, be geographically spread around the country, have various levels of market strength, and differ in their own stability and financial resources. The sales manager must decide as part of his planning process on the mix of customers to supply goods to, as well as through which available channels of distribution supply should be effected. The outcome of these considerations will usually result in a serious effort to penetrate a number of key accounts – the larger outlets for consumers or users of the products – with support sales and distribution efforts to lower tiers in the distribution chain or smaller customers (who might be serviced through the direct sales force or the distributive network established).

Pricing parameters

Whilst the marketing arm of the company will want to be involved in product pricing and positioning, the sales manager may have market views, knowledge and experience enabling him to give a very worth-while input. The pricing of products will have a bearing on the market segments that can be penetrated. Clearly a higher-priced item will have problems competing with lower-priced items unless it offers perceived or tangible benefits to the purchaser. The sales manager will have to control the special pricing and terms offered to key accounts (setting the levels of discounts, performance-related rebates and other terms and conditions of trading) to ensure that smaller customers still have an interest in stocking or using the products.

142

Sales force resources

The objectives the sales manager sets himself or accepts to be achieved through the sales force organisation will depend heavily on the resources available to him, in both the short and longer term. The resources consist largely of people, but additionally there are financial parameters (budgets) that restrict how many people he can employ, train and equip with vehicles, sales aids and support materials. An objective to increase sales by 50 per cent might be quite realistic in terms of market potential, provided a sales force exists or can be restructured to tap that potential through existing or new outlets. If the resources do not currently exist then the processes of recruitment and training become a major factor in achieving the key objective, and assume a priority as subsidiary operational objectives. Any plan, therefore, must take account of the current level and availability of necessary inputs and resources to achieve each key objective, and the time span involved in making necessary adjustments in resources.

Marketing support

Sales force success in achieving its specific objectives will for most products be a function of the marketing support provided in terms of advertising, promotions and general consumer awareness and trial activities. (Sales promotional activities will be discussed further in Chapter 5.) A pure commodity may require little marketing support if sales are very price elastic and the level of sales achieved largely dependent on the product price. The marketing team might seek to establish other purchasing criteria such as quality, availability, or other less tangible benefits. But major consideration is likely to be given to the effect on profits of reducing prices to increase sales volume – i.e. will the additional sales volume generated by a price decrease increase the gross profit contribution in spite of a loss in unit profit? A branded consumer product, whether physical goods or services (such as fast moving consumer goods, insurance or household improvements), is likely to require significant marketing support to increase sales if the supplier is not in a monopoly supply situation, or if distribution outlets are already well covered by the sales force and using or stocking the products.

Programme
implementation

The core of the sales planning process is the implementation of the plans at the level of each account or customer to achieve the desired results with that customer. The final planning stage must therefore be to go back down the chain of command and ensure that each person knows his forecasts or targets and performance objectives, has the necessary means to achieve these, and develops a system of individual account management whereby specific objectives are set that lead to the overall achievement of territory and area forecasts and other objectives.

143

On the **customer call record card** (which should be regularly used at the time of each call upon a customer) should be space to enter:

- sales forecasts by product for the customer
- specific objectives for the period of the forecast
- achievement against forecasts and objectives.

Example 10.1 is a basic customer call record card, which could be modified either by an insert or an additional pre-printed section to include a planning section as in Example 4.8.

For key accounts, the strategies and programmes developed may often be more sophisticated, require more planning and controlling, and have longer lead times than promotions that may be implemented at the level of individual users or retail outlets. The management of a key account may be required to agree subsidiary forecasts and objectives to be set within its organisation, and if it has a regional control structure then separate targets, programmes and measurements may be necessary or beneficial for each of the account's regions. Whenever a programme is introduced to a customer as a means of increasing sales or throughput then it should be presented in such a way that the customer accepts certain targets and performance criteria as operational objectives of the programme, and is committed to active participation and cooperation.

There are many interrelating factors that impact on the planning and forecasting process, yet the sales manager has one main resource – the people in his sales organisation. The sales manager may devise the policies that provide broad uniform guidelines or parameters to subsequent sales force decisions, but he is dependent on the subordinate team to implement the decisions within policy guidelines.

144

Example 4.8 Customer objective planning record

Customer: Contact: Planning period:						Territory: Salesperson:
Product	**Forecast**	**Actual cumulative performance**				**Notes**
		Q1	*Q2*	*Q3*	*Q4*	

Action plans and objectives	**Achieved/implemented**
1.	
2.	
3.	
4.	
5.	
6.	
7.	
8.	
9.	
10.	
11.	
12.	

SUMMARY

- **Planning** is necessary to give a sense of purpose and direction to subsequent sales force activities. It goes beyond sales forecasting and targeting to cover setting objectives, identifying priorities and key result areas, developing strategies and tactics, and controlling and monitoring results. Plans should have sufficient in-built flexibility to respond or permit adaption to changes in environmental factors both internal and external to the company.

- Contributions to sales planning can beneficially be obtained by the involvement in planning of other persons with additional skills and expertise in relevant aspects of market knowledge, company resources, and forecasting techniques.

- The establishment of company policies and **key objectives** serve as the guidelines for other company operating divisions, such as the sales division, to set their **subsidiary operating objectives** from which specific plans develop, including the preparation of sales forecasts and targets and the strategies and tactics that lead to the achievement of objectives.

- Objectives set at each lower level of the sales organisation must be accepted by the persons charged with achieving them as being **realistic** and **achievable** within the allocated time span, measurable, and with outcomes within their control.

- Field sales management subsidiary objectives should have a strong emphasis on personnel training and development because overall sales objectives are only achieved through a skilled and motivated sales team.

- The preparation of sales forecasts and targets is generally tackled by either or both **macro** or **micro** approaches. The **macro** approach centres round studies of general industry and economic performance and trends, and the historical company performance in relation to such relevant environmental factors. The **micro** approach starts from the base of preparing a separate product forecast for each individual customer and territory and building up to a national forecast and plan. A consensus forecast might be the result of studying the different forecasts arrived at by using both of these methods.

- In addition to forecasting the volume and value of sales (which generally will be required on a month-by-month and product-by-product basis) for each customer, territory and geographical or functional management control tier of the sales organisation, the sales manager will also normally be required to prepare budgets covering sales force operating costs and expenses, project staffing levels, contribute to forward pricing movement estimates, and make profit contribution forecasts for each customer or tier in the sales organisation.

- Forecasting needs to recognise and take into consideration any

146

seasonal or cyclical fluctuations or trends in sales or the markets for the products. Whilst randomly occurring events that impact on sales may not be predictable, there may be marketing factors concerned with the products' life cycles that need to be incorporated in sales and marketing programmes to maintain sales momentum.

- The judgement required in sales forecasting should be supplemented whenever possible or practical by more soundly based statistical forecasting techniques, such as the trend fitting techniques in **time series** studies, and the impact and inter-relationships of variables considered in some **causal** studies. In some instances a trend line fitted by inspection to historical data plotted on graphs might serve to assist in more rudimentary forecasting.

- Sales strategies designed to promote the achievement of forecasts or targets will need to take account of: the present and future product range and mix, and market segments to be targeted and penetrated; available channels of distribution; the markets and customer universe and the various commercial and geographical characteristics of each of these; product pricing and positioning in relation to competitive products; the resources in terms of people, sales aids and equipment, and finance; and marketing support in the form of advertising and promotional activity.

147

	Notes	Action

Set company key objectives

Set sales division subsidiary operating objectives

Decide on forecast period:
- short-term
- medium-term
- long-term

Check sources of data relevant to forecasting and planning exercise:
- **internal**:
  historical sales – volumes
  - values
  - month by month
  - by product
  - by territory
  - by customer
  - by geographical or functional level or job
- **external**:
  - individual performance of competitors
  - total market for the products by volume or value
  - published economic data on expenditure on the product or related product groups or categories

Develop sales forecasts at **macro** and **micro** levels by:
- product volumes
- product sales values
- month-by-month
- customer or user
- territory
- geographical management control area and functional position (e.g. key accounts)
- market sector

Consider:
- **market knowledge**
  - economic factors (interest rates, employment levels, disposable incomes, market price movements, inflation, production, distribution, exchange rates)
  - demographic factors (including population shifts and changes in age/sex profiles and ratios)
  - legislative and regulatory changes
  - political environment
  - distribution channel developments
  - import/export markets
  - market trends and changes in product preference patterns
  - seasonal or cyclical market trends

continued

Checklist   Sales planning and forecasting (contd.)

	Notes	Action
– user attitudes, perceptions and expectations – competitive prices and pricing parameters – competitive current and potential new products, and competitive market positioning and strategies • **company resources** – plant and production and any other capacity limitations – availability of raw materials and other inputs – factory labour markets and labour resources – personnel recruitment and training lead times – financial resources and limitations – research developments (new innovations and technology, in-house company research programmes, 'ready made' new products, longer-term new products and developments) – sales force resources – marketing support (advertising and promotions)		
Budget sales force operating costs and expenses, including: • wages and salaries • expenses • department operating costs • vehicles • sales aids and promotional materials • promotional activity and any pricing rebates or discounts within sales force control		
Plan sales force forward staffing levels, taking account of: • sources and recruitment lead times • training needs and lead times • management needs • changes in the needs and mix of skills, experience, characteristics, etc.		
Develop profit contribution forecasts by: • customer • territory • geographical or functional management control area or level		
Set specific objectives for each geographical or functional level of the sales organisation, and for each customer		

5 Promoting Sales

As this is not intended to be a marketing text, I do not propose to discuss marketing in general. But I do feel that the text would be incomplete without a short review of some aspects and methods of promoting sales, since it is customary in most companies for the sales manager to have a budget, independent from the marketing department budget, to cover a variety of sales promotional activities. Much of the following discussion will be applicable to industrial product promotions as well as to fast moving consumer goods.

THE ROLE AND PURPOSE OF SALES PROMOTIONS

It is not easy to identify where advertising and promotional activity separate, or to define their individual functions. Broadly speaking, a **sales promotion** is designed to promote user awareness of a product or service, increase the opportunities for current or potential users to obtain goods or services, increase trial of the product, and develop greater product usage or brand loyalty. In part, promotional activity may be aimed defensively or offensively at filling the pipeline with the company's products, perhaps resulting in users or retailers using their limited space and funds on promotional stock so that competitors have fewer short-term sales opportunities.

Sales promotional activity is frequently conducted, though not exclusively, through means or channels influenced or controlled by the company rather than through mass media, and the activity generally aims to fulfil its functions by creating activity at the point of use or sale of the products.

A sales promotion can tackle its objectives tactically through areas that are within the realm of influence of the sales force, by:

- increasing product distribution
- generating additional display activity
- increasing product trial by potential users
- limiting sales opportunities open to competitors by filling the distribution channels with additional stock (at the wholesale, retail and user levels), putting 'stock pressure' on the stockists to sell more and encouraging end users to 'stock up' on advantageous terms.

A sales promotion may be geared to impact on one or more of these strategic areas, depending on the assessment of overall needs and priorities of the products or markets made at a point in time.

150

Sales promotional activity is the main short-term tactical weapon in the sales manager's armoury. It offers a major benefit over normal advertising activity in that it can be very flexible in timing, purpose, or direction of effort and manner of implementation; and additionally can be both very cost-effective (if well planned and implemented) and results-effective. Sales promotional activity can be very variable in structure and targeted impact area and, because many forms of promotional activity need very short lead times for introduction and planning, they are a very effective supplement to major advertising campaigns, as well as providing corrective action programmes where sales results and achievements are 'off course', or where other external environmental factors (such as competitive activity) disrupt the company's basic marketing plans and programmes.

It is, of course, essential that sales managers do not turn to supplementary promotional activity at the first sign of every variance, problem or crisis, otherwise they may be guilty of 'crisis management'. The causes of problems need to be identified and recognised so that an appropriate corrective action plan be considered and implemented.

Whilst sales promotions do have very clear uses and benefits, they can also – by their very short-term nature – distract the field sales force from major objectives and activity in key result areas of the business. For example, a 'panic promotion' geared to obtaining new pioneer outlets may distract heavily from the servicing of existing outlets, leaving openings for competitors to gain entry or increased trial or market share either because buyers or users suddenly feel a degree of neglect, or because their stocks of your products fall to the extent that they are obliged to switch to competitive products. Another such situation can occur where a special very favourable promotion is offered only to one customer and not another, with a resultant loss of interest, loyalty and goodwill from the non-participating customer. As a general rule, promotional activity, subject of course to certain realistic criteria, should be available on broadly similar terms and conditions to similar types of outlets (although it would logically not always be in everyone's interest to run the same promotion in all the similar outlets at the same time). Therefore, at the stage of considering and designing a sales promotion, the sales manager should carefully evaluate the need for a special promotion at all, identify its objectives, and plan the structure of the promotion to supplement and complement the general sales force activities and objectives rather than producing any conflict.

TYPES OF PROMOTIONAL ACTIVITY

Whilst to an outsider the range and variety of sales promotions may

151

seem infinite, they generally fall into one of a number of categories, such as:

- display bonuses
- performance rebates or allowances
- trade price discounts
- consumer price promotions (including 'multi-packs')
- trade stock bonuses
- consumer competitions
- consumer 'premium' offers
- product sampling programmes
- dealer competitions
- product demonstrations
- couponing
- exhibitions
- on-pack 'give aways'
- lectures, film shows, etc.
- point of sale material
- sales force incentives
- special magazines and journals
- product merchandising
- introduction incentives
- trading stamps and similar incentives
- free product trial periods
- credit cards
- direct mailshots
- gifts for buyers
- public relations activities
- 'tie-ins' with special events
- sales and promotional literature
- promotional aspects of packaging.

The choice of technique will depend in part on the nature of the product – industrial, consumer or service.

Display bonuses

It is a common practice for producers of consumer goods, especially those that have a strong impulse purchasing element, to negotiate with retailers to pay a bonus for an agreed allocated display space in stores. The bonus might be paid by a direct cheque at the end of each display 'contract' period, or by a discount of invoice values of merchandise purchased by the stockists. Bonuses might be ongoing, or apply only at certain times (e.g. peak selling seasons), and might relate to all goods sold through the retail outlet or only those featured in special 'off the shelf' displays. Another variation on the same principle is for the manufacturer or distributor to 'rent' space and install his own custom-designed display facilities (possibly including a permanent product sales consultant or demonstrator). This technique is used by the cosmetic industry in many countries.

Where a display bonus is paid for a special space rental, it is essential that the manufacturer's own sales force make regular merchandising visits to maintain order and stock levels. If shelf stocks are low, another manufacturer's merchandising team will rarely hesitate to fill competitors' display sections with the wrong product. In addition, the retailer should have an obligation within his display bonus agreement to re-stock shelves between the visits of the manufacturer's merchandisers.

In the longer term a retailer is unlikely to find benefit in continuing to allocate an agreed display space, even for a display bonus, if the product turnover and profit contribution (including the display bonus) are not at satisfactory levels according to the criteria used by the retailer (which might be in terms of profit contribution per square foot of display area).

Performance rebates and allowances

As an encouragement to buyers to support a particular manufacturer more than competitors, another common incentive offered is for the manufacturer to agree to the payment of a retrospective bonus as a percentage of the total goods (industrial, consumer or service) purchased in a period of time, usually a calendar year. Target sales levels should be agreed with the customers and there should probably be a scale of incentives to apply at different volume or value turnover levels, say 0.5–2.0 per cent. If this is to act as a motivator then the buyer should receive regular feedback on his sales turnover performance, and additional promotional activity might provide an added means of achieving target turnover levels. The benefit of such a system is questionable if it does not encourage greater achievement each year through revised targets. A turnover (value-related) bonus should, of course, at least be adjusted for inflationary price increases year on year. It might be better to gear the bonus to unit sales volumes rather than monetary targets, although the bonus would be paid at the year end on turnover achievements for the targeted unit volume.

If several competing manufacturers are offering similar bonus schemes a shrewd buyer may plan his purchases to maximise his **total** gross return, rather than maximising purchases from just one supplier. That need not be all bad, since most marketing men accept that sales volumes per manufacturer are often higher in outlets that offer a broader variety of goods.

Trade price discounts

Manufacturers will occasionally discount prices to end users, whole-salers and retailers as an incentive to increase purchases and stock

153

levels. This 'stock pressure' approach to generating sales is only beneficial if the goods will move through the distribution chain and be sold to and used by the final consumers. Any 'stock pressure' promotion can be risky for short shelf life perishable products, especially if the supplier customarily exchanges unsold and out of date merchandise. But where the stockist can be persuaded to place more sales effort behind a product, possibly cutting his prices and increasing display or local advertising activity, then filling the pipeline through trade price discounts may generate more all-round product sales interest and activity.

Trade price discounts might be used to move older stock through the distribution chain prior to the introduction of new product varieties, or to reduce a manufacturer's inventory and turn inventory into cash, or to block competitive activity by filling trade outlets with the company's products.

Consumer price promotions

Consumer price promotions are often initiated by manufacturers who wish to boost trial of a product, encourage consumers to switch brand loyalty, or motivate users to buy higher stocks of the company's products and block competitive sales. The price promotion might take the form of a direct price reduction on a single unit of the product, or a product multi-pack or special size or variety that offers a price reduction over normal retail prices. It is customary for retailers to contribute to such price reductions in that their absolute profit margin per unit sold might not be retained but they would work on a normal (or agreed reduced) percentage profit margin, so that their normal gross level of profit would be maintained and perhaps exceeded through higher sales volumes of the product being promoted. A retailer will naturally be less receptive to price promotions if he cannot accept that the promotion is likely to increase his sales volume and gross profits. The sales manager is likely to get more commitment from buyers who make a direct or indirect contribution to the cost of a promotion, perhaps by paying for local advertising, contributing to price cuts or allocating a valuable 'key site' feature display location to the promotional product.

Where the price promotion is to take the form of a direct product price reduction over an agreed period of time then the manufacturer will need to monitor sales on a 'count–recount' basis, whereby opening stock at the beginning of the promotion period is counted, deliveries of product effected during the promotion period are added in, and closing inventory at the end of the promotion is deducted to give an accurate measure of throughput during the promotion period.

Where the price promotion is related to a change in pack size (such as the commonly seen '20% more for the same price as a 250ml canister' found in promotions for aerosol products) then there is no complicated checking system: the retailer simply buys the quantities he requires or which are allocated to him and displays the goods until they are sold.

A negative aspect of consumer price promotions is that existing product users might take advantage of the promotion discounts simply to purchase ahead of requirements and hoard stocks, perhaps leaving insufficient product on the shelves for potential new users to buy a trial pack.

Trade stock bonuses

Another technique used either to obtain new distribution or to boost stock levels in the user or distribution channel pipelines is to offer stock bonuses on purchases to the wholesale or retail trade, such as a 'buy ten cases and get one free' promotion. This approach has long been common in fast moving consumer goods markets in the United States, where retailers and wholesale distributors often expect and might even demand such a bonus prior to agreeing to list a product. However, if it is abused by buyers who purchase far more than they will move over a promotion period then the net effect is that the manufacturer has mortgaged full profit future sales for discounted present sales. Unless there is a reciprocal passing on of all or part of the bonus in the form of price cuts to consumers, an incentive or bonus that merely serves to boost the profit margins of the distributive trade is unlikely to boost buyer loyalty or market offtake. Limited funds are usually best spent on a programme of marketing and promoting that creates or increases consumer and user awareness and that benefits the final product purchaser.

Consumer competitions

The great range of consumer competitions are designed to increase product display, new consumer trial of the product, and product usage by existing product users. Such competitions are generally aimed at final consumers rather than the retail or wholesale trade, and their popularity often puts considerable pressure on stockists to buy, display and merchandise the products.

A manufacturer designing consumer competitions will get more trade acceptance the less work the stockist has to do to support and benefit from the promotion. Ideally the stockist is happiest just to purchase and display the product, and the manufacturer clearly wants the opportunity to build supporting feature displays, fix prominent point of sale promotional material, or place competition leaflets at strategic points.

Competitions that both maximise the number of potential winners (but perhaps with a few major prizes to provide the glamour) and give all product purchasers an equal chance of winning a prize tend to be the most popular. The petrol companies are well known for their competitions to 'match' items, such as two halves of a copy of a bank

155

currency note, and 'bingo' formats have found great followings. Competitions that require any significant degree of skill or knowledge will narrow the participation to those who feel competent to enter; but that need not be a reason not to consider such a format if the promoter's main objective is to generate extra product display.

To be effective, competitions often need a larger budget and have much longer planning and implementation lead times than other promotional techniques, and their use is perhaps more limited to established mass market products with an existing consumer franchise. It is essential that the organisers of any promotion comply with any local laws, rules or regulations that might impact on the promotion: for example, some countries restrict competitions that appear to have a lottery element in their design, or where purchase of a product is a condition of participation; or insist that a trade promotion is offered on similar terms to all traders in the market. Also, in designing any form of competition that involves collecting items or clues or making comparisons, it is important that the competitive inputs be concealed until an item has been paid for.

Consumer premium offers

In this section I consider a premium offer to be one where the consumer can obtain free or at a reduced price another (possibly unrelated) product as a result of purchasing the manufacturer's promoted product. The manufacturer makes a popular product available in exchange for a financial payment below the product's normal fair market value plus some 'proof of purchase' of the promoting manufacturer's products. For example, a manufacturer of suntan lotion might offer discounted beach towels or sunglasses for a cash payment below those items' normal market value plus several bottle tops or labels from the suntan lotion canister. A branded food product might make available at very favourable prices certain items of kitchen houseware along with 'proof of purchase' for the promoted products in the form of a few product labels.

This kind of promotion need not be prohibitively expensive in that the promoting manufacturer will generally be able to arrange the purchase of the premium items on favourable terms and recover the costs against the price charged. It is usually more practical to arrange for a specialist sales promotion agency to handle the mechanics of the premium offer redemptions. The key to a successful premium promotion is finding a premium item at a price that will be a real incentive to consumers to purchase more of the promoting manufacturer's products (since this style of promotion is more favoured for consumer non-durable products), and maximising the appeal of the premium by generating additional display along with point of sales material. This form of promotion can be adapted to household durables, for example 'buy a WHITE-O washing machine at the regular price and get a COOK-O microwave oven for only half

156

price'. In this situation the manufacturer is likely to want to use another company product as the premium, which would customarily be of lower value than the promoted item. Alternatively the manufacturer might give a free premium item, such as a lower-value electric toaster, with the purchase of a washing machine. Clearly the purchaser of the promoted product must see the premium as desirable or functional and as representing an attractive effective discount to the promoted product.

Product sampling

The main objective of product sampling campaigns is to promote consumer trial of non-durable products, although this can be extended to include industrial ingredient or component sampling.

Sampling may be organised in any of several ways. A demonstrator may offer samples to customers in a retail store, and attempt to make an instant sale. Another approach is to distribute mini-pack samples direct to targeted householders identified as matching the typical consumer profile. This has the advantage of ensuring that samples reach a target market group but has the disadvantage that no instant sales can accompany trial. The size of the mini-pack must be sufficient to ensure that it can both be effectively used in a home trial (a washing powder sample needs at least to be adequate for a minimum of a typical full load) and start to create a usage or preference pattern. Preparing small-scale samples may be very costly compared with the cost of manufacture of the full-size pack, and some companies might find it simpler and cheaper to give away a full-size pack, possibly by 'banding' it as a free premium with a purchase of another of the company's established products consumed by the same target consumer group.

Samples are sometimes distributed at a cost to the consumer. There are sales promotional companies that specialise in packing together a range of products that manufacturers are seeking to promote through sampling and offering these 'trial' assortment packs at very advantageous prices to consumers.

Sampling is commonly used in industrial markets to promote trial and gain approval for inclusion of the product as a component or ingredient in other processes or goods. The size of the sample may be quite large in comparison with a consumer non-durable product sample, because small-scale production trials may need to be conducted. In some industries, research-scale samples are provided free and production-scale quantities might be charged at very favourable prices.

Dealer competitions

Dealer competitions tend to have a limited value if they are organised between dealers because the level of motivation or participation may

157

then be less. However, competitions within distributor organisations can motivate increased sales activity aimed at widening distribution or boosting retail pipeline stocks. In many developing countries, competitions between retailers can be structured to motivate aggressive participation, such as display competitions where a number of attractive prizes are offered for the best product displays maintained over a period of time (coverage of this type of promotion for developing markets is given in my book *Practical Export Management*, London, Allen & Unwin, 1985), with the display activity serving to create consumer interest and awareness and product purchase and trial. On occasions display competitions can have a role in developed markets, particularly where there is a popular local theme – such as the sponsorship of a charity, where the manufacturer might donate funds to the charity for each case of product put on feature display, or for each unit of product sold from the display, and so on.

Dealer competitions and similar promotions need to be carefully structured to ensure that they are very simple to implement, participate in and control, and not likely to cause a significant disruption to the dealers' other business activities.

Product demonstrations

Demonstrations have already been mentioned in passing. They tend to be a costly exercise if used on low unit value products, and many manufacturers of mass produced consumer non-durables would find it less costly to sample through product give-away programmes. However, for products of a technical or practical nature, such as most consumer durable goods, demonstration is a way of attracting consumer attention in stores and showing the product features, benefits and ease of practical application. If the demonstration is supported by a special price for the product or other premium offer then the opportunities to motivate instant purchase are increased. Items suitable as gifts often benefit from pre-Christmas demonstration programmes.

Large consumer durables or industrial equipment may best be demonstrated at the place of final use – the home or the factory. If a salesperson can progress the sales presentation to the point of arranging a practical demonstration in the home, and can satisfy the customer on the objections that might be raised at the time of the demonstration (perhaps related to payment and the need for extended credit), then he is a long way forward to closing the sale.

A manufacturer should give great care and attention to the selection and training of store or home demonstrators to ensure they have the qualities, skills and experience to relate to the potential customers, and a level of product knowledge to demonstrate the product effectively.

158

Couponing

Coupons are used effectively in some markets with a range of house-hold consumer durable and non-durable products, to encourage both product trial and repeat purchase. To motivate product purchase, a coupon needs to offer a reasonable price reduction over normal retail prices.

There must, of course, be an effective way of distributing the coupons to the target market. Coupons are most commonly distributed by:

- direct mail drop
- door-to-door delivery using hired help
- inclusion in newspaper advertisements
- loose insertion in newspapers or other journals (including the free local journals found in some localities)
- inclusion with another package of a product for redemption against the next product purchase
- direct handout to potential product users in stores, shopping malls or on the streets
- placement of coupons at strategic locations in stores (open perhaps to the greatest potential abuse).

Coupons are very open to abuse, especially in the non-durable goods markets, and it is customary to ask retailers seeking to redeem coupons for their face value to demonstrate that they have stocked and sold sufficient of the product to cover the coupons they have accepted. Normally a rule would state 'one coupon per pack of product purchased'. Retailers or distributors accepting coupons as part payment for goods will also expect a handling allowance in many markets. Coupons are often less effective in promoting trial by new consumers than some other promotional techniques. Frequently it is established customers of a product who collect the coupons to redeem against their normal product purchases, and possibly even to stock-pile product at the discount. Couponing on commodity types of products or even brands with little in the way of strong product differentiation might prove counter-productive, merely prompting 'see-saw' brand switching. Many people simply collect any and every available coupon, treating them as non-monetary currency to be redeemed against the purchase of other unrelated products at their local stores (and many store-keepers are reluctant to refuse to cooperate with regular customers). Competitors might even offer to redeem another company's coupons against a purchase of its own products: this has been common in the 'hamburger' fast food promotional wars in the United States.

Manufacturers using couponing should therefore seek to evaluate the level of brand loyalty and new trial generated.

159

Exhibitions

Exhibitions offer an excellent vehicle for promoting a number of industrial and consumer durable products, ranging from plant and equipment to ingredients and components, household improvements, new product developments, and existing durable products not yet in common use. Attendance by a manufacturer at an exhibition must be given careful consideration to ensure that the exhibition visitors will be potential users or consumers of the products and not just exhibition 'browsers'.

The manufacturer's exhibition stand ideally needs to be in a position to benefit from the traffic flow, and not hidden in an out of the way corner, and the stand itself needs to make an impact on potential customers. Exhibition visitors should be able to identify in an instant whom the stand is representing and the product range. It is essential to have plenty of relevant product literature, samples where appropriate, suitably qualified staff to handle enquiries, and ideally a quiet spot to hold discussions with the seriously interested visitor.

A manufacturer should have clear sales objectives in participating in an exhibition and not just be there because the competitors are, or to give the sales team a break from routine. Records should be kept of all enquirers and the nature of their enquiries, and a post-exhibition sales follow-up programme developed to include further sampling, technical discussions and demonstrations. Chapter 12 extends the commentary on organising participation and involvement at exhibitions.

On-pack give aways

An on-pack 'give away' item generally relates to the main product on offer. Perhaps the best-known example of this kind of promotion is the free razor so commonly found with a pack of branded razor blades. The razor, of course, is designed to work with the manufacturer's razor blades and not those of its competitors, and the hope is that once the combination is initially purchased the user will find comfort and convenience in using the razor, and remain a loyal customer thereafter for the blades. Similar promotions can work for a number of products: toothpaste manufacturers might give a free toothbrush with a tube of toothpaste, although as the brush could clean with any toothpaste there is not the same loyalty generated through the 'locked in' effect of one part of the promotion only working in conjunction with the other.

Lectures, film shows, etc.

Lectures or film or slide shows can all be considered as tools for promoting trial or sales of a product. For example, a company producing safety aids such as reflective jackets, protective helmets and so on for cyclists might promote the sales of their products by offering free 'safety' films to schools, or having salespersons attend to

160

give safety lectures. A toothpaste manufacturer might promote his product by lecturing on oral hygiene, perhaps to the school children or their parents. If the theme of the film or lecture is of a public interest nature, credibility will be rather reduced if the content is too obviously biased to one manufacturer's products, but they can certainly be featured in illustrations, examples and demonstrations.

Many sales managers have found it to be a forceful goodwill and sales promotional exercise to encourage salespersons to lecture on business-related topics to interested groups of actual or potential consumers.

Point of sale material

Most manufacturers develop a range of point of sale material to draw customers' attention to their products in stores or even at cash and carry wholesale warehouses. Busy purchasers will pass hundreds of products every minute as they progress through a store, and pause to look at or buy very few. Any impact-making point of sales material may increase the sales opportunities by causing consumers to stop and look at products and display material. However, the design of point of sale material must be carefully thought through so that its use is acceptable in retail or wholesale stockists:

- it needs to be non-obstructive in size and shape, yet sufficiently large to make an instant impact;
- it should have a memorable yet simple message;
- it must be capable of being attached to displays or surfaces or otherwise exhibited without hindrance or hazard to anyone;
- wording should generally be clear, concise, comprehensible, non-technical, and relevant to the product.

Perhaps one of the major benefits to manufacturers in supplying the sales force with point of sale material is that it gives the salespersons a talking point at the start of a sales presentation, and also an excuse or opportunity to gain access to the product display to commence physical merchandising whilst replacing out-of-date point of sale material with the new display material.

Sales force incentives

These can be extremely effective techniques to direct sales force attention to areas that need corrective action, to counter competitive activity, or to provide added motivation in the drive to achieve sales force objectives and forecasts. This subject has been covered at more length in Chapter 2, and I would refer the reader back to the section on incentives.

Special magazines and journals

Sales promotional opportunities exist through a number of magazines or journals aimed at either the buying trade or users or consumers. A producer of sales promotional aids might advertise in a marketing journal targeted at sales and marketing managers. A supplier of building products could advertise or seek product listings in a construction industry trade journal aimed at builders, planners, architects or engineers. A manufacturer of hi-fi components might seek editorial coverage, product listings, or even paid advertisements for the products in a consumer hi-fi magazine.

Special industrial products, such as components, ingredients, plant and equipment, should be listed in the relevant trade or professional buyers' guides referred to by the industry's buyers. Such guides exist in most major countries, and many are, in fact, multinational and international in content and structure, showing international distribution sources for products or local production facilities of multinational producers. Major American and European buying directories are widely distributed throughout the developing nations. A free product listing can frequently be supported by a paid feature advertisement placed in close proximity to the listing by product category, and might beneficially include a reader enquiry card to prompt readers to seek further literature, information, samples or a direct sales contact. Listings or advertisements should ideally identify sources of supply of products. Many goods or services benefit from listings in local 'yellow pages' telephone directories or such other mass distribution buying guides as are locally available.

The sales manager should compile a list of all the trade and professional journals, special-interest magazines and buying guides likely to be read or referred to by potential product users, and develop a plan to obtain suitable listings in as many product or service categories as possible, supporting these listings with appropriate advertising where this is considered beneficial and cost-effective. The general guidelines on the format and design of sales promotional literature referred to later in the chapter may be just as relevant and applicable to the structure and design of entries in special magazines and trade journals.

Product merchandising

One of the most powerful tools the sales manager must control is his ability to merchandise product on display in trade and retail distribution outlets. The manner and method of product display has a major bearing on consumer awareness, attention, interest and purchase. Effective product merchandising is the art of making the product itself become its own silent salesperson. Most consumer goods manufacturers place great emphasis on training salespersons in effective product merchandising techniques, including attention to such aspects as:

- key site identification (the position in a store where most customers will pass or pause, such as by the cash register)

162

- store traffic flows
- product price marking (to ensure speed and accuracy and visibility)
- efficient physical case opening and shelf filling
- price feature cards (i.e. large display cards notifying shoppers of price reductions or special offers)
- feature display design and construction.

Salespersons must be seen by store managers as providing a welcome service supplementing the work of store staff in merchandising product, and therefore must not alienate store managers and lose goodwill by being excessively demanding or aggressive in seeking or taking display space. Effective product merchandising by a supplier's merchandisers should improve sales and profitability from the allocated display space, and benefit the store manager through reduced staff work loads and costs.

In training salespersons in merchandising tactics and techniques, it is useful to use some of the methods developed in Chapters 7 and 8 dealing with sales training — such as giving initial training in the theory and practice at 'in-house' sales training facilities and in simulated store environments; followed by the use of films, photographs and slides to provide a basis for case studies dealing with traffic flows and key site identification; reinforced and consolidated by demonstration and practice in the field sales environment of real retail or wholesale outlets.

The principles of effective merchandising are not just the prerogative of mass merchandising retail outlets for fast moving consumer goods. They apply equally to most products from consumer durables to jewellery, from fashion to furniture, as has been effectively demonstrated in the giant furniture, do-it-yourself, and electrical product hypermarkets that have grown in market share and dominance over the last decade.

Some companies prefer to separate merchandising functions from normal sales activity, and either have a special team of product merchandisers (often women working on a part-time basis in stores near to their homes — as has been common with f.m.c.g. companies) or contract out the merchandising support to specialist companies that provide such services to a range of non-competing manufacturers.

Introductory incentives
Another sales promotion technique that is found very useful, particularly in financial services markets (such as banking and insurance), home improvement markets, or facilities or services that seek annual membership or renewal fees (clubs, associations, credit card promoters), is to offer an incentive award or bonus to any existing product user (subscriber or club member) who introduces another person who becomes a participator in the programme. Credit card companies have long found this highly effective as a

means of attracting new users of their services, and frequently have promotions offering free gifts to persons who introduce a friend or colleague to their services. This kind of incentive scheme has scope for development in any product category or market sector where the best source of sales leads is from personal references by established users of the product or services. The technique is less used than it might be since there is no cost without sale.

Trading stamps and similar collectibles

Trading stamps were probably at their height of popularity as a promotional tool in the 1970s, almost to the extent of being an alternative currency in terms of exchangeability for goods and with a cash redemption value. They were used primarily by major retailers, and this indirect form of discounting prices was seemingly preferred by many consumers to direct price discounts, perhaps because of the receipt of a tangible additional item as a reward for spending money with the retailers issuing the promotional trading stamps. Since the late 1970s there has been a decline in the popularity of trading stamps as a promotional aid in most market sectors.

Another variation still with development mileage is the issue of coupons or certificates that motivate consumers to return to a particular retail outlet for further product purchases. Petrol companies often offer coupons with purchases of their particular brand of petrol, which are then redeemable, once enough are collected, against small-value items such as household drinking glasses. To motivate the initial purchase and regular return to the product outlet, it is generally found necessary to have an opportunity for an early redemption against small-value items, possibly with the flexibility to save more vouchers or coupons for redemption against larger-value items or complete sets of the premium gift.

Some sellers of goods and services have found merit in conducting regular raffles for attractive prizes amongst their customers. It is normal to give a free raffle ticket or a numbered cash register receipt with each purchase, and conduct a weekly draw based upon the issued numbers. Customers are supposed to be motivated to return to check their number against the draw numbers, and develop a visit and purchase habit.

Any scheme that involves an element of competition or collectibility needs to operate to the principles of:

- ease of participation
- simplicity of structure and format
- frequent prize allocation or redemption opportunities
- opportunities for many or all participants to receive direct benefits (through the award of many prizes or redemption against a range of items requiring different quantities of coupons for redemption).

164

Free product trial periods

Access to or possession of goods in the environment of use will greatly increase the likelihood of sales being consummated. On this premise many companies offer potential purchasers 'free home (or office) trial' periods, with great success. We all see the frequent advertisements (or receive unsolicited brochures through the mail) with words to the effect 'send now and we will deliver *Wonda-tool* for a free seven-day trial at home; return to us within seven days if not delighted and you will owe us nothing' (customers having generally been asked to give a credit card number at the time of requesting the free trial, or else being liable to receive an invoice subsequently if the product is retained). Such schemes and varieties of these programmes have proved of enormous benefit in marketing books and household durable products in many markets. Local stores can benefit from adapting this method of promoting by offering to let potential customers have a free home trial or demonstration.

Credit cards

A promotional technique used by many major retail chains and petrol companies is to issue house credit cards to creditworthy customers, with deferred payment terms that act as a motivator to direct the purchases of goods or services to the issuer of the credit card. This can be very cost-effective if the administrative machinery can readily be established because there is a cost in any event to accepting the credit cards issued by banks or other major credit card companies. Many issuers of such credit cards seek trade or bank references on applicants or consider the possession of a major other credit card as eligibility for issue of a house credit card. The options on deferred credit are usually either to charge a commercial interest rate, or include a mark-up in the price of the goods for credit and promote the benefit of 'x months free credit'. Purchasers of goods on credit card schemes frequently work to pay off any outstanding credit early so that they can purchase more goods at the store once they have developed the habit of visiting it.

Direct mailshots

Direct mailshots of promotional literature are a common means of supplementing personal selling efforts, perhaps as an approach to buyers who are not on regular coverage schedules. Such campaigns have traditionally been very common in the pharmaceutical industry to brief doctors on product developments, features, uses and benefits, and as a supplement to direct sales effort in industrial product markets.

Buyers receive large quantities of promotional literature through the mail, and most goes directly into the waste paper basket. If a buyer wants his mailshots to be read, they must be designed with as much care as any face-to-face sales presentation, yet without the

165

benefit that a personal sales presentation offers of being able to react to the buyer's moods, attitudes and the general selling environment. Chapter 12 extends the commentary on mailshots in the section on 'Direct mail campaigns', where it is mainly discussed in the context of alternative means of generating sales activity for a company with limited direct sales resources.

Basically a mailshot must:

- make an instant impact
- be relevant to the buyer's product needs or problems
- clearly communicate the reasons for reading the literature
- be written in language and terminology familiar to the buyer.

Direct mailshots also need to clarify how a buyer can obtain more information, samples, a demonstration, or product, and might beneficially include a reply-paid enquiry card.

Manufacturers promoting product through direct mailshots should not expect a high response – traditionally, response in the 2–5 per cent range is considered good. Mailing lists of particular target groups can frequently be leased or purchased from related sources, such as professional institutions, providers of credit, and club or association membership lists, so the benefit of mailshots is the ability of the promoter to identify his target market very selectively.

Gifts for buyers

Many companies give gifts to buyers or potential customers, particularly at the Christmas season. Care must be taken in selecting a gift. Many companies do not permit their buyers to accept a gift for personal use outside the office environment. This is probably beneficial to the gift giver because an item for personal consumption, such as food or drink, has less lasting motivational benefit than something that will constantly be seen or referred to by the buyer.

Low-value gifts can be useful as a promotional tool, and should be chosen with consideration to the principles that:

- they serve as a constant reminder of the giver and the product, possibly including a product representation or the company logo in the design
- they identify the giver with a note of the company's name and address and telephone number
- they are functionally useful on a daily basis so that they warrant a permanent position on the buyer's desk.

Many companies have developed preferences for such gift items as pocket or desk diaries, ash trays, paper weights, or writing implements including desk-top writing pads and pen holders. Non-functional items are likely to be shut away in a drawer, out of sight and mind.

Public relations activities

Public relations activity as a sales promotion tool has grown in prominence and stature over the last two decades. It is now a highly credible, effective and professional aid to direct sales activity and other advertising and promotional programmes. Manufacturers have learnt that money spent through public relations organisations to generate a favourable editorial comment on a product can often be more effective than far greater funds spent on direct media advertising. Public relations is very concerned with creating favourable corporate images – with the target market in particular and with society in general. The practising sales manager could beneficially devote a little time to reading a text dealing specifically with the subject of public relations activities, methods, benefits and practices.

Public relations activity can be designed to influence directly the attitudes and opinions of the general public or a limited target audience in a variety of ways. Political parties can use it to influence the electorate and create acceptable images of key politicians; manufacturers can use it to counter negative lobbies advocating restrictions on the use or promotion of their products. Some manufacturers prefer to subscribe to industry-wide public relations activity rather than being directly identified with any public lobbying position.

Everything a company does affects its image. Product literature and product design reflect something of corporate attitudes and self-image. The architectural and environmental considerations in designing offices and factories affect how the public views the company. Public relations activity can be geared to creating images of aggression, innovation, concern, empathy, interest in the environment, and so on, and can be used effectively in both short- and longer-term corrective action programmes. (Some manufacturers in major countries have, in the early and mid 1980s, had occasion to promote a public relations position to counter negative consumer reactions to their products after mass product market withdrawals were forced on the companies by product being the subject of criminal malicious tampering activities by individuals or minority groups seeking to make a point.)

On a national scale, public relations companies have been instrumental in encouraging major companies to sponsor public events, notably sports events, where the manufacturer benefits by the event being named after his promoted product.

At the local level, field salespersons may find occasional benefit from public relations activity in support of local causes, charities or other events of local significance.

167

Promotional 'tie-ins' with local events

This follows conveniently from the public relations section, but I have chosen to separate the two points with the distinction that public relations might often be a little more subtle in its sales motivation, whereas a promotional 'tie-in' with a public event (such as placing a product sales stand at a local sporting event, or organising a product display and soliciting customers at a public rally or meeting) is fundamentally sales- and profit-motivated. Promotions may 'tie-in' a product sales campaign with a major 'national week', such as promoting branded animal foods during a 'be kind to pets' week, or promoting child and sports safety equipment during a national 'safety' week. Sales managers should be on the look out for opportunities for any such 'tie-ins' and, if it is a charity function, may be able to persuade parties controlling sales or display space to allocate promotional space and facilities to the company in return for a share of profits or proceeds being donated to the cause the local event is promoting.

The promotional sales literature developed for and used by sales-persons is the most basic of sales promotional activities, and is critical to the process of effective sales presentations. It should be designed with as much care as is given to the actual sales training process since it is as important to the salesperson as any high-quality tool is to a professional craftsman – the sales craftsman should not be given the opportunity to blame his tools for any shortfall in performance.

The standard sales principles apply as strongly to sales literature as to any sales presentation:

- get **attention**
- create **interest**
- generate **desire**
- provoke **action**.

Well-designed and well-structured sales literature should tell in summary form the whole sales story for the product. It should:

- present the product features or attributes
- detail the benefits to the user or buyer
- give confidence in the supplier as a source of quality merchandise and efficient after-sales service
- identify product uses and functions (pictorial representation is often most effective at this stage)
- instruct simply how a product can be used
- outline product specifications that are relevant to the purchase considerations
- illustrate the product in photographic and not diagrammatic or sketch forms

- present information in such a fashion as to answer most standard questions and consumer/user objections
- generate desire to the point where the potential buyer seeks a sample, demonstration, product trial, or places a firm order.

Sales literature should not try to be too clever or fancy in format or structure. The potential buyer does not normally have the time or desire to go through mental gymnastics to work out the message of supposed 'subtleties' or innuendos. Keep it straightforward, clear, concise, informative, relevant to the product and market, meaningful and motivational. It will frequently be found beneficial to leave the sales promotion literature with the buyers.

Promotional literature should not stop at the descriptive elements of a product; it can be used beneficially to communicate advertising and promotional plans and market knowledge and information to buyers.

Sales managers of technical or industrial products can often benefit by using small 'flip charts' as a sales aid to presentations, especially to control the flow of a presentation and to impart information developed pictorially or graphically. Audio-visual aids in the form of video films or cassette tapes give great scope for development of sales promotional activity in venues where a target audience gathers but direct sales activity is impractical or inappropriate, such as at conventions, public transport centres, shopping malls, or anywhere that a captive audience is simply standing around waiting. (Chapter 7 has a section on 'sales aids' that overlaps with this commentary of promotional sales literature, and at the time of reading Chapter 7 the reader may find it useful to refer back to this section.) Generally the use of such video films, if unaccompanied by direct sales activity, needs to identify local outlets where the product might be seen and demonstrated, or where additional literature describing the products and benefits can be obtained.

Promotional aspects of product packaging and design

The design and structure of packaging for products may serve any or all of several functions, including:

- clear identification of the product to the end user and stockists (including taking account of local culture in terms of design, illustrations and wording so as not to be offensive in any way or cause any embarrassment at the point of purchase)
- physical protection against all risks and hazards in transit and at the place of final use
- compliance with all local rules and regulations concerned with the marketing and distribution of the product, including ingredient statements and representations, product descriptions and illustrations, performance claims, and labelling, safety, care and use

instructions. If a product is sold in several countries care must be taken to ensure compliance with regulations in each separate market, and the language of labelling communications must be understandable by the potential customers in each market. That may require either separate outer packages or labels for each market or a multilingual package, particularly to communicate care and use, and handling and storage instructions.

- convenience in handling and storage at each point of the distribution chain – for example, a product for sale through food stores, where many employees responsible for shelf filling activities may be females, is unlikely to be welcomed if packed in such quantities or sizes that the store personnel cannot handle the cases without help
- economising on freight and distribution costs
- the creation of a unique brand identity for the product to make an instant impact at the point of sale (the shape and design of the pack might be distinctive to the point of being protectable as industrial property)
- the provision of product information to potential users or purchasers, including care and use information, and identification of the manufacturer or source of the product.

The style, design, shape and size of the product or its packaging are essential promotional tools. The designer of products and packaging should be sensitive to the need to use design aspects in promoting products in addition to providing necessary physical protection and regulatory compliance. The inner workings of many technical products (such as household electrical goods) could be packaged in a wide range of outer casings. All too often the design considerations are largely production oriented, or simply follow a traditional pattern without innovative input. Design should take account of:

- the functional use to which the product will be put
- its place of use or storage (a garden tool may have less aesthetic design needs than a household product constantly displayed in a kitchen or bathroom), including limitations on the shape and size imposed by the normal use or storage environment
- who will use it (any physical limitations on the person's strength, weight, height, flexibility, etc.)
- effect of design on operating costs of the product (e.g. aero-dynamic automobile design to improve fuel consumption)
- the place of display or sale
- the opportunity to develop a unique brand design image around features of the product to facilitate further advertising and promotional activity.

At the design stage of both product and packaging, consumer market research can beneficially be supplemented by inputs and

170

research discussions with persons who have relevant experience, including potential users, distributors, and salespersons.

DEVELOPING A PROMOTIONAL PLAN

The promotion plan

Once a need for sales promotions in addition to media advertising is recognised then it also becomes necessary to formalise promotion planning to link with the other marketing activity. It would be rather distracting and pointless to be advertising product A heavily whilst giving field sales display activity priority to product B, even if product B was facing certain short-term market problems warranting corrective action attention and promotional support.

In many larger companies much or all of the promotional support at anything above the level of an individual in-store promotion is controlled by the marketing department. The sales managers may have flexibility to the extent that they may organise any promotions supporting product A (within budgetary and other policy or guideline limitations) whilst product A is being given media prominence. Providing a team spirit prevails throughout the company, and particularly in sales and marketing departments, there should be no unnecessary conflict or misunderstandings in the preparation or implementation of advertising and promotion plans. In industrial and service product companies, marketing is often a direct responsibility of the sales manager.

The **annual promotion plan** should take account of and include comment on:

- the timing of promotions for each product, taking account of any high or low seasonal factors or fluctuations
- the objectives of each general promotion or specific promotional activity, and the ability to control and measure performance against objectives
- special promotional media support or general media support
- promotional aids and materials needed to support the promotional activity and act as an 'ice-breaker' for the salespersons introducing the promotion
- shipping and distribution lead times for special promotional merchandise
- lead times involved in planning and ordering special promotional product packaging.

(Perhaps it is worth making the comment here that, if there is a pronounced seasonal pattern to sales, each unit of currency spent on promotional or media activity in the peak season creates more impact on sales than the same amount of currency spent in the seasonal downturn period. Many sales and marketing managers have

171

chosen to invest substantial portions of limited promotional budgets trying to combat a natural seasonal trend and create a more even pattern of demand.)

Example 5.1 shows the kind of format that might be used in planning promotional activity to support other media activity at national or local levels. Although the example is of a men's toiletries range, the format is just as applicable to any industrial or service product range.

Example 5.1   An outline sales promotion plan

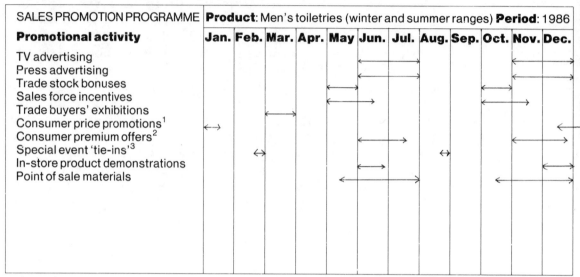

SALES PROMOTION PROGRAMME	**Product**: Men's toiletries (winter and summer ranges) **Period**: 1986

Promotional activity	Jan.	Feb.	Mar.	Apr.	May	Jun.	Jul.	Aug.	Sep.	Oct.	Nov.	Dec.
TV advertising												
Press advertising												
Trade stock bonuses												
Sales force incentives												
Trade buyers' exhibitions												
Consumer price promotions[1]												
Consumer premium offers[2]												
Special event 'tie-ins'[3]												
In-store product demonstrations												
Point of sale materials												

Notes: Summer range mainly suntan lotions and skin care preparations
Winter range mainly traditional toiletries with peak sales at Christmas
1. Assumes price discounting to reduce stocks at end of main season
2. Consumer premium offers might be: (a) beach towel with three product labels and cash in summer
                                       (b) toiletries travel bag with three product labels and cash in winter
3. Special event 'tie-ins' might relate to promotions linked to major sporting events

Setting promotion objectives

As with all sales activity, any form of sales promotion (whether at store level or at area or national sales force levels) must have clearly defined objectives, communicated to, understood and accepted by all parties responsible for planning and implementing the promotion. The sales manager needs to recognise the reason for considering or needing a sales promotion and should attempt to establish quantifiable and measurable objectives, against which the results and the effectiveness of each promotion can subsequently be compared and evaluated. (It might prove difficult to measure the direct benefit over the short term from much public relations activity, but that is likely to be a function that is less under the control of field sales managers.)

In Chapter 10, I develop a simple form that might help in planning, organising and controlling promotional activity at the level of individual stockists; it is possible to modify it for use with key accounts.

Most sales promotional activity is geared to displaying, demonstrating and selling product. The objectives set might be in terms of additional units of a product to be sold during the promotion period, generating a certain number of new leads for subsequent follow-up, achievement of a certain value of sales, expanding product distribution by a certain percentage or number of new stockists, or boosting pipeline stocks. An absolute value or percentage target should be set against each promotional objective. As always with objectives, targets must be realistic and achievable within the promotion time span, and within the control of the people charged with achieving the objectives if they are to be committed to their achievement. Feedback on performance against objectives and targets should be provided during and after the promotion.

For each promotion a separate detailed promotional programme should be prepared in written format, incorporating such information as:

- budgeted expenditure in total and by item of expense
- lead times for the preparation of each aspect of copy, artwork, design and production of each special item of packaging and promotional sales or display material
- lead times for booking advertising media space or time
- production quantities of each item of advertising and display material, packaging and product
- all rules applicable to any consumer, user, retailer, distributor or sales force competitions
- reference to the legality of any aspects of a promotion that might be questionable or require approvals, e.g. lotteries
- the objectives of the promotion and the criteria for measurement of results and for evaluating the outcome of the promotion.

Many marketing managers use simplified critical path techniques in preparing and planning promotions to ensure nothing relevant is overlooked. Example 5.2 illustrates some key stages in promotional planning.

Evaluation of promotions

Whatever the purposes and objectives of a promotion, results should be monitored both during the promotion and in the immediate post-promotional period, with a hope of seeing a change in the sales pattern. Example 5.3 shows what the sales manager would like to see from a successful sales promotion: a rise in sales during the promotion, and a sustained higher level of sales than would otherwise have been expected in the post-promotion period.

Example 5.2 Key stages in organising a sales promotion

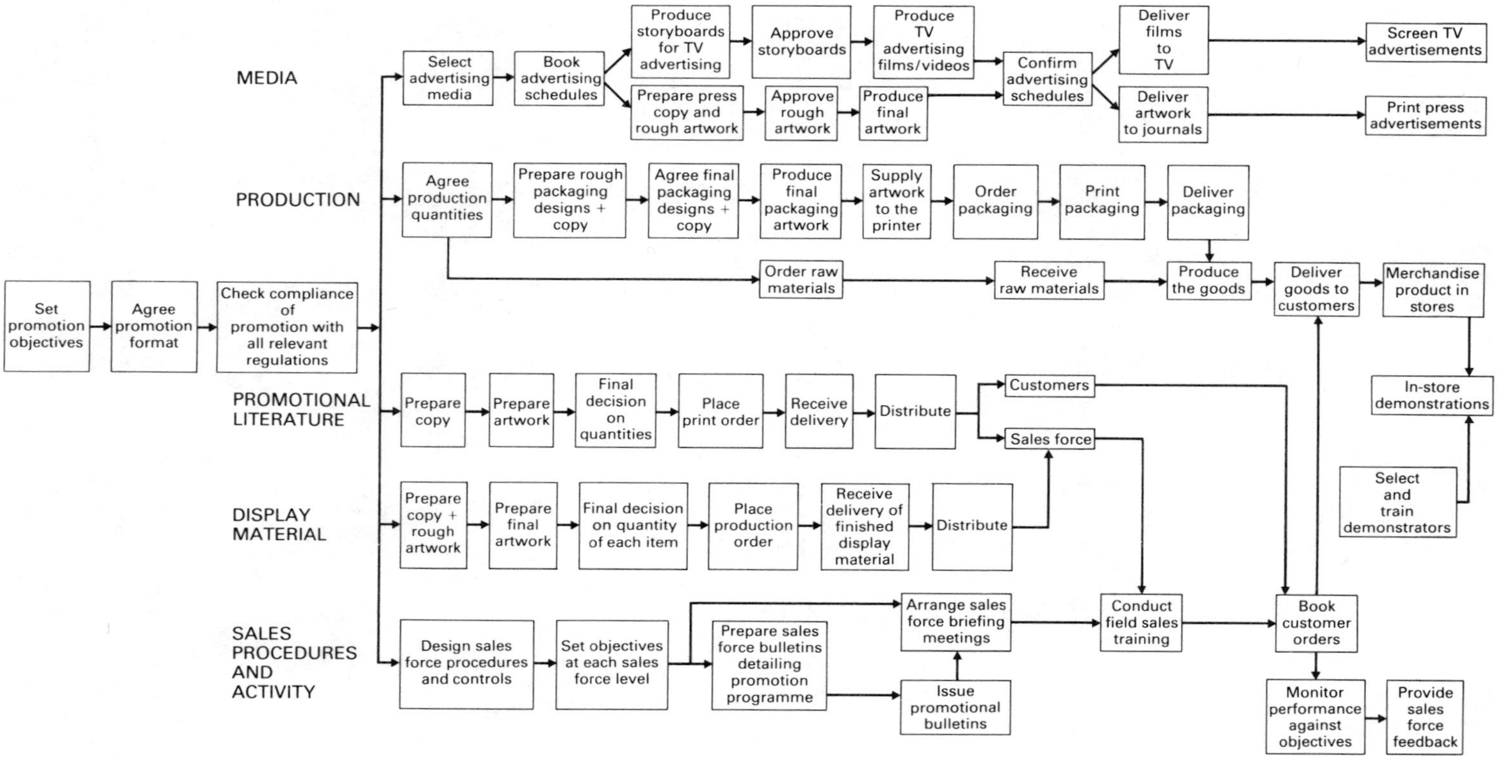

Example 5.3   The impact of a promotion on sales

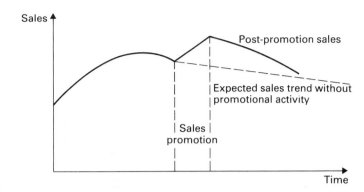

Senior sales and marketing managers should ensure that an evaluation process is part of their promotional planning in order to establish which promotional activity is effective against its objectives. For example, what is the response rate to advertisements placed in trade journals in terms of returned reader enquiry cards? How many visitors to an exhibition stand requested samples, a product demonstration, or a visit by a salesperson? What was the percentage increase in sales during the promotion period compared with a base period or a forecast that did not include the promotion? What was the effect on sales in the post-promotion period in comparison with historical sales or forecast trends?

Graphs (whether recording data month-by-month or on a moving annual basis) are one of the most effective means of instantly noticing any impact of promotional activity where sales volumes or values are plotted against time. Promotions can be noted on the graph for future reference and perhaps briefly summarised in any footnotes.

Effective sales promotions do not just 'happen'; they require considerable planning and attention to detail, and effective communication of objectives and programme details to the sales force responsible for their implementation; and additional sales training, either through area or national meetings or field training by line managers, may well be necessary.

SUMMARY

- Sales promotions are basically forms of promotional activity designed to increase market awareness, product trial or repeat usage of products or services, and widen the distribution base to increase the purchase opportunities available to current and potential users.
- Tactically, sales promotions are generally designed to achieve their specific objectives by such means as: increasing product distribution; generating additional display; increasing product trial by potential users; and increasing pipeline stocks of product.
- Sales promotions supplement and offer a benefit over normal media advertising activity in often being more flexible (and very adaptable as a tactical means of taking corrective action) in timing, purpose and manner of implementation, and in targetting particular market sectors for attention with sales force resources.
- Sales managers must ensure that promotional activity by the sales force does not:

  - distract salespersons from their goals and objectives in key result areas
  - become counterproductive either by resulting in a loss of attention to established markets, or by simply resulting in stockpiling of product by established users, or creating see-saw switches (without creating brand loyalty) between a company's products and those of its competitors
  - alienate any product stockists or distributors by conferring benefits on some and not giving equitable support to others.

- Types of sales promotions most commonly adapted to industrial or consumer product markets include: display bonuses, performance rebates or allowances, trade price discounts, consumer price promotions, trade stock bonuses, consumer competitions, consumer 'premium' offers, product sampling programmes, dealer competitions, product demonstrations, couponing, exhibitions, on-pack 'give aways', lectures and film shows, point of sale material, sales force incentives, special magazines and journals, product merchandising, introduction incentives, trading stamps and similar incentives, free product trial periods, credit cards, direct mailshots, gifts for buyers, public relations activities, 'tie-ins' with special events, sales and promotional literature, promotional aspects of packaging.
- Sales promotional literature to support the field selling activities of salespersons should be designed to: summarise product features, attributes and benefits; reassure the buyer on the product quality, availability, and after-sales service; illustrate

176

product uses and functions, and summarise specifications; show the product in photographic illustrations.

- Product packaging (including any casing containing working parts) particularly serves the functions of: identifying product end uses; providing physical protection against the hazards of the distribution chain or environment of product use; compliance with any applicable rules and regulations; facilitating ease of handling and storage; helping to create a unique brand image.

- The style, design, shape and size of products and their packaging should take account of the functional use of the product, where it will be used and stored, who will use it, operating costs, the place of display and sale, and the opportunity to create a unique brand design.

- An annual promotion programme should be prepared to link with other advertising and marketing activity to ensure correct consideration is given to the timing and planning of all promotional activity. The supporting detailed plan for each separate promotion should cover fully such matters as: its objectives; timing; media support; procedural and administrative aspects; promotional aids and materials; controls and evaluation of performance against objectives; production lead and planning times for all product packaging and promotion aids; compliance with regulations; field implementation programme; distribution of promotion materials; and budgets for each item of expenditure.

- Promotion objectives should be set at each level of the company's sales organisation and the distribution network involved in planning and implementing the promotion, right down the distribution chain to the level of individual participating distributors, and all objectives should be quantifiable and measurable.

- The results and achievements of each promotion should be evaluated against its objectives.

CHECKLIST   BASIC PROMOTION PLANNING

	Notes	Action
Agree and set promotion objectives		
Consider alternative promotion formats to achieve objectives, with consideration to: • budgetary limits • sales force resource limits • planning and implementation lead times		
Check all applicable rules and regulations on preferred promotion formats		
Decide on final format for promotion		
Fix quantities of special: • product • packaging • sales aids • promotional literature • point of sale material		
Design copy and artwork for: • packaging • promotional literature • point of sale material • other sales aids		
Order production quantities of: • packaging • promotional literature • point of sale material • sales aids		
Prepare copy and artwork and storyboards for press and television media campaigns		
Instruct advertising agencies to prepare final media campaign material		
Book media advertising schedules		
Design procedural systems and controls		
Prepare promotional communications to the sales force, including bulletins and procedural instructions		
Distribute sales force allocations of promotional literature, sales aids, and point of sale material		
Conduct sales force briefings through management meetings and other area meetings as appropriate		
Conduct sales force field training		
Set objectives for each customer		
'Sell in' promotion to customers		
Distribute promotional product		
Conduct in-store product merchandising and feature display activity		
Measure performance against promotion objectives		
Prepare a post-promotion evaluation		

178

Part II

Selection and Training in the Sales Force

6 The Sales Personnel Selection Process

Throughout this text I have taken the fundamental position that salesmen are made and not born. Hereditary and environmental factors will govern an individual's qualities and attributes at the time of selection into a sales force, but further environmental changes and specific skill training and development are necessary to create an individual who will derive success and satisfaction from a sales career. In this chapter I first consider the essential and desirable qualities and attributes of persons considered for selection into a sales force. Assessment against a number of factors will, unfortunately, often be rather subjective. Every attempt should be made at each stage of the selection process, whether of a new recruit or promotee, to seek some reasonable objective basis of measurement, comparison and judgement. I shall then review methods of identifying and selecting suitable persons. Considerable space will be given to the coverage of this subject because selection of the most suitable personnel is critical and fundamental to developing a successful sales organisation. Thoroughness at the recruitment stage will produce benefits and savings in time, money and effort at all subsequent training and management stages, and increase the likelihood of recruiting potential 'high performers'.

QUALITIES OF A SALES PERSON

The key characteristic qualities and attributes needed by a sales-person may be considered to include:

- **Integrity** The person must have the highest standards of personal integrity in his relations with his employer, his customers and colleagues if he is to build business based upon mutual respect and trust and professionalism.
- **Reliability** Managers must know that their subordinates are reliable in performing the tasks assigned to them, and customers must know that the salesperson is reliable in fulfilling commitments, obligations and promises.
- **Sincerity** Customers need to feel the salesperson calling on them is sincere in his motives and approach and will give priority consideration to the customers' interests.
- **Empathy** The ability of a salesperson to project himself into the role of the customer and his environment is fundamental in gaining respect and building good relationships.

181

- **Self-confidence**   A salesperson needs a high level of confidence in his abilities if he is to project confidence in his products and company, and influence his customers, and a strong 'ego drive' to succeed.
- **Intelligence**   The level of required intelligence, on whatever objective criteria measurement may be based, will vary according to the functions to be performed, complexity of tasks, responsibilities to be assumed, nature of products, markets and outlets, and the intellectual levels of buyers. There is no absolute standard that is necessary to perform in a sales environment, but it could be reasonably assumed that higher intelligence levels will aid learning, increase adaptability, and reduce risks of low performance.
- **Appearance**   Looking the part is the key to acceptance in the selling role. Again, there are no absolute criteria. A salesperson for financial services may find it hard to gain customer attention unless he wears a pin-stripe suit; but the same dress might not be accepted if he was selling hair-care products to trendy hair salons. The guideline is to adapt appearance to fit the standards acceptable to the more conservative buyers for any particular product or service.
- **Resilience**   The rejection rate of sales presentations is always high, and salespersons always work under considerable pressure to achieve progressively greater results. A resilient personality is essential if the salesperson is to avoid carrying the signs of rejection from one call to another. Resilience will generally develop with experience and with the ability to analyse calls and identify causes and reasons for non-success, and to plan new approaches and strategies.
- **Adaptability**   No two customers are exactly alike: each has different approaches to markets, products, and his own customers. The salesperson must be adaptable, changing to suit the occasion and customer.
- **Independence/Maturity**   Much of a salesperson's day is spent alone, driving, planning calls, completing post-call administration. He is largely without direct support, and in addition to being resilient needs to be mature and independent by nature, capable of surviving and thriving without close supervision or colleagial support.
- **Loyalty**   Loyalty to the company and management is essential to develop mutual interests and benefit.

SKILLS

In addition to the attributes outlined above certain basic skill levels are a prerequisite, along with the potential to develop these skills

182

further as necessary to perform effectively in the selling function or subsequent management positions. These skills fall into five basic categories:

- verbal
- numerical
- technical
- administrative
- interpersonal.

Clearly there will be a degree of overlap, and the level of skill will depend on the markets and demands of the job.

- **Verbal**   The salesperson must be able to collect his thoughts and make clear, concise and logical presentations that hold a buyer's interest. A salesperson who devotes excessive time to 'small talk' may lose the attention of his buyer and alienate him. Buyers will exhibit positive or negative signs in the form of words or expressions, gestures or body language, and the salesperson must learn to identify and interpret direct and indirect signals from buyers.

  Attitudes towards regional accents vary. Some sales managers believe any pronounced accent can be a distraction and detrimental; others take the approach that an accent can aid in gaining attention and interest. Perhaps as a guideline it would be worth initially adopting the position that an accent that is neutral in the selling environment will reduce the risks of distracting a buyer from the purpose of the call (i.e. a northern accent in the north is likely to be less of a distraction than a southern accent). Accents may be much less significant in a management environment or where customer contacts are at a higher level.

- **Numerical**   The level of numerical skill required will vary with the demands of the job. It may be as basic as being able to tabulate order quantities or daily sales totals. For higher-level negotiations and international transactions, a significant degree of numeracy is likely to be required to prepare quotes and product costings, evaluate risks and returns. Sales managers will need to understand basic statistical tabulations and presentations. The degree of numeracy for any job needs to be quantified and form part of the job holder specification or profile. Specialist training may be needed to supplement existing skill levels.

- **Technical**   The level of product-related technical skills is clearly a function of the complexity of the products and markets. A person selling gas turbines may need in-depth knowledge of product applications, specifications and maintenance that might be acquired only from a college education in engineering. A food products salesperson may need no specialist technical knowledge.

183

- **Administrative** Frequently little attention is given to administrative skills at the stage of recruitment. A territory salesperson may need only a minimal level of skill, but if that person is subsequently to be considered for promotion into management, the burdens of administration will increase.
- **Interpersonal** Selling and sales management are fundamentally about inspiring and influencing people. A salesperson may not need to be highly extrovert or gregarious; indeed, an extreme in this respect might be less than acceptable. But salespersons do need to be comfortable with people, able to relax and communicate with contacts, inspire and influence them. This general heading is more of a 'catch-all' phrase summing up the general acceptability to others and acceptance of others in interpersonal relationships.

MANAGEMENT QUALITIES

It may reasonably be considered that, to succeed as a sales manager, a candidate needs to demonstrate not only adequate attributes and skill levels in each of the areas previously reviewed, but also additional qualities and skills, including:

- **Leadership** This could be considered as the ability to inspire others; to obtain from others, without coercion, high levels of work effort directed towards the achievement of group and individual objectives; and to be recognised through personal example as providing a model of relevant qualities and skills.
- **Initiative** The sales manager must be able to respond quickly to changing market conditions and develop creative solutions to problems, as well as spotting and tapping opportunities for additional sales.
- **Decisiveness** As a leader of a team of subordinates, the sales manager will be expected to take positive decisions that give a clear sense of purpose and direction and inspire his subordinates to follow with confidence in the outcome of decisions.
- **Organising ability** The manager will need to be good at organising the resources under his control (mainly human, physical, financial and time-related) to maximise the returns from the team efforts and his own personal workload.
- **Selling skills** Salespersons particularly respect and relate to a manager who can demonstrate a high level of professional personal selling skills (although the manager should not permit himself to be used by his subordinates to handle problems at territory calls; rather, he should pass on his own skills through effective field sales training).
- **Determination, drive, energy** Whichever term you prefer, the sales manager should have and demonstrate high energy

184

levels for the long hours of hard, active work, and the determination to succeed in the face of adversity.

- **Empathy**   A necessary quality in dealing with both customers and subordinates, who may feel rather neglected, lonely, and perhaps unrecognised for their contributions.

- **Integrity**   It is critical that the integrity of a manager is never called in question by his subordinates if he is to manage and motivate a team effectively.

- **Enthusiasm**   Whilst each and every one of us may have an 'off day', in the selling environment that must not show through to customers or subordinates: they will have enough problems and frustrations of their own and a sales manager's moans may serve only to reduce his public image. Infectiously motivating subordinates by exhibiting confidence and enthusiasm is a basic rule. Similarly a sales manager should not be drawn into critical discussions of colleagues or support services; if there is a complaint concerning service or performance the simple approach can be to say he will investigate it and take any necessary corrective action.

- **Assimilation**   With the variety of new situations, systems and procedures inevitably occurring in a progressive sales environment, a manager needs a strong ability to assimilate information and absorb any learning situation it may represent, and effectively relate that to improving the sales performance of his team.

- **Communications**   Misunderstandings in any business environment are generally reduced where communications are made in a precise, informative and instructive fashion, whether in written or verbal format. A sales manager needs to be strong in communication skills, including the provision of meaningful feedback on performance and training.

- **Objectivity**   This is an essential attribute for a manager of people, and for the assessment of sales and marketing developments, and realistic appraisals of changing events and alternative courses of action (frequently corrective action).

- **Impartiality**   If a relationship of trust, respect and confidence in line management is to develop, subordinates should feel and believe that their line manager is impartial and without prejudice. Many sales managers have found to their cost that a flippant comment made in passing to a subordinate, whether denigrating a customer, colleague, racial group or whatever, can rapidly become known throughout the team and create an exaggerated image or reputation for certain likes, dislikes or prejudices.

THE ROLE OF A PERSONNEL DEPARTMENT

Whilst final decisions and responsibility for subordinate selection should always remain with the line manager who will subsequently

185

be responsible for training and performance, if the company is large enough to have a separate specialist personnel function the various levels of sales management can only benefit by close relationships enabling them to draw on experience and advice and practical assistance at each stage of the personnel selection process.

The personnel department can be a major source of assistance to the sales manager in such areas as:

- preparing job specifications
- preparing job holder profiles
- placing recruitment advertising and preparing advertising copy
- screening written applications from c.v. and application forms
- conducting initial interviews
- preparing shortlists of most suitable candidates
- performance appraisal systems
- job evaluations/gradings
- designing and implementing training programmes
- industrial relations
- training managers in counselling skills.

On the assumption that the all-round sales manager needs and wants a basic level of understanding and skill awareness, the text will give separate coverage to a number of these subjects, so I shall not elaborate on them at this stage.

The personnel department could perhaps be seen and used as a source of internal consultancy and, although personnel managers may have no line authority over managers in other departments, they would normally be charged with ensuring that company personnel policies and practices and all relevant industrial relations and employment laws are complied with. The personnel manager is a member of company management just as much as a sales manager, and will therefore obviously have company policies, interests and objectives also as his priority, but he must ensure good personnel practices are followed whenever disputes or conflicts arise, or employees are considered for disciplinary action by line managers. Operational line managers sometimes level the complaint against personnel colleagues that they are too soft or indecisive, but it should be borne in mind that the personnel manager is functionally useful to the line manager because of his developed position of neutrality and impartiality.

JOB DESCRIPTIONS

The first practical step in the selection process is to prepare a detailed written job description. Such a task may be undertaken by a personnel department or with their help, or with an outside recruitment agency if one is being used. A personnel manager alone is unlikely fully to understand the nature of a job, its functions, responsibilities, duties and accountabilities, and if his aid is solicited in preparing a job description he would normally hold extensive discussions with the line manager, any current or previous job holder, and possibly other colleagues.

The job description serves the function of:

- aiding recruiters in preparing job holder profiles for the ideal or acceptable candidate, so that the qualities and qualifications of applicants can be judged against the requirements contained in the job holder profile (see the next section)
- clarifying to line managers the exact nature of the duties and functions the job holder will be expected to perform, and then helping them to develop and apply measurable performance criteria
- enabling the job holder clearly to identify his functions, tasks, duties, responsibilities, accountabilities, reporting and other functional relationships and to relate these to other jobs performed by colleagues, subordinates and superiors within the organisation and to specific performance objectives he may be set as part of the overall company strategies and objectives
- providing a base against which subsequent formal and informal counselling and appraisals can be conducted, in terms of both the actual carrying out of duties and functions and comparison of achievements against standards of performance and objectives
- allowing the supervisor to compare subordinate positions with greater ease and objectivity
- aiding the process of job evaluation so that a management structure can be objectively created that reflects different degrees and levels of responsibility and accountability as part of a management hierarchy.

A very basic rule of management, as applicable in the sales environment as elsewhere, is that it is unfair to criticise a subordinate for poor performance of a task if he was not completely clear on the tasks he was to perform and the acceptable standards of performance. A poorly prepared job description or organisation structure can provoke disputes over responsibilities, cause jealousies and friction, result in unwarranted assumptions of authority by some persons, result in persons being allocated to jobs for which they are not ideally suited in terms of skills and experience, and even produce situations where rewards of job holders incorrectly reflect real responsibility and accountability within the organisation.

It is thus well worth the manager spending time and effort to produce a comprehensive and workable job description for each subordinate position, applying relevant standards of performance for all key tasks and functions, and developing specific objectives, which may apply to either the short, medium or longer term and relate to both the sales division and company objectives. Once objectives have been set, managers may then develop strategies to ensure the achievement of their objectives. It is a better management practice to discuss and agree both standards of performance and objectives with each job holder because commitment increases efforts towards achievement.

There will be as many variations in the formats of a job description as there are persons preparing them, but to make a system of job descriptions meaningful in any one organisation it is advisable to have a consistent format. A **job description** should contain at least the following information:

- **Identification** of the company, operating division, department, etc.
- **Job title**, generally descriptive of the key functional purpose, such as Area Sales Manager or Territory Salesman.
- **Reporting relationships**, e.g. position/title of the job holder's supervisor. There may also at some point be specific reference to functional relationships that are key to the effective performance of the job functions (for example, a national accounts executive would be expected to have close functional relationships with his fellow field sales managers in order to ensure field implementation of the promotions and programmes he arranges with major accounts).
- **Main purpose of the job**   It would be customary to include a one-sentence summary of the main purpose of the job or its key objectives.
- **Subordinates supervised**   The number and nature of subordinate positions to be supervised by the job holder should be identified.
- **Key skills**   Many job descriptions would identify any key management or technical skills that are essential to effective performance of the job.
- **Functions and activities**   Identification of major tasks, functions and activities would normally be included in brief descriptive format.
- **Responsibilities**, e.g. for people, financial resources, equipment, materials, budgeting, forecasting, planning, policy making, safety at work, company image, etc.
- **Relationships**   Quite separately from reporting relationships, the job description may seek to state responsibilities for the maintenance and development of other important relationships, such as with customers or trade associations.
- **Judgement**   It may be very difficult within the scope of a job description to identify how and when judgement and initiative

can and should be exercised by a job holder, but some statement may seek to establish the magnitude and frequency of judgement as a factor in decision taking, or to place limiting parameters upon the flexibility of the job holder.

- **Authority** Scope and limits of authority over both resources and people should be clarified and identified, and any procedure for authorisations outside the limits may be stated if appropriate.

Appendix 1 to this chapter contains job description examples. Using these guidelines, the reader may like to practise the preparation of an outline job description for himself, his immediate subordinate and his line superior, and possibly compare it subsequently with official company job descriptions, should they exist. It may be interesting to see how the reader's perception of the jobs compares with the descriptions prepared at some previous time, probably by other persons.

At management levels in particular, a job description will only be a guideline and not all-embracing, since a manager is expected to have and exercise discretion and initiative in dealing with tasks and circumstances which may frequently change in a selling environ-ment, or to refer matters promptly to a higher authority where his judgement indicates that corrective or appropriate action would be outside his scope of authority.

Once the job description is satisfactorily prepared in the judgement of all concerned, a proper evaluation of the job should be undertaken, possibly by an internal job evaluation committee, personnel manager or other suitably qualified person, to establish the seniority of the job within the organisational hierarchy and attach levels of rewards and benefits to it. Some larger companies have their own job evaluation system; others adopt or modify a system advocated by outside consultancy groups (such as the internationally recognised HAY system). Smaller companies may just seek to get things right by good judgement exercised by the chief executive and his colleagues. The smaller the organisation, the less pressure there will be to formalise a system as there will be less opportunity for misunderstandings to arise.

JOB HOLDER PROFILES

Following the preparation of a job description for each separately identified job function, the next task is to use that description to develop a job holder profile. (This may also be termed a personnel specification, candidate profile, or variety of similarly meaningful terms.) It should contain certain basic information, such as objective standards in the categories of:

189

- **physical characteristics**, e.g.
  - age
  - height/weight
  - race (if relevant to performance, such as working in an ethnic neighbourhood)
  - health parameters
  - general appearance
- **educational standards**, e.g.
  - minimum acceptable
  - optional additional standards
- **post-education experience**, e.g.
  - specific training received
  - previous work experience
- **skills**, e.g.
  - personal selling
  - sales training
  - administrative
  - communication
  - technical knowledge
  - line management experience
- **general**, e.g.
  - personal circumstances (family, married, single)
  - interests (social, physical, intellectual, practical, cultural)
  - driving licence.

Subjective guidelines may also be appropriate in the area of:

- **personality/disposition**, e.g.
  - drive, determination, maturity, enthusiasm, integrity, reliability, adaptability, etc.
  - leadership characteristics
  - social awareness and acceptability
  - needs and motivations, including social, income and status needs, competitiveness, etc.

Against each of the main headings or sub-headings the line manager should attempt to write a brief guide of which achievements, standards or objective criteria he would consider as essential and which as optional. The result is a 'pen picture' that can be used in screening application from curriculum vitae data, application forms, and subsequently at interviews.

As a final validation of the job holder profile the preparers should study the qualifications and experience that people who are currently successfully performing the same or similar jobs brought to those jobs at the time of their selection, and what additional training they subsequently needed or received and the effects of that training on job performance. Interviews with previous holders of the job, if it is not a new position, may also serve to highlight skills and attributes needed to perform the functions to satisfactory standards.

Appendix 2 to this chapter contains an example of a job holder profile.

SOURCES OF APPLICANTS

Whatever the level of a specific job vacancy in the company hierarchy, there are certain common sources of applicants to consider, such as:

- internal transfers and promotions
- personal contacts
- referrals
- general/trade press advertisements
- radio advertisements
- competitors
- employment agencies
- professional institutions
- management search firms
- educational institutions.

The choice may depend in part on factors such as the recruiter's need for ready experience and previously trained personnel.

Internal sources

This source should always be the first to be considered. Are there internal candidates with some or all of the skills, qualities and experience who should be considered for transfer or promotion? When an internal appointment is made, employee morale clearly benefits from such an overt demonstration of a company's commitment to staff development. A company with a strong internal sales training function may be able to develop sales persons to assume management roles with additional training in specific management skills providing that, at the initial recruitment, attention was given to selecting candidates who exhibited certain management qualities and skills or the ability and motivation to acquire additional skills.

Personal contacts

Existing employees, particularly those holding a similar or more senior position, may have contacts who, they feel, could be interested in being considered for vacancies and bring requisite skills and experience. The employees have the advantage of familiarity with the company and possibly also with the nature and demands of the vacant position, and will hopefully act as a screening agent by not referring persons whose suitability would be strongly questioned.

191

Referrals

This is an extension of the existing employee network, in that other persons with contacts in and connections to the company may also have associates, friends, or knowledge of possibly suitable candidates who could be referred to the recruiter. As the contact chain lengthens so the understanding of the job and its environment will weaken. A fuller screening process will need to be applied and so lessen the benefits to the recruiter in terms of potential time, cost and effort saving.

Advertisements

The advertising media used should depend on the nature and responsibility level of the position to be filled. A specific territory sales position may benefit from being advertised in the local evening or weekly paper covering the vacant territory. A sales management position requiring specialist skills (as might be needed in the computer, financial and engineering industries) may benefit from national coverage in a daily paper or a more clearly targeted advertisement in specialist trade or professional journals with known high readership in the target skill group. Press advertising is an increasing cost in the recruitment exercise and the more a target source market can be narrowed down the greater the likely cost-effective response rate per advertisement placed. An advertising or specialist personnel selection agency should be able to provide very specific relevant data on costs and readership profiles for any newspaper or journal.

Radio

Over recent years this has been a growing medium for recruitment advertising, but clearly the advertiser should expect a very large wastage factor since few listeners are likely to match specific job holder profiles. However, this medium has been effectively used by some companies seeking either salespersons for full-time territory sales positions or part-time store merchandisers such as are frequently employed within the food manufacturing industry.

Competitors

A rather obvious source of experienced staff is from within competitive companies. However, the advantages of experience of the industry and product types may be offset by problems of adaptation to the new employer's systems, procedures, training and management styles. In any case, line managers are often reluctant to 'poach' employees from competitors, fearing the competitor might take reciprocal action.

Employment agencies

For lower-level localised sales positions some of the many high street employment agencies may prove to be a worthwhile source of applicants, for either experienced or inexperienced candidates. Such agencies may be particularly productive in helping retail stores to identify potential store sales staff. They generally charge a com-mission of around 15 per cent of the starting salary. Some agencies maintain a register of persons expressing interest in certain career opportunities.

Professional institutions

Where specific skills are required, particularly in addition to functional selling skills, then an approach to a professional institution may give access to suitably qualified candidates. The institute may have a journal in which advertisements could be placed, or maintain a register of members seeking employment opportunities. Access to the institute's membership lists may provide an additional source of potential candidates. Professional institutes cover most key skills including marketing, export management, engineering, personnel, accountancy and finance.

Management search firms

For many senior management positions, and some lower or middle management positions, executive search firms will generally conduct a specific search for potential and suitable candidates for a fee, often around one-third of the starting salary of the appointee. Search firms normally want exclusivity on an assignment, and can offer the advantage of confidentiality in that a candidate need not initially know the potential employer's name. They can identify and target specific companies and individuals for initial approaches, conduct initial interviews, provide advice and help in preparing job descriptions, job holder profiles, and incentive and reward schemes. This is an effective but very costly recruitment method often used only for the most senior positions in companies.

Educational institutions

An excellent source of specialised talent and future management potential is through direct recruitment of students just completing higher educational courses at colleges and universities. Such candidates have demonstrated intellectual abilities, but no relevant work experience; however, they are often very trainable (if often a little idealistic initially). Induction into a sales or marketing training programme will be a good route into sales or marketing manage-ment, and give practical 'hands on' experience. Selling jobs that do not require a higher educational standard may well be filled by tapping the market for school leavers, perhaps by making direct approaches to schools in the job location vicinity, e.g. for retail sales personnel.

193

THE JOB APPLICATION FORM

As a first stage in the recruitment process the sales manager should establish if a standard job application form is in use within the company and arrange for it to be sent to appropriate applicants for vacancies. Should no such form currently exist, then perhaps the sales manager would choose to prepare one. The form will generally be completed by applicants and returned to the recruiter prior to any arrangement for an initial interview, so that applicants can be screened against the job holder profile standards.

The basic information a **job application form** might request could include:

- full names of applicant
- date of birth/age
- nationality
- sex
- marital status
- children/dependants
- address and telephone number (owned or rented)
- medical history (including information on recurring illnesses and disabilities)
- physical characteristics (height/weight)
- driving licence/driving record
- education:
  - schools attended
  - higher learning institutions/universities
  - attainments and qualifications
  - other courses attended
- employment history:
  - positions held (generally in chronological sequence)
  - dates applicable to each position
  - summary of key responsibilities and achievements in each position
  - respective salary levels
  - respective reasons for leaving positions
- trade or professional qualifications and membership of any professional institutions
- personal interests
- personal references
- linguistic skills
- supplementary information (possibly a space inviting applicants to enter any additional data relevant to their application for employment)
- period of notice in present employment.

In addition to the standard and basic information listed above, some application forms go further by asking applicants to write a

194

brief essay on why they are applying for a position and why they feel they should be considered; or possibly they are invited to write briefly on their most memorable achievement. I do not propose to act as judge on what should be included, but simply observe that whatever is requested should be seen by applicants as relevant and beneficial to support their application, and should positively contribute to the recruiter's ability to form objective judgements and to select candidates for initial interviews. Finally, the application form or covering letter should be very specific on where and to whom the completed application form should be sent, and encourage prompt response.

Appendix 3 to this chapter gives an example of a basic job application form, which could be modified to suit the needs of an individual company.

RECRUITMENT ADVERTISING

Most of the mechanical processes in seeking recruits through the various alternative sources previously listed are perhaps self-evident, but the one source requiring further attention here is the preparation of recruitment advertisements. A review of the job advertisement columns of any major newspaper will enable the reader quickly to form views on the relevance of information included in many advertisements and whether or not it encourages suitably qualified persons to respond. Many advertisements devote a significant proportion of expensive space to a subjective description of the 'ideal candidate', who may be described as 'a self-motivator with drive, determination, enthusiasm and an ability to get on with people', and 'a desire to increase his earnings in line with his real potential'. Such phraseology may generate a good response, but not necessarily from suitably qualified candidates, and could waste much of the recruiter's time in screening and responding to unsuitable applicants.

As in the case of the discussion on job application forms, this text cannot provide a fully comprehensive guide to creative advertising, but it can encourage the sales managers responsible for recruitment to satisfy themselves that recruitment advertisements follow certain normal sales presentation principles, such as:

- attract attention
- inform
- arouse interest
- create desire
- sell the benefits
- provoke positive action.

Content of an advertisement

The advertisement, whilst intended to attract suitably qualified applicants, should not be so inviting as to encourage applications from persons clearly outside the guidelines of the job holder profile. The description of requisite skills, experience, characteristics and qualifications should enable potential candidates effectively to screen themselves.

As guidelines, coverage in an advertisement should be given to:

- **The job title** This should enable potential candidates to recognise the likely function of the job, and perhaps give an indication of seniority with a phrase such as 'reporting to the National Sales Manager and responsible for 6 Area Managers and up to 30 salespersons'.
- **The company** A brief description of the company, its products, size, development or expansion plans will enable the candidate to recognise the organisation and industry, and perhaps attach a degree of status to gaining employment within the organisation. Some companies prefer not to name themselves in advertisements, either because they fear their marketplace image is not attractive, or because they do not wish employees to be aware of recruitment plans.
- **Reasons for the vacancy** It is always good to give a positive reason for a recruitment, if one exists, such as 'due to expansion of the sales force' or 'because of the promotion of the last job holder'.
- **Job functions** A brief description of the key functions and responsibilities will enable applicants to relate those to their present position and responsibilities and experience.
- **Location** A candidate will obviously want to know the geographical location of the appointment, and a comment may be made on any assistance with relocation expenses offered.
- **Requirements** The essential and desirable skills and experience or other factors identified in the job holder profile should be outlined.
- **Benefits** A short summary sentence may indicate particular career benefits and potential future prospects.
- **Rewards** General levels of rewards, including salary indicators, fringe benefits, incentive or bonus schemes, should be outlined in the advertisement. Some companies avoid reference to salary beyond the vague phrases 'commensurate with seniority and experience' or 'salary will be agreed to attract the right individual'. Many candidates already holding senior, well-paid positions are cautious of applying for positions where rewards are either vague or, they fear, inadequate. If the company has firm salary scales, it is generally best to indicate these in an advertisement.
- **How to apply** The manner and method of replying, including the name of the person to whom replies should be addressed and his location, should appear in the advertisement. (Phrases used might include: 'send a brief curriculum vitae to John Wilson at . . .', or 'Telephone John Wilson on . . . for an application form'.)

196

Inviting telephone response speeds the initial screening and application process.

I would suggest that the recruiting sales manager initially drafts his suggested advertising copy and perhaps then reviews it with experienced persons in the personnel department or the agency assigned to place the advertisement, and that he reviews his own wording, asking himself the basic questions:

- will it make an impact on a page full of other job advertisements?
- does it clearly communicate with potential candidates?
- will it arouse interest amongst potential candidates?
- does it explain the job functions and responsibilities?
- does it clarify what are the minimum requirements candidates will be expected to demonstrate?
- will it provoke response?

One of the best attention-getting openings is to precede any job title or earnings potential statement with a prominent question that arouses interest and curiosity and separates the advertisement from the bulk of routine advertisements on the page, e.g. 'Are you ready now for sales management?'.

This reviewing process is likely to result in some re-writing of copy, but it is worth the extra time and effort as advertising is generally the biggest single direct cost factor in a recruitment, and good effective copy is critical to generating response from suitable candidates. It is worth bearing in mind that you judge the success of a job advertisement not by the quantity of replies but by the quality of the applicants.

It may be a beneficial exercise for the reader to draft a job advertisement for his own job and those of his immediate superiors and subordinates, and then critically review his drafts considering the foregoing guidelines. Some examples of advertisements are given in Example 6.1, and the reader will no doubt judge which he considers to be more effective.

SCREENING APPLICATIONS

Once applications are received, whether in the form of curricula vitae, each with its own personalised style and format, or on the standard job application form provided to respondents, or in response to an advertisement inviting telephone call-in contact, each application must be **screened** to identify which correlate most closely to the job holder profile for the vacant position. At this stage of the selection process, when no direct contact has yet been made with the candidates, the recruiter should obviously be seeking objective

197

Example 6.1 Sample job advertisements

THE NATIONAL TRADE ASSOCIATION

Vacancy in the marketing division.

The staff team, based in London, is concerned in identifying market opportunities and developing market initiatives. This vacancy offers an exciting challenge to those between 25 and 35 with appropriate qualifications, flair, enthusiasm, a sound knowledge of the food industry, and practical experience in the food marketing sphere.

Starting salary will be in accordance with qualifications and experience. Further particulars from the Director of Staff Relations. N.T.A. House, London.

SALES AND TECHNICAL DIRECTOR

North West   **c.£22,000 + car**

Our client, a highly successful Manufacturer, leader in its field and part of one of the largest international British groups, requires a Sales and Technical Director based at its main UK site in a pleasant part of the North West. Total sales exceed £30 million per annum, of which over half are through overseas subsidiary companies.

This appointment is central to the Group's future development and represents an exciting and challenging opportunity to contribute to the further success of the Company.

Reporting to the Managing Director, the Sales and Technical Director will have direct responsibility for the technical and engineering departments and the UK sales function, including sales to direct export markets overseas. He/she will also provide specialist advice and guidance to overseas subsidiaries.

Managerial experience and responsibility for sales, design and development functions in an engineering environment are essential. Wider knowledge of selling overseas would be valuable. An engineering degree or appropriate professional qualification is required as evidence of the ability and contribution expected.

The remuneration package is negotiable and excellent fringe benefits are available. Future prospects for the successful candidate are exceptional.

Please write in complete confidence, giving full c.v. and present salary, to: **The Management Search Company, Commercial House, Piccadilly, London W1.**

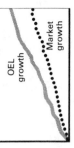

SALES PROFESSIONAL   £25K +

ARE YOU IN THE RIGHT ENVIRONMENT FOR HIGH FLIERS?

Our dramatic growth creates the urgent need for more high-flying sales professionals who have the experience and skills to negotiate successfully at the most senior management levels over several months to conclude major supply contracts, and who want to increase their earnings whilst building a successful sales career in a dynamic market-oriented organisation.

We operate at the top end of a competitive yet quality conscious market, and demonstrably continue to grow at a faster than market rate, concentrating on major opportunities with multi-user clients.

Now we need more sales professionals at several UK locations, who have relevant capital goods or office equipment experience and who will report to a Regional Director and take responsibility for major clients in a defined geographical area.

We can offer basic earnings and commission which, based upon current typical achievements, should provide first-year earnings in excess of £25k. Our renowned sales training will supplement your already developed skills, and our product range is internationally famous for quality and reliability. Fringe benefits include a non-contributory pension scheme, relocation assistance where appropriate, and a 2 litre car.

If this opportunity is for you, phone Jack Goodall on 01-234 5678 today between 10 am and 10 pm or send him your cv at

**Office Equipment Ltd,
Marketing Towers,
High Road,
London S1 2AB.**

reasons to consider applications further or reject them as outside the scope of the job holder profile. Rejections should be made only on the basis of identifiable contra-indications, such as the applicant having no current driving licence, being outside the specified age range, having no relevant experience, or not meeting other relevant criteria clearly identified as essential or desirable on the job holder profile.

Whilst screening applications, it is worth giving some attention to the area of **interests** the applicant claims to have (although these are much more useful as a discussion point at interviews), as they may provide a guide in respect of:

- stability/maturity
- active/passive personality
- depth of interests
- pattern of interests
- relevance to the job
- likes and dislikes
- skills and knowledge involved
- personal motivations.

At this stage, when even for middle sales management positions it might be common to receive over a hundred replies to a national advertisement, the recruiter should be able to identify obviously interesting applications and those that are equally as obviously unsuitable, with a further group of 'possibles' for further consideration. At this point a brief letter acknowledging the application should be sent to all applicants, since a quick response promotes goodwill towards the company. The letter could take one of three forms:

- Applications of no further interest should receive a polite rejection. The letter might thank the applicant for his interest, and comment that many replies were received, and that a number of applicants appear to have more directly relevant experience than himself. A rejection letter should be designed to leave a candidate with goodwill towards the company (as he may well be a customer for the products) and the belief that he was given fair consideration.
- The 'possible' group might receive a letter saying that many replies have been received, and further consideration is being given to each of them before taking decisions on whom to interview. Ideally it should indicate when they might expect to hear further, which will probably be after the first interviews have been held for the most suitable applicants, when the recruiter might want to review the pile of 'possibles'.
- The most suitable applicants should be invited to an initial

interview promptly, either by a letter suggesting a time and place, or by a phone call to arrange a mutually convenient rendezvous.

If it is felt more appropriate, perhaps for reasons of timing, to invite candidates to telephone in to the sales or personnel departments either to discuss the position and their suitability or to obtain a job application form, then applicants can initially be screened during the telephone conversation. In that case a brief questionnaire might be drafted to which the person receiving the telephone calls can refer. This should be designed to elicit information on facts and objective criteria only because it is not practical for any but the most experienced interviewers to probe effectively into subjective areas during a telephone conversation (and much is lost without face to face contact). Information might be sought in respect of:

- age
- present location
- experience
- education
- health
- sex
- validity of a driving licence
- present income

and any other objective parameters indicated in either the job advertisement or job holder profile. A candidate clearly considered as unsuitable could be so advised during the telephone conversation, which will reduce the need to send out application forms requiring subsequent screening.

In some companies these early stages in the selection process will be conducted or managed by the personnel department or by an outside agency.

INITIAL INTERVIEWS

Interview
objectivity

The selection process will normally include more than one interview with some candidates. An initial interview should aim to reduce the possible candidates to a manageable shortlist of perhaps four to eight persons.

There is merit in treating this stage as systematically as the earlier stages in the selection process. A busy manager may be tempted to 'slot in' interviews between other activities in his programme. This defeats the basic goal of making objective interpersonal comparisons, since such comparisons will become less meaningful if the individual candidates are seen under widely divergent circumstances at different times. The recruiting manager should treat the initial (or final) interviews as a distinct project requiring a specific allocation of time and other resources, and set aside an appropriate number of days at a venue where interruptions will be minimal (it may be better to use the facilities of a suitable hotel rather than risk office disruptions). Probably a first interview will need a time allocation of about one hour per candidate, providing the interviewer controls the pace. There will always be candidates who it is apparent within the first few minutes are not suitable: they need to leave feeling they have had fair consideration.

Interview content and conduct

The possible broad format of the first interview might consist of:

- personal introductions and reimbursement of any out-of-pocket expenses
- a brief introduction to the company, the products and the job
- the actual interview.

The conduct and content of the interview will depend greatly on the experience and style of the interviewer, but there are certain general guidelines that may be helpful to less experienced interviewers.

- **choose an informal interview environment**, such as sitting in comfortable chairs by a coffee table rather than facing each other across a desk
- **control the interview**, directing its content along lines that enable you to form objective assessments, and setting the pace
- **structure the interview round a framework**, possibly following chronological events or circumstances using the application form as a guide, and elicit information about and from the candidate that relate to his

  – impact on other people
  – qualifications and experience
  – innate abilities
  – motivation
  – adjustment

- **avoid projecting your own personality** into the interview situation – you are there to listen, gather information, form opinions and judgements, not to make a sales presentation or recount your own life story
- **project a friendly atmosphere** of warmth, empathy, sincerity and interest, but also neutrality
- **keep to a logical sequence** and avoid topic jumping in a manner that seems irrelevant to the candidate, otherwise he will suspect your motives and spend more time wondering what you are up to rather than answering the questions

201

- **link questions to replies** to encourage the flow of information
- **ask open questions** – these encourage the interviewee to expand in his replies and leave openings for further probing as appropriate and necessary
- **give thinking time** if it seems as though the candidate needs it
- **ask probing questions** that get to the issues behind the facts, e.g. 'Why did you choose to resign so soon after the new sales director was appointed?'
- **encourage the conversation flow** by linking questions and expanding comments, such as 'and what happened then?'
- **do not raise personal matters** that might seem more sensitive until after you have established a rapport
- **do not use exaggerated or distracting mannerisms**, whether physical or verbal, such as fiddling with change in your pocket or using annoying phrases (such as 'you know what I mean') that might cause embarrassment or project a prejudice
- **be sensitive to body language signals** that might project reactions and attitudes unintentionally
- **do not be afraid of silence** – it can be an excellent tool to prompt the interviewee to continue expanding on comments made
- **avoid multiple questions** – these can confuse the candidate
- **avoid ambiguous questions** – these can also seem confusing or irrelevant to the candidate
- **avoid leading questions** – these only cause a candidate to reply in a manner that he thinks fits the expected response
- **avoid technical jargon** if this is particular to your own company or industry rather than being standard technical terminology
- **avoid direct or implied criticism** either through comment or involuntary body language signals
- **avoid constant studying of the form** or just repeating information contained in the application form, as that gives the impression you have not prepared for the interview.

Just before starting each interview, the interviewer may wish to ask himself two basic questions:

- 'Do I know what I am looking for?'
- 'Will I recognise it when I see it?'

For objective assessments to be made of an individual's ability to perform successfully in a specific job function, it is necessary to study both **internal** factors, which are all particular to the individual candidate, and the **external** factors or circumstances that impact on the internal factors.

The recruiter may have his own personal style of interviewing to draw upon. If not, then a very thorough but basic technique is developed in the **seven point plan**, prepared and published

202

originally by the National Institute of Industrial Psychology and Alec Rodgers and now available in a publication from NFER–NELSON of Windsor. This encourages the interviewer to use a systematic and objective approach based on each of the sections normally covered by the job application form.

Elicit information with the constant use of open questions that require more than a simple 'yes' or 'no' answer. **What – How – Why** are the key words; for example:

'Why did you choose a sales career?'
'What prompted you to leave XYZ company?'
'How did you select your salesmen at your last company?'

The interviewer should ideally record meaningful notes under each category.

- **Physical makeup**:
  – appearance and first impression
  – bearing
  – peculiarities/habits/mannerisms
  – speech
  Look for any positive or negative factors that could affect job performance or acceptability to colleagues or contacts.
- **Attainments**:
  – formal educational standards
  – educational attainments in relation to peers, family circumstances
  – additional training sought and received
  – employment history and progression
  – tangible measurements of performance and achievements
  Look for the motivational factors, levels of achievement in relation to opportunity, actual progression and rates of progression, drive, determination, resilience, adaptability.
- **General intelligence**:
  – general intellectual capacity
  – problem-solving abilities
  – academic excellence and achievements
  Look for evidence of sufficient innate intellectual capacity to master the activities and functions of the job, and to develop the job and himself further.
- **Special aptitudes**:
  – special skills, e.g. mechanical, technical, linguistic, artistic.
  Look for evidence of strength in skill areas that would be relevant to performance of the job functions.
- **Interests**:
  – intellectual
  – social

203

– cultural or artistic
– practical
– active/passive

Look for depth of interest, patterns, special aptitudes, degree of activity. Expression of interest in a subject does not indicate expertise; that may need to be pursued in an interview if an interest area is relevant to performance of a job. Preferences may be revealed through interests and aid assessments of motivation and disposition.

- **Disposition/personality**:
  – social interactions
  – influence
  – self-reliance
  – dependability
  – acceptability to others

  Look for evidence of successful social interactions, acceptance of and acceptability to others, and an ability to inspire and influence other persons or groups. This aspect is most prone to subjective assessments.

- **Circumstances**:
  – family and home background
  – early schooling
  – early and later neighbourhoods and home environments
  – family stability, achievements, expectations
  – present situation and family commitment
  – present home environment and mobility
  – financial commitments
  – attitudes, e.g. religion, politics, social

  Look for stability, opportunities, influences, disposition and motivations and relate achievements to background circum-stances.

In addition to these seven basic assessment areas, the interviewer should throughout an interview be seeking to identify and under-stand the **motivations** that caused responses, action, or changes in circumstances.

- **Motivations**:
  – influence
  – power
  – social needs
  – recognition
  – status
  – physiological needs
  – rewards/greed
  – achievement/success

What does he recognise as his needs and what satisfactions does he seek? This can also be a subjective area.

At the end of the series of initial interviews the recruiter should feel confident that he has thoroughly screened the candidates demonstrating initial suitability for a job and obtained enough objective data and comparative information on experience, attainments, skills and attributes, motivational and personality factors and potential to decide with confidence who should be invited to any shortlist process.

THE SELECTION SHORTLIST

In an external recruitment programme the shortlist is the final stage, whereas if all the candidates are from internal company sources it may be the only stage. Even for an internal recruitment, a shortlist procedure should be conducted professionally with demonstrable impartiality and fairness, each candidate feeling he has had every opportunity to demonstrate his eligibility for transfer or promotion.

The aim of the shortlist procedure is to enable the line manager to assess the abilities and capabilities of each candidate on the shortlist clearly and objectively; he should also be aware of the personality traits exhibited by each candidate during the selection process.

By this stage, if not earlier, candidates would expect to see a full job description, and have the opportunity to discuss this.

The shortlist procedure could consist of any or all of the following:

- intelligence or aptitude tests
- personality tests
- group selection tasks
- individual tasks
- interviews
  - panel interviews
  - stress interviews
  - individual interviews
- taking references.

Tests   Some companies favour the use of intelligence, aptitude, or personality tests in the selection process. Such tests may have a role in assisting line managers to identify particular skills or potential.

Intelligence tests are possibly only of direct benefit where company experience shows a degree of positive correlation between achievement in the tests and performance of current or previous job holders. A high level of innate intellectual capacity or ability does not ensure a

205

high performance in any particular function; other motivational and skill factors would also affect performance.

Aptitude tests specific to a job and its related skills may be very useful. The test need not be in the form of a sit-down examination, but could simply take the form of a discussion between candidate and line manager on technical aspects of products or markets. For example, in the case of a company marketing industrial engineering products it would be quite logical for the recruiting line manager to go into depth discussions on technical engineering aspects of products to satisfy himself on a candidate's level of technical competence.

Personality tests are used in some countries and organisations, and are also favoured by certain major management consultancy firms. These have rarely been validated in relation to specific performance in specific companies or industries, and are therefore somewhat suspect as objective instruments for use in the selection process.

If any of the above tests are used in the selection process, then the recruiters should constantly bear in mind that any test is only one small part of the overall recruitment process, and it might be wrong to consider a test as a pass or fail criterion.

Group
selection
tasks

The use of group selection tasks, where generally from four to eight candidates are brought together at the shortlist venue and given a common project to tackle, can certainly be a source of data and inter-personal comparison under controlled identical conditions. Some candidates may resent or resist participation, particularly for more senior positions. That in itself may be a worthwhile reaction to note. Prior to attending a shortlist, the candidates should be informed about the format the proceedings will follow, and early discussions at a group selection should help the candidates to see how involvement in the full process will aid effective recruitment. The company will obviously not wish to recruit a person who subsequently under-achieves or becomes unhappy for any reason; and the candidates will learn much more of a company's style and management philosophy in the course of proceedings at a thorough shortlist.

A group task might be as simple as being given a pile of typing paper and a handful of paperclips, and asked to design and construct a paper tower within a fixed time limit and certain performance criteria (e.g. height specifications); or it might consist of being given a subject to discuss, such as the issue of aid to developing nations; or it could be a discussion on a job-related subject, such as restructuring the sales force into a grocery division and a pharmaceutical division.

The group selection process is particularly beneficial in an external management recruitment, where the individuals are largely

206

unknown quantities; it may have less relevance for existing employees with demonstrable performance records. Group tasks can be effectively used at the initial selections of sales persons, probably giving the assembled candidates a group discussion topic as a task of 10–15 minutes duration.

The aim of the observers is to evaluate the performance of each group participant, his contribution, qualities and skills as demonstrated in the task and in relation to those required of the appointee to the vacant position.

If a panel of recruiting managers is observing a group selection task, they will probably need some training from a skilled consultant or personnel manager in the observation and interpretation of the interreactions involved. This is a major subject area covered in some specialist texts, but a brief comment is warranted here, partly because an extension of the group selection process into a less competitive and more team-building environment, sometimes termed **assessment centres**, can effectively be used in management development programmes.

Two major ingredients in the group task situation are **content** and **process**. The first is more concerned with the quality of input from group participants; the second is concerned with what is happening between the group members in performing the task or project (i.e. the group dynamics).

CONTENT	PROCESS
Analysis	Morale
Logic	Feelings
Quality	Atmosphere
Judgement	Influence (and style of influence)
Common sense	Participation
Fluency	Leadership struggles
Communications ability	Conflict
Perceptions	Competition
Attitudes	Cooperation
	Projection

The group task may be analysed by the observers under several headings:

- **participation**:
  - high
  - low
- **degrees of influence**:
  - high
  - low
  - rivalries
- **styles of influence**:
  - autocratic

207

    – democratic
    – mediation
    – laissez faire

- **task functions**:
  - controllers
  - strategists
  - analysts
- **decision-making procedures**:
  - self-authorised decision taker
  - decision supporter
  - topic jumpers
  - majority decisions (votes)
  - consensus of opinions
  - unrecognised contributions
- **maintenance functions**:
  - who involves others in the task?
  - who blocks others' participation?
  - who clarifies others' comments?
  - who remains preoccupied?
  - how are ideas accepted/rejected?
  - how effective is each group member at communicating?
- **group atmosphere**:
  - who avoids conflict?
  - who prefers conflict?
  - who resolves conflict?
  - are participants involved and interested?
  - how relaxed is the atmosphere?
  - what is the pace?
- **group membership**:
  - what sub-groupings develop?
  - how do sub-groups relate to the rest of the group?
  - do developing sub-groups reflect agreement/disagreement?
- **group feelings**:
  - what physical and emotional reactions are indicated by facial, verbal or other physical expression? (e.g. anger, irritation, contempt, frustration, pleasure, warmth, affection, friendliness, enthusiasm, excitement, defensiveness, boredom, competitiveness, sensitivity).
- **group norms**:
  - what group norms develop? (e.g. are some topics avoided?)
  - who reinforces avoidance and how?
  - group formality/informality
  - group agreeability/disagreeability
  - open expressions of feelings or hiding of feelings
  - accepted styles of participation.

If a panel is observing a group selection task then obviously the

208

panel members should remain quiet whilst the task is in progress, and hold a panel review discussion privately afterwards.

Individual tasks

When a candidate at an interview is asked to perform an individual task this is often more like an aptitude test. Many recruiting sales line managers will have a practice such as handing a pen to a candidate with a comment such as 'sell me that pen'. That is only reasonable if the candidate is already professing to have selling skills. A candidate should always see the relevance of a task to the job position otherwise there is a risk he will under-perform. In selecting a sales manager it might be quite reasonable to ask a candidate to discuss a situation involving sales force discipline, or to prepare and present a case for the use of part-time store merchandisers. Such tasks are job-related and a candidate may have little difficulty understanding that the interviewer is seeking to judge his skills or experience.

Interviews

The shortlist interviews of all candidates should ideally be conducted at one sitting to ensure fair and impartial interpersonal comparisons under similar conditions. If any group tasks or tests are to be included in the selection process then these should be conducted before the final interviews to enable the panel to raise any relevant issues with candidates. The shortlist interview is likely to be much more intensive than the initial interview, as it is concerned with detailed analysis of qualifications, skills, personality characteristics and all-round suitability to the company and the job. In addition, the candidates are likely to have many questions and uncertainties that should be answered comprehensively and honestly.

Individual interviews

The principles of conducting the individual shortlist interview are as outlined for the initial interview. The interviewer may benefit by preparing some guideline notes on particular topics he feels more information is needed on, and then cover the areas of study systematically in a relaxed conversational style. If the recruiter did not conduct his own initial interviews then obviously there may be some repetition from the candidate's perspective in questions being asked of him. A chronological approach may aid the less experienced interviewer to ensure he covers the candidate's background and career thoroughly. The interviewer should have a copy of the application form at hand as a prompt, and continue to present a thorough, professional and neutral image in his interviewing role. It is generally better to avoid the use of particular company jargon or making critical comments about a candidate, his present employers, other candidates, or the interviewer's own company.

209

Panel interviews

This is an extension of the individual interview where several persons, each with a specific interest in the job vacancy (such as the line manager, department head, personnel manager), sit as a panel and put questions to the candidate (hopefully not all at the same time!). The environment is usually much less relaxed and more formal, as a panel will tend to group behind a desk or at one side of a room, and conversation flows less freely. There is also the risk that some panel members, perhaps acting out of inexperience, may ask questions of dubious relevance just to assert their presence or authority. It might be wise for a panel to agree in advance that one member acts as chairperson (although questions should be put directly rather than through the chair) just to keep communications flowing in relevant fashion. The candidate should not know at the end of the interview what any individual panel member thinks of him, although neutrality is often harder to maintain in groups.

Stress interviews

Occasionally companies feel it is beneficial to use aggressive interview situations, possibly where several panelists fire questions rapidly and simultaneously, presumably to assess a candidate's reactions under stress. This really must be a questionable purpose in such a contrived situation, and the most likely outcome is a degree of alienation of the candidate or confusion as to the direction and relevance of the questioning.

At the end of the selection process both parties should feel they have all the relevant information needed to take decisions each about the other.

Taking references

Once decisions have been reached on the candidate to whom the job offer is likely to be made, the personnel manager or prospective line manager should arrange to take up references. It is generally better to contact any personal referees and previous employers prior to the shortlist stage, but the current employer should only be contacted at the point where an offer is imminent. Some companies prefer to take all references at the same time.

References are usually best taken over the telephone. Previous employers and their personnel and line managers rarely reveal anything but factual comment in a written communication, which also results in delays whilst responses are awaited. A telephone contact gives the recruiter an excellent opportunity to probe. The recruiter will find referees more forthcoming if he can project a sincere, unaggressive, and friendly telephone manner. The recruiter should promptly establish who he is and why he is calling, and that it is with the permission of the candidate.

I would suggest that while taking references the recruiter should

210

have in front of him both the candidate's job application form and
any interview notes. Comments made by the referee may either be
noted clearly on these documents (perhaps in a different colour ink)
or on a separate and simply designed reference checking form that
might record:

- applicant's name
- position applied for
- referee contacted (name and position)
- date of taking the reference
- factual employment history, including
  - dates of employment
  - positions held
  - nature of duties and responsibilities
  - income levels
  - fringe benefits
  - timekeeping
  - comments on achievements and progress
  - reasons for leaving (if a previous employer)
  - current or previous line manager's attitude to the candidate
    leaving or seeking to change employment
  - comment on the candidate's re-employability with previous
    employers.
- character assessment, including comments on
  - integrity
  - reliability
  - independence
  - motivations
  - team spirit and ability to work with colleagues and customers
  - leadership
  - influence
  - flexibility and adaptability
  - strengths and weaknesses.

As part of the relaxing process, early questions are best aimed at
confirming the facts of previous employment, including employment
dates, job titles and responsibilities (as we all have a tendency to
exaggerate a little in this respect). Then lead into the character
reference area with open questions; the referee's response will
quickly indicate if much probing is needed. A question such as 'What
is your opinion of Bill as a salesman?' might elicit a stony silence
requiring a different approach if any information is to be obtained, or
it might produce an enthusiastic outburst of 'The best performer and
team member I ever had', which can readily lead into a discussion on
strengths and weaknesses with a follow-up question 'Oh! What made
Bill stand out so much in your team?'.
A reference should always seek to establish why a candidate did or

is leaving a company, and if he would be considered as re-employable
– was he an asset or a liability? When a recruiter can get no further
than a factual statement that the candidate was employed for a
certain period he should attempt tactfully to probe further to
whatever extent is practical and acceptable, and then decide if there
are issues to be raised further with the candidate prior to confirming
a provisional offer. It should not automatically be assumed that
silence or reticence reflect a negative attitude to an employee or
former employee: some companies have internal policies of doing no
more than confirming the fact of employment and not giving further
references; and, in the case of previous employers, it is possible that
the candidate's line manager has also left the employ of the company,
leaving a personnel officer to supply a reference with no guidelines
except the cold details in a file.

MAKING THE APPOINTMENT

Whatever the complexity of the selection process and the number of
stages used, in the final analysis each candidate should be viewed as a
'whole' person, rather than a number of separate parts or qualities as
identified at any stage in the proceedings, and judgements made
accordingly on the most suitable person to be appointed. In this text I
have devoted considerable space to the selection process because
recruitment of the right individuals to sales and sales management
positions is critical in an environment where the emphasis is always
on achievement of objectives, forecasts, targets and growth in
absolute and market share terms.

The appointment offer to the selected candidate would generally
be made by the new line manager rather than a personnel manager,
but it should always be checked to ensure that it is comprehensive in
detailing the terms and conditions of employment (which may form
part of a separate contract of employment). Generally a mutually
acceptable starting date will be agreed, and assistance offered in
locating suitable accommodation if this is required. Relocation terms
should have been discussed at an earlier stage, but confirmed at the
time of making an appointment. If the appointment is conditional in
any way, such as upon a satisfactory medical or references (which
should be pursued and checked promptly and thoroughly), that
should be made clear. More than one company has faced the
embarrassment of not clarifying certain conditions, and finding that
the candidate has given notice to a current employer to learn
subsequently that a conditional offer cannot be confirmed.

After the appointment offer has been accepted, the line manager
then has the task of designing a personalised induction training
programme to ensure that the new manager's arrival is met with the
continued professionalism demonstrated throughout the selection
process.

Example 6.2 will aid the reader in designing and implementing an effective recruitment system to cover each of the stages of the recruitment process discussed in the text.

Example 6.2 The recruitment process flow chart

Identify the vacancy → Prepare a job description → Prepare a job holder profile → Review alternative sources of applicants → Prepare and place media advertisement → Receive application letters and c.v.s → Send application forms and job descriptions to applicants → Receive completed application forms → Invite to initial interview → Conduct initial interviews → Select shortlist → Final shortlist interview process → Final candidate evaluations → Make offer to 1st choice candidate → Offer acceptance

Appoint from these sources if suitable candidate identified

Candidate self-screening process

Reject unsuitable applications

Candidate self-screening process

Reject unsuitable applications

Hold possible applications

Candidate self-screening process

Reject unsuitable candidates

Further candidate self-screening

Reject unsuitable candidates

Hold 2nd favourite on reserve

Check references

Company medical

Release reserve with polite rejection letter

SUMMARY

- Key qualities needed in a salesperson include good standards of: integrity, reliability, intelligence, sincerity, empathy, self-confidence, appearance, resilience, adaptability, independence and loyalty. Managers need additionally to demonstrate qualities of: leadership, determination, enthusiasm, influence, assimilation, objectivity and impartiality as well as excellent personal selling and communication skills.

- Salespersons need certain skill levels – depending on the nature of the products, markets and seniority – in verbal, numerical, technical, administrative and interpersonal skills.

- The first stage in the recruitment process is the preparation of a comprehensive job description and job holder profile, both of these being required to ensure that candidates' qualities, experience and skills can be objectively measured against the requirements of the job.

- There are several sources of potential candidates for any vacancy, including: present employees of the company, personal contacts, referrals, media advertising, competitors, recruitment and employment agencies.

- To aid the recruitment process at the initial screening stage it may be advantageous to request all applicants to complete and return a standardised job application form that solicits information that may be compared with requirements of a job holder profile.

- Any recruitment advertising should aim to attract attention, inform about the job, arouse interest, create desire and motivate the submission of applications from suitable parties. It should state job titles, responsibilities, the company, location, to whom the job reports, minimum candidate qualifications, rewards and benefits, and how to apply.

- Applications should be screened objectively by comparing qualifications, characteristics and skills with requirements in the job holder profile.

- Initial interviews ideally should be conducted in a relaxed, informal environment, and a systematic approach followed designed to elicit information relevant to the applicant's capabilities and abilities to perform the job functions effectively. Interviewers may prefer to work through the information contained in a c.v. or application form using a questioning approach of **how? why? what?**.

- A shortlist may be drawn up of most suitable candidates after initial interviews. The final selection process should be designed to enable direct comparisons and objective assessments and measurements to be made; it might include some of: tests of intelligence, aptitude or personality; group or individual tasks; and further interviews.

CHECKLIST   QUALITIES AND SKILLS AUDIT

Below is a list of the main qualities and skills likely to be needed to varying degrees by salespersons and sales managers. A weighting should be attached to each item (and any others the reader wishes to add) on the two separate lists, such that the weighting points total 100 on each list. Each individual can then be personally rated on the scale from 1 to 6 against each factor. In the last column multiply the weighting by the scale rating, enter the result, and then total up all the figures in the last column to give a grand total at the bottom.

An average score would be 350, and internal considerations might aid the sales manager in assessing at what level his subordinates should score.

Factor	Weighting	Rating score 1 2 3 4 5 6	Weighting × score
Qualities Integrity Reliability Sincerity Empathy Self-confidence Intelligence Appearance Resilience Adaptability Independence Maturity Loyalty Leadership Initiative Decisiveness Enthusiasm Determination Energy/drive Objectivity Impartiality			
TOTAL	100		
Skills Verbal Numerical Technical Administrative Organisational Communicating Interpersonal Personal selling			
TOTAL	100		

CHECKLIST   RECRUITMENT STAGES

	Action	Notes

Job description
Is it current?
Has it been checked against functions of job holders?

Job holder profile
Is it current?
Has it been checked against successful job holders?

Sources of applicants
What sources have been checked and researched:
- internal?
- personal contacts?
- advertisements?
- competitors?
- employment agencies?
- professional institutions?
- management search firms?
- educational institutions?

Job application form
Is it suitable for the job?
Does it ask relevant questions to facilitate pre-interview
  screening?
Has it been sent to all applicants?

Advertisement
Does it:
- attract attention?
- inform?
- arouse interest?
- create desire?
- sell the benefits?
- provoke response?
- state the job title?
- identify the company?
- give reasons for the vacancy?
- give key functions and responsibilities?
- give location?
- identify candidate qualifications?
- state rewards and benefits?
- tell how to apply?
Has the advertisement been placed with the media?

Telephone screening
Is it appropriate?
Has a screening question form been prepared?
Does the advertisement give the phone-in details?

Application screening
Have application forms been sent to candidates?
Has all screening been conducted by comparison with
  the job holder profile?
Have application acknowledgements been sent?
Have interview invitations been sent?
Have rejection letters been sent?

Initial interviews
Have dates been arranged?
Have locations been agreed?
Have all interviews been conducted?
Have rejection letters been sent?
Have shortlist invitations been sent?

Shortlist
Have dates and locations been arranged?
Have recruiting panel been advised of details?
Interviews conducted?
Tests:
- intelligence?
- aptitude?
- personality?
Have rejection letters been sent?

References
Have former employers been contacted?
Has present employer been contacted?
Have other personal referees been contacted?

Appointment letter/contract
Has a conditional offer letter been sent?
Has company medical been satisfactorily completed?
Has final offer/contract been:
- sent?
- accepted?

217

Category	What? How? Why?
Physical make-up	
Appearance	
Bearing	
Speech	
Disabilities	
Peculiarities/mannerisms	
Attainments	
Formal educational standards	
Educational attainments	
Additional training	
Job history	
• reasons for taking jobs	
• progress (absolute and relative to peers)	
• tangible results	
• reasons for changing jobs	
• relationships with colleagues and supervisors	

continued

Checklist   Interview notes (contd.)

General intelligence General intellect Width/depth of interests Problem-solving abilities Academic excellence Achievements Rate of assimilation	
Special aptitudes Mechanical Technical Linguistic Artistic	
Interests Intellectual Social Cultural Practical Active/passive	
Disposition/personality Social interactions Influence Self-reliance Maturity Dependability Acceptability	
Circumstances Family background Early schooling Environmental upbringing Stability Family circumstances/expectations Present circumstances Family commitments Financial commitments Mobility Attitudes (religious, social, economic)	
Motivations Influence/power Social needs Recognition Status Physiological needs Rewards/greed Achievement/success	

219

In principle, the more senior the position the broader the terms of reference used in the body of a job description and, conversely, the more junior the position the more detailed and specific will be the terms of reference.

Example 1

Department: Sales

Job title: National Sales Manager

Responsible to: Managing Director

Responsible for: All sales personnel both located at the head office and within the field sales force (approximately 70 persons); sales volumes of about £50 million; total sales force and promotional budgets of around £5 million; company vehicles, equipment and other tangible assets of around £2 million.

Main purpose of the job:
To achieve the plans, forecasts and targets agreed with the main board, and control budgets within the limits of the annual financial plan. To provide leadership and create an environment and system for the recruitment, training and motivation of subordinates to ensure they have the qualities, abilities, skills, desire and determination to perform their job functions with a level of productivity that ensures the achievement of objectives, plans, forecasts and targets.

Key functions and responsibilities:
1 To prepare monthly and annual sales forecasts, targets, plans and budgets acceptable to the board and in line with company objectives and procedures.
2 To be responsible for achievement against all sales forecasts, plans, programmes and budgets, and the implementation of company policies as they relate to the sales organisation.
3 To design and develop a sales force structure and organisation that can effectively implement all programmes and plans necessary to achieve the forecasts, targets and budgets.
4 To provide leadership to the sales force, at both management and territory personnel levels, and to develop and maintain high standards of morale.
5 To recruit and provide all necessary training for all subordinate personnel to ensure that each has the qualities, abilities and skills needed in his particular job function to perform satisfactorily and aid in the achievement of the overall forecasts, plans, targets and programmes, and to contribute to the development and implementation of strategies that promote the achievement of company objectives.
6 To develop the abilities and skills of each subordinate through training, counselling, appraisal, etc., with the aim of creating a pool of promotable talented individuals to ensure the management succession of the sales division.
7 To prepare, develop and implement other programmes and strategies, including sales promotional activities, within budgetary limits, that support the marketing effort and aid the achievement of objectives, including in-store promotional activities, exhibitions, display material, sales aids, etc.
8 To develop systems to develop and monitor performance of all subordinate functions and the sales organisation as a whole against objectives, forecasts, plans, targets and budgets, and to provide feedback to subordinates on individual and company performance.

9   To liaise with the Marketing Division to develop and implement terms of trade, including pricing structures, rebates, discounts and allowances that are acceptable and comparable with normal trade custom and practice whilst also ensuring the profitability of products.

10 To organise the sales force to provide optimum coverage of all established customers and to identify and develop new potential outlets for company products.

11 To develop sales support functions such as Customer Service and Order Processing departments that will liaise with field personnel and operate alongside other sales office functions to maximise customer goodwill through the provision of support services.

12 To develop a key account function meeting the special needs of the company and customers who operate with multiple unit or branch operations with the objective of optimising sales through such organisations.

13 To develop good communications both within the sales organisation and with other company departments, and with customers.

14 To develop and recommend corrective actions and implement corrective action as appropriate where deviations in performance below plans occur in any market sector, or where other problems occur that affect sales or customer goodwill.

15 To manage the sales organisation according to company policies including those contained in the Personnel Practices Manual.

Authority:

1   To hire and terminate the employment of any subordinate subject in compliance with the company's personnel practices and procedures and within the limits of manning levels agreed and including in the annual plan and budget.

2   To remunerate and reward subordinates within the limits imposed by current salary scales contained in the annual plan and budgets.

3   To approve the expenses of all subordinates up to a limit of £1000 per individual on any one weekly expense claim.

4   To spend and account for such sums as are specified in the annual plan and budget, including capital equipment, administrative costs, salaries, sales force promotional activities, other rebates, discounts and allowances.

Example 2

Department: Sales

Job title: Area Sales Manager

Responsible to: National Sales Manager

Responsible for: 6 to 8 territory sales representatives

Main purpose of the job:
To manage the area sales team to achieve the company plans and objectives and sales forecasts applicable to the area.

Key functions and responsibilities:

1   To provide leadership and manage, motivate and control subordinate territory salespersons.

2   To recruit territory salespersons, in liaison with the Personnel Department, to ensure scheduled coverage can be maintained, selecting recruits from persons considered to meet the essential requirements of the job holder profile for the position.

3   To provide field sales training to ensure that all subordinates have the requisite skills and abilities to perform all their job functions competently and professionally.

4   To assist the sales training manager in designing and developing head office induction and initial sales training courses and to attend such courses as necessary to assist with the actual training.

5   To provide feedback, counselling and appraisals to all subordinates with the objective of maintaining and improving individual morale and performance, identifying personal development training needs and to provide ongoing training to meet individual development needs. Formal appraisals should be conducted at least every six months.

6   To prepare territory and area sales forecasts for each territory under his control, and liaise with the Sales Planning Department to agree specific sales forecasts and targets in line with the overall company plans and objectives.

7   To manage, motivate and control the area sales team to ensure all plans, forecasts, targets and other objectives are achieved.

8   To develop specific promotional activity within budgetary limits with individual accounts to aid in achievement of forecasts and plans.

9   To achieve the area's distribution and display objectives agreed with the National Sales Manager, including the setting of subordinate territory distribution and display objectives, and to monitor performance against objectives.

10 To maximise customer goodwill and maintain a high company image of professionalism, competence, efficiency and concern with customers.

11 To provide reports and feedback to the Sales Planning Department on competitive activity and market intelligence, including information on prices, products, promotions, advertising, sales force organisations, etc.

12 To communicate with territory salespersons by means of bulletins, occasional area meetings, etc., to maximise job involvement and commitment and ensure an understanding of company policies, plans and programmes.

13 To assist the Sales Planning Department as required in the organisation and conduct of national sales conferences.

14 To maintain scheduled coverage of existing outlets and identify and develop new potential outlets for the company's products.

15 To liaise with Customer Service Department on matters of customer credit, and monitor the payment of all accounts as due within the area limits to minimise overdue accounts.

Authority:

1   To recommend compensation levels of subordinates within current salary scale limits, approval coming from the National Sales Manager.

2   To authorise expenses of subordinates up to a limit of £500 per individual on any one weekly expense claim form (higher claims to be referred to the National Sales Manager).

3   To commit to and authorise expenditure within budgetary and plan limits for specific promotional activity with individual accounts subject to satisfactory sales performance according to the agreements made with the particular customers.

4   To recruit for vacant territories to ensure maintenance of scheduled call coverage.

5   To recommend the termination of subordinates to the National Sales Manager on grounds of unsatisfactory performance or conduct, or other relevant reason, after compliance with normal company personnel practices relating to disciplinary matters.

6   To appraise, counsel or issue formal warnings to subordinates in accordance with company personnel practices.

Example 3

Department: Sales

Job title: Territory Salesperson

Responsible to: Area Sales Manager

Responsible for: Achievement of territory sales plans, forecasts and budgets; increasing product distribution and display in line with objectives for the territory; maintenance of customer goodwill.

Main purpose of the job:

To maximise sales volumes, display and distribution of the company's products in outlets within the boundaries of the assigned territory, and to provide call coverage of all outlets according to the territory journey cycle schedule. To identify and develop new outlets and customers for the company's products.

Key functions and responsibilities:

1 To call on each customer in the assigned territory at the prescribed frequency detailed in the journey cycle schedule to obtain orders for the company's products in relation to the potential of the customers.

2 To maintain and improve the display of the company's products in each outlet visited, and particularly to seek displays at key traffic points in retail outlets.

3 To maintain and increase levels of distribution of the company's products in existing outlets and new potential outlets.

4 To identify and develop new potential outlets for the company's products.

5 To set and develop specific objectives for each outlet in the territory and to work towards the achievement of those objectives, maintaining records of progress and activity.

6 To liaise with the Area Manager to develop and achieve overall territory objectives in respect of sales volumes, display and distribution levels.

7 To organise sales promotional activity with suitable accounts in accordance with guidelines laid down by the Sales Planning Department or the Area Sales Manager, including feature displays and consumer special offers.

8 To comply diligently with all administrative requirements of the job, including:

- maintenance of accurate customer records of stock, orders, promotional activity, calls made, buyer contact details, etc.
- completion of Daily Activity Reports
- weekly submission of expenses to the Area Sales Manager for approval
- daily despatch of orders received to the Order Processing Department
- completion of such other administrative requirements as may be specified by head office departments and the Area Sales Manager.

9 To conduct himself in a professional manner at all times, including the maintenance of good appearance acceptable to customers and management to maximise customer goodwill towards the company and the salesperson.

10 To care for and maintain all company documents, materials and other equipment under his control, including customer record cards, display and sales aids, manuals, and the company vehicle (which should be serviced according to the manufacturer's recommendations and by authorised garages and dealers).

11 To restrict customers' credit within agreed credit limits and seek payment of invoices outstanding beyond normal terms and periods of payment.

Authority:

1 To negotiate sales promotional activity within prescribed limits and budgets in liaison with the Area Sales Manager and subject to post-promotion approval of rebates and allowances by the Area Sales Manager.

2 To identify and open new creditworthy accounts within credit limits that might be imposed by the Customer Service Department.

224

3   No authority to vary standard prices, terms and conditions of trade, to offer inducements to customers in any form other than specific approved promotional allowances, or to offer or provide any guarantees or warranties in addition to those specified on the wrappers or packaging of products or contained within the terms of trade appearing on the company's standard order forms.

APPENDIX 2   JOB HOLDER PROFILE

Company: Computer Services Ltd,

Position: Export Sales Manager

Reporting to: Sales Director

REQUIREMENTS

Factor	*Essential*	*Desirable*
Physical characteristics		
Age	• 28 to 40	• 30 to 35
Height/weight		• 5′ 10″ to 6′ 2″
Health	• no recurring illnesses • no visible physical disabilities	• low sickness incidence
Appearance	• well groomed	• Caucasian/Arab
Attainments		
Education	• first degree	• computer science or related first or higher degree
Languages	• English	• Arabic
Employment	• 2 years experience in computer field, with systems or operations work	• domestic and international selling experience • computer consultancy experience
Special aptitudes	• highly numerate • good communicator	• good report writer, planner & organiser
Personality	• self sufficient • independent • high integrity • self-motivator • creative in identifying market opportunity	• adaptable • flexible • requires minimum supervision
Interests	• problem-solving • intellectual	• physically fit through exercise • well versed in current international affairs • sociable • practical involvements
Disposition	• acceptable to clients • team member	• outgoing but not flippant
Circumstances	• flexibility to travel extensively • must live within 1 hour of office • general family circumstances conducive to travel • immediately available	• single or married without children, or with teenage children

Note: It is very possible that the job holder profile might beneficially be expanded to give qualitative measures to subjective areas.

APPENDIX 3   A BASIC JOB APPLICATION FORM

NATIONAL FOODS COMPANY PLC.	EMPLOYMENT APPLICATION

Applicant's full name:

Present address:	Tel: Home
	Business

Rented/owned:	Period of residence:

Last previous address:	Tel: Home
	Business

Rented/owned	Period of residence:

Date of birth:	Sex: Male ☐ Female ☐	Height: Weight:

Nationality: At birth? Now?	Do you hold a current driving licence? Yes ☐ No ☐

Marital status: Single ☐ Married ☐ Date Divorced ☐ Date	Detail any current or previous endorsements or driving convictions:

Dependants: Number of children Ages Number of other dependants	
	Medical history: Previous illnesses and operations Present state of health
Are you prepared to relocate? If yes, which are your preferred locations?	Recurring illnesses or disabilities

Position applied for:

Source of application:

Do you have now, or have you ever had, any relatives working for us?
Yes ☐   No ☐   If yes, who?   Relationship?

Have you ever applied for a position with us before? Yes ☐   No ☐
If yes, position   when

FOR COMPANY OFFICE USE ONLY
Date application form sent: Date received back:
Action taken:

PLEASE PRINT OR TYPE ALL INFORMATION YOU ARE SUPPLYING

227

EDUCATION

	Names and location	Dates attended From	To	Examinations and qualifications	Special achievements
Primary schools					
Secondary schools					
Universities and higher education					

MILITARY SERVICE
From: To:
Service: Branch: Rank on discharge:
Main duties:
Special training received:

Main interests whilst attending full-time educational establishments:

EMPLOYMENT HISTORY	Are you currently employed? Yes ☐ No ☐

List in reverse chronological order

Name and address of employer	Position held	From	To	Main responsibilities and duties, including number of subordinates	Reason for leaving
				Starting salary £ Final salary £	
				Starting salary £ Final salary £	
				Starting salary £ Final salary £	
				Starting salary £ Final salary £	

Give details of any other positions previously held on a separate sheet of paper and attach to this form

Summarise any part-time employment undertaken whilst you were still attending full-time education

1.   2.   3.

INTERESTS
Give details of your current main interests and activities outside of the working environment

LANGUAGES
Please note any foreign languages you speak or write and indicate the level of your fluency (e.g. basic, average, good, bilingual)
    1.
    2.
    3.

REFERENCES

List whom we may contact at your present or past employers for references. No contact will be made with your present employer without your prior agreement.

Person to contact: *Company*   *Telephone no.*
1.

          Position
2.

          Position
3.

          Position

Give the details of two personal referees (not employers or relatives) who have known you for at least 3 years, and whom we may contact for personal references.

Name and address of person to contact: *Relationship*   *Telephone no.*
1.

2.

SUMMARY OF EXPERIENCE AND SUPPORTING STATEMENTS
Please summarise your work experience, special achievements and skills which will support your application for employment with us. You may also wish to note any other factors relevant to your application.

Period of notice
How much notice will you be required to give your present employer?

I confirm the above information supplied by me is correct, and understand that incorrect statements could result in the termination of employment should I be employed as a result of submitting this application. I also understand that any offer of employment would be conditional on my submitting to and passing a company medical examination and satisfactory references being obtained.

Signed: Date:

Return the completed form to the Personnel Department,
National Foods Co. plc, P.O. Box 123, Manchester.

7 Basic Sales Training

The training of subordinates has been mentioned frequently in this text as a fundamental responsibility of the sales manager. He can delegate that responsibility to a sales training manager or, since each line manager is held accountable for the performance of the persons he manages and controls, to the specific line manager of any individual within the sales organisation. This chapter will review the areas of basic sales training that might be covered at the initial entry into a selling career.

THE ROLE OF TRAINING

Why train?   The purpose of training is to:

- impart knowledge (of the company, its products and its markets)
- create or change attitudes that affect performance
- develop skills that increase performance
- develop habits that contribute to improved performance.

In the selling environment skill training may more specifically be directed towards:

- better territory/account management, including identifying potential outlets and planning call coverage
- more efficient time utilisation
- improved negotiating skills, including making presentations, handling customer objections and closing the sale
- managing the administration associated with the territory
- setting call objectives and managing by objectives
- post-call analysis resulting in self-appraisal of performance and self-development programmes.

Training may have a major benefit in reducing the amount of supervision subsequently needed by salespersons, which might enable field sales managers to widen their span of control and accept responsibility for additional subordinates, wider geographical areas, additional functions and so on, with obvious cost benefits to the company. Training may well also have the benefit of reducing sales force turnover as the sales team improves performance and thereby their satisfactions with the job in terms of status, recognition, rewards, promotion, prospects and management.

231

The training required by any individual will really be a function of:

- his existing knowledge, experience and skill levels
- his aptitude for the job
- his attitude to the job
- his rate of assimilation
- his adaptability and flexibility
- his ambitions and motivations
- the 'training gap' between the standards required and his actual performance.

The amount of training needed is not necessarily a function of age, although field sales managers are often sensitive to longer serving salespersons who they feel are under-performing or 'off the boil'.

It is assumed here that the persons requiring training have been identified as having the basic aptitudes, attitudes, and other characteristics relevant to the job, otherwise the training may prove a long, arduous, and possibly relatively unproductive process.

The next consideration in assessing training needs is what current levels of skills and experience the trainee has, and what previous training has been experienced. A complete newcomer to selling may be included on basic induction and introductory sales training programmes. The training of a person who has previous selling experience or skill levels needs to be planned with consideration to:

- frequency of use of those skills
- recency of use of the skills
- rate of assimilation of new information
- adaptability
- level of interest and personal motivation.

If the skills have been regularly used, then formal sales training may be less necessary than a programme of analysis and feedback at the field level, following a brief induction to the company and the products.

Identification of the performance deficiencies of individual salespersons should be objectively conducted by the line managers, giving attention to such aspects as:

- achievement against objectives (assuming objectives were both realistic and achievable)
- analysis of the conversion rate of orders to calls
- analysis of call rates compared with standards or average achievement of the sales team
- identification of new potential customers
- success in obtaining new product listings, key display sites, feature displays, etc.

- effectiveness of sales presentations
- ability to overcome objections and objection handling techniques
- techniques and success at closing the sale
- customer relationships
- relationship between territory cost of operations and sales values compared with standards or averages
- ability to comply with and compliance with company administrative requirements and procedures.

It is particularly beneficial for a line manager to ask his subordinates for their own views on their training needs, strengths and weaknesses, and to relate this to the manager's views and assessments so that they can work together to develop a training programme to improve skills and performance to an agreed timetable. Most line managers become quite sensitive to 'the cries for help' from their subordinates, manifest sometimes by increased rates of sickness, absence or late starting.

In assessing training needs and developing individual programmes managers should be aware of the difficulties of creating a 'new person'. It is easier to build on strengths than change personality or totally overcome weaknesses. Provided that all essential skill requirements are at least at a satisfactory minimum level, the sales training effort might actually contribute more to overall improvement of performance if directed to developing strengths further, rather than to imparting skills in an area of particular weakness. The line manager himself must be flexible in identifying training needs and assessing the relative improvement potential from any training effort, and sensitive to the overall objective of maximising individual and team performance from limited resources in terms of training time.

Whilst training is critical to developing skills and improving performance, it is only one factor in the overall achievement of results. The others are:

- motivation (personal, and by management)
- objective setting and measurement
- rewards and incentives
- feedback and performance appraisal.

Who to train and when

If skills are to be increased, performance improved, and individuals to adapt to changing markets, business conditions and work environments, everyone should be trained all the time, with constant review of needs.

New salespersons need training in company orientation, products and basic selling skills. Established salespersons need ongoing training in developing new business, territory management, more advanced selling skills, refresher courses in basic selling skills, and personal development training to fit them for promotion. Problem salespersons need guidance and training to correct deficiencies specifically identified as correctable. Managers need training in management techniques, including motivation and training.

DEVELOPING INITIAL SALES TRAINING PROGRAMMES

A basic training programme can be designed around imparting and developing skills in:

- company knowledge
- product knowledge
- developing a sales sequence
- selling techniques
- use of sales aids
- communicating effectively
- administrative aspects of the job
- pace control
- journey planning.

Company knowledge

It is customary in most training programmes for new employees to have a period of induction training during which they are familiarised with:

- **the company**:
  - its management structures, organisation, reporting relationships
  - its role in the industry
  - company history and development
  - company performance
  - objectives for the future
  - management philosophies and style
  - personnel policies and practices
  - tours of plants and facilities
- **the products**:
  - historical product development
  - current product range, including design aspects, packaging, specifications
  - legal aspects relating to the products and markets, such as health, safety and labelling regulations
  - manufacturing operations
  - product development and expansion plans
  - competitors and their products, with relevant operational and benefit comparisons
  - the markets for the products
  - marketing programmes and support.

234

This serves to reduce uncertainties and make the new employee feel a welcome member of the team. It may be considered opportune and useful to:

- provide basic materials relating to the company such as: published accounts, product literature, samples, organisation charts, statements of company philosophy and policy and company objectives, personnel practices guidelines or manuals, job descriptions (likely to have been provided previously during the recruitment process, but a further copy may facilitate discussion on duties and responsibilities)
- have individual aspects of the induction programme presented by a variety of different managers from relevant departments. This serves to let the new starter meet a number of colleagues and associates and relate their roles and functions in the organisation to his own function, thereby promoting more team spirit and awareness; it is particularly beneficial for salespersons who do not have a day-to-day opportunity to meet with colleagues, relying more heavily on written or telephone communications.

The process of selling

Selling is concerned with satisfying the needs of customers and presenting solutions to their problems. This involves communicating the product benefits to customers and not just listing product attributes or features. Training in the selling process involves imparting skills in identifying customer problems and needs and relating these to product benefits derived from product features. Whether the salesperson is involved in high technology industries or mass market consumer goods, the basic steps in the selling process include:

- identifying potential customers and their internal decision-making processes
- analysing their product needs
- setting relevant objectives for the customer
- obtaining a meeting with the decision maker
- presenting the products and product benefits in relation to identified needs
- responding to any objections in a manner satisfactory to the customer
- closing the sale by asking for the order
- completing post-call administration and follow-up.

These steps should be expanded into a system or **call sequence** that can form the basis for initial sales training. Salespersons trained to follow the sequence are less likely to miss any stage important in the process of obtaining an order or achieving a call objective. The

Example 7.1 Call sequences

F.M.C.G. PRODUCTS

1 **Prepare for the call:**
   - establish call objectives
   - check sales aids and samples
   - study call records of recent performance
2 **Make the approach:**
   - relax the customer
   - identify the purpose of the call
3 **Check product display:**
   - condition
   - volumes
4 **Gain access to stocks:**
   - check stock levels
   - identify products in stock but not on display or with inadequate shelf stocks
5 **Additional merchandising:**
   - refill allocated shelf spaces
   - build agreed feature displays
6 **Analyse order requirements:**
   - prepare an order related to offtake
7 **Present a positive order:**
   - include regular replacement stock, new products and promotions, in the presentation to the buyer
8 **Overcome objections:**
   - use appropriate objection handling techniques
9 **Close the sale:**
   - use appropriate variation of the closing techniques
10 **Complete post-call administration:**
   - update call record cards
   - complete order forms, etc.

INDUSTRIAL PRODUCTS

1 **Preparation:**
   - set call objectives
   - prepare sales aids
2 **Approach:**
   - identify and relax the buyer
   - establish purpose of the visit
3 **Analyse needs:**
   - review buyer's current systems and practices
   - identify unsatisfied needs
   - relate needs to seller's products or processes
4 **Survey the facilities:**
   - survey customer operations to identify equipment needs, possible location sites, costs
5 **Present positive proposal:**
   - based on survey and needs analysis
6 **Overcome objections:**
   - listen
   - identify real objections
   - provide suitable responses
7 **Close the sale:**
   - agree supply terms and conditions
   - obtain the order or supply contract
8 **Complete post-call administration:**
   - complete necessary paperwork
   - liaise between all departments to ensure commitments are honoured.

call sequence may be specific to a company or industry, although some stages in the sequence are common to any industry or sales situation, whether in consumer goods, industrial or retail sales environments.

Possible sales call sequences for a fast moving consumer goods company and an industrial products company might look like the examples in Example 7.1. In a typical f.m.c.g. selling environment all stages of the sales call sequence would be conducted consecutively over a short time span whilst at the customer location.

For many major industrial supply contracts, the various stages of the call sequence may be spread over several meetings, depending on the time needed to progress satisfactorily through each stage (it takes time to complete and evaluate surveys of customer facilities, and complicated offers require careful evaluation by customers). A logical sequence is still necessary to reduce the risk of sales being lost because of poor planning and presentation. Such call sequences can just as readily be developed for a salesperson of double glazing, insurance, or any goods or services.

Prior to commencing the training of salespersons the sales manager should give time and effort to developing his own sales call sequence relevant to his market, customers and products; this may satisfactorily form the core of initial sales training courses.

Techniques in selling

Specific training must be given on each stage of the sales call sequence to provide clear understanding and skills. I am here assuming that a formal initial training programme is being conducted internally at the company's offices or training facilities. It is, of course, perfectly possible for similar training to be provided in the field selling environment under the supervision of the appropriate field sales manager.

For untrained recruits it is often desirable to commence with a period of theoretical training, role playing and consolidation before entering the 'real world' of actually calling on customers. This serves to build a degree of knowledge, confidence and basic skill levels. A larger company may have sophisticated sales training facilities, including simulated shops or sales environments. A small company may simply have to make do with a meeting room and prepared 'flip' charts. Wherever the training takes place, the most suitable trainers are experienced sales managers – either field sales managers alone, or a staff **sales training manager** aided by field sales managers. They can create confidence amongst trainees, imparting knowledge and skills seen as relevant to the actual sales environment and its problems.

Training should ideally be very **participative** and **practical**, with an emphasis on **doing** and **role playing** to maximise learning over a given period of time.

237

Preparation

The key to a successful call is often found at the preliminary stages of preparation and making the approach to the customer. Trainees need to be familiar with the sales aids available to them, such as price lists, catalogues, other brochures, samples, display material, advertising outlines. From the perspective of personal preparation and organisation it is useful to train and encourage salespersons to consolidate all standards information in a **sales presentation folder**, which could be taken into every call along with other aids and documents specifically related to that call. The salesperson needs practice in checking his customer call records to establish the business history and buying habits, identify the buyers and other key people involved in purchasing decisions, and in setting **call objectives** prior to entering the call. If the company advocates the use of a standard customer call record card by salespersons then the system of recording and interpreting data should be taught and practised if good administrative habits are to be developed.

Approach

During the approach stage the salesperson is initially concerned with identifying the decision maker with purchasing authority (if not already known), gaining access to him rapidly, making a favourable impression and creating a professional rapport to enable a sales presentation to be made along the lines of the pre-set call objectives. It is at this stage that the first tests of resilience and adaptability may occur, as a buyer often keeps a salesperson waiting, which in itself may put pressure on the salesperson. When contact is finally made, the salesperson needs to be polite, positive and enthusiastic, and in relaxed control of the interview. Role playing in a training environment aids the acquisition of skills in making the initial approach.

Merchandising and stock-checking activities

These stages mainly apply to the consumer goods markets, and are a prerequisite to preparing and presenting an order to the buyer. Once initial contact has been made at the buyer's office, permission will normally be sought to check product displays, obtain access to stock to replenish displays, and then count stock levels (also checking for damaged merchandise), all before returning to the buyer to present a proposed order. Displays need to be checked for location, condition of merchandise, volume of merchandise on display, compliance with any special display agreements made with the customer, supporting display material, and additional feature display activity. At the initial training stage, new trainees need to familiarise themselves with the company's products and competitors' products, and learn to identify products quickly, count stocks accurately, price merchandise (if they will be working in an environment where goods are priced at the display points), and build displays quickly and efficiently. These are largely time-consuming mechanical functions where slowness can be costly in terms of reduced call rates.

Preparing an order

The salesperson will need to use his stock count to estimate the order requirements. Basic theoretical training can be given in the techniques of estimating average sales and product movement of repeat purchase products over any given period, such as the last three call periods, and of calculating orders. For example, if the call record card shows stock and order levels at the time of each call, average product movement over a regular call cycle (say one month) can be calculated by simple mental arithmetic. If there have been out of stock positions at the time of recent calls then clearly the quantities ordered need to be adjusted to correct that situation since both parties are losing potential sales volume. If stocks are building up then an analysis needs to determine whether that is purely the result of over-ordering or whether it is related to some other factor such as inadequate or incorrect display, product merchandising or pricing. Allowance must also be made for the lead times from ordering to delivery plus some reserve contingency stock.

If an example is taken of a call on a four-weekly cycle where delivery lead times are normally two weeks, and reserve stocks are set at an additional two weeks, then minimum stocks at the time of making a call should equate to four weeks' average sales throughput. The salesperson should balance orders such that stock at the time of the call plus the order placed would equal eight weeks' average sales.

It might be wise to develop clear guidelines and a basic formula to aid in order calculation and avoid lost sales. If deliveries of standard products can be effected within one week, then the presented formula might look like:

Average weekly throughput
times
Number of weeks between calls
plus
Delivery lead time allowance (1 week's throughput)
plus
Reserve stock (1 week's throughput)

Thus in a four-weekly call the opening stock and order should equal six weeks' average throughput; and in a two-weekly call it might be four weeks' average throughput. Practice in the training environment will enable a new recruit quickly to get used to the estimation of order requirements.

Even in industries where there are no systems of standard repeat sales, such as door-to-door selling of home improvements, the salesperson needs training and practice in preparing accurate estimates if

239

sales are not to be lost. Customers will surely seek alternative estimates and may lose confidence in a salesperson who returns with the claim that he made an error in initial quotes.

In some larger f.m.c.g. companies computers have taken over the function of keeping customer stock and order records. Order forms can be computer generated in response to the information entered on the form containing the last order placed. Such a computer order form might require stock levels to be entered along with the order, so that average throughput by product over any specific time period can be advised on reprints of the order form.

Presenting a positive order

Once the salesperson has estimated the order requirements, or prepared his estimates and quotes, it is time to seek the buyer's attention again and present a **positive order**. The buyer's response will in part be influenced by the confidence of the salesperson. Training therefore needs to concentrate on techniques of presenting a positive order. It is all too easy for the experienced manager to assume that discussion of the theory of any step in the sales call sequence substitutes for practice, because the experienced sales-person has a good knowledge base upon which to build and therefore possibly a faster assimilation rate. An inexperienced recruit will need coaching in such basic steps as laying the suggested order in front of the buyer (correctly positioned so that the buyer can read it) and opening the presentation with such simple lines as 'I've checked your stocks, Mr Buyer, replenished the displays on the fixtures, and estimated that you need these quantities to cover your needs until my next call', or 'I've measured your windows and patio doors, Mr Householder, and estimated your secondary glazing requirements, and can quote you an all-inclusive installed price of . . .'. Once the salesperson can actually present an order with confidence he can be trained to modify it to take account of any adjustments needed in the order, for example to allow for likely increases in sales in response to advertising and promotion or seasonal or cyclical fluctuations in offtake or usage.

Overcoming objections

In the training environment it would be normal for the trainer acting in the buyer's role to introduce typically encountered objections into the role playing situation in order to develop skills in handling objections.

The trainee needs much practice in objection handling techniques so that presentations can be successfully closed. If the buyer feels he is being given scripted responses, he is likely to react negatively. A sequence in handling objections is better than a scripted series of answers to standard objections. One simple sequence is:

240

- lessen the objection by listening
- indicate understanding and acceptance of the matter as a worthy consideration
- pause (show concern and interest in the customer and his particular problem)
- clarify with the buyer the key objection
- turn the objection into a question
- represent the relevant benefits that answer the objection or provide solutions acceptable to the buyer.

The trainee needs to learn not to respond either aggressively or flippantly and without apparent concern, because it is likely that the point raised by the buyer is a matter of serious concern. With training and experience the salesperson will learn to distinguish genuine objections from stalling tactics designed to avoid taking decisions or placing orders. Sometimes, particularly in industrial selling situations, objections are centred round the buyer's need for additional information, and this may involve the salesperson in subsequent research and repeat sales presentations.

Closing the sale

As there are many occasions when a straightforward positive presentation may not be expected to close the sale, trainees need coaching and role playing experience in the different closing techniques and in judging which technique to use. Training and role playing should cover:

- **confident close**: just asking for the order with confidence
- **concession close**: allowing the buyer the opportunity to adjust the order in some respect, the salesperson probably having assessed where the adjustment is likely to be made
- **alternative close**: presenting the buyer with a choice that assumes he wishes to place an order but has a decision to make on an aspect such as final quantity or delivery time, e.g. 'would you like 20 or 15 cases this time?', or 'would you prefer delivery this week or next?'
- **fear close**: generating a degree of fear in the buyer that if he does not order now he will lose some benefit, e.g. 'Orders not placed before Friday will not qualify for the promotional allowance'.

Post-call administration

Obviously it is essential that the sales team are fully trained in company administrative systems and procedures, and this topic is covered more fully later in this section.

Use of
sales aids

Particular attention may need to be paid to training in the correct effective and timely use of sales aids, such as brochures, catalogues, samples, display material, and promotional literature. Now that selling is becoming more sophisticated, many companies are developing additional sales aids for product launches and more technical presentations of products and services, including video films, cassettes, and portable presenters (perhaps built into a carrying case) designed on flip chart principles. The trainee salesperson has much to practise and assimilate in a short initial training course, and will, of course, rapidly gain experience in the field selling environ-ment; but at the role playing stages of a central training programme the trainer should ensure from the outset that all sales aids are available and used in demonstrations and exercises so that the trainee acquires good habits. The trainee should learn the need to appeal to as many of a buyer's senses as possible in order to control a presentation, retain interest and avoid distraction by surrounding activities. Field training often needs to reinforce the use of sales aids to continue the development of good habits.

To be effective, sales aids should be relevant to the subject of the presentation and aid and increase understanding, not complicate it. Information needs to be presented in a fashion that promotes interest, encourages buyer participation in the presentation, and aids assimilation of the information being presented. (Chapter 5 has a section on 'promotional sales literature' that could beneficially be read with this section.)

Effective communicating

Communicating is a two-way process. New salespersons need to be trained to watch and listen in the selling situation – to observe the buyer's verbal and non-verbal communications, including gestures, mannerisms and eyes. Observation, along with a good questioning technique, helps identify a buyer's attitudes, needs and motivations. The greater the understanding of the buyer and his needs the easier it is to relate product benefits to the perceived needs.

Communicating also involves the use of the telephone and written communications, and salespersons benefit considerably by training that improves skills in these forms of communication.

Administrative training

Most companies have quite a number and variety of documents and forms that pass to and from the sales team, including:

- customer record cards
- order forms (several copies may be routed to different recipients)
- product uplift notes
- credit notes
- daily activity reports
- journey planning documents
- sample request forms
- expense forms

- stationery request forms
- invoices
- product movement/despatch notes
- quote forms
- internal memo pads
- contact report forms
- in-store promotion control forms,

to mention just a few frequently found in one format or another. Of course, ideally there should be as few pieces of paperwork as possible to reduce the administrative burden and concentrate time and effort on practical selling. To increase efficiency during the working day and to minimise time given to administration during the day and at home in the evenings the initial training course should give time and attention to the correct use and completion of all standard administrative documents in use within the sales organisation. Training in the use of any particular form may be linked to a relevant point in the practical role playing exercises to put the item's use in context. Study and practice with forms and documents provides a useful short evening exercise during any residential training course.

Pace control

Initial training can give some emphasis to the need of salespersons to treat **time** as their scarcest resource. They must learn to control the pace of sales activities and presentations to maximise the effective selling time during the working day. The key phrases to remember are:

GET IN – GET ON – GET OUT

Journey planning

In a large company a salesperson may be taking over a regular established territory where all journey coverage plans have been previously prepared. In a smaller company or new sales organisation the sales training programme may beneficially incorporate guidelines on journey planning to minimise driving time and maximise selling time (Chapter 9 gives further coverage of this topic). If the nature of the product and markets is such that there are no set journeys, as with non-repeat sales products such as financial services or home improvements, then the training programme needs to cover the identification and pre-call screening of contacts and assignment into priority call categories according to relevant criteria.

Whilst these basic selling techniques, procedures and processes can be applied to any sales environment, training needs to be modified to suit a particular product, industry, company or market.

243

FURTHER CONSIDERATION OF THE INDUSTRIAL SELLING PROCESS

The markets
Although a sales sequence for industrial selling can be developed, as has been outlined in the previous section, there are differences between consumer and industrial and specialty markets. An industrial salesperson is usually offering to supply:

- plant or equipment (e.g. major or minor operating machinery)
- raw materials (e.g. essential basic material inputs)
- components (e.g. parts for inclusion in a finished product)
- supplies (e.g. packaging materials, stationery, etc.)
- services (e.g. financial, legal, insurance, cleaning, security).

Some of these inputs are productive, in that they are used as an input in the production process; others are simply a contributory overhead to the business operation.

Industrial markets differ from consumer markets in several respects that impact on sales opportunities and therefore on training:

- **Transaction size** Industrial or service supply contracts (including other services such as finance/insurance) often involve much greater sums of money than the consumer salesperson regularly deals with.
- **Purchasing motives** The professional buyer of industrial supplies is often much less concerned with emotive buying factors (such as status) and more with rational factors (such as value for money, functionality, quality, guarantees, after-sales or technical support service, supply continuity, operating costs, spare part availability, product reliability, delivery lead times).
- **Long-term supply agreements** Since an industrial user clearly cannot be left short of any input, the tendency is to fix prices, quantities and delivery times contractually for longer periods than is normal in consumer markets (6–18 months being quite common). A new prospective supplier usually has to wait until a supply contract renewal point to compete, and the present supplier always has an advantage.
- **Service support agreements** A manufacturer who buys or leases equipment that needs operating supplies (such as a photocopier) is usually obliged to purchase these from the original equipment supplier even if other sources have compatible and competitive products. (The initial lease may have been on particularly favourable terms in exchange for higher prices on operating supplies.)
- **Price negotiations** Whilst in consumer goods markets suppliers tend to fix supply prices according to standard terms and conditions, in industrial or service industries price may be a

244

negotiable factor dependent on quantities, product specifications, product modifications, distribution costs, seasonal availability factors, payment terms, etc.

- **Negotiation lead times** Supply contracts may take a long time (frequently many months in the case of complex products, customer requirements, or extensive product testing programmes) to negotiate. An order is rarely achieved with one visit.
- **Technical assistance** The potential buyer may need considerable technical assistance to incorporate the product in processes, or to adapt it to existing systems or existing systems to it, and this may involve a team of specialists working closely with the client for considerable periods before and after a sale and delivery to ensure correct specification, incorporation and functioning.
- **After-sales service** Industrial supplies may require service after delivery, or regular maintenance as part of price-inclusive guarantees or separate maintenance contracts, and a product likely to need continuing service is unlikely to be attractive to a buyer without the supplier's own service support.
- **Special relationships** It is quite common for a supplier of one product to another company to reciprocate by taking its own requirements for that company's products from that company. In the case of these (usually unwritten) 'favoured supplier' relationships, an outsider has his work cut out to win supply contracts even where the product offers competitive advantages.
- **Cash availability** Suppliers of industrial products are faced less often with major cash shortages within their customer groups (although all buyers seem to believe it is their right and duty to take maximum time to effect payments!) than are suppliers of consumer goods to the retail trade or direct to end users.
- **Cyclical fluctuations** Industrial demand depends on final user demand, but changes in user demand often impact with a lag in industrial demand, and in some industries the fluctuations are less severe (demand is more inelastic). In consumer goods markets, retailers will simply stop ordering and live off inventories as long as possible during a market downturn in offtake. Moreover, as the industrial concern is likely to be supplying output nationally, any particular regional fluctuations have less impact on a salesperson's market or performance.
- **Market coverage** Unlike consumer goods market outlets, the manufacturing industries in most countries are more frequently concentrated in certain geographical regions near to essential supplies, facilities or markets, and where there is identifiable cost benefit in location. This may make coverage of prospective customers simpler to organise.

Training programmes developed for salespersons specialising in industrial or other specialty markets therefore need to take account of any particular market structure factors.

We should consider briefly other key sales environment factors that may differ between consumer and industrial markets.

Customer identification

In addition to there often being fewer customers for industrial or specialty products and services, it is often a little easier to identify them and ascertain their suitability for further contact as well as to assign a priority in the contact-making programme. Advertisements in specialist journals will often produce enquiries from professional buyers or specialist customers with a particular interest in the product or service. Other potential customers may be readily identified through directories, trade associations, exhibitions and other trade gatherings. The training programme can possibly include a section concerned with:

- identifying potential customers and users
- ranking prospects for priority of contact according to factors such as: current usage of competitive products, potential usage, balance of time and quantities outstanding on existing supply contracts, and any other relevant data that can be elicited at initial contact stages.

Relationships

While the consumer goods salesperson may often be selling to a single buyer or decision maker (except, as discussed in the text, perhaps at key accounts), this is unlikely to be the case in industrial sales situations. Therefore considerable time and effort will need to be devoted to cultivating relationships not just with the buyer but also with all the other individuals and departments concerned with the product testing, specification, approval and final utilisation. For many products this is likely to include scientists, technicians and engineers. The salesperson may need not only technical expertise in order to relate to the specialists, but skill in cultivating relationships with those who have a direct or indirect influence on buying decisions. The limits of each person's authority and influence need to be identified and acted on in the selling process, and training programmes developed accordingly.

Some additional comments on the **sales sequence stages** illustrated in Example 7.1 above may be helpful.

Preparation

This is a stage at which thoroughness is essential in industrial and

246

specialty selling. Frequently the very last point of this stage is the actual preparation for the presentation of a proposal. The call objectives will have been set early, maybe many months ahead of submission of a proposal. The preparation stage should include:

- analysing the customer's needs and problems
- identifying possible solutions
- surveying facilities as necessary
- presenting standard or modified product samples for testing
- assisting with the conduct of any appropriate tests and product evaluations.

In general, industrial and specialist salespersons may find their current and prospective customers more forthcoming with information helpful to the preparation of proposals, as both buyer and salesperson recognise each other's information needs.

Approach
The physical approach is likely to be less stressful in that the buyer is aware of the project under study and wants regular progress reports, and visits are arranged by appointment, with both seller and buyer having a professional interest and attitude.

Presentation
This may occur over several visits as proposals are developed or modified. The initial proposal will often be in written format, covering:

- problem analysis
- evaluation of identified alternatives
- proposed solutions
- equipment/product specification
- costings
- cost–benefit (to buyer) analysis
- financial considerations, e.g. investment payback analysis
- timetable to supply and implement
- contractual considerations.

In some instances the proposals may even be a joint matter, with representatives of both seller and buyer making valuable inputs to each stage of a proposal for consideration by the decision makers in the buying organisation. Above all, proposals must be thorough, accurate, factual and credible.

Objections
The main objection to large-value purchases is budget. But if the sales-person has been fully involved in the evaluation and proposal

preparation he is likely to have elicited enough information about the customer's own business that can be used in handling objections.

Closing the sale

Again, although this may not be a clearly defined section of the selling process, the same principles and alternatives apply as previously discussed, and a positive closing review of the proposal with the customer, to ensure it is fully understood, is a good general style.

Post-call follow-up

There may not be specific call record cards to complete for 'big deal' sales, but there will be significant post-call follow-up to ensure that contractual obligations and other commitments are met, modifications made, equipment installed and commissioned, maintenance programmes established, and so on.

Although the training principles and needs are generally just as applicable to industrial selling and specialty sales environments, all too frequently in-company training is most heavily biased towards product knowledge training. Courses in negotiating skills may be particularly beneficial to develop personal 'big deal' sales skills. Such courses might be organised internally or involve external trainers. And, of course, direct field coaching has an important role in skill development.

VARIETY AND DURATION OF EFFECTIVE TRAINING

Training
techniques

Effective sales training programmes can include a variety of media and techniques, such as:

- lectures
- films
- role playing
- closed circuit video television
- feedback reviews and discussions
- printed handouts.

Each of the modes adds a dimension and variety to the training programme, and helps retain the interest of trainees. The trainer should remember that selling participation in the training programme is no different from selling any other product, and that best results will come from getting **attention**, creating **interest**, arousing **desire**, and provoking **action**.

There are advantages and disadvantages in using each of the above training media and methods.

248

Lectures

These are often an excellent method of involving an audience, if it is not too large, as they can be quite personal, with a speaker able to answer questions and control the pace to the apparent rate of assimilation. The lecturer can use wall charts, question and answer techniques, slides, overhead projector facilities, summary hand-out literature, and any other simple communication aids that promote interest and involvement of the audience. However the audience's span of attention to any one speaker will be limited, and it is usually necessary to change the speakers frequently (possibly every two hours or so unless practical exercises break the routine).

Films

Viewing a film of a realistic sales situation is perhaps a less intense learning activity than sitting before a lecturer, who might at any time ask questions, and films can be judicially used to break the routine and change the pace of training. Many good sales training films are available (advice may be available through consultants or professional institutions) that illustrate different selling environments and sales techniques. They will often depict both good and bad sales presentations, and trainees should be invited to discuss and analyse each selling situation (the **case study** approach) to see if they can identify aspects such as the film salesperson's objectives, preparation, approach, presentations, use of sales aids, objection handling techniques, closing techniques, style and mannerisms and other factors the trainer wishes to highlight. Trainees are initially often more willing to comment and criticise film situations than live role playing situations because they do not want to risk offending anyone present, and each trainee is well aware that if he is critical of a fellow trainee's role playing he risks reciprocal reaction.

Role playing

This is very practical work involving each trainee in simulated sales situations. Usually the trainer will initially act as the buyer, but as each trainee gains confidence and enters into the spirit of the exercise, they can be involved as both salesperson and buyer. The trainees are likely to be rather cautious and self-conscious at first, concerned that they might perform poorly and face criticism from the other trainees. If the trainer can introduce a little humour into some of the situations this frequently helps relax the participants. Practice of each stage and technique is generally necessary until each trainee can respond correctly and with confidence to situations. As group and individual confidence grows, and participants develop an understanding and minimal level of skill at each stage of the sales call sequence, the trainer can introduce more variables and techniques.

A large part of any training course can advantageously be given to the practical sessions, with new factors being introduced by lectures,

249

films, etc. The main risk of role playing in simulated environments is that with some participants it can create over-confidence to the point that their reaction to any initial failure in the field is more acute; and the field manager must carefully provide the confidence and morale boosts needed during the early days of field training.

Closed circuit video television

This is a most useful tool in providing feedback and aiding learning in the role playing situations. Each trainee can see himself in the simulated call situations, observe progress, and note strengths and weaknesses, techniques, styles, habits and mannerisms, and attitudes. A trainee may initially feel less than comfortable seeing himself on the screen during a post-call analysis, but this reaction is soon overcome, particularly when a few humorous situations occur and he sees that colleagues are no more perfect than he.

Feedback, reviews and discussions

Little needs to be said on this as the benefit of feedback and discussions at each stage of training to aid learning has already been frequently mentioned. The trainer and manager should remember that if a positive attitude is to be created, feedback should be not just critical but also complementary and positive. A trainee will more readily take note of a suggestion to improve a technique or change a practice if such comment follows a sincere compliment and praise on a good point. The process of feedback from the trainer or line manager should also be extended to develop the salesperson's own ability to analyse situations and techniques as part of ongoing self-assessment and self-development.

Handouts

Printed handouts relevant to the subject matter of initial training will greatly aid learning and retention, and avoid the loss of attention that could occur during sessions as trainees attempt to keep up with note taking. The main handout that can summarise virtually all the training and sales operations is the **sales manual**, which should be prepared by the sales manager and his team to act as a permanent reference guide to all field sales force personnel. It should ideally cover:

- the company
- the products
- job descriptions
- practical and comprehensive guide to all administrative procedures and documents
- comprehensive guide to all the sales call sequences and selling techniques adopted and taught within the company
- summary of company personnel practices and policies.

250

The sales manual provides a constant source of reference, review, and ongoing personal training.

In addition to the above media and methods of training there are always others that can be successfully used, such as programmed texts on subjects suitable for presentation and learning in this manner (such as product and company knowledge, sales theory, legislation). Consolidation and review are essential at each learning stage, and simple tests might be conducted by the trainers at appropriate points in the training programme.

Specialist
training

Where a sales function is particularly specialised in some manner, then a more complex or longer initial training programme may need to be designed. Such specialist training is quite likely in areas of industrial selling, where in-depth knowledge about the product, its specifications and applications is essential to work effectively with customers to satisfy their needs — as in selling processing or production plant and equipment or specialist ingredients or components. The recruiting line manager should draw up a formal training programme that includes time spent in all relevant departments (such as research, engineering, marketing, finance and production departments) and agree specific learning and training programmes and objectives with the appropriate trainers in each department to ensure that the trainee is not just left 'kicking his heels'.

Use of training
consultants

Whilst larger companies will probably have the facilities, experience and manpower resources to plan, organise and implement tailor-made training programmes for salespersons at all levels, smaller companies and many industrial products companies are likely to have much more limited resources. But that does not lessen the need for or benefits of thorough professional training. One approach is for such a company to recruit people with previous sales experience in similar products or industries, thereby only having to concentrate training on areas of product and company knowledge.

Another approach is to use the services of external consultants and training establishments, of which there are many. Some specialise in sales recruitment; others in sales training. Professional institutions can often give leads to established consultants, who can analyse the company's specific needs and develop an individual training programme to meet identified needs, or who can organise internal or external courses to impart sales skills. There are also a number of very reputable companies and organisations that produce and run regular training courses in aspects of selling. These may be suitable for both new recruits and established salespersons in companies that do not have adequate internal facilities or that are seeking variety in training inputs. Managers and sales operatives should be exposed whenever possible to new ideas and developments that increase

251

awareness, improve skill levels, introduce new techniques, or simply serve as motivators. Attendance on external personal development courses can in itself be a major motivator worth the costs to the company.

Length of training courses

The length of a course will, of course, depend on the content, but it is likely to be from two to ten days. If the course is too short it may not allow enough time for assimilation and consolidation of knowledge and skills. If it is too long the attendees may lose interest and give lower commitment and performance. Sometimes there can be benefit in splitting a course into two or more parts: a theoretical part (with role playing) to impart very basic skills; a part that might consist of intensive field training under the guidance of a field sales trainer or area sales manager; and possibly a third part back at the training centre designed to refine techniques and consolidate learning.

A typical outline for a five-day initial sales training course might look something like Example 7.2, encompassing both theoretical and practical training.

The initial sales training programme, whether conducted internally or externally, should be followed immediately by an intensive period of field sales training (see Chapter 8). If time and resources permit, a refresher or consolidation training period back in the sales training facilities after several weeks in the field would aid skill development as the theory and practice are reviewed, and help in reinforcing good techniques and habits.

Example 7.2   An initial sales training programme

DAY 1

The company:
- history
- market position
- organisation
- tour of facilities
- introductory presentations by other departments

The products:
- range of products
- historical product development
- product attributes and benefits
- marketing support and programmes
- new product developments
- competitive products
- applicable rules, regulations and legislation

DAY 2

The sales call sequence:
- preparation for the call
- the approach to the buyer
- stock checking and product merchandising

Territory organisation and journey planning

DAY 3

The sales call sequence:
- calculation of order requirements
- presentation of the positive order
- overcoming objections

Effective communicating

DAY 4

The sales call sequence:
- overcoming objections (cont.)
- closing the sale
- sales administration

Sales force administration

DAY 5

The sales call sequence:
- the complete call

Personnel practices and policies

Questions and answers

Issuing manuals, sales aids, administrative stationery, and other relevant
equipment

Note: Evening work assignments can include case studies, developing role playing,
practice at complying with the administrative requirements of running a territory.

SUMMARY

- The training of subordinates to perform the functions of the job is a fundamental responsibility of each line manager.
- Training imparts knowledge, creates attitudes, develops skills and habits. Sales skill training may centre on territory management, time utilisation, negotiating skills, administration, management by objectives, and self-development through post-call analysis.
- Training required by an individual is a function of existing knowledge and skill (including frequency and recency of use), aptitude, attitude, rate of assimilation, adaptability, and motivations.
- Training should be supplemented by management and motivation, objective setting, suitable rewards and incentives, and feedback and performance appraisal.
- New salespersons need training in company and product knowledge, basic selling skills and techniques, operating to systematic sales call sequences (if relevant to the product), and complying with company administrative procedures, policies and practices.
- If a sales call sequence can be developed it should act as a framework rather than a script, probably including such stages as: preparation; approach to the buyer; stock checking and product merchandising (or surveying facilities and requirements for industrial goods); order/quote preparation; presenting a positive order; overcoming objections; closing the sale; completing post-call administration and follow-up.
- Industrial and specialty markets differ from consumer goods markets: transactions may involve larger sums of money, professional buyers may respond more rationally, and contracts may take considerable time to negotiate because of existing supply contracts, special relationships, lead times for product evaluation, technical support requirements, etc. However, a sales sequence approach still has validity, although the individual stages may be less distinct and take longer to progress.
- Sales training courses may include any or all of: lectures; films (and slide presentations); role playing exercises; closed circuit video television facilities; feedback; printed literature and handouts; and such other aids and media as provide variety and aid learning.
- Whilst training is an ongoing function and requirement to maintain and improve performance, there is a limit to the beneficial length of any formal training course in terms of attendees' attention span, interest and retention, and the amount of new information that can be successfully imparted and assimilated. Short refresher courses at regular intervals may prove more effective than longer less frequent courses.

254

CHECKLIST   THE BASIC SALES TRAINING PROGRAMME

	Notes	Action
Have the levels of training needs and skills of new recruits been assessed?		

Has an initial training course to cover needs been developed?

Does the initial training provide sufficient knowledge and skills in:

- company knowledge?
- product knowledge?
- basic selling skills?

  - preparation?
  - objective setting?
  - approach to customers?
  - product merchandising?
  - stock checking?
  - preparing orders?
  - presenting the order?
  - handling objections?
  - closing the sale?
  - post-call administration?

- use of sales aids?
- effective communicating?
- administration?
- territory organisation?
- pace control
- journey planning?

Does the training course effectively use a combination and balance of:

- lectures?
- films?
- role playing?
- closed circuit television?
- feedback?
- discussions?
- printed handouts (including manuals)?

8 Field Sales Training

THE ROLE AND PURPOSE OF FIELD TRAINING

As every sales line manager rapidly learns, there is no substitute for practical selling experience and field sales training, whether in consumer goods, industrial or service industries. Formal school-type training courses can essentially provide an insight into theory, basic product-related knowledge, and rudimentary selling skills; as buyers become more professional, and the market place more competitive, so the sales team needs to develop more expertise in practical aspects of their chosen profession, and a more professional attitude of mind. The term 'representative', usually shortened to 'rep', has connotations of an order taker. The line manager has the opportunity to create an atmosphere and environment of professionalism that raises the self-image of his team members. His training and management can instil confidence and pride in their performance, skill levels, status and role in the broader business environment, and create a desire constantly to improve performance and professional standards and standing to levels that ensure continued success in a competitive environment. Movement up the promotion ladder – perhaps from a territory salesperson to a key account executive – demands far greater sophistication and business maturity in addition to more refined selling skills as the environment changes from basic 'selling' to 'negotiating'.

Training can be aimed at a number of aspects of selling, including:

- imparting marketing skills to increase effectiveness at the fulcrum of the marketing effort – the point of sale
- increasing professional presentation and negotiating skills such that both the salesperson and the company derive tangible benefit
- improving the understanding of the buyer, his motivations and objectives
- increasing adaptability to different buying/selling environments and situations, including one-to-one head office presentations and buying committees, buying techniques and buyers' analysis of products, their benefits, costs and mix suitability with other products
- developing administrative and organisational skills, initially to ensure effective and efficient territory management and subsequently to develop the salesperson for increased responsibility
- developing expertise in aspects of human relations relevant to selling

256

- developing expertise in the identification or creation of customer needs and subsequently in the satisfaction of those needs.

Training stages — Field sales training can aim to improve skills and performance in all of the foregoing areas by:

- discussion
- demonstration
- explanation
- practice
- consolidation.

Discussion

Whilst discussion does not substitute for demonstration, the traditional **kerbside conference** approach — where the sales manager reviews and discusses a salesperson's performance, activity, skills and techniques and then coaches in methods and processes that should improve effectiveness — does have a place in field sales training. It is often particularly useful in sales environments where it is not practical for the field sales manager personally to demonstrate points (perhaps because of the risk of disrupting relationships or the flow of communications, as with key accounts or industrial buyers).

Demonstration

No amount of discussion or explanation can substitute for a practical demonstration of the point that is the focus of the training session, although an initial explanation on a training aspect can beneficially precede a demonstration presentation so that the trainee understands the objective of the call presentation, the strategy to achieve the objective, and the activities and style of the presentation. The field manager, when making a demonstration presentation, needs to be careful not to be side-tracked by peripheral issues raised by the buyer, otherwise the trainee may lose sight of the training point and not benefit from the demonstration.

Explanation

Immediately after conducting a demonstration of a training point the sales line manager should conduct a brief review discussion with his trainee to establish if the trainee understood and perceived the difference between his own style or format of presentation and that of the manager, and is aware of the improvement in achievements to be gained by adopting the new approach. The tangible benefits to the trainee might be in time saved or other results achieved. The trainee needs to understand the specific modifications needed in his present methods or style to duplicate the manager's demonstrated techniques.

257

Practice
Each trainee needs to practise what is taught and demonstrated to develop skill and confidence and improve performance. Line managers will generally find that one single practice exercise is not enough to produce lasting benefit or form a habit in using a technique. Some patience is often needed at this stage, particularly if the existing style, habit or technique has long been part of a trainee's method of operating. Repetition aids learning.

Consolidation
At each stage of the training process the manager will need to ensure that the training point has been consolidated to the stage where it becomes a new habit as strong as the former habit or style. Other training points should ideally not be introduced into the exercise until the training line manager is happy with the degree of consolidation and performance improvement. Unless a trainee begins to see results from a particular training point he will be sceptical of adopting further changes in his style and method of operating.

ASSESSMENT OF FIELD TRAINING NEEDS

The previous chapter discussed aspects of assessing training needs. At this point consideration should be given to the role of a field assessment in identifying problems and developing corrective action.

There are four facets of job performance where field training can be instrumental in improving performance:

- functional activity
- sales techniques
- organisation
- personal attitudes.

Only functional activity lends itself to performance measurement in absolute or comparative terms or criteria. The other three are open to qualitative interpretations and assessments. Field managers themselves will need experience and training in assessing the training needs of individuals in these areas, and in developing and implementing subsequent corrective or developmental training programmes.

Functional
activity

Quantitative or objective measurements can be made of most aspects of functional activity in the sales job. It is perfectly practical physically to observe each activity the salesperson undertakes in the course of a day and his use of time in relation to each activity, and to form judgements and conclusions on the satisfactoriness of performance in each area, including making comparisons with other team members. While some functional activities may apply only in consumer goods markets, most will apply, in modified form, to industrial and service industry markets as well.

Use of time
Time is the key limiting resource of the sales force, so the first analysis might consider:

- time of first call
- time of leaving last call
- amount of time driving (i.e. between calls)
- pre-call planning periods
- post-call administration periods
- lengths/frequency of inter-call breaks (e.g. meals)
- waiting time at calls (e.g. to see buyers)
- time spent checking stocks
- time spent merchandising displays
- time given to effective selling activities (e.g. presentations).

From this observation and analysis it may be identified that training, management or motivation are needed in certain aspects such as:

- **starting time**:
  - is the salesperson starting promptly?
- **pre-call preparation**:
  - does he do adequate preparation at home for the working day?
  - or does he await arrival at each call before beginning his preparation?
- **journey planning**:
  - has he planned his journey in the most time-effective manner and sequence to avoid unnecessary driving, repeat call-backs, etc.?
- **rest breaks**:
  - does he take excessive (in length or frequency) breaks or rest periods during the working day, and if so is there any apparent reason?
- **waiting times**:
  - does he spend time unproductively waiting at calls or does he

use waiting time effectively in preparation, planning, stock checking or merchandising?

- **relationships**:
  - are his relationships such with the buyers that he can use waiting time on associated activities, and have significant influence because of mutual trust and respect on the outcome of repeat order presentations and/or new proposals?
- **stock activities**:
  - is he thorough, accurate and efficient at stock checking and related merchandising activities?

Functional tasks

The second stage of the functional activity analysis can encompass the functional tasks of the job, including:

- **preparation**:
  - what preparation is done prior to the call (quality/quantity)?
- **sales call sequence**:
  - does the salesperson adhere to a recommended sales call sequence?
  - how effective is he in using it to control the call situation and enhance performance?
- **call rate**:
  - how many calls does he make daily (average)?
  - are there significant variations from the average (highs and lows) and apparent reasons for variations?
- **conversion rate**:
  - what is the average relationship between orders to calls (percentage conversion)?
  - does this vary significantly at times; if so – why?
- **stock checks/merchandising**:
  - does he perform the functional activities relating to checking stocks and merchandising product and displays at all calls?
- **job description**:
  - does he perform all the other functional activities detailed in a job description, or required by management as specified in other communications?
- **administration**:
  - does he competently and promptly complete all administrative tasks?

A review of the particular job description will enable a line manager to identify key functional areas where relevant performance analysis is appropriate.

An experienced field sales manager will have sufficiently developed personal selling skills to identify weaknesses in sales techniques, and to have credibility with his subordinates to propose changes and provide corrective training. Where a company lacks resources or management experience it may be that outside sales consultants can conduct a training survey and recommend and implement suitable training.

A skill audit could give attention to such aspects of selling techniques as:

- **approach**:
  - is it professional, confident, warm and enthusiastic?
  - does the salesperson have the appearance and bearing to command attention and respect as an equal?
  - does he create a favourable impression of himself and the company?
- **identifying decision maker**:
  - does he identify and gain access to the decision maker in the buying organisation?
- **opening**:
  - is the salesperson positive in taking the initiative to relax the buyer and lead quickly but acceptably into the business discussions?
- **control**:
  - does he control the interview situation or is he led by the buyer?
- **listening**:
  - does he listen to the buyer and recognise signals reflecting the buyer's moods, attitudes, interest and responsiveness?
- **identifying needs and problems**:
  - does he establish the buyer's needs and problems in relation to the products being offered, his market or operations, and adapt his presentation to recognise and satisfy needs or problems?
- **creativity**:
  - does he create opportunities and needs in the buyer and offer solutions to satisfy those needs, or is he purely an order taker reacting to stimuli from a buyer, perhaps simply reciting product attributes in scripted fashion?
- **objection handling**:
  - can he recognise objections, clarify them, and respond with appropriate objection handling techniques?
- **benefit selling**:
  - does he sell product benefits or simply list attributes?
- **communications**:
  - is he an effective communicator in clear, concise, logical, informative and interesting terms?
- **closing techniques**:
  - does he effectively present a positive order and close the sale,

using such techniques as confident, concession, alternative or
fear closes?

- **use of sales aids**:
  - does he prepare his sales aids for a presentation and use them
    effectively throughout the presentation to aid communication
    and control and to influence the buyer?
- **knowledge**:
  - has he adequate company and product knowledge to present
    products effectively and answer product-related questions,
    including those concerning specifications, performance,
    servicing, availability and pricing?

Once the skill audit has identified the relative strengths and
weaknesses, and these have been discussed and accepted by the sales
person, a specific and personalised training programme can be
developed.

Organisation

The field sales manager's audit of training needs should extend to
cover organisational aspects of the job, such as:

- **information storage and retrieval**:
  - has the salesperson organised his files and call records in a
    fashion that aids storage and retrieval of information?
- **sales aids**:
  - does he check and prepare his sales aids prior to making each
    call?
- **journey planning**:
  - is his journey planned in the most time effective manner?
- **appointments**:
  - does he make prior appointments with buyers where this might
    be beneficial?
- **vehicle maintenance**:
  - is his vehicle kept in fully maintained and serviceable condition,
    and clean and tidy?
- **accessibility of sales equipment**:
  - is all sales equipment, including records and aids, kept in tidy
    and accessible fashion at home or in the vehicle?
- **briefcase**:
  - are sales aids and call paperwork organised and accessible in a
    briefcase or other carrying case to give easy access for use and
    reference at the calls?
- **administration**:
  - is post-call and pre-call administration carried out promptly and
    efficiently?
- **communications**:
  - are communications and correspondence with customers,

colleagues and other internal and external contacts handled in a timely and efficient manner?

- **commitments**:
  - does he record, follow up on, and honour commitments given to customers and colleagues?

Attitudes This is perhaps the most subjective area of all in a training audit; assessments of attitude may be influenced by personal feelings, prejudices and preferences. The field sales manager needs to feel sure he is making impartial assessments in this qualitative subject area, if only because it is hard to train a person to change his or her attitudes. It needs to be recognised that often a manifest attitude problem has a more basic underlying cause. For example, a sales-person might become sceptical of a company's 'indoctrination style' of making sales presentations, mainly because they lack the confidence and skills necessary to implement the recommended sales call sequence and selling systems. The field sales manager should therefore recognise that skill training in the areas of more objective assessment, providing that the salesperson actually sees that he can improve performance, will frequently produce modification in attitudinal problems.

The attitude audit might cover aspects such as:

- **warmth**:
  - does he exhibit warmth and friendliness?
- **empathy**:
  - can he project empathy with the buyers when discussing their problems?
- **enthusiasm**:
  - does he project enthusiasm for the company, its products, and his job?
- **loyalty**:
  - is he loyal to the company and his superiors and colleagues?
- **positiveness**:
  - has he the right positive mental attitude to the job and life in general?
- **team spirit**:
  - is he a good team member and participative at meetings and conferences?

The training audit As part of the assessment or audit discipline the field sales manager should develop his own discipline by preparing an audit or assess-ment form to be used as a guideline and completed on each occasion that he works with a member of his sales team. The results and interpretation of the analysis can and should be reviewed with the salesperson involved, and specific priority areas identified for further practical field training that will make a real measurable difference to performance and results. A sample of a simple sales training audit form is given in Example 8.1. This can be modified and developed to suit any particular company or manager. To reduce the risk of confusion caused by a long list, it could be simplified to the point that only main headings appear, and the trainer inserts his own sub-headings to highlight the strengths and weaknesses appropriate to the time.

An attempt should be made to standardise the terminology, measurement criteria and rating scales used by field managers in preparing training audits and conducting performance assessments. This is clearly not an easy task, and is a function of the skill and job training given to managers. Any one manager should demonstrate consistency in his ratings and measurements. Terminology will be influenced by training and company jargon: the word '*satisfactory*' may in one company mean that a person is performing in a manner that is perfectly acceptable and that there is no question that he makes a positive contribution to results; in another company, the same term may be taken to mean that he is seen as just 'getting by' with minimal effort and results. Senior sales managers need to train subordinate managers in the acceptable interpretation and terminology to use to reflect levels of performance such as: outstanding, excellent, good, satisfactory, unsatisfactory. ('Satisfactory' would seem to suggest that the job functions are being performed or results are at a level where continued employment of the person is not in question, but there is room for improvement.) Once managers are clear on the meaning and interpretation put on training and appraisal rating phrases and words, then they must ensure that the same understanding is communicated to subordinates so that they may fairly and appropriately respond to an assessment audit or appraisal.

In giving a rating assessment on a training audit, as an alternative to the use of subjective phrases such as 'good' and 'satisfactory', it is often beneficial to allocate a rating score from 1 to 6, as in some of the other audit formats developed in this text. By using a six- (or ten-)point scale the assessor avoids the common tendency to score too many persons or factors just at the mid-point of the scale, as might occur on, say, a 1 to 5 scale. The training audit should ideally have a section where the trainer reports on what training he gave the trainee on that day as part of a record system of ongoing training.

CONDUCTING FIELD SALES TRAINING

An assessment of performance strengths and weaknesses and of training needs should always be discussed promptly with the sales-person involved, and generally will be better received if it can commence with some favourable comment on strengths and performance. As training needs may frequently involve attention to

264

Example 8.1 Example training audit form

TRAINING AUDIT		
Date:	**Salesperson:**	
Trainer:	**Territory/function:**	
	Rating	**Notes**
Functional activities Use of time Journey planning Relationships Preparation Sales call sequence Call rate Conversion rate Merchandising Administration Other:		
Sales techniques Approach Identifying decision maker Opening Control Listening Identifying needs Creativity Objection handling Closing techniques Benefit selling Communications Use of sales aids Product knowledge Other:		
Organisation Call records Information retrieval Sales aids Journey planning Appointments Vehicle Administration Communications Other:		
Attitudes Empathy Enthusiasm Loyalty Positiveness Team spirit Other:		
Training given:		

comparatively fine points of technique and performance-related tasks it is wiser to separate in the trainee's mind the difference between a training audit and a formal annual appraisal. The training audit is based on analysis and judgements at a specific point in time, and is aimed at improving skills and performance over the short and longer term. A formal appraisal will measure performance against agreed standards and objectives and other relevant criteria, and is historically based over the time interval between appraisals.

Priority training

When the field sales manager discusses the training audit with the trainee or territory salesperson he should identify one or two key aspects to isolate immediately for practical field training, and concentrate on those points for the duration of that training session. The manager's priority should be to create change through improving skills and attitudes in areas that will increase the results of the individual and thereby the company. It is unlikely to be particularly productive to spend long periods lecturing a salesperson about minor matters such as car care; that kind of subject can be covered in an end-of-day review of any sundry matters. In any case, the trainee probably has a more limited ability to grasp and learn new techniques and points than the experienced manager. If more than two or three training points are raised at one training session, the trainee will probably not respond adequately to the explanations and demonstrations and so will not effectively consolidate learning and modify performance on all points.

Feedback

The provision of feedback at each stage of training is essential if performance and behaviour are to be modified. Feedback – by which I mean the frank communication and open discussion of a salesperson's performance, abilities, skills, standards and methods of operating – serves several purposes:

- it lets the salesperson see that his supervisor is interested in him and his ability to perform the job
- the salesperson recognises consistency in the behaviour of his supervisor towards him and the job, and learns to expect counselling and training; as he comes to learn that the supervisor does not expect perfection but respects effort, he may come to ask for assistance
- it helps the salesperson to improve his self-analysis of performance aspects and develop self-training projects
- it leads to awareness that changes in behaviour and performance improvement lead to greater acceptance, respect and satisfaction exhibited by the supervisory manager
- it aids maintenance of high morale as it can and should refer to the positive as well as the negative, producing praise as much as or more than criticism

266

- it will come to be seen not just as criticism (or constructive criticism – since none of us really accepts criticism as constructive) but as ongoing counselling that increases satisfactions and rewards if it is properly presented.

There are a number of guidelines in conducting training that it might be helpful to enumerate.

Where?

To be most effective, training should be conducted in the environment to which it directly relates. In the case of selling that basically means at the locations of customers during the course of real sales presentations and situations.

How?

Effective training, as has been mentioned frequently before, is best conducted by demonstration of the training point, post-demonstration reviews and comparisons between the trainer's style and results and the trainee's style and results, practice by the trainee, and subsequent consolidation of the learning process through repetition, understanding and incorporation in standard methods of operating.

Benefits

If a salesperson cannot see or accept that he is under-performing or incorrectly operating to a sales call sequence he may come to see his manager as picking on him when discussions on performance and techniques commence. The trainee will open his mind to a training situation only if he is given cause to see personal benefit to himself. That benefit may be in terms of job satisfaction, improved personal rewards, promotion prospects, pleasing his manager (and having a little less aggravation in the process!), or simply fear that he will lose his employment by non-compliance or continued under-performance.

The primary task of the manager is then to find one single aspect of the job functions where the salesperson can be persuaded by demonstration that there is an alternative approach and one that is easier or more productive. It may simply be that the man likes to avoid excess work at home, and that a period spent rearranging his call record and administrative systems reduces his home time allocation to work-related activities. Once the line manager has identified a motive that will encourage learning and assimilation from the training situation and demonstration has promoted acceptance of change in some job-related area, training can progress at an appropriate rate into other higher-priority areas.

Because each salesperson is a different combination of skills and attributes, it is essential that training objectives for the day are

realistic and likely to improve standards and performance in the eyes
of the individual trainee. The manager must gear his training
objectives to the learning abilities of any one trainee, and his
knowledge of the trainee's response and attitude to previous training
sessions.

Frequency

A salesperson will be more receptive to training sessions if these
occur frequently and at regular intervals (by which I mean once or
twice a month, but not on a fixed day or at a standard interval). As he
comes to accept this management function because it improves his
performance and benefits in tangible ways, training days will become
more of a welcome change in routine than treated with suspicion.

**The training
framework**

The trainer's approach to a training day needs thought, preparation
and planning. A review of previous training audits and the line
manager's own knowledge of each of his team members may
indicate likely training needs, and a framework should be developed
within which the training will take place.

The **training framework** should give consideration and attention
to:

- the salesperson's understanding and implementation of company
  programmes, policies and strategies as manifest in marketing and
  sales activities and programmes, including new product launches
  and sales promotions
- previous experience of the trainee's ability to perform job
  functions, activities, and sales techniques, including organisational and attitudinal aspects as they relate to performance and
  the accomplishment of objectives
- the trainee's response to and assimilation of knowledge and
  experience imparted during previous training sessions; the
  trainer needs to evaluate progress made on previous training
  points before proceeding to new training points or priorities.

Training on courses, whether internally organised or at external
venues, may seek to impart knowledge and skills in theoretical or
practical aspects of selling within the limits imposed by a classroom
environment, where several trainees attend and each has individual
experiences, needs, learning rates, motivations and performance
levels. Training in the field sales environment can and should be
totally personalised to the individual being accompanied that day.
The manager should make the trainee aware that it is *his* day, and that
he can make an input into the day's training programme.

Once the manager has developed his broad training framework it is usually useful for him just to observe the salesperson's performance in the first few calls, and build a rapport that gets the salesperson into a relaxed frame of mind. Perhaps during the initial part of the day, training could usefully centre on any aspects of communications, bulletins, policies or procedures that the salesperson might have questions about, and this will help in creating the receptive environment the trainer needs to home in on practical priorities.

It is very useful also in this initial 'warming up' period to get feedback from the salesperson on any particular problems he is currently encountering and how successful he feels he has been at implementing previous training points, and to establish if he has identified any points where he would like coaching. It would be unwise to cast a cloud over the training day at the outset by presenting criticisms of work standards, performance, techniques or achievements at too early a stage. These can all be covered as the day progresses and as the receptiveness to counselling grows, particularly as practice following demonstration starts to produce obvious tangible benefits to the trainee.

After the initial 'warm up' period, it is time to establish and clarify the day's training programme and objectives. It may be that the line manager, acting in his role as trainer, simply says 'let me do the next call' and performs all the sales function in that call whilst incorporating a demonstration of the point or technique he wishes to emphasise in training. Full participation in a sales call is easier and more acceptable at lower selling levels, such as calling on a store or customer in the home, although the manager should take care not to risk alienation of any subordinate by acting in a fashion that reduces the status or authority of the salesperson with the buyer in a call. It is more difficult at key accounts, head office calls or industrial sales presentations, where the salesperson must clearly be seen as in charge of business with the account, and not just a trainee. In such situations the sales manager may prefer just to slide into the presentation at an appropriate point, without appearing to take it over, make his training point without the buyer realising his motives, and then withdraw from active participation again. Rather than surprising the salesperson with his intervention, the manager may feel it is wiser to discuss and agree his participation and its objectives. There is always the risk that the salesperson will see the success of the manager in making a presentation more as a function of his status and seniority being recognised and acknowledged by a buyer than as actually being different in style or format. This can only be countered by ensuring that the salesperson perceived some difference between his own techniques and those of his manager. Post-call discussion should rapidly establish differences in style and technique and results, and help the trainee recognise benefits that at least justify him experimenting in subsequent calls. He should then be encouraged to practise the same method in several subsequent calls. Post-call reviews, and possibly some more practical demonstrations by the manager, aid understanding and learning. A compliment from the manager on the way the trainee picks up a point will produce a more receptive attitude to other comments on aspects the trainee has not fully understood or implemented as the day progresses.

If the trainee is actually a very experienced long-serving employee or salesperson the manager must particularly beware of 'talking down' to the person, and making reference to his 'training needs'. That kind of approach, especially if the manager is younger than his trainee salesperson, is only likely to cause an experienced salesperson to 'tune out' of the learning process and only go through the motions of physical participation in the training exercise. The manager might choose to lead into a demonstration with some introductory comment such as: 'I see old Joe Smith didn't buy our promotional offer there. I wonder if there is some other way we might get the benefits overs. There is a thought in my mind on another alternative way to explain the programme. Would you mind if I try it out in the next call?' The demonstration will then show the problems and possible solutions rather than the field manager simply listing them.

The field sales manager will earn more respect from his subordinates by helping them to develop and grow with the job than by simply relying on his authority to demand results. Pulling rank is an ineffective motivator and unlikely to produce lasting performance benefits. The salesperson who feels his manager understands his job environment and the problems associated with achieving objectives and standards, and really has a sincere interest in helping him develop and achieve his personal satisfactions and goals through improved performance, will give more loyalty to his manager, be a more committed team member, and respond positively to training and motivation.

Practical points in the field training process can be summarised as:

- **prepare a training framework** based on the salesperson's understanding and implementation of programmes and policies, effective levels of sales skills, and historical response to training
- **relax the salesperson**, just as you would relax a customer, in the early part of the training day (perhaps with some sincere praise on accomplishments), and let him know you will be there to provide help, guidance and training throughout the day
- **observe performance** of functional activities and skills in several calls and the incorporation of training points from previous recent training days
- **identify key training priorities** for attention that day
- **introduce the priority points** by means of practical demonstrations and discussions

- **review differences in techniques** and results in post-call discussions
- **obtain acceptance and agreement** of the need to change style or modify techniques or methods of operating
- **encourage practical application** of the alternative methods or techniques until familiarity and practice result in improved performance, greater self-confidence, and recognition of tangible benefits
- **provide feedback** after each practice call, always trying to precede criticism or negative comment by compliments and positive comment
- **maintain regular contact** between training days with each salesperson to encourage discussion on progress, needs and problems, and aid development of the process of self-analysis and self-development
- **maintain training records** to monitor improvements in performance over time, the effectiveness of training, and the receptiveness to training. This also helps the trainer to evaluate his own abilities and success as a trainer, and establish if he needs guidance and training to train.

The basic rule for the field sales manager seeking to influence and inspire improved performance through training is:

DEMONSTRATE, MOTIVATE, DON'T DICTATE.

INITIAL FIELD TRAINING

Where a salesperson is quite new to the sales job, the general training approach will have to be modified to reflect the more intensive and basic training needed at the field sales call level. The trainee may have undergone induction training (company and product knowledge) at the head office or sales training facilities, and possibly received some basic sales training as part of an induction programme. The field sales manager has to accept responsibility to turn these elementary knowledge and skills into effective performance mechanisms rapidly if a new sales trainee is to gain confidence, achieve initial successes and develop in the sales environment.

The first training week is critical in the development of good practices and habits. The field sales manager should formalise his approach to the training exercise and create a professional environment with which the trainee will feel proud to be associated. The trainer should ensure that he spends full days with the trainee, rather than arriving mid-morning or leaving mid-afternoon, as a new trainee needs to see that his manager works as hard as him and is committed to his training (he may not appreciate at that time that his

271

manager has many other functions to perform). Good examples by supervisors encourage good standards and performance by subordinates.

If company and product knowledge and basic sales skills have not been imparted as part of an initial induction programme, then the first step is to set the starting day aside for full discussion of these, including the provision of all necessary sales materials, equipment and manuals.

To instil the discipline of pace and time as a scarce resource the field sales manager should ideally take the first selling day as a demonstration model, and personally perform all the requisite tasks and functions – making all the calls, and doing the preparation and administration. The trainee then has a chance just to observe and assimilate the mechanics of the job in a practical environment prior to commencing his own practical training. If the sales manager has developed a sales call sequence, then a copy of this should be given to the trainee at the outset, and the sequence explained so that the trainee recognises the importance of each stage in the successful completion of a call and the sales presentation.

If the recruitment of 'ideal' candidates was successful, then it is highly likely that as the demonstration day progresses the trainee will be pushing to be allowed to try a sales call. Generally speaking it is probably best to avoid the trainee's participation until the second day, so that the trainer clearly demonstrates the procedures, systems, techniques and achievement of standards such as daily call rate.

On the second morning the trainer may like to start the day with a demonstration call to refresh the trainee's memory on activities and call sequence, and then hand over to the trainee to make a few calls. At this point some trainers feel strongly that the trainee should make his initial few calls alone in order to get the feel of the job and develop an initial level of confidence. The pattern for the rest of the training day might consist of trainer and trainee alternating in making the calls, with regular post-call brief reviews. This pattern could continue for several days, with the trainer doing fewer calls each day and the trainee doing more calls.

If the field line manager has managed to devote the entire first week to training his new starter, then in the second week it would be appropriate to leave the trainee to work alone for a few days to practise and consolidate his skills. The trainer may then accompany the trainee in the latter part of the second week, and for part of the time in the subsequent weeks until he is confident the trainee has the skill levels to perform and work alone, apart from the regular review training days. It is during the early days and weeks that the field sales manager has the greatest opportunity to influence skills, perform-ance, motivation, attitudes and habits, and he should clearly accept the training of a new starter as his fundamental priority during that period.

SUMMARY

- Field training can aim to: impart marketing skills; improve professionalism of sales presentations; increase understanding of the buying function; develop adaptability to different selling environments; develop administrative and organisational skills; increase skills in human relations; and improve skills in identifying and creating needs with customers.

- Field training can improve skills and performance through **discussion, demonstration, explanation, practice** and **consolidation**.

- Training can improve performance in respect of functional activities, sales techniques, organisation and attitudes. A **training audit** can be conducted that analyses: use of time; performance of functional tasks; sales techniques and skills; in addition to studying organisation and attitudes: from this a personalised training programme can be developed with both short-term and longer-term objectives and priorities.

- Field training should: identify priority training topics where improvement can impact positively on results; provide feedback on performance and progress; be conducted as a regular practice and frequently; and provide tangible benefit to the trainee in respect of results and current or future (direct or indirect) rewards and satisfactions.

- The trainer should develop a **training framework** taking account of a trainee's understanding and implementation of company policies and programmes, his performance history, his previous response to training, and his rate of assimilation.

- Actual training should commence when the trainee is relaxed and receptive, and after his current performance has been observed, so that the training presented is seen as relevant to current activities. The manager should maintain regular contact between training days to review progress, and develop a system of keeping training records to monitor progress over time.

273

Part III

Management and Control of the Sales Force

9 Territory Management

In times gone by, when salespersons were not recognised as being skilled professional individuals contributing to the efficient marketing and distribution of goods and services, the usual image of a 'rep' was of the man who was virtually his own boss, free to work or play as he pleased, make customer calls and obtain business on a friendship and 'old boy' basis, and sit back and count his commission. It is unlikely that any readers of this text have that misapprehension. In this chapter I propose to consider aspects of managing a sales territory, since that is basically what the professional salesperson does, and the relationship of particular job functions to the overall productivity and management of the territory.

MANAGEMENT OF RESOURCES

The salesperson has three basic resources to manage and whose productivity he must maximise:

- time
- company resources
- himself.

Time   This is the one irreplaceable resource available to the salesperson, and often the most difficult to manage. There are many demands and pressures on his time, some much less critical or productive than others yet still a necessary part of the workload. An effective selling day in most industries spans the hours from 9 a.m. to 5 p.m. with extensions often from around 8 a.m. to 7 p.m. to cover pre- and post-call driving and administration. Within the working day the major time consuming activities are:

- driving
- call preparation/planning
- waiting time at calls
- pre-presentation activities such as stock checking and merchandising
- sales presentations
- post-call administration
- meal breaks.

In addition there will be occasional area sales meetings and other

277

conferences to attend, which in most companies occupy about a day per month on average.

The salesperson is constantly under pressure to utilise time to optimise call coverage and maximise time given to effective sales presentations and order-producing activities; yet the other time-consuming activities are ever-present. In a typical working day in most industries most salespersons discover they are likely to devote only around two hours to actual selling out of a day away from home of probably around ten hours. Another two–four hours may be spent driving and parking, probably up to an hour on pre-call preparation in the car, an hour for meal breaks, and perhaps two hours in non-selling call activities (stock checking and merchandising). The actual amount of time given to effective selling varies less than is at first often realised between industries and seniority of salespersons, such as key account executives. Key account executives generally make fewer calls and must give far greater time to planning, preparation and other account monitoring activities.

Efficient journey planning and call coverage are thus critical to optimise the time available for sales-related activities. The importance of training in effective selling skills assumes a new urgency and dimension when we realise how little of the day is devoted to the key result-getting activity, and how much must be accomplished within that brief time span.

Company resources

The company resources the salesperson is charged with managing can be divided into tangible and intangible resources.

Tangible resources will include aids and equipment such as:

- the company vehicle
- financial resources (e.g. expenses and contributing to optimising returns from company investment in existing and new products, and plant, equipment, etc.; customer credit)
- advertising, marketing and sales promotions
- sales aids and materials.

Intangible resources include:

- company goodwill and product goodwill arising from historical reputation, brand names, etc.
- time

Self

The salesperson must manage himself in terms of functional activities, skills, performance, self-development, his ability to utilise and optimise returns from the tangible and intangible resources at his disposal, motivation, morale, and attitudes. Much of his working time is spent alone; most of the balance of time is spent not in the more relaxing company of colleagues, but in the more stressful

278

environment of customers, with the accompanying pressure to achieve tangible results from a concentrated sales effort.

ACTIVITIES

The salesperson's activities can broadly be allocated to one or other of the functional activities of:

- planning
- selling
- communicating
- administering
- decision making.

The territory manager/salesperson needs skills in each of these operational areas in addition to technical skills specific to the products and markets. As an extension of the initial training of new recruits in fundamental selling skills and the ongoing field sales training by the field line manager, sales managers may decide to develop internal or external courses and training programmes to increase skills and competence in aspects of planning, communications and the decision-making process.

Planning The planning functions of the salesperson include:

- new call identification
- journey planning
- appointment scheduling
- making travel plans
- setting call objectives
- sales presentations
- preparing sales aids and equipment
- post-call planning.

New call identification
If new outlets or potential customers are expected to contribute to some or all of the territory's business growth, then considerable planning time will be needed to identify outlets and contacts that are current or potential users of the product, and then to follow up and contact these outlets to schedule calls and presentations.

Journey planning
Careful attention to journey planning is essential to ensure the best use of time in systematically covering calls at prescribed frequencies where such coverage is essential to maintain distribution – as with fast moving consumer goods. In the interests of efficiency and

279

control, the salesperson should develop a master plan to cover a journey cycle, and it would be normal for his manager and head office to retain a copy of this set of documents. The salesperson can then confirm each week in advance to his line manager which days' work from the master journey cycle plan he will actually cover the following week. The journey cycle plan would normally be based on the time span between those calls receiving the minimum coverage frequency, which might be every 8 or 12 weeks, with other calls with higher potential or volumes receiving more frequent coverage during the journey cycle, possibly as frequently as weekly. The actual construction of a coverage plan will be discussed in more detail later in this chapter.

Appointment scheduling

It may not be necessary to make appointments prior to visiting a customer if calling on smaller outlets in the f.m.c.g. industries, such as food markets where a store keeper or manager is generally available all day, and where much time in the call is devoted to product merchandising and repeat order activities. With industrial selling, visits to head office buyers, or selling to the professions (such as doctors, lawyers, architects, etc.) it would be customary to schedule appointments to ensure the busy buyer will be available at the time of calling. If the call is of a regular nature it may be the practice to schedule the next meeting at the close of a current meeting. Some buyers may specify regular times and days when they will receive salespersons without a prior appointment and operate on a first come, first seen basis. As a general rule an appointment should be made if it is likely that the buyer might be otherwise occupied at the time of a call.

Making travel plans

Quite apart from the basic scheduling of calls and making customer appointments, planning time and effort may need to be given to the mechanics of arranging inter-city travel and hotel accommodation, as the field sales manager may wish details of arrangements to be included with journey plan data.

Setting call objectives

This is a key planning function for each territory salesperson: effective territory call objective planning separates the territory manager from the ordinary sales order taker or 'rep'. Identifying and setting objectives in relation to the customer potential, and then managing the presentations and achievements of those objectives, is one of the two main ways a sales territory grows – the other being the identification of additional outlets that can add business to the territory.

Whatever the industry or product range being offered, the sales-person should never make a call or schedule an appointment without having a specific purpose or objective as the focal point of that visit, and aimed at increasing mutual business and benefit.

A call objective may be as basic as deciding to work towards the listing of a new product or pack size, to install a particular piece of display material, or to move the product display from a secondary display site to a primary 'key point' display site within the store. It could be to upgrade a customer from an old or obsolete model of machinery or equipment (whether bought or leased) to a newer more effective and efficient model. (We might all be embarrassed as professional salespersons to admit how often we have had a customer ask 'What's new?' or 'Have you got a new model which will save time and staff operating it?'.) How often does a salesperson, whether selling photocopiers or cars, go back through his customer lists and renew contact to advise and make presentations on the new models?

Sales presentations

Sales presentations are not normally spontaneous occurrences. They require careful thought and preparation to ensure that all the studies or proposals required by a buyer are finished and available, and that all necessary sales aids (including catalogues, specifications, costings and price quotations, samples, etc.) are in the briefcase. Planning must also ensure that all historical customer knowledge is available and can be used to advantage. If it is known that the buyer has particular reactions or objections, the planned presentation may anticipate some of the objections by incorporating appropriate comments. Likely objections should always be anticipated and responses prepared with any supporting material. Skill comes in knowing when to introduce each selling point or objection handling technique or response. The poor salesperson shoots all his arrows before he sees the target and uses up his possible responses to objections before identifying what, if any, objections there are, and may create the problem of putting objections into the buyer's mind. Objections should be anticipated but the buyer should be left to raise them, so that the salesperson can respond by giving sincere thought and consideration to the buyer's problem before delivering an answer.

Preparing sales aids and equipment

These do not just appear in the call, but have to be requisitioned or obtained according to the company's practice, and therefore will only be available with a lead time. As part of the planning and territory management process the salesperson should survey his require-ments weekly and indent for standard sales aids in sufficient quantity to allow for lead times.

Post-call planning

Depending on the outcome of any presentation, the salesperson should, in his post-call review and analysis, seek to set future objectives for the account. Also the outcome of the presentation may result in a need for further planning and action to deliver the goods and honour commitments.

Selling

The selling activities of the salesperson encompass the stages of objective and presentation planning outlined in the previous section, and particularly cover the **in-call** skill activities of:

- identifying the decision maker and gaining access
- making the sales presentation
- handling/responding to objections raised
- closing the sale.

Chapters 7 and 8 cover the particular sales call sequence stages and techniques involved in the above activities.

Depending on the customer, market or industry, final in-call preparation may be necessary before actually making the sales presentation, handling objections and closing the sale. For example, prior to making a sales presentation in a repeat order situation, it will be necessary to check current stock levels, enter stock levels on a call record card, and make a calculation of current order requirements related to product movement and promotional activity.

Communicating

Much of the salesperson's activity involves *communicating*, either in person, by telephone or through correspondence, and skill training may be beneficial in each of these areas to maximise the effectiveness of communications. Making appointments over the telephone may prove difficult in cold canvassing situations; it requires skills related to selling to get attention, arouse interest, and get the appointment to make the presentation that will create desire and provoke action.

There is a risk in any form of communication of misunderstanding, and **brevity, clarity** and **simplicity** are basic guidelines that reduce that risk. A typical salesperson's communications involve:

- his customers and contacts
- his line manager
- head office support functions
- liaison with distribution points;

and include such basic tasks as:

- arranging appointments with customers
- communicating journey plans
- reading, interpreting, understanding, and implementing com-

282

munications from head office and line managers, which frequently may relate to matters such as: customer payments/credit, marketing and promotional activity, new products, price changes, terms of trading, performance analyses of accounts or territories, deliveries, production matters (such as those related to production scheduling), product specifications, and so on

- distilling relevant aspects of communications originating from head office into action plans or subsequent communications for specific customers
- communicating the contents of sales presentations and marketing and promotional activity effectively to the buyers
- liaison with head office support services on aspects relating to particular customers, such as order lead times, product availability, and payments.

The process of communication needs to be **efficient** and **timely**, and records kept for subsequent referral or follow-up. It is customary to keep copies of exchanges of written correspondence (often in the form of self-carboned copies of order forms and other standard company documents). In addition the salesperson should, for his own records and reference, keep notes on any other contacts or communications, such as telephone conversations, in which agreements or commitments are made. At the level of a retail sales call the only record system necessary may be notes added in appropriate places on the customer call record card. For meetings with major accounts, industrial customers, or in any selling situation where the selling process or negotiation is ongoing, the salesperson would be wise to adopt a system and discipline of preparing brief post-call **contact reports**, which should summarise the content of discussions, agreements reached, and further action required to progress negotiations. These contact reports should largely be an internal document, generally with copies going into the salesperson's file on the customer, to the line manager for supervisory control purposes, and possibly to other persons or departments required to take specific action on the contact report.

Administering

Administering the sales territory places time burdens on the salesperson, and should therefore be kept as **simple** and **minimal** as effective management and control permit. Wherever possible, the use of standard forms and record systems may aid efficient and effective administration and reduce the risks of neglect. Standard forms may often be developed to aid field communications, such as:

- customer call record cards or folders
- journey plan forms
- order forms
- daily activity reports

283

- credit/product uplift notes
- advice of visit/appointment postcards
- contact report forms
- internal memo forms
- quote forms
- special store promotion activity forms
- payment due notes.

Many of these documents could be produced in the format of self-carboned pads, which aid use and storage.

The manager designing administrative systems should do so in the knowledge that the more time that is given to administrative paperwork the less time is available for selling, and that he should minimise intrusion into the private time and home life of his sales team by designing forms and systems that can largely be completed immediately after calls have been made rather than requiring an hour or two at home in the evening.

Decision
making

The decisions a territory salesperson makes may not be as large in magnitude or impact on the overall company business as those of the sales director, but they are as frequent and require the same processes in arriving at a judgement on a course of action. Whether the decision required simply concerns re-routing for the day to take account of a particular traffic problem resulting from road works, or whether it involves possibly offering a special price or promotion to a customer to prevent the loss of an order, the basic decision-making process should consist of:

- recognise, identify and define the problem
- analyse and identify causes of the problem
- identify possible alternative courses of corrective action
- evaluate each alternative and any limiting parameters (such as scope of authority, corporate policies, time limitations)
- decide on the best solution or course of action
- implement the action
- monitor to ensure satisfaction, effectiveness, or the need for further corrective action.

Specific training in decision making may well be considered as a constructive extension to the regular sales training programme, particularly at more advanced stages of ongoing training and refresher courses. It is comparatively easy to develop a number of case studies, both relevant to the job and more neutral, and have trainees develop decisions and action plans within the above framework. Individual decisions can then be reviewed within the group training situation to arrive at consensus decisions and action plans,

284

which often produces variations in thought processes and consider-ations, resulting in a consensus on a better corrective programme. This type of group discussion and training aids team building as individuals learn to recognise the benefits of discussion, sharing information, and willingly seeking involvement with and help from colleagues.

Example 9.1 The decision-making process

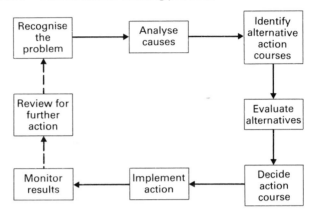

MARKET INTELLIGENCE

An important function of every salesperson, which involves communication but which I prefer to cover separately, is the gathering of information relating to competitive activity in the sales territory or with key accounts, including information such as staffing levels, new products and packs, prices and promotional activity, or tenders for supply contracts on industrial products or services. The salesperson often incorrectly assumes that what goes on within his territory limits is the same as everywhere else and already known to management, forgetting that new products and packs or advertising programmes are frequently tested in a smaller area initially to measure acceptance and effectiveness.

Field sales managers may well wish to develop a system where each subordinate submits a weekly report (of at most about one page) on market intelligence. This could cover points made above, and other factors affecting business with customers and contacts and competitive activity. Many an astute sales manager has saved himself bad debts because an alert salesperson heard from a competitive salesperson that a certain account was getting behind on payments; or perhaps the territory salesperson became aware of reductions in stock holdings.

If the reader uses this weekly market intelligence report system, then I would advocate that if any salesperson has learned nothing of interest he should still submit a 'nil report' to ensure that the task was

285

not simply forgotten. A field sales manager can then analyse and collate information from his subordinates' reports, develop an overall area report to submit to his superior, and plan local action on any factors he may feel he should be acting on (such as obtaining feature displays on his major products to compete for sales against a competitor's new product). If a salesperson makes a particularly interesting report or observation, that person should receive full recognition for his contribution, perhaps with a special mention in the next area bulletin, as that will motivate that individual and encourage the balance of the team to be alert.

OVERDUE PAYMENTS

I believe this topic warrants a separate section because of my view that if a customer fails to pay for goods on time and within agreed terms it is the responsibility of the territory salesperson who opened the account or booked the order to raise this matter with the account and seek early settlement from the customer involved. Most companies send a polite reminder when an account has an outstanding balance for a certain period, perhaps 7 or 15 days overdue. Companies may have a rule that further shipments must cease until past due accounts are settled, which puts pressure on the salesperson and his manager to ensure that payment is received because they are losing the sales volume in the interim until debts are cleared. It is easy initially for the territory salesperson to raise the matter with the customer by saying something to the effect, 'I received a copy of the reminder note that your last payment was due a week ago. I thought I would mention this as you always do pay promptly, and I did not want this to come to the area manager's attention because we have this internal rule that prevents us shipping further orders when payments are late. Can I collect your cheque and post it off with my other documents?'

It is important from the aspect of territory management that each field manager and territory salesperson is aware of the commitment of company assets in the form of credit extended to customers under his control. A company operating a computer accounting system may be able to produce a weekly summary of information relating to despatches to each area and territory or key account group, including:

- value of orders received that week
- value of invoices outstanding for goods despatched, categorised by time lapsed from payment due or invoice date (e.g. 7, 14, 21, 28 days).

The actual system is perhaps less important than the fact of having some system to alert field personnel to overdue payment situations

286

and to prompt corrective action, and also to make management and salespersons aware of the sums of money and company assets for which they have an involvement and responsibility. Is the salesperson aware, for example, that an interest cost of, say, $12\frac{1}{2}$ per cent on an average £200,000 outstanding for a year would alternatively yield the income to finance another salesperson?

PLANNING TERRITORY CALL COVERAGE

The subject of call coverage has been touched on several times in the text so far, and as this is a fundamental factor in sales and territory management where repeat outlet coverage is the practice it warrants further discussion at this point.

Coverage is the planned calling on customers and potential customers for a product or service. When considering consumer goods and general products sold through retail outlets, the above definition can be extended to be considered as the **planned calling on customers and potential customers for a product or service according to a system of regular scheduled call frequencies related to the needs and potential of each customer and outlet.**

Journey
workload
analysis

The first stage in developing coverage is to divide the market into units, according to the workload that each salesperson can manage in terms of calls per day and per journey cycle. The number of calls a salesperson can potentially make depends on such factors as:

- distance between calls and driving time
- the pre-call preparation required
- the functions to be performed at the call
- the average length of sales presentations
- post-call administration.

A salesperson with a consumer goods company calling on smaller retailers in close proximity to each other may manage 12–15 calls per day. If calls on supermarkets are involved, with extra merchandising activities needed, the call rate may well fall considerably, even to around 6–8. A key account executive or industrial salesperson might be able to schedule only from 2 to 4 calls per day.

Each outlet in a geographical area should be identified and classified according to the **frequency** of call it requires. High-volume outlets would be expected to require more frequent calls, perhaps once a week or every two weeks; calls with lower potential can be scheduled for less frequent coverage.

The **length** of a journey cycle will be governed by the minimum frequency at which it is felt a call can justify remaining as a direct account. Outlets with very limited potential that do not justify the

287

costs of direct calling and that would not be able to make minimum order requirements even at the minimum call frequency within the journey cycle may, when encountered, be referred for supplies to an approved distributor or wholesaler. The cost of making a direct call is high. Some sources have considered that the overall costs may be in the order of three times the direct costs of the salesperson making the call by the time management and the provision of support functions is taken into account. Most companies find that a very small percentage of outlets account for the vast majority of sales – the often-quoted 80%/20% rule. Sales managers need to estimate for their own company the average costs of selling and distribution, and assess minimum order quantities that justify a direct call rather than routeing sales and orders through wholesale distributors.

All the calls in a geographical area can be added up on a list to estimate at what point the workload reaches the limit of one territory salesperson (Example 9.2). It may be convenient and useful either to invent arbitrary time spans, which can be termed '**work units**', or simply to assess the number of minutes a call will take including all time required for driving and other work related activities. A 'work unit' might be set, say, at 10 minutes, and it might be decided at the early planning stage that 20 minutes or two work units are added to each call to allow for driving time, pre-call preparation and post-call administration. In Example 9.2 a superstore may require four work units (40 minutes) for in-call activity plus two work units (20 minutes) standard allowance for the other call-related activities. On a 12-weekly journey cycle, based on a 40 hour working week (excluding early morning and evening driving to and from first and last calls), one salesperson has 2880 work units of 10 minutes available. By adding up cumulatively, we can establish at what point a single sales territory reaches maximum workloads. In the example, the territory might comprise 263 separate customers based on the identified outlets and assigned work units per call per journey cycle. At this point no allowance has been made for finding new potential customers (pioneer calling) or attendance at area or national sales meetings. I generally prefer at the planning stage to assume that a territory will have a fully planned and committed workload, and that time lost on holidays or attending meetings or for any other cause can be covered by a relief salesman.

In any larger sales force it is generally necessary, if not ideal from the point of management and motivation, to have certain 'relief' or 'floating' salespersons who do not have their own permanent territories but cover other territories during absence or other problems. Experience will indicate the necessary ratio of relief salespersons to territory salespersons. Relief salespersons are a necessary evil, but only 'evil' in that they are often neglected for regular training, management and motivation. Any area manager may neglect the relief salesperson by thinking of him not as an established team member, but purely as a 'work horse' to help the area through a coverage crisis. Internal procedures and rules should identify which field manager is to be held responsible for the management and training of any relief salesperson. It is unwise to leave an individual in this floating category for too long as it is hard to hold him account-able, to measure contributions and results, and therefore to counsel and appraise fairly and objectively.

Example 9.2 Journey workload analysis

Customer name and address	Annual potential sales volume[1]	Expected call frequency (weekly)	Calls per cycle	Work units per call	Work units per cycle	Cumulative work units
1. J & J Superstore, Newtown	1,000	2	6	6	36	36
2. Acme Hypermarket, Newtown	900	2	6	6	36	72
3. Wilsons Market, Newtown	1,000	2	6	6	36	108
4. Jones Supermarket, Newtown	950	2	6	6	36	144
5. Cash & Carry Ltd, Newtown	2,000	2	6	7	42	186
6. Johnson Wholesale, Newtown	1,700	2	6	5	30	216
.						
.						
.						
29. Newtown Foods Ltd, Newtown	800	4	3	5	15	965
30. Ali's Store, Newtown	600	4	3	6	18	983
31. Corner Shop, Newtown	500	4	3	6	18	1,001
.						
.						
93. Anyshop, Newtown	300	6	2	6	12	1,490
94. Browns Grocery, Newtown	240	6	2	6	12	1,502
95. A&B Stores, Newtown	120	6	2	4	8	1,510
.						
.						
260. Star Grocery, Newtown	100	12	1	4	4	2,868
261. Moon Grocery, Newtown	80	12	1	4	4	2,872
262. X&Y Supplies, Newtown	70	12	1	4	4	2,876
263. Khan General Store, Newtown	60	12	1	4	4	2,880

Note: 1. Assumes minimum delivery of 15 cases per order.

289

Once each call has been allocated a call frequency and the territory workload assessed, the territory salesperson should then prepare his territory journey cycle schedule.

The schedule can initially be built by allocating the right amount of time at specific call intervals for the most frequent calls, and then adding in the less frequent calls, so that any one working day will consist of a mixture of, say, weekly, two-weekly, four-weekly and eight-weekly calls. The schedule may consist of a master form, laid out perhaps as in Example 9.3 where a separate sheet is used for each day's work in the journey cycle – say 40 sheets for an 8-week cycle or 60 sheets for a 12-week cycle. Each day's work would be recorded against a journey day number based on a 5-day working week (1–40 for an 8-week cycle; 1–60 for a 12-week cycle). Each call name and full address is recorded, along with notes on call frequency, time or work units allocated to the call, and perhaps other relevant facts, such as if there is an early closing day. In an 8-week journey cycle, a two-weekly call would appear on the journey sheets for perhaps days 1, 11, 21 and 31; a four-weekly call might appear on journey days 3 and 23; and an eight-weekly call would appear on the journey sheet only for one single day. The calls should be written in the best calling sequence for the particular journey day, i.e. the exact order in which the territory salesperson plans to make the calls.

Many salespersons like to start the day's work at the furthest point from their base, doing the bulk of distance driving in the early morning when they feel fresher, and working inwards towards home as the day progresses. That system is likely to result in a good amount of criss-crossing over the same routes or ground during the day, which might be especially frustrating if it includes a lot of city centre calls. The allocation of calls into daily workloads and calling sequences should be influenced by the need to plan the scheduled call order logically within each day to minimise driving time and distances and facilitate call-backs if calls are missed for any reason, such as a buyer being out for a short while.

The traditionally recommended system is to treat the territory in a circular fashion, and divide it into five roughly equal segments, one for each of the working days in the week. The focal point should be at or near the centre of the territory. In this method the salesperson would never be far from any call that was missed on its scheduled day for any reason, enabling him to pick up missed calls perhaps the next day or on the same day of the week in the following week. This can be further refined, as in Example 9.4(a), where the salesperson could cover the calls over a 20-day period as illustrated; however, as certain calls would be covered weekly or perhaps two-weekly there might be a degree of overlap in the journeys.

Within each day's work, to avoid the criss-crossing that generally results when a start is made at the nearest or furthest point, it is again useful to make the calls in a circular fashion, starting at a call nearest base, working outwards and then back inwards to finish at a call near base. This also facilitates picking up a call later in the day that had to be missed at an earlier point. Whenever practical it is useful to mark the specific location of all territory calls on suitably large-scale maps as an aid to efficient journey and route planning (and additionally useful if the map shows one-way traffic systems). Rough segment lines can then be added if that will aid the salesperson in planning the days' journeys, possibly using a chinagraph pencil on plastic overlays as that makes alterations simpler. This format of planning daily journeys might not suit all industries or market circumstances, but the principles will, i.e.

Example 9.3   Journey cycle planning sheet

Territory: 45 – Central Area   **Journey cycle day**: 11

Call	Work units	Early closing	Frequency[1]
1. Acme Supermarket, The Mall, Newtown	6	—	2
2. Giant Market, Broadway Centre, Newtown	6	—	2
3. Ali's Grocery, 10 New St, Newtown	4	Wed.	8
4. A&B Foodstores, 35 New St, Newtown	4	Wed.	8
5. Khan's Cash & Carry, 46 Central St, Newtown	6	—	4
6. The Corner Grocery, 12 Broad St, Newtown	4	Thurs.	4
7. Star Markets, 29 High St, Newtown	5	—	4
8. Wilson, 65 New Rd, Newtown	4	Thurs.	8
9. Banks General Store, 69 New Rd, Newtown	4	Thurs.	8
10. Star Markets, Victoria Ave, Newtown	4	—	4
11.			
12.			
13.			
14.			
15.			
16.			
17.			
18.			
19.			
20.			
	47		

Prepared by: **Approved by**

Territory salesperson   Area sales manager

Notes: 1. Frequency of calls means 2-, 4- or 8-weekly call on the outlet.

- to minimise distance between consecutive calls
- to be able to pick up calls missed with minimum disruption
- to maximise time available for effective sales functions
- to aid field control by line managers.

Example 9.4   Segmenting a territory for journey planning

(a) Divide the territory into five main segments, one for each weekday, and subdivide each daily segment into four further segments. This aids call planning on a 20-, 40-, or 60-day journey cycle (numbers indicate the journey day).

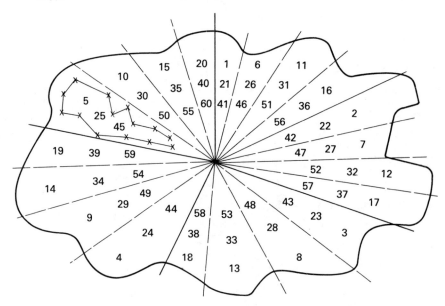

(b) Divide the territory into segments for sequential calling in a sales operation where all calls are made at the same standard interval.

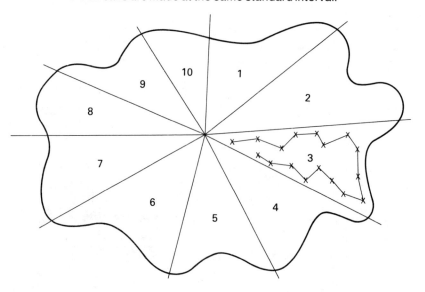

Where all calls in any territory are made at the same frequency, as might be the case with certain merchandising or wholesaling operations or with cash van selling systems, there is no real need to divide the territory into segments for each day of the week or to plan to be in each segment each week. Instead, the territory may be divided into segments to represent each day's work in the journey cycle, although the principle of working in an elliptical fashion each day should be observed for efficiency reasons. In Example 9.4(b) I have assumed a 10-day cycle for a wholesaler's sales territory. This system will give the salesperson the opportunity to pick up any missed calls on the following day.

Another way of building up territories is to start the geographical division by using a system known as **sales bricks**, where the country is divided up into geographical sections of similar size in terms of certain standard parameters. Each sales brick can be analysed for its workload content applicable to any particular industry or type of outlet. The individual workloads for sales bricks in close proximity can be added together until the maximum workload that can be handled by a territory salesperson is reached.

Similar analyses can be developed to plan coverage of any market. A start might be made by considering the preferred internal organisation for market sector coverage. If the company is selling electrical switches, with different salespersons covering the professional market (architects), distributors and the building trade, then the respective territories within each market sector may well be of differing geographical size. Where a product has a once-only sales opportunity, double glazing perhaps, yet another approach to coverage might be for a sales 'commando' team to visit each area of potential and cover that geographical area intensively before moving on to the next blitz area. Alternatively, the territory salespersons might be allocated geographical areas of similar demographic characteristics in terms of number of households, ratio of owner-occupied property to rented accommodation, income distributions, or other relevant characteristics, and then left to develop leads independently or from enquiries generated from advertising or through strategically located retail outlets.

Once outlets are identified and call frequencies allocated in relation to sales or potential, it is possible to estimate the necessary size for a national or regional sales force to provide adequate coverage. From such an estimate can be estimated the supporting numbers of field sales managers required to provide effective management, taking account of the span of control and other limitations discussed in Chapter 1.

However, the actual system of organising coverage and the sales force in the early days of developing a sales organisation may be less important than the fact that a system and an organisation exist and function.

Once a salesperson is allocated to a territory or sales function it is unwise to change the boundaries of that territory or to switch salespersons between territories or to change persons between sales functions too often and without careful thought to the risks of disrupting coverage and limiting the accountability and performance measurements of the salespersons involved in change. Continuity of coverage is important, as is continuity of the persons making contact with customers to maintain and develop relationships. The salesperson given specific responsibility for a territory and accounts needs time to build relationships, develop business towards potential, achieve measurable results and work towards setting and achieving objectives.

COLD CALL CANVASSING

I use the term cold call canvassing to refer to the type of selling where the salesperson must identify and develop his own leads and turn these into potential and actual customers for the product or service, with conversion of sufficient leads into sales justifying his continuing employment (unless he works purely for a commission on sales). In many industries where a significant amount of initiative from the salespersons is required to generate leads and contacts, it is common for income to include a strong element of commission, although a basic living wage may be provided along with expenses and possibly a company vehicle.

The management controls (which will be reviewed in Chapter 11) and disciplines needed in journey planning are still essential to effective planning, performance and management, although a permanent journey cycle schedule to be followed in consecutive journeys will not exist. The salesperson in such circumstances will be more likely to operate on short-term journey plans sent perhaps weekly or monthly to his line manager. The line manager should seek to set some guidelines and objectives to ensure market coverage of potential contacts and that the salesperson is working constructively and productively. In such forms of selling, conversions of calls to sales may be low. During periods of limited sales success or seasonal downturns, morale may suffer as well as income, and supervisory neglect of training, motivation and planning disciplines may accentuate staff turnover problems.

The salesperson should be encouraged to plan his work programme to incorporate a mixture of qualified calls developed from such sources as:

- personal contacts
- referrals from previously satisfied customers

294

- enquiries generated in response to company advertising (the return enquiry cards usually included with advertising material)
- callers to company-owned retail sales outlets
- visitors to stands at exhibitions and conventions
- local 'market' research by the salesperson into potential customers or neighbourhoods likely to yield potential customers according to known customer profile information.

Priority attention might be given to leads from sources most usually found to be productive (say, referrals and enquiries in response to advertising or at company retail outlets), and to calls that are 'qualified' as matching profiles of known customer types against objective parameters such as income, home location, socioeconomic class, and so on. Even though in certain markets (such as the home improvement markets for double glazing, extensions, insulating, roofing, etc.) it has become the preferred practice to sell by direct home or office calls on potential customers,significant leads can be developed by strategically located retail outlets displaying the company's products, which can handle enquiries both from casual impulse callers and those who have already decided to make changes but are seeking product comparisons.

THE COSTS OF SELLING

The direct costs of a salesperson, and the approximate cost per call can be measured fairly simply. A cost analysis might look like the following example (for the United Kingdom market):

	Annual cost £
Salary, commissions & bonuses	12,000
Fringe benefits (life assurance, pensions, national insurance contributions, etc.)	2,500
Company vehicle (including leasing costs, depreciation, insurance, maintenance, running costs, etc.)	5,000
Entertainment	700
Lunch allowances	300
Telephone & postage	300
Accommodation & subsistence away from home	2,000
Sundry costs	1,000
Samples	1,200
	£25,000

This figure may be divided by the number of effective working days in a year to give an average per day cost. Allowing 143 days to cover weekends, statutory public holidays, annual holiday entitlement and attendance at meetings, we would arrive at 222 effective working

295

days, or an average direct cost of approximately £113 per day. If the average salesperson does ten calls per day, that gives an average cost per call of £11.30. Orders produced must generate a contribution to at least cover that cost, in addition to the actual costs of manufacturing and distributing the product plus a share of general overheads.

In looking at the direct costs per call I have clearly not made estimates for the costs of support management and functions, and other equipment and materials used in the selling process, considering these as general overheads. The company's cost accountants will help the sales manager to identify and attribute costs to the selling and distribution of goods in order to arrive at appropriate minimum order levels. Initially the company will be limited to some extent by trade custom and practice, competitive trading terms and the size of its product range. It might be quite unreasonable for a one-product company to seek a minimum order of 15 cases of one item on a monthly call frequency when no competitive product moves at that volume offtake rate; but that might be a very reasonable minimum drop for a multi-product company.

The costs of running a direct sales force are frequently in the order of 5 per cent of turnover for an established product and company, but this figure may vary, depending on the nature of the goods and markets, what are included as sales force costs, and a host of other variable factors. Therefore it is not really reasonable to give any target cost/sales value ratio.

Where it becomes clear that it is not worthwhile for a salesperson to call on a particular account, but the sales manager wants to maintain some contact or distribution, alternatives to be evaluated can include:

- wholesale distributors
- telephone selling
- brokers
- postal orders
- delivery through a head office warehousing system or voluntary buying group warehouse for branches of multiple retailers or members of voluntary buying groups.

These are further considered in Chapter 12.

In the industries where repeat orders are not the rule, similar cost exercises are just as necessary, but sales values per effective call may need to be that much higher to cover the costs of a larger number of unproductive calls. For example, if a salesperson works in the home improvement industry and makes an average of eight calls per day, with the same total costs as the consumer goods salesperson but with a conversion rate of calls to orders of eight to one, then that successful call must bear the whole day's direct selling costs of £113. If the product has a gross margin after manufacturing costs and central overheads but before direct sales expenses of, say, 20 per cent, then the minimum order needed to cover just direct sales costs would be £565. It might be that the average order is in fact several times that, and therefore the direct sales operation is readily justified and cost-effective.

- The salesperson is responsible for the management of the territory to maximise productivity of such key resources as **time**, company **tangible** and **intangible resources**, and himself. Time must be effectively managed to provide scheduled call coverage and maximise the time devoted to effective selling activities.
- The activities of the salesperson can be broadly categorised into **planning, selling, communicating, administering** and **decision-making** functions.
- Planning will include: identification of potential customers, journey planning, appointment scheduling, travel planning, setting call objectives, preparing sales presentations, preparing sales aids, and post-call planning activities to progress business.
- Selling activities include: identifying the decision maker, making effective sales presentations, handling objections, and closing sales.
- Communications will involve contact with customers, line managers, head office support functions, and perhaps liaison with distribution depots. Verbal and written communications should ideally be brief, to the point, simple in structure and clear, to avoid misunderstandings. Records should be kept as appropriate for future referral or follow-up.
- Administering the territory is aided by devising standard forms and paperwork systems to facilitate communication and the preparation and flow of information.
- Decision making involves: recognising the problem (the need to make any decision), analysing the causes, identifying alternative courses of action, deciding on the best alternative, implementing the action plan, and monitoring the results, including reviewing the outcome and possible need for further corrective action.
- Territory management includes market intelligence activities, and responsibility to pursue outstanding customer payments.
- In an industry with repeat calling activities on established outlets it is beneficial to develop a planned call coverage system, the **journey cycle schedule**, arranging calls at various frequencies related to the potential business to be obtained from each customer.
- In product markets where there is little likelihood of repeat sales and/or local leads must be developed through cold call canvassing, whilst it may not be practical to develop a regular journey cycle schedule, a journey planning system can be developed and used by management to control activity. Such a journey plan might include leads developed from: personal contacts, referrals from previously satisfied customers or other contacts, enquiries developed in response to advertising or through callers to company-owned retail outlets or visitors to

company stands at exhibitions or conventions, and other market research sourced leads.

- The costs of direct selling are high and ever-rising, and should be evaluated and monitored by management to ensure the cost effectiveness and profitable viability of direct calling on customers, and to assess minimum order levels that justify direct calling and direct accounts. If direct selling is not practical or cost effective, the alternative means of obtaining sales coverage and distribution can be considered and evaluated.

	Notes	Action

Planning

Are new customers identified,
contacted and developed?

Is journey planning both efficient
and effective?

Are appointments scheduled as necessary
in the most time-effective manner?

Are call objectives pre-set for
each customer and contact to be
visited?

Are sales presentations pre-planned
and objections anticipated?

Are all sales aids and supporting
materials prepared and available?

Selling

Are decision makers identified
and contacted?

Are sales presentations prepared,
effective and related to pre-set
call objectives?

Are objections handled competently
and professionally?

Are all sales-related functions
completed at the calls?

Are all sales presentations closed
in a manner that seeks positively
to elicit an order?

Communicating

Are telephone communications
effective?

Are communications and liaisons
with head office support functions
timely, efficient and effective?

Are communications with the line
manager thorough, informative,
accurate and sufficiently frequent?

Are communications with customers
timely, efficient and mutually
beneficial?

Administering

Have the standard information and
communication needs of the company
been identified?

Do standard forms exist to aid
compliance with information and
communication needs?

continued

Checklist   Functional activities (contd.)

	Notes	Action
Are personnel trained to comply with administrative requirements and procedures?		

Are administrative tasks and
requirements promptly and
efficiently handled?
Are accurate and up-to-date files
and records maintained?

Are incoming mail and
bulletins read daily and
information distilled to relevant
actionable points?

Decision making
Can and does the salesperson
take decisions?

Is the decision-making cycle
understood and adhered to, i.e.

- recognising a problem
- analysing causes
- identifying alternatives
- evaluating alternatives
- taking a decision
- implementing the decision
- monitoring results
- reviewing results for
further corrective action?

Market intelligence
Does a formal system of gathering
market intelligence exist?

Is it effectively operated or
complied with?

Are inputs reviewed and studied
in relation to any impact they
might have on company plans
and programmes?

	Notes	*Action*

Time

Is driving time minimised
(effective journey planning)?

Is pre-call preparation thorough?

Is waiting time at calls necessary,
excessive, or effectively used?

Is stock checking and merchandising
efficient and quickly completed?

Is post-call administration completed
promptly and accurately?

Are breaks too frequent or too long?

Company resources

Is the vehicle well maintained, clean
and effectively organised as a mobile
office?

Is maximum use made of and benefits
gained from marketing and promotional
activity in the sales situation and at
the point of sale?

Is there a cost-conscious attitude
to the use of resources?

Are expenses controlled and reasonable?

Are customer payments and credit
controlled within prescribed terms
and limits?

Self

Are the skills present to perform all the
functional requirements?

Is the salesperson self-motivated?

Has the salesperson the right positive
mental attitude to the job and himself?

Is morale high?

Is the salesperson a willing and
effective team member?

Are standards being achieved in all
aspects of the job?

10 Sales Force Administration

BASIC ADMINISTRATIVE CONTROLS

Apart from the forms used in planning and preparing a territory journey cycle discussed in the previous chapter, any company will need to develop certain minimum administrative records and procedures in standardised form. This aids all those involved in managing, controlling, measuring, analysing, interpreting and planning within the sales force and using data provided through the completion of forms and documents by members of the field sales force. The needs may vary by company, industry and market (consumer goods companies traditionally requiring more standard reporting and control documents), but likely basic documents required by a field sales force and its management structure would include:

- customer call record card
- journey plan notifications
- order forms
- daily activity reports
- credit/product uplift request notes
- advice of visit postcards
- contact report forms
- internal memo pads
- sales planning slips
- store promotional activity forms
- quote forms
- expense forms.

Sample designs of major items will follow in the text, and these may be adapted to suit particular company requirements depending on the nature of the industry or markets.

In addition, the head office support functions are likely to issue a number of standard documents that may be routed to field sales personnel, including:

- acknowledgement of order receipt
- invoices
- advice of despatch notes
- product uplift notes
- credit notes
- payment overdue notes (including computer printouts giving accounts' payment status).

Example 10.1 Customer call record

Name:	**Buyer:**
Address:	**Other contacts:**
Telephone:	**Early closing:**
Company display units:	**Buying hours:**
Other display notes:	**Special delivery notes:**
Type of account:	

Sales history: Year:	198	198	198	Forecast 198
Cases:				
Values:				

Date of call	Product							Objectives/Notes
	Stock							
	Order							
	Stock							
	Order							
	Stock							
	Order							
	Stock							
	Order							
	Stock							
	Order							
	Stock							
	Order							
	Stock							
	Order							
	Stock							
	Order							
	Stock							
	Order							
	Stock							
	Order							
	Stock							
	Order							
	Stock							
	Order							

Notes:

304

Customer call records — These could be in the form of either a double-sided record card, or, as I generally prefer for most companies operating regular calls on established customers, a record folder or envelope in which can be kept copies of current documents such as order notes, credit and payment notes, copy invoices, etc. The basic information normally required to be recorded on the customer call record would include:

- trading name of the customer
- ownership (if relevant or not apparent otherwise)
- full postal address
- telephone number
- buyer's name (and names of other key parties)
- early closing days/trading hours/special calling or delivery times
- stock/order records
- notes on display or merchandising aids or facilities
- call objectives
- other relevant call notes.

Example 10.1 illustrates a basic design for a customer call record. Salespersons should be trained in the disciplines of using the customer call record as a planning aid, setting call-by-call objectives, recording details of stocks, orders and promotional activity.

Journey plans — A journey plan should be submitted in advance of a day's or week's work to the line manager as a control that the salesperson has a specific work programme, and to enable the line manager to arrange to work with the territory salesperson or conduct a field follow-check on call activities, or to enable head office departments to contact the salesperson if necessary.

In an industry where set journey cycles are not possible or practical, or for an account executive who is calling on key multiple accounts, the journey plan may simply be an advance list of the calls and contacts to be made the following week (Example 10.2(a)).

A territory salesperson working to a regular journey cycle schedule, of which the field supervisor has a copy, might complete a journey plan similar to the one in Example 10.2(b). By simply referring to the appropriate day number in the master copy of the journey cycle schedule the field supervisor can establish the exact calls to be made that day and the effective calling order, and can then meet the territory salesperson at any point in the working day.

Another simple system of journey planning where calls are pre-identified and can be planned several days or a week or so ahead is for the salesperson to complete the essential name and address information of calls in planned calling order on the **daily activity report** ahead of time. He can then tear off the back copy and post it to his line manager as a journey plan preferably with a note of specific

305

call objectives. He can complete all the other information at the time of actually making the calls. Alternatively a format such as that in Example 10.2(c) might be developed and used.

Order forms The order form will generally need to have at least three copies, one each for the customer, the head office order processing department, and the salesperson's files. The style and format will vary with the nature of the goods, size of product range and pack variations, company information needs, and the company's administrative preferences, but essentially it is likely to show such information as:

- name and full delivery address of the customer
- billing address, if different from above
- customer's reference number (if relevant)
- company reference number
- sales person's name and territory number
- special delivery instructions
- list of goods being ordered, including names of items, pack sizes, quantities
- prices of goods being ordered (may be preprinted if the product range is also preprinted)
- total order quantities and values.

Companies with a very standard product range are likely to find it simpler to pre-print the entire product range, pack sizes, case prices, and any other standard data, thus minimising the actual writing by salespersons. It is also advisable to print clearly on the customer's copy of the order form all standard terms and conditions of trade, limitations of warranties, etc., and to have the customer sign the order form acknowledging that he has seen and placed the order as prepared and read all applicable terms and conditions.

Some customers provide their own order form as part of their own internal processes, so the supplier of goods should satisfy himself that the conditions specified on the customer's order form are compatible with his own terms of supply, or are superseded when his salesperson transfers order details to the supplier's order form and has the customer acknowledge the order with a signature.

Of course the situation is not as straightforward when orders are taken by telephone, but it might be the practice to post an order acknowledgement to the customer prior to despatch of goods. With regular supply situations to established customers there is customarily a strong element of goodwill in all relationships, and the supplier will have a particular interest in resolving any problems or disputes in a mutually acceptable manner.

Computerised order and stock control systems may be extended to include information on stock levels on the order form at the time of ordering by product. This may enable a head office computer-

Example 10.2   Journey plans

(a) *A simple format of a journey plan*

JOURNEY PLAN	**Week commencing:** 1 April 1986
Salesperson: Charles Wilson	**Function/territory:** Key accounts

MONDAY	10 a.m. Acme Supermarkets (John Smith), Newtown Rd, Bradford (0274-00000)
	2 p.m. A & B Hypermarkets (Jim Brown), Bradford Rd, Leeds (0532-00000)
TUESDAY	9 a.m. Giant Markets (Mike Jones), Coral St, Bradford (0274-11111)
	1 p.m. Jack Parrish – Manchester area sales manager Airport Hotel, Manchester (061-123 4567)
WEDNESDAY	a.m. Store checking branches of Huddersfield Co-op.
	1.30 p.m. Huddersfield Co-op (Fred Jackman), High Rd, Huddersfield (0484-22222)
THURSDAY	Monthly key accounts review with National Sales Manager at Head Office Overnight: Swank Hotel, Newcastle (0632-33333)
FRIDAY	Northern Division Sales Conference Swank Hotel, Newcastle (0632-33333)

(b)

JOURNEY PLAN	**Week commencing:** 1 April 1986
Salesperson: Jim Warton	**Function/territory:** 45

MONDAY	Journey schedule day 6
TUESDAY	Journey schedule day 7
WEDNESDAY	Journey schedule day 8
THURSDAY	Journey schedule day 9 Overnight: Swank Hotel, Newcastle (0632-33333)
FRIDAY	Northern Division Sales Conference Swank Hotel, Newcastle (0632-33333)

307

Example 10.2   Journey plans (contd.)

(c) A comprehensive journey plan

Salesperson/Account executive:

Territory/Function: **Week commencing:**

Customer name & address	Time	Objectives/notes	Last call	Overnight location
MONDAY 1. 2. 3. 4. 5. 6. 7. 8.				
TUESDAY 1. 2. 3. 4. 5. 6. 7. 8.				
WEDNESDAY 1. 2. 3. 4. 5. 6. 7. 8.				
THURSDAY 1. 2. 3. 4. 5. 6. 7. 8.				
FRIDAY 1. 2. 3. 4. 5. 6. 7. 8.				

generated order form to be issued each time a new order is received, which shows average order levels (product movement) by product and prints out stock levels on the last or other recent visits. This effectively reduces the need for some call record data being maintained by the territory salesperson. Extensions of such systems can link customers' stock and order records, as maintained or recorded by the supplier's salespersons, to the supplier's inventories and production scheduling programmes. This aids more accurate sales forecasting and better production and inventory controls and schedules, with likely financial benefits to the supplier.

Daily activity reports

Some form of daily activity report should be required from all types and levels of salesperson, including territory salespersons (for consumer goods, industrial or service products), key account executives and field sales managers, partly as a record of activity and partly for management control purposes.

A key account executive or industrial salesperson is likely to produce his activity report in the form of **contact reports**, which are basically brief summary notes of each key account contact made, indicating who was met, the content of the meeting discussions, summaries of agreements and proposals reached, and any subsequent action required (including a note of who should progress the action).

Any field sales manager working with a subordinate with the objective of monitoring performance and providing training and motivation should prepare a brief training review record noting strengths and weaknesses observed and training given. This record should be kept as part of ongoing performance review and development programmes.

If a field sales manager is making visits to retail or other customers with a view to establishing levels of display and distribution, he should record his observations on a simple form to be reviewed with the appropriate salesperson as soon afterwards as is practical. Prompt feedback is an essential element in the training and development process if the feedback is to have current relevance to activities and performance.

When a field sales manager is conducting a **follow-check** on a recent day's work by a territory salesperson (which is particularly appropriate in many consumer goods markets) the best recording aid is to use the manager's copy of the relevant daily activity report, and mark findings on the copy as appropriate.

At the level of a territory salesperson, the daily activity report is most important to:

- identify exactly who was visited during the working day
- provide the salesperson's statement of his work activity

309

- provide a summary record of orders received, enabling perform-ance statistics to be prepared and conversion rates of calls to orders to be monitored
- enable other relevant in-call activity to be monitored as reported by the salesperson, e.g. quantities of goods merchandised, display levels and activity
- provide a post-call control enabling the field sales manager to check and monitor performance and identify training needs
- enable calls made to be compared, either manually or by computer (if the company has sophisticated computer controls and systems), with journey schedule plans and call frequencies, and call coverage monitored accordingly
- provide a record of reported activity that may be checked by field sales managers who conduct post-call follow-checks.

The information required by a company on its daily activity report will depend on the information and control needs of the business and the resources available to process, and analyse the information, and to take action. Information should be collected that is meaningful, useful and actually used in the management of the business. A typical daily activity report might identify:

- the salesperson's name and territory number
- the date
- time of first and last calls
- time spent at each call (in minutes or work units)
- name and address of each call visited in the sequence calls were made
- in-call activity:
  − products on display
  − products merchandised
  − orders received.

So that field management can identify new accounts or pioneer calls, the company might request that any such calls be entered from the bottom of the daily activity report working up. All entries on a daily activity report should be made immediately a call is completed while the information is fresh in the mind of the territory salesperson, and any information requested should appear relevant to the call activity or sales and marketing programmes. An illustration of a fairly basic daily activity report is seen in Example 10.3.

Credit and product uplift notes A salesperson will occasionally have reason to issue credit notes or arrange for the uplift and transfer of goods, perhaps because of a wrong delivery or merchandise damaged in transit. Some companies prefer the salesperson to request the uplift of goods, using an

Example 10.3 Daily activity report

DAILY ACTIVITY REPORT	Date:
Name:	**Territory:**
Mileage: Close	**Time in–first call:**
Open	**Time out–last call:**
Day	

Customer's name & address	A		B		C		D		E		F		1	2	Cases merchandised	Cases ordered
	S	O	S	O	S	O	S	O	S	O	S	O				
1.																
2.																
3.																
4.																
5.																
6.																
7.																
8.																
9.																
10.																
11.																
12.																
13.																
14.																
15.																
16.																
17.																
18.																
19.																
20.																
21.																
22.																
23.																
24.																
25.																
Totals																

Notes: The letters A–F might represent the particular products offered by a company.
S = stock recorded in inventory on entry
O = order quantity placed
Columns 1 & 2 might be used flexibly for any current particular recording requirements, possibly relating to sales and promotional activity.

311

appropriate form; after goods are collected and checked, the head office will issue a credit note. This may provide a more efficient and strict control against abuse of credit notes. However, in many f.m.c.g. markets there are many occasions where small amounts of goods are broken or otherwise unsaleable, and the salesperson needs to arrange credit. A store may have its own policy of 'no orders before damages are credited'. In such events the territory salesperson might have authority to remove goods personally and either issue a credit note or send a product uplift note, which will generate the credit subsequently, noting that goods have already been collected and destroyed. As a management control it should be insisted that any goods credited are removed from a customer's premises, so that they are not part of any future claim for credit, and that unsaleable goods are destroyed. Field sales managers should require their subordinates to send them copies of all product uplift or credit note forms or requests, and check for unusual frequencies of such notes, as the abuse of credit note systems is not uncommon as a means of bribing customers to place orders or even as a means of salespersons exchanging credit notes against fictitious damaged goods in exchange for personal benefit, such as other goods.

Each company will need to develop a system and design forms that suit its needs, administrative systems and sales force controls.

Advice of visit postcards

In industries where it is customary for salespersons to make appointments with buyers or advise customers of a scheduled visit date it is useful to design and print a standard 'advice of visit' postcard, which can be despatched ahead of time by the salesperson to give the date and time of the call, and might also request the buyer to have stock levels checked prior to the call.

Contact report forms

Certain sales managers – such as key account executives calling on major buyers and other contacts in the company's major accounts or export sales executives visiting overseas markets and contacts – should produce their activity reports in the form of a contact report. A simple memo pad can be designed to include:

- name of the manager preparing the contact report
- addressee to receive the report, e.g. National Sales Manager
- parties to whom copies should be supplied, e.g. appropriate field sales manager in the case of a report by a key account excecutive
- date of report
- note of persons to take action
- date of next appointment or deadline dates for actionable points.

See example 10.4 for a sample layout.

Example 10.4   Contact report form

CONTACT REPORT	From:
Contact:	**To:**

	Copies:
Objectives:	**Date:**

Notes on discussions and agreements	Action
Signed:	

The report should identify:

- who was met
- the objectives and purpose of the meeting
- the summary content of the meeting, including agreements reached and further action programmes and plans to develop business.

The design and use of internal memo forms or pads is purely a domestic matter for each company. Generally they are simply used as a means of informing of events or occurrences relevant to the operations of the company, or requesting action from specific departments or persons. As most field sales operatives might not have facilities to type memos, particularly if notes are being prepared in a car or at a customer's premises, it can be useful if, say, a three part self-carboned memo form is available.

313

Sales planning slips

Sales planning slips are a very basic and useful tool in the stock-checking and order-taking process. Their use is certainly not limited to consumer goods salespersons; they can be designed to suit any product or service, acting as a checklist during a presentation. They would normally consist simply of a list of the company's products with several columns for general use, such as noting the level of stock of each product or the suggested order quantities. They are a most useful aid during a sales presentation to hold a buyer's attention, and to draw his attention to specific promotional offers or special offers (which might even be highlighted on the sales planning slip with the use of a different colour ink). Where an objection is raised to any item or quantity, it then becomes easy to home in on the objection, re-present the benefits, and close again with positive, concession, alternative or fear closes as appropriate.

Example 10.5 shows a basic format for a sales planning slip.

Store promotion programmes

In many companies where promotional activity is normal, and is frequently organised by the territory salespersons at the level of the individual store or wholesaler, some form of documentation needs to be developed to control the promotion in respect of:

- costs
- quantities
- commitments
- performance.

A form may be designed that suits internal management and control requirements, and that can be used by the territory salesperson in planning and negotiating special promotional programmes and activity with customers.

Example 10.6 illustrates how such a form might be used in respect of a promotion programme for a soap product. The particular store has agreed to match the manufacturer's 10 per cent price rebate on sales during the agreed period of the promotion by giving a 20 per cent discount to consumers making purchases during the promotional period, with the objective of increasing consumer trial and generating a higher level of repeat sales. The salesperson would agree with the store buyer or manager to have appropriate special promotional display space allocated during the period of the promotion, and use suitable display aids, which might either be designed by the store or supplied by the manufacturer. The form enables the opening stock at the start of the promotion, orders delivered during the promotion and closing stock recordings to be used to assess the monies due as the manufacturer's rebate contribution. The increase in average sales can also be measured, and it is always useful as a control to measure any change in the average

314

Example 10.5 Sales planning slip

Supakleen Products Plc		Stock	Order		
Supasoap	Large	15	**20**		
	Medium	10	**30**		
	Small	20	**50**		
Ultrawash	Large	20	**50**		
	Medium	10	**60**		
	Small	15	**30**		
Wondawhite	5kg.				
	2kg.				
Supastarch	500g.				
	250g.				

WORLDWIDE INSURANCE	Present cover	**Recommended minimum**

Home contents:
    standard
    'new for old'
    accidental damage
	10,000	} **15,000**

All risks: valuables	3,000	**5,000 revalue**

Extended cover:
    televisions
    pedal cycles
    credit cards
    cash
    personal effects
    visitor cover
	✓
	✓
	×
	×
	×
	×
		✓
		✓
		✓
		✓(200)
		✓(200)
		5,000

Public liability	100,000	**250,000**
Life assurance: whole life		

Automobile:
    comprehensive
    third party
    owner/driver
    any driver		

Note: The entries in these columns would actually be made by the salesperson at the call.
The pre-printed sales planning slip would have blank columns for flexible use.

315

volume in the few weeks following the promotion to assess whether the promotion actually did produce new trial and customers, or whether it simply produced an element of advance purchase and hoarding by established customers (resulting in a post-promotion downturn in sales).

Example 10.6 Store promotion programme – control form

Customer: Acme Supermarket 123 High Street Newtown				**Salesperson:** J. Warton **Territory:** 45 **Promotional period – buying dates:** 20 March 30 April **selling dates:** 1 April 30 April					
Product	**Normal case sales**	**Planned promotional case sales**	**Normal case cost**	**Promotional case cost**	**Normal retail price**	**Special retail price**	**Post-promotional analysis**		
							Actual promotion sales	**Actual cost**	
Supasoap – large	100	200	£30 (12's)	£27	£3.00	£2.40	180	£540	
Supasoap – small	50	100	£34 (24's)	£30.60	£1.75	£1.40	140	£476	

Notes: 1 Rebate of £3.00 and £3.40 per case on sales volumes during the promotional period as noted above to be paid retrospectively.
2 Store agrees to match the rebate and to discount consumer prices by full amount of matched contributions.

Signed:	**Approved:**	**Accepted:**
Salesperson	Area sales manager	Store manager

A form such as in the example might be routed to the field sales manager for approval and control purposes, and then passed to the appropriate head office department for payment.

Quote forms In industries where it is customary to quote to supply goods or services, then the suppliers may want to design a simple standard quote form for quotes to be prepared at the buyer's location by the salesperson. Such a form is likely to contain blank spaces for products, quantities, prices and delivery dates. Basic information needed on a quote form includes:

- supplier's name and full address details (and any regulatory company registration details)
- date of the quote
- period of validity of the quote
- name and signature of person authorised to prepare and submit the quote
- goods quoted on:
    - description and specifications of goods
    - quantity or volume involved
    - prices of units/cases or merchandise
    - rebates, discounts or allowances
- method of ordering/accepting the quote (i.e. signing and returning a copy)
- guarantees or warranties attached to the goods or contract to supply
- general terms and conditions of trade or related to the specific offer
- timing and terms of shipment or delivery of goods, or installation of plant or equipment
- payment terms, including deposits required on acceptance of the quote.

A quote is unlikely to be of indefinite validity as prices may vary frequently or significantly, particularly if there is a strong commodity element of inputs, or a significant proportion of imported parts or materials. If the quotes involved are international in nature then the reader may find it useful to refer to the relevant section of my companion volume *Practical Export Management* (London, Allen & Unwin, 1985), which elaborates on aspects of international trade. The quote document should clearly show the date on which the quote will lapse if not accepted, and might also have a clause stipulating that delivery must be effected within a certain period.

To avoid mistakes or misunderstandings the supplier should clearly describe the goods or services in specific terms, and not just rely on general phrases such as 'small' or 'large'; the supplier's brand name, generic name, broad specifications, pack sizes/weights/volumes might all be included along with the number of shipping or individual units. Prices must show whether they refer to ex-factory, delivered to customer's premises, installed, or such other details as clearly indicate where and when they will be delivered or ownership transfer, which may depend on the practice of the trade, nature of the goods, or buyer's requirements. Practice is very different in the

317

United States from the United Kingdom: in the United Kingdom much merchandise is sold on the basis that it is delivered by the supplier to the buyer, whereas in the United States it is common to quote on goods delivered only ex-factory, free alongside rail, free on board truck, and so on.

If there are any applicable discounts or rebates, the terms under which these can be earned should be stated on invoices – such as '2% discount for payments received within 15 days of invoice date'. The reverse of the quote form might suitably be used to detail all general terms of supply, order acceptance and delivery, but if this is done a note on the front of the quote document should draw attention to conditions exhibited on the reverse.

Expense forms

This is one of the essential cost and management control documents used by field sales managers. Integrity is a vital quality in the sales force, where salespersons generally have more independence and more opportunities to abuse systems than do head office based personnel. Abuses are usually very small, such as claiming lunch for customers when the real guest was a personal friend, or exaggerating parking fees. But, whatever the abuse, once it is identified it must be stopped quickly and firmly and appropriate disciplinary action taken if standards are not to be compromised.

An expense claim form is necessary as a company record of business expenses incurred in the pursuit of orders, as a control, and as part of internal accounting and auditing procedures. Some companies prefer to give fixed allowances on certain standard items of expense, such as lunch allowances, parking fees, telephone costs, mileage allowances for petrol, car washing costs, and possibly for overnight accommodation and subsistence. Providing the allowance levels are realistic and set at a level that permits the performance of all necessary job functions, I favour a standard allowance approach to expenses wherever practical as it encourages economy and reduces the risks and opportunities of abuse, leaving management control time a little freer for more productive activities. Standards of acceptable overnight hotel accommodation might vary with seniority, as will the type of company vehicle provided. Car maintenance costs clearly can only ever be reimbursed as actual costs incurred, unless the salesperson is using his own vehicle and paid a more generous rate of allowance per mile. When salespersons are required to provide their own transport there is always the risk that the vehicles will be less well maintained than company-owned vehicles, with possibly more time lost through maintenance problems. Business mileage for territory salespersons can be monitored if standard journey cycle schedules contain a mileage estimate; additionally, the daily activity report can request a notation of actual mileage claimed daily.

It would be customary as a management control for each line

318

manager to have responsibility for checking and authorising the expense claims of immediate subordinates, perhaps up to a prescribed limit of budgetary authority before it is referred to higher management. Where expenses are customarily high in relation to income levels it would be wise for the company to consider providing a float or, possibly, company credit cards.

A simple expense control form is illustrated in Example 10.7 and this might be used by field salespersons on a weekly basis. Obviously the type of form finally used should be acceptable to the company accountants and auditors to comply with their standards and practices.

Example 10.7   Sales force expense control form

Name: **Function:**

                                          Week ending:

Date:	Sunday	Monday	Tuesday	Wednesday	Thursday	Friday	Saturday
Lunch							
Other meals							
Accommodation							
Entertainment							
Car maintenance							
Petrol & oil							
Telephone							
Postage							
Other travel							
Other (specify):							

Signed: **Approved:**

Note: Attach all receipts to the top copy of this form.
  Top copy – to line manager.
  Bottom copy – retain.

GENERAL FORM GUIDELINES

Each company will develop systems to meet its internal administrative requirements and controls in managing sales force operations. However, all documents should be designed with the ease of comprehension and administrative compliance in mind, to minimise

319

time given to administration, to facilitate prompt action on receipt of a document by the appropriate party or department, and to standardise systems and procedures internally. The basic guidelines in designing forms are:

- keep the layout simple
- only ask for relevant information that aids management, control, performance measurement, and planning
- encourage the completion of forms immediately after the activity to which it relates is completed
- wherever possible note any special instructions relating to the completion or submission or routeing of copies on the form (e.g. 'top copy to order processing department' or 'yellow copy to area manager').

Whenever a form is being designed it is wise to submit the drafts both to the persons who will be expected to complete and submit it, and also to persons receiving or analysing the data, to ensure they agree it is simple, relevant, and easy to complete, analyse, control and interpret.

ESSENTIAL CUSTOMER COMMUNICATIONS

At this point of the text some brief commentary is appropriate on the essential company-produced literature that is generally supplied to customers in standard formats:

- product price lists
- product specification sheets
- catalogues and brochures
- advertising and promotional information sheets.

Each of these documents is intended to communicate information, create attention and interest, and instil in the buyer a desire to pursue contact with the salesperson to the point where an order is placed.

Product price
lists and
specification
sheets

These may be separate or combined, but essentially need to include information on:

- product names and/or descriptions and reference codes
- pack sizes (e.g. number of units per carton)
- package weights and dimensions
- price quotes per shipping unit to point of change of ownership (e.g. ex-factory or delivered to customer)

320

- standard terms of sale, payment terms and conditions
- warranties and exclusions
- period of validity of price list or quote.

The specification sheets may also cover product technical data, possibly including illustrations, drawings, designs, wiring diagrams (for electrical goods), maintenance data, etc.

Catalogues and brochures

These are intended to show the product to a prospective buyer, although they cannot substitute for a practical demonstration and presentation of a sample. Illustrations should be in photographic form and not just a line drawing, although those can usefully aid a presentation where they show the workings or functions of a product.

Advertising and promotional programme information sheets

These are most commonly used by suppliers of consumer goods who wish to motivate additional display and distribution by demonstrating the extent of their advertising and promotional support for products. A suitable summary leaflet, to be used by the sales force in presentations and which can also be left with buyers, will normally illustrate the product and the extent of media support through the use of simple diagrams, illustrations, comparisons, tables, graphs, etc.

Presentation guidelines

The reader may find some of the principles and guidelines expounded in Chapter 3 on communications relevant to the presentation of information to customers. Suffice it to say at this point that:

- each document should include the information necessary to enable a buyer and his specialist advisers to evaluate products and take decisions
- the content should be presented in readable, concise, clear, instructional format and avoid obtuse subtleties that distract from its purpose.

321

- The standardisation of administrative systems and procedures aids those involved in managing, controlling, measuring, analysing, interpreting, and planning using data provided through the completion of forms and documents by members of the field sales force.

- Sales force documents and forms are likely to include some or all of: customer call records; journey planning forms; order forms; daily activity reports; credit/product uplift request notes; advice of visit notes; contact reports; internal memo pads; sales planning slips; store promotional programme forms; quote forms; and expense forms.

- Forms and documents should be designed to aid understanding and administrative compliance, to minimise time given to the administrative functions, to facilitate prompt action on their receipt, and to standardise internal systems and procedures.

- Forms should be simple in design and structure, ask only for information relevant to the management process, encourage accuracy through the prompt completion of administrative documentation, and wherever possible include instructions relating to correct completion, submission and routeing of copies.

- Literature that may be supplied to customers in standard format might include: product price lists; product specification sheets; catalogues and brochures; and advertising and promotional information sheets.

CHECKLIST   STANDARD FORMS AND ADMINISTRATIVE DOCUMENTS

	Useful	Necessary	Prepared
Sales force documentation			
Customer call record card or folder			
Journey plan notification form			
Journey schedule planning sheets			
Order forms			
Quote forms			
Daily activity reports			
Product credit and/or product uplift request notes			
Advice of visit notification cards			
Contact report forms			
Internal memo pads			
Sales planning slips			
Store promotional programme control and planning forms			
Expense control forms			
Invoices			
Despatch notes			
Credit notes			
Product uplift notes			
Late payment notifications			
Confirmation/acknowledgement of order			
Customer literature			
Price lists			
Product specification sheets			
Catalogues & brochures			
Advertising and promotional programme information sheets			

323

11 Sales Management Control

CONTROL PRINCIPLES

A major function of managers is to exercise control over the performance and functions within their sphere of responsibility, and to ensure that performance and results relate to and comply with the plans, programmes and policies of the company. Managers are especially concerned with maximising the productivity of the scarce or limiting resources under their control – i.e. people, time, and the company tangible and intangible resources.

However, a control cannot exist in a vacuum. Before controls can be developed and implemented, it is essential first to identify and highlight **key result areas** that can be subject to control in quantifiable terms and then to set realistic **standards of performance** against which productivity and activity can be measured. It is also necessary to identify and communicate policies and procedures affecting job holders at each tier of the organisation and to define the scope of jobs, including limitations on authority and responsibilities.

In the sales environment, controls can be exercised at the levels of:

- field sales managers (field controls)
- sales office general management (performance and planning controls).

Generally the field sales manager will be concerned with practical controls that enable him to monitor performance in relation to standards and objectives at the territory and call level – the **micro** level. The sales office general management will normally be more concerned with controls at the **macro** level, i.e. monitoring how the whole sales force performs against company standards and objectives and plans, but will, of course, supply micro-level data to field management for its local controls.

Control, like training, is an ongoing management function. Controls can be **continuous** in nature, that is, designed to monitor that salespersons or managers are doing the tasks and duties assigned to them, and to reduce the risk of problems occurring (prevention is always better and usually much less costly than cure). Continuous controls can be developed to monitor objective factors in such aspects of job performance as quantity, quality, cost, and time.

Because circumstances frequently change, and deviations from plans do happen, often for reasons outside the control of operating managers, another tier of controls can be designed to operate as

warnings. In some project planning and programmes, critical path analyses are used to monitor that each stage of the project is reached at the right point in time. In the sales environment the most common warnings are numerical in nature, thrown up from the manual or computer analyses that record progress and results in each key result area. A control might be a printout showing an overspend against budget at a point in time, or a significant shortfall in sales volume against targets at a key point in the year. Because such warnings need to operate rapidly in key result areas if managers are to have the opportunity to identify the nature and causes of problems and develop and implement corrective action, it is more critical that the warnings identify the direction of deviation and give an order of magnitude than that the warning is totally accurate.

Commonsense must prevail in building warning systems. In some industries, sales do not flow in a steady stream, and to avoid the constant 'flashing' of warning lights it is wise to build into a warning system levels of tolerance that are normal or acceptable. If a budget is broken down into 12 equal monthly amounts, but expenditure is heavily biased towards the first half of the year, there is little benefit in having a warning at the half-year mark; perhaps the realities should be recognised and budgets aligned with expected expenditure periods.

Control can be assisted by the use of computer printouts (where computer resources exist), graphs, charts and tables that may serve to alert the recipient to deviations from norms or plans in key result areas.

It is particularly important to concentrate control in the sales force on key result areas because of the natural tendency we all have to concentrate effort on those aspects of a job that get noticed or are emphasised in training, bulletins or other verbal or non-verbal communications. A sales manager who gives too much attention to cosmetic factors, such as car care and maintenance, risks distracting his subordinates from the key result areas of making effective sales presentations, increasing distribution or improving product display. That does not mean that standards should not be set for maintenance of company equipment, including vehicles – standards should be set in all areas where quantifiable or objective measures of performance are possible and practical.

All personnel should be familiar with their standards of performance so that they can check and evaluate their own performance against known objective factors and criteria. **Self-control** is generally the most effective control, if only because the individual is aware of all he does whereas a manager sees only part of the activities. It is useful to encourage salespersons to keep their own simple running records in key result areas, such as call rates, or case or volume sales against targets, and to ask the salesperson to summarise his performance and achievements against key result areas. Self-control is also encouraged

325

where a territory performance target is broken down to the level of each call. For example, when a target is set for the territory to sell 1000 cases of the special offer in the month there is far greater likelihood the target will be achieved if at the monthly area planning meeting the salesperson is given the task of assigning a case target on each customer's call record card that needs to be achieved on the next call (of course, the call target would relate to its realistic potential).

One philosophy of management that I, like many practising sales managers, particularly subscribe to is the principle of **management by exception**. If standards of performance, objectives, plans, budgets and tactics all interrelate, and managers have in-built continuous controls, management time and effort can be devoted to identifying exceptions or deviations from the norm and taking corrective action when they are significant. A salesperson who makes only five calls one day against a standard of ten may not require special attention from his line manager if he normally achieves standards. Perhaps his car broke down, or he had an unusual amount of stock merchandising to do. The manager's main concern is that the lost calls be picked up, and the salesperson may be confident he can do that over the next day or two. However, if the salesperson is consistently falling short of the standard call rate on which the territory journey cycle schedule is dependent, then the manager must investigate more thoroughly, plan corrective training or take such other action as becomes necessary to ensure coverage is maintained.

MANAGING TIME

At several points of the text, including in this chapter, I have made reference to management of the scarce resource of **time**. In Chapter 9 on territory management some coverage is given to time management in respect of efficient journey planning as it relates to markets where set journey schedules are the normal coverage method. But that system is not universally applicable, and makes no allowance for the management time planning exercise.

Use of time for most salespersons, key account executives and those serving industrial and specialty markets can be studied under the categories of:

- preparatory
- productive
- unproductive
- personal
- call management.

Example 11.1 illustrates the design of a single form which shows how a salesperson can analyse his time use by identifying the particular activities that fill his normal working day under the general headings identified, and surveying how time is being utilised over a period of, say, two to four working weeks. The results will generally show that very little time is devoted to productive activities that actually generate business or even to the main preparatory functions that lead to productive activity. This self-awareness exercise may assist in better organising time and functional activities.

Example 11.1 Sales activity time management analysis

Activity	1	2	3	4	5	6	7	8	9	10	Total	Ave.	%	Plan %
Preparatory														
Customer knowledge	10	120			40				90	40	300	30	7	10
Proposal preparation	10			60	40	20	40	40	40	40	290	29	7	10
Target planning	20		60			20			30		130	13	3	3
Productive														
Contact making	60	20				100	20	60	40	20	320	32	7	8
Proposal presentation	30			60	80	20		80	20	40	330	33	8	10
Unproductive														
Travel	80	60	20	90	120	120	20	150	110	60	830	83	19	18
Waiting at calls	40	20		30	60			20	20		190	19	4	2
Routine administration	20	30	150	30	20	40	180	20		60	550	55	13	10
Complaint handling	0	20	30			20	40			40	150	15	3	3
Meeting attendance	0		120				60			30	210	21	5	5
Personal														
Meal breaks	60	30	60	60	80	40	60	50	40	60	540	54	12	10
Other		20						20			40	4	1	0
Call-management														
Post-sale account servicing	30	60	40	40	30				50	60	310	31	7	5
Evaluation of programme results	30	40				40	40			20	170	17	4	6
TOTALS	390	420	480	370	470	420	460	440	440	470	4360	436	100	100

Note: Use of time recorded in minutes to nearest 10-minute interval.

Sales managers' time management A similar exercise can be performed for a field sales manager (or any other sales management function for that matter). Example 11.2 illustrates how a time analysis might be structured for a typical month of 20 working days, assuming each identified activity is independent

Example 11.2 Sales manager's time use analysis

Activity	Day 1	2	3	4	5	6	7	8	9	10	11	12	13	14	15	16	17	18	19	20	Total	%	Plan %
Management																							
Field training:																							
territory 1	4											4									8	4	6
territory 2				4											6						10	5	6
territory 3			6								4			4							14	7	6
territory 4																8	8	8			24	12	6
territory 5								6											3		9	5	6
territory 6						4									4						8	4	6
Field audits:																							
territory 1	2										2										4	2	2
territory 2			2									2									4	2	2
territory 3										2											2	1	2
territory 4									3												3	1	2
territory 5								2													2	1	2
territory 6				2										2							4	2	2
Recruitment		8																			8	4	3
Customer queries				1		1				1									2		5	3	2
Bulletin preparation		1			1															1	3	1	1
Sales meetings					2		4														6	3	3
Counselling									2				1								3	1	3
Personal accounts	1					2					1	1							2		7	3	4
Distributor contacts	1			1					2	1				1					1		7	3	2
Administration																							
Report preparation	$\frac{1}{2}$		$\frac{1}{2}$	$\frac{1}{2}$		$\frac{1}{2}$		$\frac{1}{2}$	$\frac{1}{2}$		$\frac{1}{2}$	$\frac{1}{2}$	$\frac{1}{2}$	$\frac{1}{2}$	$\frac{1}{2}$			$\frac{1}{2}$	$\frac{1}{2}$		$6\frac{1}{2}$	3	3
Correspondence		1			2		1	$\frac{1}{2}$		2		1		$\frac{1}{2}$	3	1	1		1	$2\frac{1}{2}$	$16\frac{1}{2}$	8	5
Journey planning					$\frac{1}{2}$					$\frac{1}{2}$					$\frac{1}{2}$					$\frac{1}{2}$	2	1	1
Personal expenses					$\frac{1}{2}$					$\frac{1}{2}$					$\frac{1}{2}$					$\frac{1}{2}$	2	1	1
Credit control	1														1			1			3	1	1
Driving/travel	1	1	$1\frac{1}{2}$	$1\frac{1}{4}$	1	$1\frac{1}{2}$	3	1	$1\frac{1}{2}$	1	$1\frac{1}{2}$	2	1	2	1	2	2	2	2	$\frac{1}{2}$	$29\frac{3}{4}$	15	15
Planning																							
Sales forecasting					1					1				$\frac{1}{2}$						1	$3\frac{1}{2}$	2	2
Promotion planning					1					1					1					2	5	3	3
Territory target/ objective setting					1				1				1				$\frac{1}{2}$			1	$4\frac{1}{2}$	2	3
TOTALS	$10\frac{1}{2}$	11	10	$9\frac{3}{4}$	10	9	8	10	10	10	9	$10\frac{1}{2}$	$9\frac{1}{2}$	$10\frac{1}{2}$	$11\frac{1}{2}$	11	$11\frac{1}{2}$	$11\frac{1}{2}$	$11\frac{1}{2}$	9	$203\frac{3}{4}$	100	100

of others. By becoming more aware of how time is used in relation to priority functions management should be more effectively directed to devote time to key result areas such as training.

Obviously not all management activities occur at regular intervals or with the same frequency. There are certain tasks the sales manager might perform only at infrequent intervals. As a useful time control it might be worth preparing a list of the main infrequent tasks and noting in which months action will need to be taken, as in the diary format in Example 11.3. This long-term planning exercise can then be incorporated in the particular month time management programme when appropriate.

Example 11.3   Sales manager's key task diary planner

	J	F	M	A	M	J	J	A	S	O	N	D
Annual sales forecast										×		
Annual cost budgets										×		
Annual sales force objectives											×	
Annual sales promotion plan											×	
Annual sales conference	×											
Manpower planning schedule										×		
Regional sales conferences				×			×					
National trade convention						×						
Field sales managers' meeting		×		×		×		×		×		×
Sales force appraisals							×					×
New starters' course	×			×				×				
Salary reviews							×					×
Vacations							×					
Quarterly performance review	×			×			×			×		

FIELD CONTROLS

At the outset of any discussion on field controls it is important to make the point that over-control can be a major demotivating influence on salespersons. Nobody likes to have his supervisor breathing down his neck, and performance is likely to suffer where salespersons feel excessive pressure. In any case, a manager has a limited amount of time available for allocation between the major management functions of controlling, training and planning; and, within each function, time is best allocated to those aspects having the most impact on results. In non-key result areas, field managers

329

should generally limit their control time to the occasional but thorough random check of such factors for each of their subordinates. Spotting the occasional exception and commenting on or raising it with the person involved maintains an awareness of the need for accuracy and honesty, provided always that over-control on peripheral matters does not distract from key result area performance. An important control over the activities of the salespersons is thus simply the reputation of the manager for having a 'nose' for the irregular, unexpected and unacceptable.

Remember, the purpose of control is to monitor deviations from standards and plans, and to alert the manager to the need to consider and take suitable corrective action. Once the need is recognised, the course of action must be identified, evaluated and implemented.

Identifying key result areas and setting standards of performance

Once overall plans, forecasts or targets and objectives have been established and communicated, the first stage in a first or second line manager developing and exercising controls within the field sales force environment is to break down all such plans to tactics and strategies and develop matching forecasts and objectives at the lower organisational tiers, such as areas, territories and individual accounts. This breakdown gives a measurement and achievement base to which the first line manager and territory salesperson can relate.

The next stage is to recognise the **key result areas**, and then to set **standards of performance** in all aspects of the job that are objectively measurable in terms of quantity, quality, cost or time.

Meaningful results-oriented standards of performance within the sales organisation can usually be set in respect of:

- standard daily call rate (i.e. minimum acceptable)
- average daily call rate (measured over a longer period such as one month or a journey cycle)
- minimum order size in volume or value
- average order size in volume or value
- total daily, weekly, monthly or annual sales volumes and values (forecasts or targets) − which can be set and measured by customer, territory and area, etc.
- identification of and contact with new prospects
- conversion ratio of calls to orders
- distribution by product, which can be monitored by customer, territory, area, etc., to national levels
- product display, where display is relevant as a measure of achievement and where the daily activity report measures aspects of display achievement
- achievement of scheduled call coverage
- pre-call setting of call objectives.

Standards of performance can also be set for factors that may have less or little impact on key result areas, such as:

- compliance with administrative systems and procedures (such as completing all reports daily and posting them in the evening in time for a last mail collection)
- maintenance and updating of customer call records
- submission of journey plans by set deadlines
- salesperson's appearance
- satisfactory maintenance of company equipment including a vehicle
- pre-scheduling of appointments with customers
- customer complaints or claims against warranties (where this is a factor within sales force control, possibly in certain installation contracts)
- staff turnover (sales managers only).

A standard of performance may be expressed as an absolute number, such as 'to achieve an average of 10 calls per day and 100% of scheduled call coverage each journey cycle', or in ratio terms, such as 'to convert 40% of calls made to orders'.

If a standard of performance is to have credibility and acceptability, and serve as a motivator to the person held responsible for achieving it, it must have a basis in historical performance and achievement. It must be seen to be both realistic and achievable by all those committed to achieving it as a result of their functional responsibilities. Equally, standards of performance will normally only be effective as motivators and controls in respect of factors that are subject to measurement within the company's systems and procedures. It would be of no benefit to set a standard of performance in respect of pioneer calls, say, if there is no system or procedure for separately identifying such new prospects within the broader reporting systems.

Standards of performance, once set, must be communicated both to the persons held accountable for achieving them, and to the managers responsible for controlling performance against standards.

Sources of control data

Once the need for and principles of control are understood and accepted by the field sales manager he should look for meaningful key result area and sundry control information from sources such as:

- journey plans
- customer call records
- daily activity reports
- credit notes
- expenses records
- discount and allowance (pricing) data.

331

Information can only be as useful as it is accurate. Managers, therefore, must emphasise the need for strict accuracy in all recordings, and this can often be verified by territory follow-checks (to be discussed subsequently). Errors and inaccuracies must be discussed promptly, and if there is a reason, such as misunderstanding of recording instructions communicated in bulletins, such misunderstandings need clarification. The larger the sales force the harder it is to standardise all recordings on reports and other forms or documents; each person makes his own interpretation of instructions even though each believes he is acting with total objectivity and clarity. Where there is room for misinterpretation of instructions (and even managers sometimes experience doubt on the intentions or meanings of communications), then the field sales manager must seek clarification from the sales head office and at least ensure that all his subordinate team are consistent in recording and interpretation, so that he can exercise control in an environment of consistency.

Journey plans

The line manager should ensure that he always receives his subordinates' journey plans sufficiently ahead of the period to which they refer so that he can take them into account when planning his own work programme. In general, if journey plans are submitted weekly in advance, then the manager would need to receive plans by the Wednesday or Thursday of the preceding week.

From the point of view of control, the field sales manager should be seeking to establish that:

- calls are actually scheduled to be made
- appointments have been made where beneficial or necessary
- appointments actually make the best use of time during the working day (i.e. appointments start at around 9 a.m. and are thereafter set at regular intervals, rather than starting at, say, 10.30 a.m. or in the mid-afternoon, with much of the working day thus being lost)
- scheduled journey calls actually match any particular scheduled journey day as detailed in a master journey cycle schedule
- pre-call objectives have been set (if the sales force systems require journey plans to note call objectives – especially important at the level of key account selling)
- the salesperson has given any relevant overnight accommodation or contact details so that he may be contacted should that be necessary.

Customer call records

When a field sales manager is working with a salesperson on a training day that is always a good time to conduct a review of customer call records. The salesperson should come to expect this as a normal part of the training day and accept that his manager will monitor that he is:

- keeping all records current
- operating a call objective system
- recording all requested data on reports and other records
- keeping customer record cards for all calls listed on the master journey cycle schedule
- not neglecting any particular product or part of the product range
- actively seeking additional volume and distribution, particularly to support promotional activity and advertising programmes.

When a salesperson is picked up on journey by a line manager who has not forewarned the salesperson of his visit, as is common in some f.m.c.g. companies, then a random call card check will generally indicate the normal standard of record keeping and planning. It might be particularly worth checking the call cards for any calls made earlier that day, and one or two other days recently worked (especially if a follow-check on any recent calls has been conducted) to establish that recent activity relates to current priorities communicated through bulletins and meetings.

The experienced field sales manager will find a wealth of information during his control checks on work activity and records. It is not uncommon to find accounts that have not received a scheduled call for quite considerable periods. Indeed, cards may simply be missing for particular customers – usually the small, more difficult to handle, and geographically remote calls. A manager is often alerted to check that call cards exist if a computer printout is from time to time issued showing which previous customers have shown no recent sales activity. When computer data systems permit, then it is very useful to have a printout once every journey cycle to show:

- that all calls due on any customer during the journey cycle were made on schedule (i.e. when the last call was due and when the last call was actually made)
- whether any scheduled visits made did not produce orders (i.e. should consideration be given to reducing that customer's call frequency?)
- when all customers still on the head office direct account list last placed an order.

A survey of the call record cards also helps a manager spot distribution weaknesses (which might be apparent also from field checks), lack of promotional activity or planning (objective setting) weaknesses – objectives recorded may simply not be pursued and acted on, may be unrelated to prescribed current priorities, or might

333

be quite unrealistic for that particular call. Where call cards reveal just very routine repeat orders, it might be worth the line manager visiting a few such customers to satisfy himself that calls are actually being made on schedule (rather than repeat orders being taken over the phone).

Daily activity reports

The daily activity report (D.A.R.) provides a source of control data in several respects to both field sales managers and the sales head office, and managers should exercise control over facets of the selling operation that are the subject of recordings on the D.A.R.

The first useful control is to compare actual calls made with those previously planned, whether on the journey plan for that day, or on the master journey cycle schedule if that system is being used, or on the pre-planning copy of the D.A.R. (the system whereby the names and addresses of customers are entered ahead of time on the D.A.R., and the back copy of the D.A.R. is sent to the first line manager a few days ahead of the work day to act as a form of journey plan). This comparison should be made by the first line manager promptly after the receipt of the D.A.R. (and salespersons should be instructed to post these daily in time to catch the last post). The field sales manager needs to monitor variations from the scheduled coverage, identify the nature of the variations, and try to establish any pattern or cause.

It is common to find that a salesperson (particularly one making a number of cold contacts on new prospects) schedules more calls than are actually made. Calls are possibly missed because no appointments had been fixed with the contact, or because other factors resulted in more time being given to calls made than was planned (or might have been warranted). If calls are missed, then there may be a pattern: perhaps they are the more geographically remote calls, or the ones where the buyers are considered less cooperative; or smaller customers are neglected in favour of the larger clients; or pioneer calls are simply not made, perhaps because a salesman paid mainly on commission is reluctant to miss a regular repeat order on the offchance of opening a new account at a small pioneer call.

Attention should be paid to any calls that were not made as planned. The salesperson might be requested to delete calls not actually made, and should also be asked to explain missed calls. Field managers can ask that missed calls be picked up on another day, but if workloads are balanced between days then that might not be too practical, and help from a relief salesperson might be needed.

The D.A.R. also enables call rates and the conversion ratio of calls to orders to be compared with standards and averages. If the D.A.R. requires any special recordings in respect of display and distribution, then these recordings should also be compared with standards and targets.

If pioneer calls are to be separately noted or identified on a D.A.R.,

334

then a control will be to note that such calls are being made and in sufficient numbers to meet standards, and that a reasonable number are being converted to active calls.

If the D.A.R. records daily mileage figures, these can be compared with any pre-planned mileage estimates appearing on the master journey cycle schedule, and variances discussed if significant. For example, if mileage is unusually high but call rate is down, then there may have been a degree of 'calling back' on customers where the buyer was initially unavailable. The manager must control that such 'call backs' are worthwhile, justifiable and more productive than missed calls. If mileage is significantly high, yet all calls appear to be made according to plans, is there an element of private mileage being included with the business mileage?

Should the D.A.R. require the recording of the time of first or last calls, then this information may be used in any field follow-checks (with consideration to the comment made later in this chapter on the limited recall accuracy of customers found during follow-checks).

It is always better for the salesperson himself to enter any relevant totals at the bottom of columns on the D.A.R. in order to make him aware of achievements and give a basis for self-assessment and self-control. Many field managers like to transfer such summary data onto tables, charts or graphs to help them communicate with their team on their individual and overall area achievements in key result areas (such as call rates, orders to calls, average order sizes/volumes/values, distribution, pioneer calls, etc.). These visual aids help to ensure that the field manager and his team are aware of results and activities, and can plan necessary corrective action, whilst aiding the control process by ensuring that the manager is analysing, interpreting and using information available to him.

Credit notes

If salespersons have any authority to arrange for credit notes to be issued then field managers should exercise control by:

- requiring copies of all credit notes or credit requests to be sent to the field manager for his approval
- laying down strict guidelines on the occasions or reasons when credit notes might be issued
- ensuring that if credit is given for damaged or wrongly shipped merchandise all such merchandise is uplifted from the customer's premises prior to the granting of credit
- controlling the issue of the blank credit note books or forms (which ideally should have pre-printed serial numbers on them)
- checking the credit note book or forms when working with the salesperson to ensure that he has previously personally seen all the credit requests coming through for his approval.

The field manager must be aware of any possible abuses within the crediting system operating within his organisation, exercise firm positive control, and deal equally firmly with abuses identified.

Expenses records

Expense recording and control were covered in some depth in Chapter 10. Controlling expenses rarely has a major or significant impact on the key result areas, but it remains an essential management function and duty. Generally it is better wherever possible to reduce the time needed in exercising controls over expenditure by fixing standard expense levels or guidelines for normal cost-incurring activities such as lunch allowances, postage, telephone costs, car mileage, overnight hotel and subsistence, and so on.

Where abuse of expenses is identified and confirmed after investigation then managers must always respond with firm action according to the company's disciplinary practice; a blind eye can never be turned to any lack of integrity.

Discount and allowance data

Where the salesperson has any flexibility to modify prices or quotes to obtain business, the field manager should be aware of any scope for abuse and satisfy himself that no such abuse is occurring. Rebates that relate directly to sales volumes and are paid at the end of any fixed period such as a year are in general less subject to abuse, although some customers may choose to increase order levels close to a year end to achieve the next level of discount or rebate. The supplier may have little control over that, even though it may mean he is obtaining a slightly lower price for goods that will not be sold immediately; however, customers are well aware of the costs of financing inventory, and in general will not overbuy unless they can move goods through quickly.

Field checks or audits Field checks by line managers of f.m.c.g. companies or producers of other goods or services offered through retail outlets or direct to the consuming public offer an excellent opportunity to keep in touch with the market and customers, and to monitor the performance and activities of the members of the sales team. Broadly speaking there are two fundamental types of field check:

- the general check or general audit
- the follow-check or audit.

The general check or audit

Field managers can beneficially conduct a general check or audit on outlets within their geographical area or market sector to observe and note:

- levels of product distribution in called-on and uncalled-on outlets
- display achievements
- coverage of outlets, i.e. regularity of calls on existing customers, and uncalled-on or pioneer outlets apparently worth an initial visit from a salesperson
- awareness of the products and supporting marketing effort
- use of sales promotional materials to highlight displays
- competitive activity in respect of display, distribution, pricing, product range and presentation, and promotional activity.

The field manager should obviously make notes on his observations. It is generally best to identify a limited number of objective study points to be reviewed during the field audit, such as the use of point-of-sale display material and feature displays, and draw up a simple recording sheet where the criteria are recorded by outlet visited (see Example 11.4). On a field audit day the manager's aim is to see as much as he can in a short space of time, and he should therefore avoid getting distracted from his purpose by being drawn into lengthy discussions with customers. With f.m.c.g. products in wide general distribution a manager can frequently cover 10–12 outlets in close proximity per hour, and a half-day field audit gives a good overview of activity and achievement in a territory or area.

Follow-checks or field activity audits

A field activity audit is normally used as a control on the activity, results and recordings of an individual territory salesperson. It should be used not as a policing exercise but as an aid to assessing performance, training needs and response to prior training, or the ability of the salesperson to interpret and act on communications through meetings and bulletins.

A follow-check audit can be conducted on the same day as calls are actually being made by the salesperson, using a master journey cycle schedule or other journey planning document that indicates the sales-person's route and call list for the day. Notes and observations can be made on the field check form developed in Example 11.4, where the manager would simply note the details of the calls and his observations against key criteria or in-call activity. To highlight current strengths and weaknesses in distribution, display activity, and the communication of current sales and marketing promotional activity, it can often be beneficial for the field sales manager to visit a few calls due to have been made early in the day by the territory salesperson prior to picking up the salesperson on journey to work with him.

The follow-check audit may be based on a very recent day's work, taking, for example, the latest daily activity report the field sales manager has received from the territory salesperson, and then

Example 11.4 A basic field check form

FIELD AUDIT FORM **Outlet name and address**	Call ✓ No call ✗	Supa Soap	Feature display	Promotional material	**Notes**
Acme, High Street, Newtown	✓	✓	✓	✓	Excellent feature display
Giant, Newtown Rd.	✗	✓	✗	✗	Call missed this week. Why?
The Corner Shop "	✓	✓	✗	✓	
Wilson's Cash + Carry, "	✓	✓	✓	✓	Good end display. Can we get price cut?
Khan's store, High St, "	✗	✓	✗	✗	Due for call next week. Cooperative
Newtown Coop, " "	✓	✓	✓	✓	Good. Excellent deep cut price
Newtown Coop, New Rd, "	✓	✓	✗	✓	Why no feature?
A+B Stores, New Rd, "	✗	✓	✗	✗	Pioneer call. Visit needed

visiting a number of the outlets listed as having received calls. The manager can make his own notes alongside the salesperson's recordings on the daily activity report. Sometimes the manager may find a recording that a feature display was left at the customer's

338

premises, but no sign of it exists. That should not be taken to mean that it was not left there, since many a retailer lets a salesperson have his way while in the call, only to remove the masterpiece shortly after. The real point to be made is that a field sales manager must exercise judgement and experience in assessing what has or might have happened. A few pertinent questions often help in establishing what did go on in a call, and the benefit of the doubt should be given to the salesperson unless clear patterns of misrecording appear.

Obviously the field sales manager should not make customers aware that he is conducting a follow-check audit; that produces negative reactions and throws doubt on the integrity and credibility of the salesperson. A simple opening phrase such as 'I'm from Supasoap, just conducting a survey to see if we are calling on all the stores in this area, and giving you the necessary level of service. Do you get a call from our local salesman?' This leads to a response such as, 'Oh, he was in here only this week', which allows the sales manager to make and record a few observations (usually just mentioning to the retailer that he would like to check the products on display and make a few notes) and ask a few more leading questions, such as 'Did you hear about the new product we are launching later this month?'.

A follow-check audit will reveal very rapidly if the salesperson is correctly interpreting and acting on any special or regular daily activity report recording instructions. The less experienced sales manager is often shocked at how often customers make negative comments on coverage, such as 'Haven't seen your salesman in months', but a little probing might well reveal good reasons for that, such as that the wife runs the shop in the mornings when the salesperson would normally make his call. So, whenever a negative point does arise, the experienced manager, rather than accepting it as fact and jumping to conclusions, should probe a little deeper; the span of recollection of a lot of busy retailers, who may each see a dozen or so salespersons a day, is often short. The manager will usually see signs of display and merchandising activity in a f.m.c.g. environment that confirms a visit and in-call activity.

A general field check or follow-check is of little use unless the findings are communicated promptly to the appropriate salesperson, and also used as a training assessment aid. Usually the salesperson can be found later on journey if his journey plans have been accurately communicated. It is important always to communicate the good as well as the bad – or perhaps it is all good. Since the salesperson is always at a disadvantage or taken by surprise suddenly to be confronted by his line manager waiting outside his next call, it is important for the manager to relax him quickly, and create an impression it is just a routine training visit if the salesperson is not to be put off his form in subsequent calls. Excuses such as 'I was just passing this way' are unnecessary and lack credibility. A few well-chosen compliments on observations from a preceding field audit often help, such as 'I was looking round the town centre this morning and was absolutely delighted with that feature display you built in Acme'. Other comments can then be covered subsequently as appropriate, or may simply lead into some practical training or kerbside discussions, perhaps clarifying bulletin communications or recording instructions.

HEAD OFFICE PERFORMANCE AND PLANNING CONTROLS

Sources of
information

Generally there are two main sources of information available to the sales manager and the information team assigned the responsibility of analysing and presenting data relating to field performance and measurement against objectives, plans, forecasts or such targets as are set:

- the daily activity report
- the customer order form.

The daily activity report

In addition to the field analysis conducted by the first line manager in respect of all recordings and information, the daily activity report can be analysed by the head office support information team. Whereas the field manager is concerned with honesty and accuracy of recording and the performance of functional activities, the head office analysis normally assumes accuracy and is more concerned with measuring against the plans and looking for deviations that impact on the overall performance of the company. Data are generally provided at each tier of the sales organisation to facilitate control by each level of line manager.

Head office analysis is easier if the format of the daily activity report aids coding and sorting of information. Some companies, particularly in the United States, have moved towards a card system, with one card for each call; the salesperson uses special pencils to make recordings so that the markings can be picked up directly in the computer coding and sorting operations, and all relevant information is tabulated and presented in the reports. This limits the immediate control information available to a field sales manager.

If a master computer file is kept on all scheduled calls and their coverage levels, then the recordings from the daily activity reports and the customer order forms can be compared to provide a master printout, probably only monthly or less frequently. This can summarise calls made compared with calls due according to the master journey cycle schedule for each territory. If the management

340

by exception principle is followed, field managers need only receive a printout listing those calls receiving fewer or more visits than are warranted according to the master journey cycle schedule; they should then seek to identify the reasons for incorrect coverage or to observe if patterns exist.

The printout can extend to show if any regular customer is not ordering on each call. If this is a repeat occurrence, computer analysis can highlight the failure of the customer to generate enough business to warrant the scheduled call frequency. It is then up to the field sales manager to establish whether the customer's business has declined to the extent that he needs a reduced call frequency, or whether some other factors have a bearing on the poor performance.

If the daily activity report records stock situations at the time the call is made, then computer analysis can highlight any regular occurrence for any particular customer, which can serve to alert the appropriate field sales manager that either the salesperson is not booking sufficiently large orders or the call should receive more frequent coverage to maintain in-stock positions.

If certain calls are seasonal in nature, these can be added into the computer files at the beginning of the season and extracted at the end to avoid distorting the coverage analysis.

Where recordings of product distribution are made, analysis can extend to total the distribution by product for each level in the sales organisation. This is, of course, biased towards over-stating true distribution, compared with a random survey, because only called-on outlets are included, and because of the often over-optimistic recordings found in any self-reporting system. However, such a distribution base measure is still very useful.

Similarly, if display is a key result area monitored by the daily activity report recordings, figures for product display percentages can be built up from territory and area to national levels, but with the same limitations referred to above when compared with a neutral and random market survey.

The limitations of self-recorded sales force documents as measures of performance do not negate the value of such controls and measurements. As managers improve the standardisation of interpretations and recordings, the data become more meaningful.

Customer order forms
These will generally be capable of analysis to show:

- total volumes and values of orders by customer, territory, area, and each higher tier to the national sales force totals
- comparisons between actual sales at each tier and forecasts, plans and targets.

341

The comparisons might be made in respect of:

- actual sales during a specific period this year versus the same period in the previous year, e.g. the same calendar month or accounting period
- actual sales as a percentage achievement against forecast in the present year period versus the previous year period
- cumulative actual sales versus the cumulative forecast to the current point in time
- cumulative actual sales versus the cumulative actual sales to the same point in the previous year (usually shown on tables as a this year/last year comparison)
- moving annual totals of sales by customer, territory and the higher tiers in the sales organisation, in order to give a clearer indication of trends as seasonal and other unusual fluctuations in performance are smoothed out over the longer term.

It is generally necessary for all comparative sales analyses to note performance both in volume (real) and value terms (which include the inflationary element of any price increases during the time period) so that real growth can be separated from inflationary growth and correct analysis and interpretation made.

Analysis can also be conducted:

- on a product-by-product basis to show gains and losses in distribution by customer, territory, area, etc.
- to draw attention to new distribution, i.e. how many new customers were found for each product over a given time period, say a journey cycle, and the results can be compared with any standards of performance relating to increases in distribution
- to identify new customers (pioneer calls converted to active accounts) and relate them to standards of performance
- to separate out new products for special analysis of results and performance, including sales to calls rates, order volume levels, and distribution
- on gross profit contribution by customer, territory, area, etc., using standard costing parameters applied to the product-by-product volumes ordered and despatched.

Key result areas Head office control systems, even more than field controls, should concentrate on the key result areas. Systems and procedures can be designed to give measurements and readings (as appropriate to the particular industry, markets and company information needs) in all of the following areas:

- scheduled call coverage
- pioneer calls
- sales to call ratios
- distribution
- sales volumes and values
- display achievements
- trends
- response to advertising and promotional activity
- profit contributions.

Scheduled call coverage
Are calls being made as scheduled? Missed calls may mean missed orders and irrecoverable losses of sales volume as consumers switch to competitive products until the salesperson makes the next call due within the journey cycle schedule.

Pioneer calls
Are new outlets being identified and called on to assess potential and solicit orders?

Sales to call ratios
This can give a measure of the effectiveness of the sales force in making presentations, the effectiveness of field training, and efficiency in identifying and pre-screening pioneer calls. Any standard of performance must relate to historical levels and the nature of the sales operation. For example, in an f.m.c.g. company making regular calls on established outlets, a sales to calls ratio of 80–90 per cent might be quite normal. In a cold canvassing situation, such as selling insurance or home improvements, the conversion rate might be very much lower, in the 5–20 per cent range. Obviously in this most critical area of performance evaluation the sales manager must give consideration to other factors or results. The key priority is always to maximise the effective use of salespersons in making productive calls and conversions of contacts to orders. If the conversion ratio is low for pioneer calls is this because of poor sales training, incorrect marketing information on target markets, inadequate pre-screening of leads against profiles of existing or previous customers, incorrect assessment of product benefits in relation to customer needs, incorrect targeting of advertising, or inadequate provision of sales aids and supporting material and information? If the conversion ratio for pioneer calls is low in relation to the sales ratio to established customers, then perhaps the training of the salesperson in basic techniques needs reviewing (as he may have become more of an order taker); or possibly the problem is one of motivation, in that the salesperson possesses the necessary selling skills yet makes little effort in a pioneer call.

Every effort must be devoted to increasing productivity through corrective training by the field sales manager. If standards of performance are realistic and a salesperson does not improve performance in response to training, the point will come where the line manager will need to take more permanent and positive action, using the company appraisal and disciplinary procedures.

Distribution

Distribution analysis is key to measurements that impact on market share. Most companies have specific market share objectives (which might actually conflict with profit maximisation objectives if such are actually set at the corporate level). Ideally the market distribution should be assessed through randomly conducted market research audits of all potential outlets. Practicalities may dictate a narrower measurement of distribution based only upon reportings of called-on outlets from the daily activity report. A selected panel may be used by a market research agency, with a representative cross-section of all levels and sectors of the distribution network, to assess distribution. Analysis that might be aimed at prompting corrective action can particularly seek to identify lost distribution (customers who cease buying a product) and possible gains in distribution (because wider distribution may warrant further marketing support and pro-motional activity).

Sales volumes and values

Measurements of sales volumes (probably in terms of units or cases of the items) and turnover levels by product should be developed so that comparisons can be made as an ongoing exercise, with warnings at any significant variation from the programme or plan. Data can be sourced from order forms and prepared at territory, area or national levels, so that each person in the sales hierarchy can see his performance position and progress in relation to standards, objectives, plans and forecasts.

Display achievements

In an industry where display is key to creating offtake – as in most f.m.c.g. markets – measurement systems can be developed from self-reporting on daily activity reports on aspects of display, possibly with a simple code system, e.g.

- 0 = product out of stock on entry to the call
- 1 = product in stock on entry to call, but not displayed
- 2 = product both in stock and on display on entry to the call.

(A minimum level might be set that constitutes 'in stock', e.g. at least one case of the product.)

Trends

Analysis of each of the factors such as sales volumes and values and distribution achievements needs to be extended to indicate any underlying trends. Such knowledge is essential in the evaluation of marketing programmes, including sales promotions, advertising, product mix and pricing policies. A useful system is to compare the cumulative figures for the current year with the results at the same time one year ago (or any two comparable time periods). **Moving annual total** tables can also be produced (to be discussed later in this chapter), which have the advantage of smoothing out anomalies such as seasonal factors and fluctuations.

Response to advertising and promotional activity

Either standard or special recording procedures used on daily activity reports or customer order forms might highlight distribution or display activity in response to promotional support or activity. It is always important to evaluate the immediate response to promotional activity, and to measure the more lasting effects in the post-promotion period (did the promotion actually produce permanent increases in trial and sales, or just result in hoarding in response to discount prices?). Head office analysis, particularly where computer systems are used, can assist by separating out data on particular products involved in promotions, relating them to any sales force recording of volume, value, distribution and display, and comparing actual results with targeted results.

Profit contributions

Where it is possible to cost products, either on the basis of an individual contract quote (as with the supply of many industrial products such as plant and equipment) or using standard costing techniques, then it is a very useful exercise to measure the profit contribution at each level of the selling chain, i.e. by individual account, by territory, by area, and nationally. Whilst it may not be helpful or practical to make such calculations each month, it certainly would be useful at the end of each journey cycle or quarter. Different product mixes for each customer might have a dramatic effect on overall profitability and gross contributions, and awareness of such factors may produce marketing strategies to change the product mixes sold through some or all accounts, or change the emphasis on certain markets or customers. It will not generally be very productive to try and allocate sales costs to individual customers, although it is an important measure in certain fields such as tendering for major supply contracts (where considerable supporting technical service might be essential), and possibly in some key account sales activities (where the field costs of sales merchandising support might be higher than really justified at the level of certain branches).

Guidelines to consider in the production of statistical data can include the following:

- information should contribute to or measure actual performance compared with plans, forecasts, targets, budgets or standards of performance
- information should help in identifying underlying trends
- information should give warnings of significant variances from plans and programmes in sufficient time that in key result areas corrective action can be developed and implemented in time to impact on results within the plan's time frame
- information should aid the sales organisation in the performance of its functional activities and assist in the recognition and acceptance of training needs.

Information that is not likely to be constructively used in one of these ways probably has little value in the sales management control process, and might not justify the time and effort involved in developing the systems and producing the information. In most sales environments information that is not needed and produced on at least a monthly basis usually has little contribution to make. (There are exceptions: for example, it is often only useful to produce updated call coverage analyses at the end of every journey cycle or quarter; similarly with any analysis of account or territory gross profit contributions.) Senior sales management need to give guidance to the less experienced members of the management team on where management control time should concentrate to promote change that will improve performance.

Budgetary control The main items of budgetary control within the sales organisation relate to:

- salaries and fringe benefits
- direct selling expenses
- purchase (or leasing) and maintenance of company vehicles
- sales promotional costs (production of sales aids and promotional materials, and other promotional costs)
- promotional allowances (discounts and allowances, rebates related to volume/value or other performance criteria, or in respect of specific promotional activity).

A monthly printout or analysis table can provide detail for each tier in the sales organisation. The field sales manager may need to pay little attention to factors that at his level are largely fixed-cost items outside his control (salaries, equipment, sales aids and display material) and may prefer to monitor his direct selling expenses and the costs of various promotional schemes and allowances (particularly if he is measured on gross margin contribution from the territory or area). The national sales manager will need to give attention in varying degrees to each element; however, assuming he needs to maintain full coverage, he may be particularly concerned to ensure that all territories are manned but without an excess of relief salespersons.

When sales forecasts are not being met or budgets are otherwise exceeded it is normal for the financial division to urge cuts and expenditure restrictions. Certainly it is wise to tighten control under such circumstances, but at the sharp end of the company's drive for volume – the sales force – it can be less rather than more constructive to push cuts in manpower and promotional support (including advertising) too far. There are usually other fringe service areas, possibly including development projects, consultancy, and so on, that have less short-term impact on business if expenditure is temporarily restricted.

It is none the less extremely important if sales forecasts and targets are not being met, yet were historically based and considered reasonable, to identify causes for the shortfall and develop a corrective action programme. Shortfalls occur for many reasons, including: delays in launching new products; production stoppages; undermanning in the sales force; inexperienced sales management; training needs in the sales force; shifts in market acceptance of the products; competitive activity; wrong pricing policies; distribution problems; and so on. Any shortfall that produces less revenue and gross profit contribution must result in a review of budgeted expenditure and sales and marketing programmes.

Performance statistics
: The most commonly used range of performance statistics, all of which can be produced either manually or using computer systems, are:

- sales volume by product and in total
- sales value by product and in total
- distribution by product
- market share data
- company turnover
- company profit performance
- profitability by account, organisational tier, or function.

Figures in each of the first three categories can readily be provided (since they are produced by a build-up from inputs relating to specific calls as recorded by territory salespersons on order forms and daily activity reports) for each of the tiers in the organisation – e.g. territory, area, regional and national levels. To be constructive and

347

Example 11.5   Presentation of sales performance data

TERRITORY 45 Performance analysis	Jan. Vol.	Val.	Feb. Vol.	Val.	March Vol.	Val.	April Vol.	Val.	May Vol.	Val.	June Vol.	Val.
Supasoap Large												
TY forecast	1,000	30,000	1,000	30,000	1,400	42,000	1,200	36,000	1,100	34,650	1,000	31,500
TY actual	1,010	30,300	960	28,800	1,600	48,000	1,400	42,000	900	28,350	950	29,925
%	101%		96%		114%		117%		82%		95%	
TY cumulative	1,010	30,300	1,970	51,900	3,570	107,100	4,970	149,100	5,870	177,450	6,820	207,375
LY actual	950	27,075	970	27,645	1,200	34,200	1,200	34,200	1,050	29,925	1,000	30,000
LY cumulative	950	27,075	1,920	54,720	3,120	88,920	4,320	123,120	5,370	153,045	6,370	183,045
% TY/LY actual	106%		99%		133%		117%		86%		95%	
% TY/LY cumulative	106%		103%		114%		115%		109%		107%	
M.A.T. actual TY	12,430	366,270	12,420	367,425	12,820	381,225	13,020	389,025	12,870	387,450	12,820	387,375
M.A.T. actual LY	12,120	340,530	12,130	342,255	12,180	345,405	12,230	348,555	12,280	345,980	12,330	352,905
M.A.T. % TY/LY	103%	108%	102%	107%	105%	110%	106%	112%	105%	112%	104%	110%

Notes: TY = this year
LY = last year
M.A.T. = moving annual total
Vol. = volume in cases
Val. = value in pounds sterling.

meaningful, each level of analysis or information table should relate the figures to such comparative reference points as:

- the appropriate plan or forecast achievement due by that point in time
- performance over the same period in the previous calendar or company year (this year/last year comparisons).

Figures can show actual performance in a specific period (say one month) and cumulatively this year (company or calendar) to date, and on a moving annual total basis to smooth out seasonal or other fluctuations and to highlight trends. It can be particularly helpful to present figures both in standard tabular formats and with the help of graphs or other pictorial illustrations. Also, it generally aids under-standing and interpretation to see the key results expressed in both absolute numbers and percentage terms, i.e.:

	Forecast	Actual	Percentage
April	1,000	900	90%
May	1,000	1,100	110%
Year to date	5,000	5,200	104%

As a further example, cumulative sales this year to date might be shown in relation to forecast as:

volume	98%
value	105%,

July		August		Sept.		Oct.		Nov.		Dec.		Year	
Vol.	Val.	Vol.	Val.	Vol.	Val.	Vol.	Val.	Vol.	Val.	Vol.	Val.	Vol.	Val.
900	28,350	900	28,350	1,000	31,500	1,100	34,650	1,100	34,650	1,200	37,800	12,900	399,450
1,000	31,500	1,050	33,075	1,050	33,075	1,090	34,335	1,170	36,855	1,250	39,375	13,430	415,590
111%		117%		105%		99%		106%		104%		104%	
7,820	238,875	8,870	271,950	9,920	305,025	11,010	339,360	12,180	376,215	13,430	415,590	13,430	
850	25,500	900	27,000	950	28,500	1,050	31,500	1,100	33,000	1,150	34,500	12,370	363,045
7,220	208,545	8,120	235,545	9,070	264,045	10,120	295,545	11,220	328,545	12,370	363,045		
118%		117%		111%		104%		106%		109%		109%	
108%		109%		109%		109%		109%		109%		109%	
12,970	393,375	13,120	399,450	13,220	404,025	13,260	406,860	13,330	410,715	13,430	415,590		
12,380	352,605	12,380	356,955	12,360	357,810	12,380	359,955	12,360	361,035	12,370	363,045		
105%	112%	106%	112%	107%	113%	107%	113%	108%	114%	109%	114%		

indicating that the customer has purchased fewer units but at higher prices. A more detailed customer analysis might then show a change in the product mix towards higher-value products (assuming that the 7 per cent differential was not accounted for entirely by price inflation). Similarly the moving annual total comparison for volume might be expressed as a percentage, e.g. 105% TY/LY, indicating that there has been a real growth in volume over the last year to this point in time. This can then be looked at in relation to changes in value and any appropriate interpretations made, including corrective action plans if trends are not considered healthy.

Example 11.5 illustrates how data can usefully be prepared, as they might be presented from a computer printout. A manual preparation and presentation might, for ease of compilation, separate onto different tables such results as the moving annual total figures and comparisons or the cumulative data and comparisons.

The data can be built up to show a total for all products for each level of the sales organisation where performance is measured. However, it is not really necessary for a manager to receive the statistical data and other analyses for any but his own level and one level lower. So the area manager would receive the territory and area tables, and a regional manager would receive each area's figures and the regional totals.

The **moving annual total** (M.A.T.) is such a useful measure of trends and performance on a year-on-year rolling basis that it is worth demonstrating how it is constructed so that managers appreciate the benefit of the smoothing out of unusual fluctuations,

Example 11.6   Moving annual totals

	Volumes[a]								
	1983 Actual	1983 Cum.	1983 M.A.T.	1984 Actual	1984 Cum.	1984 M.A.T.	1985 Actual	1985 Cum.	1985 M.A.T.
January	980	980		950	950	12,120	1,010	1,010	12,430
February	960	1,940		970	1,920	12,130	960	1,970	12,420
March	1,150	3,090		1,200	3,120	12,180	1,600	3,570	12,820
April	1,150	4,240		1,200	4,320	12,230	1,400	4,970	13,020
May	1,000	5,240		1,050	5,370	12,280	900	5,870	12,870
June	950	6,190		1,000	6,370	12,330	950	6,820	12,820
July	800	6,990		850	7,220	12,380	1,000	7,820	12,970
August	900	7,890		900	8,120	12,380	1,050	8,870	13,120
September	970	8,860		950	9,070	12,360	1,050	9,920	13,220
October	1,030	9,890		1,050	10,120	12,380	1,090	11,010	13,260
November	1,120	11,010		1,100	11,220	12,360	1,170	12,180	13,330
December	1,140	12,150	12,150	1,150	12,370	12,370	1,250	13,430	13,430

Notes: a   volume in cases
b   value in pounds sterling.

such as seasonal peaks and troughs. Moving annual totals are taken by looking at the cumulative total for the previous 12 months (or 13 periods if the company operates on 13 equal four-weekly accounting periods) at any point in time. So, for example, the M.A.T. at the end of April includes the 12 months from May of the previous year. To calculate the May M.A.T., all that is required is to add the current May actual sales figure for volume or value, as appropriate, and deduct the equivalent figure for the month of May in the previous year. It may be seen as a rolling measure of performance. Similarly, in comparisons it is useful to produce a moving annual forecast with which the actual moving annual sales may be compared in both absolute and percentage terms. Example 11.6 illustrates an M.A.T. compilation to match the sales performance figures illustrated in Example 11.5. It has been assumed for the purposes of the exercise that the company had no sales history prior to 1983, and the first M.A.T. figures were therefore available only from the end of 1983.

In the graphical illustrations of Examples 11.7 and 11.8 the data for actual sales, cumulative sales and moving annual totals have been transferred from Example 11.5 to demonstrate how much easier it is to spot trends using graphs (or bar charts). Most sales managers have a preference for graphs and other charts as the method of illustrative presentation to aid comprehension and assimilation.

Each company should aim to provide feedback and performance measurements in a manner that: is meaningful; aids the measurement of performance against plans and objectives within that

| | | | | **Values**[b] | | | | | |
| | 1983 | | | 1984 | | | 1985 | |
Actual	Cum.	M.A.T.	Actual	Cum.	M.A.T.	Actual	Cum.	M.A.T.
26,460	26,460		27,075	27,075	340,530	30,300	30,300	366,270
25,920	52,380		27,645	54,720	342,255	28,800	59,100	367,425
31,050	83,430		34,200	88,920	345,405	48,000	107,100	381,225
31,050	114,480		34,200	123,120	348,555	42,000	149,100	389,025
28,500	142,980		29,925	153,045	345,980	28,350	177,450	387,450
27,075	170,055		30,000	183,045	352,905	29,925	207,375	387,375
22,800	192,855		25,500	208,545	352,605	31,500	238,875	393,375
25,650	218,505		27,000	235,545	356,955	33,075	271,950	399,450
27,645	246,150		28,500	264,045	357,810	33,075	305,025	404,025
29,355	275,505		31,500	295,545	359,955	34,335	339,360	406,860
31,920	307,425		33,000	328,545	361,035	36,855	376,215	410,715
32,490	339,915	339,915	34,500	363,045	363,045	39,375	415,590	415,590

Example 11.7   Sales performance graph – current year

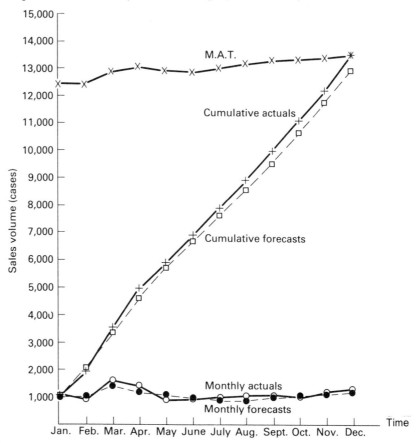

351

company's market, structure and environment; helps identify progress and actual or potential problems; and is within the technical resource capabilities and general resource limitations of the company. The provision of information is not an end in itself but purely a tool to assist management control and planning. Generally a company should seek to assess and fulfil the minimum information needs rather than the maximum; each extra data sheet adds to the complexity of the control process, is likely to distract further from priorities and key result areas, and burdens the limited management resources of the company.

Example 11.8   This year/last year performance comparisons

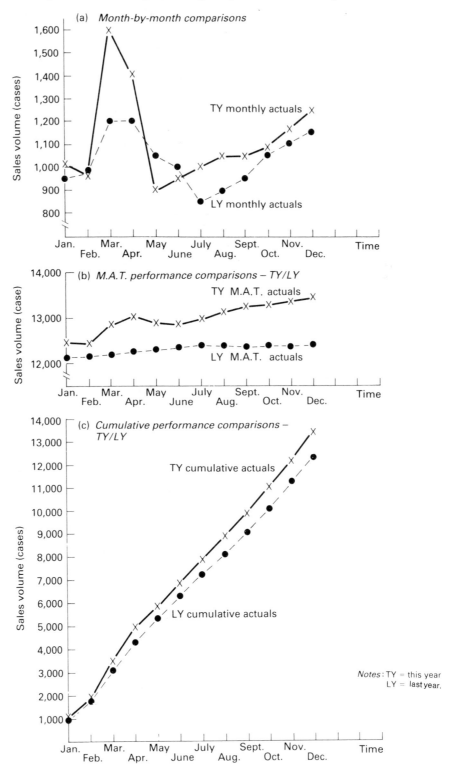

(a) *Month-by-month comparisons*

TY monthly actuals

LY monthly actuals

(b) *M.A.T. performance comparisons – TY/LY*

TY M.A.T. actuals

LY M.A.T. actuals

(c) *Cumulative performance comparisons – TY/LY*

TY cumulative actuals

LY cumulative actuals

Notes: TY = this year
LY = last year.

- A key management function is to exercise control over the functions and performance of subordinates to ensure that results positively relate to agreed strategies and objectives, plans, forecasts and budgets.
- As part of the control process, **standards of performance** should be set and communicated in respect of all functions and performance areas that can impact on or are **key result areas**. Such standards should generally be historically based, realistic and achievable.
- Controls generally will be either **continuous** in nature, monitoring performance of functional tasks to maximise productivity and giving objective measurements of quantity, quality, cost and time, or designed as **warnings** to highlight results that are off course in key result areas.
- Field controls exercised by line field sales managers can encompass monitoring activity and information provided in respect of journey plans, customer call record cards, daily activity reports, issue of credit notes, expenses, and such other reporting processes and procedures, and the flexible use of trade terms and allowances.
- General field audits and field activity audits (follow-checks) provide an important source of data on activity in relation to: effectiveness of and needs for training; implementation of marketing and promotional programmes; functional activities such as coverage; performance against plans, targets, forecasts and objectives, recording of data, display and distribution achievements; and should be used where appropriate as a control that gives an overview of field activity and performance.
- The main sources of information in a head office analysis are usually the daily activity report and the customer order form, which can be designed to record most of the data relevant to key result area performance analysis.
- Performance and planning controls exercised by head office should concentrate on measurements related to key result areas, and can include: providing statistical data related to scheduled call coverage, pioneer call contact, sales to call ratios, distribution and display achievements, sales performance in volume and value; achievement against plans, forecasts, targets and objectives, etc.; trends; effectiveness of promotional programmes; profit contributions by account and the various tiers in the sales organisation.
- Information should not be produced for its own sake, but should: contribute to performance measurement in key result areas compared with plans and forecasts and objectives; help in identifying and analysing trends; give warnings of variances from

354

plans; and aid in the control of sales force operations. Generally the production of data not needed as an essential control or measure of performance on a monthly basis should be questioned.

	Notes	Action

Key result areas

Have the key result areas been identified
   for the sales force in such areas as:

- call rate?
- sales to calls ratio?
- minimum order levels?
- product distribution?
- product display?
- call coverage?
- pioneer calling?
- sales objectives?
- price level achievements?
- sales targets, forecasts and plans
  (in volume and value)?
- profitability?
- budgets?
- product range and mix?
- other? . . . .
  . . . .
  . . . .
  . . . .
  . . . .

Standards of performance

Have standards of performance been set and
   communicated in each of the above key
   result areas?

Field controls

Do systems and controls exist and operate
   effectively in respect of:
- accuracy of recordings?
- journey plans
  – scheduled call coverage?
  – appointments?
  – pre-call objectives?
  – contact details?
- customer call records
  – are they up to date?
  – pre-call objectives?
  – buyer contact details?
  – promotional activity?
  – coverage?
  – product distribution?
- daily activity reports
  – scheduled call coverage?
  – call rate?
  – sales to call ratios?
  – display/distribution achievements?
  – pioneer calls?
- expenses?
- other? . . . .
  . . . .
  . . . .
  . . . .
  . . . .

	Notes	*Action*

Performance and planning controls

Are statistical measures relevant and
useful, and do they exist in each of the
key result areas listed above?

Do analyses measure:
- variances from plans and forecasts?
- trends?
- promotional and advertising effectiveness?
- profit contribution by account,
territory, area, etc.?

Do analyses give comparisons with
achievements over the same period in
the previous year?

Are moving annual total analyses relevant
and prepared in respect of such key
result areas as:

- product sales volumes?
- product sales values?
- distribution?
- market share?
- company turnover?
- company profit performance?
- profitability by account and/or tier
level in the organisational structure?

Are such figures prepared for each product,
geographical or structural tier in the
organisation, and compared with:

- M.A.T.s of the relevant plan or forecast?
- previous year's achievements to the
same point in time?

Is each item of data being presented in the
most meaningful and easily interpreted
manner for action?

357

Part IV

Further Development Opportunities

12 Alternative Sales or Distribution Operations

TELEPHONE SELLING

As an alternative to direct sales calls by consumer or industrial salespersons it is possible to use telephone selling, either in emergencies or as a regular system.

If a territory salesperson is unable to make all his regular calls on the journey cycle schedule, perhaps because of sickness or meetings, and where no relief salesperson is available, he could set aside a day to telephone customers to identify stock levels and obtain repeat orders. Clearly this is likely to be much less effective than a direct call, as it is harder to 'sell' special offers or promotional activity over the telephone, and much of the results will depend on the salesperson's relations with his buyers. In fact he may have to telephone twice: once to ask the buyer to count stock levels; and then to obtain those data and relate them to order requirements. In the case of fast moving consumer goods, such telephone calling also loses the opportunity to merchandise stock and create display activity. Because of its limited effectiveness, and because it removes the pressure from the territory salesperson to complete requisite call rates to ensure effective coverage, telephone selling should not be encouraged by managers. Managers are well aware that it is not uncommon for some less than honest members of a sales team to follow this practice occasionally without permission when various factors prevent them from making physical calls; and management field controls are intended to identify such problems.

There can none the less be significant benefit in a head office department being organised to specialise in the functions of telephone selling, providing sales support in the tasks of:

- initial cold contacts
- replenishing stocks
- emergency cover
- small accounts or geographically remote customers.

Initial cold contacts

Suppliers of industrial and consumer products, including those marketing directly to the end user (e.g. home improvements and financial services) might develop telephone selling to make initial contact with potential customers, possibly for follow-up by direct sales calls. Possible contacts might be identified from reader enquiry cards returned in response to advertisements, from trade directories

361

or professional journals or registers of members of a society or professional body, telephone directories, or from other sources of leads, including specially purchased lists of likely product users. Such telephone calls should seek to establish use of or need for the product or service, and the possible level of interest, as well as to identify the decision maker in the home or business who should be contacted, either by a direct salesperson who might make a fuller presentation, or with additional literature despatched by post. Such initial cold contact can usefully conclude by asking for suggestions of other possible contacts (and might even offer a gift or other reward for leads that result in sales).

Replenishing stocks

Where a product (industrial or consumer) has repeat sales potential and a customer is already well-established and operates good stock and order control, and where the re-order frequency is greater than the call rate that could be justified for a direct selling call by the territory salesperson, then it might be decided that it is cost-effective to supplement direct sales calls with telephone sales calls to obtain stocks and orders. For example, if a weekly order is required by a wholesale distributor, cash and carry warehouse or other retail outlet (which might be badly located for a weekly physical call), and it is not necessary to perform other in-call activities each week, line management might assess that it is more cost-effective for the territory salesperson to call, say, only once each month, with interim orders being obtained by the telephone sales department.

When the territory salesperson does call, he should then perform all the in-call physical merchandising activities, check actual stock levels to compare with the figures given over the telephone, sort out any special problems, such as returns of damaged merchandise, make special presentations of promotional activity, including advertising and consumer or trade promotions, and other special offers or new packs and products, note competitive activity for his market intelligence report, and probably book an order for current needs. It might be wise for the territory salesperson to schedule his physical call for the same day of the week as the scheduled telephone sales call, and then possibly telephone in the stock and order to ensure prompt despatch and the updating of records.

Where physical merchandising is a necessary activity, as in mass merchandising retail or cash and carry outlets, but the costs of a direct sales call are high, the telephone sales calling function can be supplemented by developing a team of independent specialist part-time merchandisers, either actual part-time employees under the control of the field line manager, or self-employed, or they might even work through a specialised merchandising service or agency. Such merchandisers can undertake basic shelf-filling and display-building activities in outlets conveniently located to their place of residence. This sort of work often suits married women with limited home commitments during part of the working day. The use of part-time merchandisers and telephone sales departments frees the more costly and skilled territory salespersons for more essential sales development activities.

Emergency cover

The telephone sales department may also effectively act in the capacity of a relief salesperson to make telephone sales calls to customers when there is no salesperson available to make the normal scheduled physical call at the due time, perhaps because of sickness, holidays, or a vacant territory. This is a poor substitute for a direct call if a personal visit is needed to develop sales and other in-call activities.

Small accounts or geographically remote customers

Where business volume is too small to justify a direct sales call or there is no other effective means of gaining and maintaining distribution (i.e. no satisfactory local wholesale distributive outlets), then it might still be cost-effective to maintain direct distribution at the lower sales cost levels of the telephone sales department. The customers will need motivating and training to note stock levels before the scheduled telephone sales call, which should always be at the same day and time to create consistency and habituate the customer to being prepared and available. In such situations the customer may simply state his own estimate of order levels and requirements, or the telephone sales department may seek to elicit stock levels and suggest the order levels after estimating product movement rates and taking account of advertising and consumer promotional activity or seasonal trends.

Telephone selling, therefore, has a place in consumer and industrial goods markets and in the sale of services. A well-trained telephone sales department can be very cost-effective, and particularly beneficial in companies where there is a low conversion rate of calls to orders on first contact by a salesperson, because the cost of making that first cold contact can be significantly reduced. (Some companies assess the costs of making contact through a telephone sales department at around one-third of the cost of a direct sales call by a territory salesperson.)

Obviously, when establishing a telephone sales department, two key aspects must be considered:

- records and systems
- training.

Records and systems

Contact lists should be developed from such sources as have already been identified above in the section on initial cold contacts. Records basically need to note who was contacted, when, and the outcome. Some form of customer call or contact record needs to be maintained for positive leads to ensure follow-up, which could be in the form of a direct call from a salesperson, or the despatch of literature or samples to promote interest and develop sales. A company might prefer to maintain all contact through the telephone sales department, in which case, if the product is of a repeat use and purchase nature, a form of stock and order record should be developed. The telephone sales staff need to have a system of generating the order resulting from an enquiry, and may have an internal order form to be routed to the order-processing department.

Additionally, if orders are being generated then there must be a system of credit checking and control. Direct sales to private individuals should preferably be by credit card to avoid the risks involved in direct invoicing after despatch of goods. If credit cards are not being used, the company may request payment by cheque prior to despatch of merchandise. Sales of goods and services to established companies are likely to require the normal extension of credit, subject to satisfactory credit checking.

Telephone sales departments in industrial, service and consumer goods companies can make considerable use of computers and desk-top visual display units as data sources. If regular customers are called to solicit repeat orders, a programme can be developed that retrieves previous stock and sales activity, enables current stock levels to be built in, and can calculate a suggested order based upon average movement; it can also be refined to adjust order levels to take account of seasonal trends in offtake and special advertising and promotional activity. Automatic calling systems can save much time and reduce errors and costs resulting from mis-dialling.

Training
The telephone sales team need training to meet their special functional duties and responsibilities just as much as the field sales team. Training needs are likely to be identified in such areas as:

- making 'cold contact' calls to potential product users
- identifying decision makers
- techniques of penetrating through staff and subordinates or other family members to the decision maker
- quickly and effectively relaxing the contact to create a receptive atmosphere
- gaining the contact's attention and creating interest to enable the conversation to progress to a brief telephone presentation
- use of questioning techniques to elicit interest or potential product needs or use
- making effective telephone sales presentations

- dealing with objections over the telephone
- closing the sale or arousing interest to the point where the contact is willing to receive literature or a direct sales call from an experienced member of the sales force
- recording results of telephone calls.

Telephone salespersons are more likely to be received positively if they:

- have voices that project warmth, friendliness, sincerity, authority and maturity
- are clear, concise and logical communicators
- are good listeners, patient and able to lead the direction of conversation
- present the subject in a conversational manner (without giving the impression of following a script)
- establish at the outset of each call if the contact is free to talk (he may be in a meeting or having a meal) and, if he is not free, seek to arrange a specific time to place another call. A contact will generally be more receptive to a 'cold canvass' telephone call if the caller establishes that the call is a result of a reference from another party.

Trial calls by the telephone sales supervisor will elicit likely response reactions and patterns and enable a telephone presentation script format to be developed. As an inflexible script tends to be rather limiting and obvious to the contact, a degree of in-built flexibility might be achieved by developing a **telephone sales sequence** along the lines discussed in Chapter 7 on Basic Sales Training.

A head office telephone sales department may be as basic as one girl at a desk with a single telephone doing all the functions in a smaller company; or it could be a bank of desks with multiple line and computer facilities, manned by a highly trained team of telephone sales specialists using 'hands free' telephone aids and visual display units.

A sales manager should certainly investigate the costs and benefits to his organisation of establishing a basic telephone sales operation, but its effectiveness will be a function of the training, disciplines and systems provided to develop requisite telephone sales skills.

WHOLESALERS, DISTRIBUTORS AND BROKERS

Where a product user or stockist does not warrant a direct call from the manufacturer's sales force, perhaps because of low volume orders

365

or remoteness of location, another alternative is to introduce the customer to a **wholesale stockist** or other **distributors** who can provide the merchandise. Such distributors will normally take title to the goods and resell them. They might have a formal territorial franchise or distribution agreement with the supplier, or simply buy goods on a non-exclusive wholesale basis. Exclusive distributors may be more aggressive in pushing the supplier's product range, but often have the limitation of not covering all potential outlets within any geographical area or market sector.

Smaller companies that have limited sales volume initially or cannot justify the cost of a direct sales force may well find that an answer is to work through distributors and have a small team of managers or other sales executives responsible for the development of business through each distributor, including providing all training at distributor field force and management levels.

An extension of wholesale distributors could be the appointment of specialist **sales brokers**, who act as sales agents on a fee or commission basis without taking title to the goods, although they might also have facilities to handle physical distribution and customer invoicing and credit control. Smaller companies with limited resources should investigate this alternative as a means of expanding representation and distribution.

A broker will normally specialise in the products of one industry, or products being sold into one form of distribution channel (such as, say, industrial chemicals, electrical supplies, food stores or the 'do it yourself' markets). Because the broker sells a number of suppliers' products to the same outlets, he can often quote a fee or commission scale that would be less than the supplier's costs of operating a direct sales force.

There are, however, limitations imposed by:

- the lack of direct line authority over the staff within the organisations of the distributor or broker
- the diversity of products represented or sold by the broker or distributor
- the conflicting pressures on the distributor or broker to maximise his own earnings from the limited resources of time, personnel and finances (with the result that generally more effort is put behind the major products to the detriment of minor and new products)
- possibly lower motivation, interest and/or skill levels within the sales organisations of a distributor or broker.

Selection   On the assumption that there are sufficient brokers and distributors operating in the market sector to offer a choice to the manufacturer or principal, the first consideration is whether to use a broker or a distributor, or perhaps a combination.

The alternative flow of goods distribution models are illustrated in Example 12.1.

Example 12.1 Alternative distribution models

(a) *Model I: Distributor only*

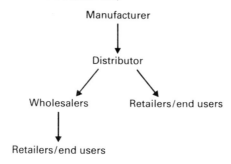

(b) *Model II: Broker only*

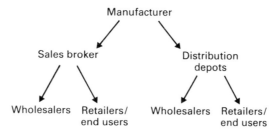

(c) *Model III: Combined broker/distributor*

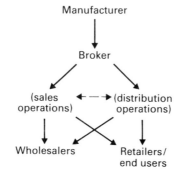

In model I it is assumed that the manufacturer appoints a network of distributors who will each handle all sales and the physical distribution of goods to specific geographical areas or specific market sectors. In this case the manufacturer will generally have few delivery and invoicing points, and lesser needs for administrative support services and direct salespersons. However, there is an opportunity for sales management to work with the distributors in developing product knowledge and selling skills, and assist in gaining distribution and coverage, with particular emphasis on key accounts. (It might be that certain major accounts are excluded from a distributor arrangement, which is likely to be convenient if such accounts have their own central distribution facilities.)

Model II assumes that the manufacturer appoints a broker to solicit orders and handle all sales functions, in return for a sales commission, but that the manufacturer processes the orders and makes the physical distribution from depots. The manufacturer is responsible for extending credit to customers, and would reserve the right to approve or disapprove customers on grounds of credit ratings and payments history. The manufacturer in this case needs a more sophisticated internal organisation to manage the administrative and support functions associated with order processing, distribution, and payments control. It is possible that, whilst all support services are provided from the manufacturer, the actual delivery of goods and warehousing at strategic locations might well be more cost effectively contracted out to specialists.

Model III assumes that the manufacturer appoints a broker to handle his sales functions, and that the same broker can also handle the warehousing and physical distribution, probably with all supporting invoicing and payment control services. The broker might either take title to goods, or act purely in an agency capacity in the services provided. The broker would probably work on a sales commission and fee basis to cover services and costs and, by providing similar services to a number of companies in complementary product ranges or market sectors, would offer each single manufacturer a more cost-effective operation than could be managed directly by the smaller manufacturers. As a variation, the broker might sub-contract distribution through truckers and warehousing companies. However, under this system the manufacturer would again have limited direct delivery and billing points.

Which system, or any other modification, is used will depend in part upon the internal resources available within the manufacturing operation, including people, finance, and warehousing and distribution facilities. Obviously there are trade-offs between cost savings, widening the base of sales and distribution, and effective control over sales and distribution; whilst each manufacturer might prefer totally to control his own sales and distribution through own resources, that is not always practical in the growth stages of smaller to medium-sized companies.

If the preferred alternative to direct sales and distribution involves a distributor or broker, one must be selected. If suitable companies are not already known to the manufacturer, it is likely he can identify potential contacts through an appropriate trade or professional organisation covering the distributive, wholesaling, selling or marketing functions for the industry in particular or the market in general.

Research into appropriate distributors and brokers should include:

- correct legal title and company address
- identification of ownership of the company
- size in terms of capital and turnover
- financial accounts, credit status reports and trade and bank or other references
- internal management organisational structure and staffing levels
- sales organisation, structure and size, and market coverage data
- market sector and outlets covered and frequency of coverage
- number and geographical spread of effective distribution depots and other facilities
- actual existence of all reported resources (including personnel and premises)
- products and manufacturers presently represented and period of representation
- performance and other achievements in relation to products currently or previously represented
- administrative systems and controls
- company policies and strategies
- training policies and programmes
- the company's ability and willingness to implement the manufacturer's marketing and sales policies and programmes, to cooperate in preparing and providing data and information as required by the principal, and to permit the principal's sales management staff to assist with training, including company and product knowledge and sales techniques and skills, etc.
- distribution facilities including those for the handling of products with any special needs, such as air-conditioned or refrigerated storage and delivery
- abilities to provide after-sales service to retailers, other stockists or consumers if the nature of the product is likely to require that.

The manufacturer will need to visit all of the broker's or distributor's facilities in his evaluation process, to satisfy himself that they both exist and are suitable to the function they perform. He should ideally spend time working with the organisation and their sales team visiting contacts and customers, and it is usually useful for the principal to conduct his own market outlet checks on products currently represented by the broker or distributor by contacting end users or stockists. An outlet check serves to identify:

- strengths of competitive products (user attitudes, usage, distribution and display)
- which distributors, brokers or manufacturers are most effective in obtaining display and distribution (and possibly how they achieve

results, e.g. use of display aids, display or promotional allowances, merchandising support, etc.)

- which distributors and brokers are known to customers and respected
- market practices in any product category in respect of display, merchandising, pricing and promoting products
- competitive market pricing, customary trade terms, promotional programmes and policies
- achievements of your potential broker or distributor with products already represented and in relation to other manufacturers' products.

The broker or distributor should satisfy the principal on the following criteria:

- that they have high standing and reputation in the local business community and are seen as experts in the products they represent
- that they have no conflicting interests of similar agency lines or management or financial involvement with other parties that could limit the principal's marketing and market development
- that they have the organisation and facilities to perform to the principal's standards and requirements
- that they have sound financial standing and resources to pay for goods, extend customer credit and grow with the business.

To reduce the risks of missing factors or aspects in discussions it might be useful for the manager responsible for evaluating brokers and distributors to prepare a checklist or questionnaire relating to all the points that need to be investigated or answered in research and evaluation of brokers and distributors.

Contracts A distributor or broker may require a formal contract covering the terms and conditions of his relationship with the principal. Although it may be necessary to draw up such an agreement with the aid of a lawyer, the initial discussions and drafts of terms are likely to be conducted by the principal's sales manager, who should identify commercial matters to be covered by the agreement, possibly including:

- territorial exclusivity
- product exclusivity and product range, including range extension should new products be launched in the future
- special handling and storage requirements
- reservation of rights to supply 'house accounts' or to restrict supplies to any user or stockist

370

- rights, responsibilities and duties in respect of any stocks of merchandise or spare parts held on consignment
- promotional responsibilities, including the apportionment of costs between the parties, and responsibilities for the provision of sales and marketing aids, including display material, product and servicing manuals, etc.
- reporting/marketing information reports
- performance clauses (minimum sales requirements)
- payment terms and/or commission arrangements and fees
- any costing or pricing arrangements subject to the agreement
- the rights and responsibilities of the principal in providing initial and ongoing training to management and sales and other personnel employed by the broker or distributor
- any factors affecting protection of industrial property rights, e.g. patents, trademarks, copyrights
- confidentiality clauses protecting the manufacturer's confidential data from misuse or unauthorised disclosure
- duration of the agreement and guidelines for renewals or extensions
- handling of disputes, e.g. arbitration
- assignability of the agreement, e.g. in the event of changes in the ownership or management of the broker or distributor
- grounds for early termination of the agreement and the disposition of any stocks or equipment in the event of termination of the agreement
- the other rights, responsibilities and duties of the broker or distributor and principal.

(*Note*: This subject matter is covered more fully in my companion work *Practical Export Management* (London, Allen & Unwin, 1985) and those responsible for business through distributors and other agents may well find the appropriate chapters useful supplementary reading.)

It is important that the principal establish if any laws apply in the country of distribution or representation giving ongoing rights or protection to distributors, brokers or other agents in the event of termination of the agreement for any reason. Some markets have laws giving protection in the form of guaranteed commissions in respect of accounts originally introduced by the agent.

All the terms and conditions of representation by a distributor or broker or other agent should be clarified in writing at the outset of a relationship to reduce the risks of misunderstandings and disputes. The best agreements are those that are simple in format, style and language; as the agreement is a two-way definition of the rights, duties and responsibilities of both the parties, the final agreement should be seen as balanced and fair to each party.

Training The training of the sales team of a distributor or broker is just as critical to results as the training of a manufacturer's own sales organisation.

The manufacturer can assist in providing training to the management and sales teams of the brokers or distributors (within the limits of his own resources), particularly in the areas of:

- basic sales skills, including but not limited to the use of company sales aids, operating to a sales call sequence (on all products represented), handling objections and closing sales, and product merchandising (or servicing, for industrial products)
- company and industry knowledge and developments
- product knowledge (especially important for industrial and 'hi-tech' products)
- territory organisation and management
- design and use of effective information systems and sales force administrative documents and systems
- conducting sales meetings and conferences, and effective participation at exhibitions and conferences
- man-management skills, motivation, field sales management and controls, decision making, planning and forecasting, and such other areas where the principal may be seen as having more developed or specialist skills.

A broker or distributor will want to limit the time he permits any principal to take for training because of his responsibilities to other principals to maintain coverage and produce tangible sales results, and there are often several principals competing for training time or the opportunity to make presentations at sales meetings. The principal can perhaps concentrate training in two respects: first, by adopting the principle of '**little and often**' and providing shorter training programmes more frequently to retain interest; secondly, by concentrating a proportion of training time and effort to development training of the managers of the brokerage or distributive organisation, because they, in turn, will train their subordinates.

The management of the broker or distributor will generally respond more positively to manufacturer-sponsored training programmes where there is also benefit in respect of the other lines represented, and if the key persons feel very much an integral part of the manufacturer's own organisation − they can beneficially be invited, when appropriate, to meetings and training programmes conducted by the principal at his facilities, and their advice and opinions solicited (and acted on) in respect of sales and marketing developments.

Sales information systems should be developed that are mutually communicative and beneficial to the principal and broker or distributor in analysing business developments, trends, levels of

372

usage, distribution and display, and market shares. Market share and market research information that becomes available to the principal might usefully be shared with the broker or distributor if not of a particularly confidential nature as this increases mutual under-standing and exploitation of markets and opportunities. The principal should clearly limit his demands for information and reports to such data as are clearly relevant to the analysis and development of the markets, identification and interpretation of trends, and identification of problems that might require corrective action.

Sales managers charged with responsibility for managing distributors and brokers need a high level of patience, tenacity and tact, in addition to the management characteristics previously covered. They also need a particular ability to manage and motivate for results in situations where there is no line authority over the persons actually responsible for the field implementation of programmes and policies and for achieving the sales-related results.

OTHER ORDERING OR DISTRIBUTION METHODS

Multiple account branch delivery systems

Amongst some retailers with multiple consumer outlets, orders are shipped to a central warehouse and redistributed to branches, which place their own orders with the central warehouse. The supplier benefits by lower distribution costs and possibly maintaining distribution to smaller outlets that might not otherwise justify a direct call and direct deliveries. However, the supplier faces the dis-advantage that if his own sales team are not visiting the branches it is hard to maintain display and distribution at optimum levels and to communicate promotional activity. Many larger suppliers respond by arranging for the territory salesperson to call on branches at reduced frequencies or for reduced time periods (fewer work units, if that system is being used) for the purpose of:

- maintaining distribution by seeking branch orders through the central distribution system
- checking and helping with display and merchandising activities
- providing updated display material and point of sale aids
- communicating new products, special offers, advertising and promotional programmes
- demonstrating interest in that particular branch and maintaining goodwill.

Alternatively, the necessary service might be provided by a merchandising call by a member of a specialist (part-time) merchandising sales force.

Voluntary retail buying groups, such as can be found in some

373

countries in the food, pharmaceutical or hardware businesses, can be similarly covered by occasional calls on members of the buying group where this has tangible benefit and can be considered as cost-effective. Members of the buying group can similarly be introduced to new or existing products, informed of advertising and promotional activities, and motivated to place orders through their buying group central office or branch warehouses.

Exclusive retail stockists

A manufacturer of specialist products (such as perfumes and cosmetics, home computers or fashion goods) may not require either a large sales force or a distribution system because the nature of his market may rule against mass market distribution. Such a manu-facturer may operate solely through a network of appointed exclusive retail stockists, who might order either directly when stock is needed, or through the manufacturer's representative, or possibly through an in-store sales consultant, paid for in part or total by the manufacturer. The stockist might buy on standard pricing terms and conditions, or expect a scale of discounts, allowances or rebates to reflect the volume of sales. In some circumstances the retail outlet might actually prefer to sub-let a display and selling area to the manufacturer in return for a rental, either fixed or related to sales volume.

Postal orders

Small customers, or those with limited seasonal trade or located in remote geographical regions, might also be serviced, albeit in a very impersonal fashion, by a postal system of soliciting orders. Whilst this is likely to be less welcome than telephone selling and ordering, it might be practical where it is necessary to despatch samples, product or trade literature in any volume or to detail new product ranges. Customers might be requested to check stocks at regular intervals and to post in their current order requirements; a new order form can be despatched with merchandise.

Direct mail campaigns

A refinement of the general use of mail to send regular order forms to stockists is the direct mail sales campaign. This is commonly used with significant success to promote sales direct to end users, especially of consumer durables or items often termed as 'special offers'. The mailshot should be limited by whatever consumer marketing demographic parameters are considered relevant (age, employment, social class, geographical location, income levels, etc.) to minimise wastage, but there are restrictions on how narrowly a market can be identified and selectively targeted. Target users and consumers may be identified from directories, membership lists for clubs and organisations, professional registers, and a variety of relevant mailing lists that can be purchased or leased.

Wherever possible, mailshots should be addressed to specific named people and be accompanied by a personalised letter

374

requesting the reader to study the literature and contact the source for additional data, demonstrations, samples, etc. In general, material relevant to a person's job or performance has a good chance of being read prior to disposal. A marketing manager will usually seek to supplement mailshots with advertising or favourable editorial comment in appropriate trade, professional or technical journals.

A direct mailshot should be prepared with certain basic guidelines in mind:

- simplicity in structure and content
- illustrative photographs (not drawings) of the product and product uses, possibly highlighting special features
- clear presentation of the product attributes and user benefits, specifications, uses, after-sales servicing support, warranties and guarantees relating to the product or performance, prices, availability (ordering lead times, or names and addresses of distributors), etc.
- maintenance requirements or intervals
- provision of a mail response card or cut-out reader enquiry card bearing the address to which it should be posted to obtain additional information or to request a demonstration and visit from a salesperson (telephone numbers may also beneficially be included), or to place an order by post.

A broader target market can sometimes be reached by having a leaflet or brochure distributed by loose insertion between the pages of a magazine or journal.

Mail order catalogues

Mail order catalogues seem to rise and fall in popularity. They can be useful both for increasing sales of general products (particularly durable goods such as jewellery, clothes and household goods) and to promote special products to special target markets (such as coins, stamps, seeds, collectables and other hobby-related items). Their effectiveness will be a function of how closely the catalogue company have defined and identified the target markets and individuals to receive the catalogue.

Ideally, purchase through a catalogue should offer the purchaser some tangible benefit over purchases at other distributive outlets to gain interest and encourage action to the point of placing an order. The benefit may be in terms of:

- **price** – lower prices than for similar goods offered in retail outlets
- **product range** – a broader product range of specialist products than might generally be available in retail outlets
- **scarcity** – such as unusual collectables or exclusive products available only through the catalogue source

- **convenience** – ordering without leaving the home
- **payment** – extended payment terms to creditworthy customers, or use of approved credit cards
- **ordering** – ease of ordering on a preprinted order form
- **guarantees** – money-back guarantees to unsatisfied customers in addition to manufacturers' warranties
- **trial** – delivery and trial before invoicing and payment due.

The construction and layout of catalogues is more a subject for a marketing than a sales text, but the guidelines given in the previous section on direct mail campaigns can equally apply.

Direct home distributors

Over the last decade or so several companies, particularly in the United States, have achieved effective distribution and high sales volumes by selecting and appointing distributors who operate from home on a part-time basis. Local distributors may take stocks either to use as samples or to resell at a mark-up within a local area or circle of acquaintances. In some instances they may buy samples but book orders for direct shipment from the principal and payment to the principal, and receive a sales commission. Specialist products or exclusive product ranges (including certain household durable items, health foods, dietary plans, cosmetic ranges, costume jewellery) may lend themselves to this system of distribution where the investment in stock by a distributor is not high.

Companies operating in this manner need a core of full-time professional field sales managers to select, train, motivate and manage distributors within any agreed parameters of exclusivity.

If correctly operated, this system and variations on it differ from the ill-reputed 'pyramid selling' systems, where product stocks are basically passed down a chain of distributors and sub-distributors without finding a final consumer.

Exhibitions

Exhibitions are another way to promote, demonstrate and sell products either to the consumer or other end user of goods and services, or to distributors and retail stockists. In some exhibitions (such as major automobile shows) the intention is less to make immediate sales than to have a forum for presenting the latest technology and models – orders perhaps being subsequently placed through agents or distributors. Other exhibitions concentrate on marketing direct to potential users and consumers (such as office equipment and home improvement marketeers) and may motivate prompt ordering by offering special discounts, allowances or bonus terms to people placing orders at the exhibition.

Planning and managing a stand at an exhibition is a time-consuming and often frustrating task. The sales manager will need to concern himself with:

- selecting exhibitions that are likely to satisfy sales and marketing objectives
- setting objectives for the exhibition and monitoring results
- planning the details of attendance at the exhibition
- organising post-exhibition follow-up.

Selecting the exhibition

The sales manager may have the alternatives of trade-only exhibitions for his products or user/consumer exhibitions. As the budgetary allocation to exhibitions is likely to be rather limited, selection might take account of:

- cost of participation (either total or per attendee)
- location (proximity to the exhibitor's centre of operations and markets and access to public transport)
- relationship between the company's products and target market and the known parameters of the exhibition's visitors (job functions, industries, interests, etc.)
- reputation (national and international) of the exhibition
- quality and quantity of other exhibitors
- competence of exhibition organisers and promoters
- timing of the exhibition (in relation to the company's market sales cycles or new product launches)
- suitability of the facilities for the display and demonstration of the company's products.

Exhibition objectives

Participating in an exhibition without objectives should be as alien to the salesperson as entering a new call without samples. Objectives should be quantified and might include:

- booking orders at the stand
- obtaining new leads for subsequent follow-up and product demonstration
- showing and demonstrating a new product (product launch promotion) to prospective users/consumers
- contact with existing agents/distributors/customers
- identifying potential new agents/distributors in selected market sectors or regions
- testing acceptability of and obtaining feedback on products.

As a supplementary activity or objective, the exhibitor might devote some time and attention to assessing competitive products, prices, promotions and marketing activity and relative strengths and weaknesses. In most instances, an exhibition objective will be for profits from sales made as a result of the exhibition to exceed the costs of exhibiting.

Exhibition planning

This must commence very early if participation at an exhibition is to be effective. Some recommendations for the sales manager are:

- Delegate overall responsibility for the entire exhibition project to one manager who has full authority, budgetary control and access to the necessary resources of people, time and money.
- Book participation as early as possible (sometimes a cancellation clause will permit withdrawal at little penalty cost to a point in time) in order to select the most suitable exhibition stand location.
- Prepare a list of all necessary stand equipment, display aids, promotional literature, etc., and establish what can and will be provided by the exhibition organiser. Particular attention must be given to special needs of displays, such as refrigerated storage or rotating stands. All other requirements must be designed, ordered, received by the exhibitor and delivered to the exhibition site to meet the critical lead times. The longest lead time to produce any particular requirement governs the entire timing schedule of the project.
- Plan the manning of the exhibition stand, preferably using competent sales and technical personnel rather than temporary hired help, and ensure staffing is such that the stand will never be left unmanned. It may also be necessary to hire interpreters at foreign exhibitions and to have foreign language versions of sales literature. It is often wise to rotate stand personnel every few hours, enabling all to benefit from attendance at the exhibition.
- Notify existing customers and known potential users of your products of your participation at the exhibition, perhaps through personal letters and advertisements in trade journals.
- Ensure supplies of sales literature and samples are adequate to meet expected needs, but at the same time there is no need to be wasteful giving expensive literature to casual browsers.
- Have a system of noting and recording exactly who visits the stand and the nature of their interest and enquiry (possibly using a pre-printed enquiry card that also seeks to establish the enquirer's status and decision makers in his organisation).

Exhibition follow-up

If the exhibition has been successful in generating leads, considerable follow-up is needed to turn leads into sales. Visitors to stands normally make rather general enquiries, which must be pursued by direct meetings to relate specific products to needs. The sales manager should follow the exhibition with a programme that:

- quantifies the results in terms of leads generated and orders taken in relation to the costs of participation
- analyses the enquiries/leads into priority groups for post-

exhibition follow-up, including product sampling and demonstrations, to ensure that those most likely to produce sales are contacted promptly (knowledge of markets, industries and companies may provide the basis for lead prioritisation)

- commits suitably qualified (technical) salespersons to pursue leads and to relate the needs of prospects to the company's products and assess levels of usage of competitive products.

The amount of post-exhibition activity will depend on the nature of the product. A standard home durable product, such as a washing machine, may require only a single home demonstration to complete a sale; an industrial machine may require modifications to suit particular environmental factors; an ingredient or component may require lengthy testing to confirm its suitability in particular end products.

Participation in exhibitions has a place in the sales manager's armoury of promotional weapons if used effectively, and can sometimes be a powerful way to reach a targeted market, particularly in international marketing. The reader especially interested in this aspect of sales promotion may wish to pursue the subject further in more specialised texts. For others the brief Exhibition Planning Checklist at the end of the chapter may prove of use, particularly if modified for particular situations.

Conventions

Suppliers of specialist products aimed at one industry, trade or profession may find benefit in attending appropriate conventions, either just to renew or make contacts, or as exhibitors, should any limited display facilities exist. Planning and follow-up need to be just as thorough as at any larger or more formal exhibition. It is usually a good practice to advise by letter, or invitation to visit a stand or hospitality suite, all current customers and contacts, and those known to be useful contacts or potential customers.

Sales conventions and exhibitions likely to be of benefit to any company should be identified at least a year ahead, and attendance programmed into the sales and marketing plans and budgets.

Computer-linked ordering systems

Many mass merchandising retailers currently control stock levels through computer recording of sales passing through checkouts. Similarly, computer controls over stock levels are exercised by most industrial users of materials and parts. In time, suppliers and purchasers of goods might agree to direct computer links that generate automatic repeat orders of products at certain critical stock levels. This will clearly have inventory control benefits to the buyers, and production planning (including inventory control of inputs) benefits to manufacturers. Salespersons will still be needed to fulfil

379

the selling and communication functions and will actually have more time to spend on the more sophisticated selling tasks.

The growth of the home computer market facilitates the direct marketing of goods and services through computer links to central marketing services. In the future, consumers will be able to access more product data and place orders through the home computer links to a far greater degree, possibly with payment by credit cards. As these systems develop, suppliers may choose more often to give contact point details so that potential customers can follow up computer-initiated enquiries by telephone contact to suppliers' own staff for further information, direct ordering, or to request direct sales and demonstration visits.

FRANCHISING

Over the last two decades, and particularly during recent years, the system of licensing or, as it is more commonly becoming known, franchising has grown rapidly, and is predicted to account for a most significant share of total sales of goods and services by the 1990s — some estimates being as high as 30 per cent. When a **franchise** or **licence** is given to a party, whether an individual or company, the franchisor or licensor is granting the recipient the rights to use a trademark, know-how, business operations system, or technology, or to produce or distribute a distinctive product or service. This method of expansion offers great scope for increased sales and distribution to a variety of industries and product groups. This subject is treated at some length in my earlier book *Practical Export Management* (London, Allen & Unwin, 1985) and also in my article 'Developing markets through licensing' in *Export* (journal of the Institute of Export, March 1985), but because it can also have a major impact on domestic sales expansion I feel some particular attention is warranted in this text.

Why license? A manufacturer or supplier of goods or services may seek to license products, services, know-how, technology, trademarks or a business format domestically for a number of reasons:

- he has insufficient capital and internal resources to expand to take advantage of market potential and opportunities
- there is an unacceptable relationship between the cost of freight and general distribution and the achievable market price structures (i.e. there are clear cost and price advantages in having goods produced in the immediate distribution and marketing locations)
- a product has a short shelf-life and normal shipping and distribution lead times would result in the product having too

380

short a balance of shelf-life for effective distribution and marketing
- products are too delicate to withstand the rigors of shipment over long distances, possibly with several modes of transport
- the nature of the goods or services is such that the licensor feels that entrepreneurially owned and operated franchised units will actually produce more sales and profits than would company-owned and managed units
- a product is not mutually exclusive but would necessarily form part of another complementary product or service
- there is benefit in or a need to link with another company with effective distribution channels serving the same potential users or consumers
- one party controls access to essential ingredients or raw materials needed in the licensed product or know-how.

Larger companies might choose to structure and develop a licensing team incorporating such functions as marketing, finance, research, production, technical service, training and legal, whereas smaller companies with more limited resources may only be able to develop through a single individual. A number of consultancy firms now exist that specialise in offering total services to potential and new franchisors, including feasibility studies, evaluation of markets and opportunities, and preparation of contracts and manuals.

A licensee must see tangible benefits to himself when taking a licence, such as:

- improved sales volume and earnings potential
- measurable cost savings (e.g. better yields, lower material costs, lower energy use, better quality control, less maintenance, lower staffing levels, lower staff turnover, etc.)
- acquisition of national or internationally recognised trademarks and brand names that will enhance the existing or potential sales and reputation of the licensee
- significant savings in start-up costs or investment in research or developing know-how from own sources and resources (which might be very limited)
- easier access to business start-up capital and financial services when a licensee of a major established franchising organisation
- ability to obtain key sites in busy commercial centres as a licensee of an established organisation with proven sales, goodwill and market acceptance
- acquisition of a new product or service that might complement an existing product or service or would sell through existing outlets
- inclusion of new technology or know-how in existing or new products or services, giving additional marketing strength and tangible product advantages over competitors.

What to license	A company may seek to license a **product, copyright work, process, technical know-how, business format, trademark** or business **brand name**, which a licensee might accept has a value or use on its own or if incorporated in another product or service. Whatever the licensor wishes to license must have a recognisable degree of exclusivity and not be in the public domain if it is to have a value. If a product or other industrial property is protected by patent or copyright laws, the potential licensee may feel no need to enter into a licensing agreement with ongoing royalties if he thinks he can circumvent the protection and duplicate the goods or services alone. That is where there is considerable benefit to the licensor in having a strong and recognisable trademark and image created through marketing effort, because a licensee can generally recognise the benefits of being part of an established successful operation rather than starting from scratch with a 'me too' venture.
How to license	A licensor may sell a licence for a once-only fixed fee, but is likely to benefit by that approach only if he really believes his product has a very limited life. More usually a licence is granted for a fixed period, which should always be long enough to ensure that a licensee will recover his investment and make a return on the capital over and above the initial investment. Many licensors initially grant a licence for periods of from five to twenty years, depending on the nature of the product and markets, and the initial investment required. The licensor will normally seek an initial licence fee to cover his costs of helping to start the new licensee in the business, including all training, administrative support, finding suitable locations, planning and site design services. Thereafter it would be normal for a royalty to be payable related to the level of output or turnover.

Where a product formulation is being licensed, the licensor may additionally seek to protect his exclusive product or know-how by only agreeing to supply a base ingredient or product mix, without revealing the actual specifications or formulations. Part of the returns to the licensor can then be obtained by a mark-up on ingredient supplies. Licensors may actually seek to control the source of all materials or inputs through themselves, either because of concern over input quality or as a means of generating additional profits by mark-ups that are possible through the licensor's strong buying power. Not all countries will accept that a licensor may be the sole source of inputs and/or take a mark-up on them.

Where a business format is being licensed, then the licensor should seek to maximise his protection by developing the most thorough manuals, which are protected by copyright, to include all aspects of the business operations, such as:

- recruitment systems and procedures
- staff training and discipline

382

- financial systems and procedures
- administrative systems and procedures
- production or process systems and techniques
- quality control practices and methods
- sources and standards of inputs and raw materials
- factors concerned with the licensor's image, such as design, layouts, use of trademarks.

It is likely that the contents of all operational manuals will form part of the master agreement between the licensor and licensee. The licensor also needs to be able to provide full start-up training in every aspect of opening, managing and operating a franchise outlet according to the business format developed. Support services are generally necessary to cover marketing and market research (including advertising and product development), financial advice (bookkeeping, stock controls, cash flow, budgets, income statements, etc.), personnel (recruitment, training, employment regulations, discipline), quality control over both inputs and outputs, and central purchasing of inputs (and distribution if stocks must be taken from the central purchasing unit).

Clearly a licensor does not want licensees to fall foul of the agencies concerned with ensuring compliance with any enforceable regulations, nor does he want the embarrassment of licensees closing operations because of non-compliance or financial mismanagement. The licensor will therefore need to establish that his products and services or processes comply in every way with all applicable rules and regulations operating in any market, including health, labelling, packaging, safety, ingredient usage or composition. All trademarks and patents or copyrights should be registered in the licensor's name. The licensee must in turn, be obligated by contract to comply locally with all by-laws, rules and regulations affecting the running and operation of his business as a licensee, including employment laws, health and safety regulations, packaging, labelling and ingredient regulations, and any rules on hours of operating or opening, company registrations, and rules relating to filing tax returns and any other required business statements.

Finding a licensee

Finding suitable licensees is a task requiring great effort in time and resources to ensure that the marriage of licensor and licensee is not a mismatch. Both parties need to have a good degree of commonality of objectives and a commitment to work together to their mutual benefit and profit. Some guidelines can be developed, which clearly will be influenced by whether it is a manufacturing process being licensed or a business format for a retail establishment.

383

Manufacturing process

Points to take into account in seeking a licensee for a manufactured product, process or technology include:

- for a specific process for treating a raw material, ingredient or waste product, identify producers or users of the ingredient or raw material, or generators of the waste item
- if a raw material involved is produced or sold only through certain private or government agencies, then enter discussions with those agencies to establish which of their customers might have applications
- for mass market items, seek to identify those companies that presently produce similar goods, or that distribute to suitable outlets, and that might benefit by expanding a product range to include a national or international brand
- if production requires certain ingredients, seek out producers of the ingredients to establish if they have an interest in expanding into end uses of the ingredient or raw material
- if a product is in a specific market category, such as an automobile component or a camera accessory, consider approaches to producers of such items who might benefit from range extension
- if a product must be an integral part or component of another product, logically there may be merit in an approach to current producers of the other product who might find technical or earnings benefit by incorporating the item.

Potential licensees for such manufactured products, processes or technology should be evaluated according to certain basic criteria and data collected on:

- the size of the company (turnover, assets, staffing)
- production and distribution facilities and capabilities
- current product ranges and product volumes
- market share data and marketing capabilities
- financial performance history
- ownership and corporate structure
- any major shareholdings
- key officers and personnel.

A business format

If a franchisor wishes to franchise a retail business or service, which might include trademarks, or tried and proven business formats (such as fast food outlets, car rentals, hotels and motels, personnel services, cleaning services, car servicing centres), he will most likely be seeking small privately owned companies or private individuals to form the core of franchisees. The franchisee benefits from the training, ready-made systems and procedures, the business format and the franchisor's support on a scale no single individual franchisee could contemplate even for an independently operated business in the same field.

The franchisor needs to evaluate each single potential franchisee most carefully against detailed relevant criteria, which can be established from experience in the categories of:

- **education**
  - does the franchisee have the level of formal education needed to assimilate the operations and know-how of the business and to operate successfully as a self-employed business person?
- **skills**
  - does the business require any special skills or aptitudes (e.g. for photography, printing, business services, engineering, car maintenance)?
  - does the potential franchisee have the requisite skills?
- **experience**
  - is any particular type of previous experience necessary to operate effectively as a franchisee (e.g. man-management, selling, bookkeeping, stock control, fashion merchandising, catering etc.)?
  - does the potential franchisee have the relevant experience?
- **personal characteristics**
  - is the franchisee suited to serving customers and to being self-employed?
  - has he the requisite interest, commitment, temperament and other character traits demonstrated by successful franchisees as necessary or ideal?
- **financial resources**
  - has the franchisee got the necessary financial resources and stability both to open and operate a franchise?
  - has he the reserve resources to meet personal and family needs until the franchised unit produces positive earnings and cash flows?

The franchisor should also prepare an initial prospectus package providing information to potential franchisees on such matters as:

- fees and royalties
- capital requirements
- pro-forma earnings and cash flow projections
- the products or services
- the markets and franchisor's performance history in the markets
- training programmes and support
- aid in site selection and evaluation
- design services for the franchisee's unit.

Potential franchisees should be encouraged whenever it is practical to spend time at the location of another franchisee or company unit (but the former is perhaps preferable) in order to assess if that particular business will satisfy the needs of the franchisee.

Both the new franchisor and franchisee may benefit at the initial stages of investigating franchising as a means of developing in business by making contact with such recognised trade associations as the British Franchise Association of 75a Bell Street, Henley-on-Thames, Oxon RG9 2BD, England, or the International Franchise Association of 1025 Connecticut Avenue N.W., Washington DC 20036, United States. These associations can provide invaluable advice and information, including on such matters as laws and regulations currently in force within their geographical spheres of interest.

Elements of a licensing agreement

The length and complexity of a licensing agreement will depend on such factors as the nature of the product, process, service or know-how being licensed, the rights, duties, obligations, commitments and programmes of the respective parties, and the legal requirements of the particular markets or countries. Obviously the company's legal advisers will have a major input into the construction of an agreement, which will generally not subsequently be negotiable to any degree with any individual licensee. An agreement must be, and be seen to be, fair to both parties. If at first glance the agreement appears to consist mostly of the franchisee's duties, obligations, commitments, etc., then perhaps the franchise manager should sit down and redraft it so that the respective commitments look more balanced on paper. The agreement will generally at least have clauses to cover:

- what is being licensed
- the period the licence is granted for
- commitments to starting dates or time spans
- terms for extensions or renewals
- initial fees and ongoing royalties, and the timing and manner of payments due (possibly with penalty clauses for late or non-payment)
- the basis on which fees and royalties will be assessed (such as on unit volume or turnover)
- audit and control, enabling the franchisor to verify fees and royalties
- territorial limitations to the licence or other basis for exclusivity
- licensee's rights or lack of rights to grant sub-licences
- quality control, covering both inputs and outputs

- secrecy, preventing the licensee from disclosing know-how, systems, procedures and practices considered as the industrial property of the licensor
- rights of assignment by either party to another
- performance, involving minimum sales or royalties
- responsibilities in respect of compliance with all relevant and applicable rules and regulations governing the offering of the goods or services in the market (both parties may have separate responsibilities)
- registration and protection of patents, trademarks and copyrighted industrial property
- product development programmes, exchange of information, and rights of ownership and marketing resulting from developments by either party
- supply and pricing of components, ingredients, or exclusive formulations
- pricing of the final product on offer to consumers or other end users
- marketing assistance and programmes to be provided by the licensor and the supply of marketing materials, and the arrangements for the financing of all such programmes (e.g. a levy on sales values)
- licensee's responsibilities to obtain and maintain all local permissions and certification to operate the business at the agreed location, and to comply in every respect with local and national laws, rules and regulations affecting or concerning the operation of the business
- any restrictions on the use of the agreed site or business location for other domestic, private or business purposes by the licensee or his associates
- investment responsibilities relating to the necessary plant and equipment both for the start-up and for replacement due to wear and tear or obsolescence
- mutual development of marketing and market development programmes and involvement of the licensee and licensor in preparing plans and programmes, possibly with details on the membership, structure, role and authority of any licensee advisory panel or committee
- procedures for the handling of disputes
- details of the support services and programmes to be provided by the franchisor
- licensee's rights in respect of the range of and access to support services
- causes for premature termination of a licence, and the respective responsibilities, rights and duties of each party to the other in such circumstances
- the licensee's rights to sell the licensed business unit

387

- limitations on the licensee, both during the period of the licence and subsequently, to operate in competing businesses
- maintenance of insurance cover to protect both parties' interests in respect of goodwill, royalties, earnings, replacement cost of all capital equipment and direct investments in the business unit, etc.
- applicable laws to be used in interpreting and enforcing the agreements (particularly relevant if a licence is being granted from one country to another).

Licensing is a subject the modern sales and marketing manager should be aware of and consider in relation to his own company's aspirations, resources, products and markets, because it may offer a practical way to grow more rapidly, and with higher net earnings potential, that may offset to some degree the limitations upon control encountered once a network of independently owned franchise units form the core of a business.

- Salespersons can beneficially use telephone contact to make initial contacts and identify potential consumers and users of goods or services; to obtain repeat orders from established customers; as a means of effecting emergency cover and contact when no relief salesperson is available; to maintain contact and solicit orders from small or geographically remote customers.
- A specialist telephone sales department might be established to make regular contact for repeat orders, requesting stock levels and gearing orders to stocks and product movement levels, including making adjustments for seasonal trends and promotional activity. Such a department can also be extremely useful at the stage of identifying contacts as part of a cold canvassing operation, and identifying potential needs or use for goods or services, along with making arrangements for direct visits by sales personnel.
- Telephone sales staff will need intensive and specialist training in selling skills, including relaxing the contact, identifying and gaining access to decision makers, using questioning techniques to arouse interest and identify potential needs or use, handling objections, and closing sales presentations. Supporting administrative systems should be designed for the specific needs of the telephone sales department staff.
- Distributors and brokers offer alternative means of achieving sales and distribution, with limitations imposed by the lack of direct line authority of the supplier, the diversity of products represented or markets catered for, conflicting pressures from a multiplicity of principals, and lower levels of skills, knowledge, interest and motivation.
- Selection of brokers and distributors should include careful depth research into the company's markets, facilities, organisation and operations, with thorough field checks into achievements on products already represented. The appointee should have sound financial standing, no conflicting interests, and the organisation, facilities and funds to meet his obligations to the principal and maximise growth and market development.
- The relationship between principal and broker or distributor may be recognised and formalised in respect of mutual rights, duties and responsibilities in a formal contract or other mutually acceptable exchange of correspondence. Such a document should include reference to the principal's rights and responsibilities in respect of training of the broker or distributor's management and sales personnel, and the mutual information needs of the parties.
- Apart from a manufacturer's direct sales force or telephone selling operations, orders can also be solicited through such means as: branch deliveries through central warehouse facilities

of major retailing or distributive groups; exclusive retail stockists; postal orders; direct mail campaigns; mail order catalogues; home distributors; exhibitions and conventions; and computer-linked information and ordering systems.

- Franchising or licensing offers an alternative mode of expansion to manufacturers or other suppliers of goods or services, particularly where the franchisor has limited financial or other resources but has a product or service with a clear market potential, and where an individual or corporate licensee can see tangible benefit in operating as a licensee. The franchisor may license products, processes, technology, know-how or other business formats that have a recognised degree of exclusivity.

	Remarks	Action

Telephone selling

Is there a need or role for a telephone
  sales department for:

- making initial cold contacts?
- replenishing stocks?
- emergency call cover?
- small accounts?
- remote geographical customers?

Has a telephone sales call sequence been
  developed?

Are telephone sales staff trained in:

- cold call telephone canvassing?
- identifying decision makers?
- gaining access to decision makers?
- relaxing contacts?
- identifying customer needs?
- presenting the goods or services?
- handling objections?
- closing sales?
- arranging direct sales visits?
- questioning techniques?
- recording notes on results of contacts
  made and complying with administrative
  procedures?

Have support internal administrative
  systems been developed for:

- identifying potential customers?
- ordering?
- arranging payment?
- invoicing?
- arranging direct visits by field personnel?
- recording information (such as stock
  levels) obtained as a result of telephone
  contact?

Other alternatives

Do any of the following offer alternatives
  to or complement a direct sales
  organisation:

- wholesalers?
- distributors?
- brokers?
- exclusive retail stockists?
- distribution to branches of multiple
  retailers or members of voluntary
  buying groups with central warehousing
  and distribution facilities?
- postal ordering?
- direct mail campaigns?
- advertising producing direct orders and
  enquiries?
- mail order catalogues?
- direct home distributions?
- exhibitions?
- conventions?
- computer-linked ordering systems?
- franchising?

391

	Notes	Action
Select the exhibition Consider: • access to public transport (air/road/rail) • proximity to customers/markets • reputation of exhibition • competence of organisers • compatibility of visitor profile with target market profile • timing		
Objectives Set objectives: • obtaining orders at the stand • product launch • contact with existing customers/distributors • identifying new customers/agents/distributors • general marketing promotion • market evaluation • evaluation of competitive activity • others:		
Planning Set budgets: • participation fees • stand design costs • delivery/handling/storage of exhibits, etc. • hire of furniture, telephones, etc. • stand cleaning expenses • sales promotion literature & other aids • samples • foreign language interpreters • locally hired demonstrators, etc. • staff travel & subsistence expenses • advance publicity & public relations • insurance of exhibits, etc. • customer hospitality • others: Facilities check: • electricity supply sources • lighting • stand location (proximity to traffic flow, competitive stands, etc.) • ease of access for bulky exhibits • catering • security • communications (telephones/telex, etc.) • other: Action: • develop a critical timetable • appoint exhibition project leader • book stand		

Checklist   Exhibition planning (contd.)

	Notes	Action
• decide on exhibition theme		
• design stand and place order		
• design promotional & other literature and order		
• decide on exhibition manning requirements		
• book hotels and travel for company personnel		
• book hospitality suites		
• plan and book advance publicity		
• notify existing and potential customers		
• prepare and implement public relations campaign		
• prepare exhibits		
• ship exhibits to the exhibition		
• prepare & ship samples to exhibition		
• hire interpreter & local support staff		
• prepare stand manning rota		
• check despatch of all equipment, materials, etc.		
• other:		

Post-exhibition

• compare achievements with objectives		
• compare budgets with actual costs		
• prepare and implement an enquiry follow-up programme		
• evaluate competitive and market information obtained		
• other:		

393

13 Developing International Markets

Within many companies the responsibility for finding and developing international markets rests with the company's sales director. This could be either because the company is too small to warrant a separate export division with board level representation, or because the nature of the goods or services being offered to foreign markets is such that the domestic and foreign sales are best managed by the same team. Many home market sales managers find an attraction in considering transfer to the export sales and marketing operations of a company, yet have little insight into the key export functions and responsibilities. In this short chapter I do not propose to dwell on the complexities of export and international business operations but to bridge the gap between this text, which deals more specifically with home market sales management operations, and the more specialised export management functions.

WHY EXPORT?

Export confers benefits at the macro level on nations in political, economic and social terms. International trade is **politically** important in building permanent relationships, loyalties, dependencies and spheres of influence. **Economically**, trade results in specialisation and a cross-flow of goods and services from the country with the greatest economic advantage in production and other resources to the country with the needs that cannot be satisfied domestically. **Socially**, trade brings about change and progress by transferring skills, services and products from more advanced to less advanced economies.

Individual nations benefit from export activities by improving their balance of payments positions through increased foreign exchange earnings, and by maintaining higher levels of employment, gross national product, individual earnings and increased taxes on profits and incomes, which, in turn, can be used for further domestic benefit.

The individual company benefits from exports through increased plant utilisation, which, in turn, gives more secure employment opportunities, better labour force morale and training, and a better profit base to reward shareholders and employees or to provide additional funds for reinvestment.

THE ROLE OF THE INTERNATIONAL SALES MANAGER

The international sales manager has the primary functions of:

- identifying foreign markets that offer expansion opportunities for the company and its products, know-how, technology and business formats and other resources. International growth might come through the direct export of goods and services, or through other arrangements such as foreign acquisitions and mergers, subsidiary companies or joint ventures, or the granting of licences to foreign entities

- ensuring that the goods or services offered for sale to foreign markets comply with all the applicable rules and regulations in each foreign market, including those that relate to labelling, ingredients, components, structure, design, health and safety

- arranging that the goods are packaged in a manner that ensures their arrival in the foreign market and with the final user in the desired condition, free of damage, defect or deterioration caused by the hazards of international transit

- selecting, appointing and training such agents, distributors and their sales teams or other representatives as are appropriate to each separate target market

- overseeing the preparation of all international sales contracts, and all agency, distributor or licensing contracts, and ensuring that these are both acceptable to the contracting parties and enforcable according to the laws of the applicable countries

- preparing marketing and sales plans and programmes for each product and market, including all advertising and promotional activity; this could also include the planned modification of existing products to suit local market conditions and user needs, or the development of special products for particular foreign markets

- ensuring that all necessary export, transit and import documentation is prepared accurately, promptly and efficiently to meet all the requirements of both exporting and importing nations' customs and other interested authorities, the customers and the shipping lines or other providers of transport or financial services to enable the goods to pass from the exporter to the final customer through such foreign countries as might be necessary without undue delay in transit

- ensuring that payment will be received for goods despatched either by documentary letters of credit or by such other means of payment as might be agreed between the exporter and importer from time to time. The risks of default in international transactions are substantially greater than is normally the case in the home market, and particular skill and attention is needed in this area because exports are frequently made on a marginally costed

basis where one loss can dramatically affect export profits on a large volume of transactions or merchandise
- provide personal selling support to the agent or distributor
- negotiating the terms and conditions of all sales and shipments with customers, agents and distributors to ensure both that the exporting company makes a profit on each transaction and that the export pricing structure is such as to be of interest to potential customers and competitive with similar products from other sources.

In order to perform these functions, the international sales manager needs all the personal selling and management skills of the home market sales manager and more. In addition to any necessary linguistic skills, he must expand his sales and management skills to include a good level of marketing expertise (because the planning of market research, advertising and promotional activity and fore-casting will all be his responsibility), and also acquire the specialist knowledge required of any exporter in the areas of export documentation, international distribution and shipping, foreign payments, the financial aspects of negotiating and managing a business, and the many legal and quasi-legal aspects of international trade. Some of these additional skills can be acquired through internal training; some by attendance on external courses and management development programmes; and some will simply be acquired over time through experience on the job.

Sales and export managers have frequently asked me what are the priorities in skills and experience required in international sales management. That is not a question that can easily be answered. However, I have often found that the most successful and contented export sales managers have come from a strong home market sales background before choosing to specialise in international selling, and have then set about acquiring the necessary export expertise. Linguistic skills, which frequently have an important place in the skill mix, are insufficient on their own to make a successful international marketeer – in the same way as technical expertise in the mechanics of exporting does not replace sales and marketing skills.

The selection of managers for international sales responsibilities needs to be undertaken with careful attention to the functions, activities and specialist skills required in addition to a thorough assessment of the profile of general characteristics and skills normally expected of a person in a sales and marketing management position. Chapter 6 gives structured guidelines on preparing job holder profiles once detailed job descriptions have been prepared, and the job holder profile for an international sales management position can be developed from these guidelines. It must be particularly born in mind that decisions will often need to be taken during market negotiations and that the international sales manager is generally operating away from the home base for long periods and will not have ready access to the expertise of colleagues. Partly for that reason he needs a higher level of skills or understanding in many peripheral management functions, including knowledge of financial and production matters that impact on the company's production capabilities and flexibilities. Additionally, he needs to be decisive and able to work with minimum supervision, communications and colleagial support.

EXPANSIONARY OPPORTUNITIES

Exports in the marketing mix

Mention has already been made of some of the social and economic benefits of exporting. Exports provide additional benefits in the marketing of products.

The marketing mix is concerned with the production, promotion, presentation, pricing and profitability of products offered for sale to markets that have identified or perceived needs met by the products concerned. The mainstream marketing thrust is generally behind products for the domestic markets. But the marketeer and sales manager should not lose sight of the additional opportunities offered in export markets.

One of the major costs in marketing is developing new products. The launch of a product in any market normally results in a sales pattern that shows a post-launch peak in sales, with a subsequent decline after the novelty has worn off and distribution and usage reach saturation or the product's market share settles down. Frequently sales settle at a plateau level, perhaps with gradual decline as the product life cycle progresses, technology advances and new products appear on the market. An illustration in Chapter 4 (p. 131) shows a typical life cycle pattern. Occasional boosts to sales may result from promotional activity (as illustrated in Example 5.3), which serves to distort the longer-term life cycle pattern. Finding suitable export markets can extend the profitable life cycle of a product because a well-established and dating (in terms of technology or stage in the life cycle) product on the domestic market may be new to many a developing market, or have particular functional or reliability characteristics that commend it to foreign users.

The main likely export opportunities are to:

- seek export markets for the standard home market product without adaptation for foreign markets except in minor respects (such as a voltage change, packaging or presentation, labelling or language of instructional leaflets)
- modify a product in any practical way (including shape, size, design and functionality) to suit the particular needs and regulations of the foreign markets

397

- develop a new product exclusively suited to the foreign markets but that capitalises on the exporter's present technology, production facilities (which might require minimum modification for the export production runs), labour force skills and raw material inputs. For example, a manufacturer of electric house-hold appliances might develop an electric wok targeted at oriental markets (and which might also have minor home market sales potential).

Any of these routes might serve to generate additional sales opportunities, utilise spare production capacity, reduce the costs of production and increase profit contributions from any particular production or assembly line. Goods offered to export markets may frequently be priced below the equivalent domestic market price for the same or similar products if the foreign market pricing structure (including freight distribution and other trade margins and import duties) dictates a need to ship at lower price levels in order to compete in the foreign market. Provided that the unit sales value exceeds the marginal costs of production, the project may still be very worthwhile to the exporter, with additional benefits other than just profit contributions.

The exporter should not expect that a major home market product will find a similar niche in any foreign market. What might be an everyday consumable or durable item at home may be a luxury status symbol in a developing nation. But building a brand awareness now may create the potential for a substantial export marketing effort (or local manufacture under licence) as incomes and demand grow.

At this point it is worth drawing the attention of home sales and marketing managers to the import opportunities that might contribute to growth and profitability. Once you have a home market sales and distribution operation in place, the organisation may have spare capacity to market, sell and distribute additional products. It might well be worth seeking complementary foreign products, especially if they are not restricted by import quotas or licences, to sell alongside the home-produced range. Goods could either be sold under the foreign manufacturer's brand names, which could be an advantage if the foreign brand names have an international standing, or they could be packed as private own-label products under the importer's brand names, which would be beneficial if the importing company might eventually want to produce similar products locally. Many sales managers have found that handling a limited complementary range of products to be offered for sale to the same target outlets as the company's own products enables them to expand a sales operation more rapidly than could have been possible on the basis of the home product range alone. An expanded product

398

range, particularly if some of the products are sold under already established brand names, might serve to give home market access to some buyers who would otherwise be reluctant to grant appointments to the company.

The real point here for the home sales manager is that he should resist the dangers of being parochial or inflexible, and always seek ways to utilise the spare sales force and distribution capacity to increase overall company profits without disruption to the sales and marketing efforts put behind company-produced products.

ALTERNATIVE WAYS OF DEVELOPING EXPORTS

Direct exports The larger companies, and many smaller companies with specialist products (such as components or ingredients, or services) that do not require major marketing effort, prefer to develop direct exports to the foreign markets, seeking to appoint a network of **agents** or **distributors** in each of the target markets identified as worthwhile for management attention and effort. This method gives the greatest degree of direct control by the exporter over the foreign market sales and marketing effort of the agents and distributors. Where a product or service is sold to few end users in a foreign market then even the smaller companies frequently find they have the resources to export directly and provide necessary after-sales service.

Indirect exports The smaller company or one with limited human or financial resources may find that it cannot readily develop a direct export operation. In that case do not rule out exports as a source of additional sales volume but consider indirect exports. There are a large number of specialist companies that will provide a range of export services to smaller companies. Some companies may provide a service where they act as **export agent** only, with representatives travelling the world seeking orders in exchange for fees and commissions; the manufacturer in such cases would normally be responsible for the other aspects of exporting such as documentation and credit (although finance may be available through banks against confirmed orders). Other companies, such as those often referred to as **export houses**, may actually take title to the goods and pay the manufacturer, in turn handling all the documentation and extending credit as necessary to foreign customers; such export houses are frequently found to have a traditional strength through contacts in certain geographical regions. A sales manager charged with finding export markets but who does not have the necessary experience can start by making contact with the local regional offices of the British Overseas Trade Board (B.O.T.B.), which is quite expert in providing advice and information.

399

Managing the sales and marketing effort through foreign agents and distributors requires all the skills of the home market sales manager and more, because the foreign representative will normally represent quite a number of principals, probably in several product categories, and will be motivated to maximise his own income rather than any one principal's sales volumes.

Foreign agents or distributors, particularly in developing nations, tend not to have the benefit of sophisticated management training. Therefore the international marketeer can work through training to develop the average level of selling and management skills within each foreign agency or distributor organisation. This will serve to raise performance for all of the product ranges represented by the agent or distributor, thus increasing his total sales and income, yet giving greater potential loyalty and commitment to the company providing the training. There is therefore great merit in treating a foreign agent or distributor as an extension of the home market sales force when it comes to matters of training. The international marketeer responsible for any market should:

- conduct sales and management training courses for the management and sales force of the agent or distributor in the market wherever possible
- provide field sales training support for both the managers and salespersons in the agency or distributor organisations
- conduct field audits regularly in each market to monitor sales activity including distribution, display and promotional activity, and use this information to provide feedback to the representative's management and to develop further sales and marketing plans and programmes. Generally field audits should be conducted when the export sales manager can be accompanied by a field sales manager or other management representative of the agency or distribution organisation so that both parties clearly see and interpret the same market conditions
- prepare sales and marketing plans, forecasts and programmes in conjunction with the management of the agency or distribution company to which all parties are committed and which clearly state objectives and plans and timetables for the implementation of programmes
- develop systems with the agent or distributor for monitoring the results of all the programmes and plans against targets, forecasts and objectives
- design and develop stock, order and inventory control systems that suit the needs of the products, importers and market conditions, customs and practices.

400

Frequently a manufacturing exporter will benefit directly or indirectly by providing management assistance and training to importers, agents and distributors in a number of service areas such as financial controls and internal information systems, in addition to specialist training in product handling, storage, distribution and product servicing.

The international sales manager or marketeer has the added complication that he is frequently working in markets where his own language is not the local means of communication, even if the management of the agency or distribution company speak English. Because much is often lost in translation, greater time, effort and repetition are often essential to produce the requisite modification in behaviour.

The key to developing foreign agents and distributors is to concentrate on training their management personnel, who can then adapt the training to local needs and market conditions and communicate it to lower levels of the sales organisations. Many larger companies that run internal management and sales training courses find considerable benefit in inviting key personnel from their agency or distribution organisations to attend occasional internal manage-ment development courses. This cross-fertilisation of skills and experience is both interesting to the home market managers and builds greater commitment, loyalty and skill levels within the foreign representative's organisation.

The sales director charged with international sales responsibility should pay particular attention to the integration of the international sales management team with the home market sales management team to promote the overall best interests of the company. All too frequently conflicts arise because the domestic and international sales teams do not adequately communicate, cooperate or under-stand each other's markets, pressures and problems. An export order might take many months to negotiate, particularly for the provision of capital goods, and if, when the order finally materialises, product is not available to meet the customer's delivery schedule then, naturally, the export marketeer involved in obtaining the order will be extremely frustrated, just as any home market sales manager will be if he cracks a tough account only to find delivery delays. If regular meetings are held within the export and home sales management teams then there is merit in ensuring that each team is represented at the other's meetings to provide input on the respective activity of each department and build a better team spirit geared to maximising the return from sales and overall growth.

In this text, concentrating on home market sales management and development, I do not propose to try and condense into summary form the many intricacies of exporting and the development of inter-national business, beyond making the senior sales managers aware of these important additional avenues for growth and expansion. Export is a complex subject, and many managers perhaps treat it as a mystical subject that they are nervous to venture to understand. I would urge the sales or marketing manager charged with developing further sales internationally, yet with limited personal exporting experience and expertise, to read selectively from the work I have previously produced on the subject of international business development, and referred to at intervals in this text (*Practical Export Management*, London, Allen & Unwin, 1985). I believe it offers a very readable yet comprehensive introduction to the complexities of exporting in one practically orientated volume.

SUMMARY

- Political, economic and social benefits can accrue to exporting and importing nations. Companies can benefit from exporting through fuller use of plant capacity and an extended product life in new markets, increasing earnings and profits, giving a more secure employment base with resultant benefits in improved employee morale.

- The international marketeer must: identify potential foreign markets; ensure exported products comply with all regulations governing their use and importation to each foreign market; ensure that protective packaging is adequate; select, appoint and train foreign agents or distributors; oversee the preparation of all contracts and agreements with foreign parties; prepare sales and marketing plans in liaison with foreign representatives; ensure that all export and import documentation is prepared accurately and in timely fashion; ensure that payment terms are secure; give personal selling support to the foreign agent or distributor; negotiate and agree all sales terms and conditions.

- The international marketeer needs well-developed personal selling and management skills and additional expertise in export documentation and shipping procedures, international marketing and distribution, foreign payments, product costings, legal and quasi-legal aspects of trade and contracting.

- Whilst export markets might present opportunities to extend plant utilisation and product lives after sales in the home market have peaked, imports of complementary products also offer a means to utilise spare sales force and distribution capacity, and to strengthen the company's position in supplies to the home market.

- Where a company does not have the internal resources to develop direct exports an alternative is indirect exports using the specialist services of export agents or other export buying houses.

- International marketeers need to develop sales and management skills within the foreign agency or distribution organisations to increase growth within the foreign market. Field check audits are just as relevant to control and training in the foreign markets. In addition to sales and marketing training an exporter can assist his agent or distributor in developing other financial and information controls and systems.

- Morale and motivation within the home and export market sales teams will generally be improved if there is regular contact and integration in planning and training meetings.

Index

407